CICS

J. Ranade IBM Series

ISBN	AUTHOR	TITLE
0-07-051244-2	J. RANADE	VSAM: Concepts, Programming, and Design
0-07-051143-8	J. RANADE	Advanced SNA Networking: A Professional's Guide for Using VTAM/NCP
0-07-051144-6	J. RANADE	Introduction To SNA Networking: A Guide to VTAM/NCP
0-07-051265-5	J. RANADE	DB2: Concepts, Programming, and Design
0-07-009816-6	M. CARATHANASSIS	Expert MVS/XA JCL: A Complete Guide to Advanced Techniques
0-07-009820-4	M. CARATHANASSIS	Expert MVS/ESA JCL: A Guide to Advanced Techniques
0-07-017607-8	P. DONOFRIO	CICS Programmer's Reference
0-07-050691-4	N. PRASAD/J. SAVIT	IBM Mainframes: Architecture and Design
0-07-054529-4	S. SAMSON	MVS Performance Management (ESA/390 Edition)
0-07-032673-8	B. JOHNSON	MVS: Concepts and Facilities
0-07-032674-6	B. JOHNSON	DASD: IBM's Direct Access Storage Devices
0-07-028682-8	G. GOLDBERG/P. SMITH	The REXX Handbook
0-07-023686-0	G. GOLDBERG/P. SMITH	The VM/ESA Systems Handbook
0-07-040763-0	M. MARX/P. DAVIS	MVS Power Programming
0-07-057553-3	D. SILVERBERG	DB2: Performance, Design, and Implementation
0-07-069460-5	A. WERMAN	DB2 Handbook for DBAs
0-07-002553-3	G. HOUTEKAMER/P. ARTIS	MVS I/O Subsystems: Configuration Management and Performance Analysis
0-07-033727-6	A. KAPOOR	SNA: Architecture, Protocols, and Implementation
0-07-014770-1	R. CROWNHART	IBM's Workstation CICS
0-07-036111-8	R. LAMB	Cooperative Processing Using CICS
0-07-015305-1	C. DANEY	Programming in REXX
0-07-034600-3	P. KIESEL	REXX: Advanced Techniques for Programmers
0-07-037040-0	J. KNEILING	Understanding CICS Internals
0-07-022453-6	A. FRIEND	COBOL Application Debugging Under MVS: COBOL and COBOL II
0-07-006583-7	H. BOOKMAN	COBOL/370: For VS COBOL and COBOL II Programmers
0-07-008606-6	L. BRUMBAUGH	VSAM: Architecture, Theory, and Applications
0-07-041793-9	B. MERROW	VSE/ESA: Performance Management and Fine Tuning
0-07-054977-X	J. SAVIT	VM/CMS: Concepts and Facilities
0-07-018994-3	T. EDDOLLS	ASO: Automated Systems Operations for MVS
0-07-018303-1	T. BARITZ	AS/400: Concepts and Facilities
0-07-035869-9	J. LEBERT	CICS Essentials for Application Developers and Programmers
0-07-050623-X	J. PORTER	AS/400 Information Engineering
0-07-041984-1	L. TRINDELL	NetView: A Professional's Guide to SNA Network Management

To order or receive additional information on these or any other McGraw-Hill titles, please call 1-800-822-8158 in the United States. In other countries, contact your local McGraw-Hill representative.

CICS

Capacity Planning
and Performance
Management

Ted C. Keller

McGraw-Hill, Inc.
New York San Francisco Washington, D.C. Auckland Bogotá
Caracas Lisbon London Madrid Mexico City Milan
Montreal New Delhi San Juan Singapore
Sydney Tokyo Toronto

Library of Congress Cataloging-in-Publication Data

Keller, Ted C.
   CICS : capacity planning and performance management / Ted C. Keller.
      p.   cm.
   Includes bibliographical references and index.
   ISBN 0-07-033783-7
   1. CICS (Computer system)   2. Computer capacity—Planning.
I. Title.
QA76.76.T45K43   1993
005.4'3—dc20   93-14510
                                                                                        CIP

Copyright © 1993 by McGraw-Hill, Inc. All rights reserved. Printed in the United States of America. Except as permitted under the United States Copyright Act of 1976, no part of this publication may be reproduced or distributed in any form or by any means, or stored in a data base or retrieval system, without the prior written permission of the publisher.

1 2 3 4 5 6 7 8 9 0   DOC/DOC   9 8 7 6 5 4 3

ISBN 0-07-033783-7

The sponsoring editor for this book was Jerry Papke, the editing supervisor was Joseph Bertuna, and the production supervisor was Donald F. Schmidt. It was typeset in Helvetica.

Printed and bound by R. R. Donnelley & Sons Company.

Information contained in this work has been obtained by McGraw-Hill, Inc., from sources believed to be reliable. However, neither McGraw-Hill nor its authors guarantees the accuracy or completeness of any information published herein and neither McGraw-Hill nor its authors shall be responsible for any errors, omissions, or damages arising out of use of this information. This work is published with the understanding that McGraw-Hill and its authors are supplying information but are not attempting to render engineering or other professional services. If such services are required, the assistance of an appropriate professional should be sought.

I would like to dedicate this book to my family, who had to put up with me over the past two years, and especially to my wife, Jane, without whose support this book would not have been possible.

Contents

Preface   xiii

Chapter 1. Introduction   1

  1.1 Objective   1
  1.2 General Contents   2
  1.3 Capacity Planning, Performance Management, and Tuning   5
  1.4 Why Do Performance Planning?   5
  1.5 Why Large CICS Systems Face Constraints   7
  1.6 How To Use This Book   8

Chapter 2. CICS Architecture and Performance Characteristics   11

  2.1 Overview   11
    2.2.1 Primary Audience   12
  2.2 CICS Background and History   12
    2.2.1 A Short History of CICS Systems   12
  2.3 CICS/VS and CICS/MVS Internal Dispatching   14
    2.3.1 MVS Task Scheduling   14
    2.3.2 CICS/VS and CICS/MVS Use of MVS TCBs   15
    2.3.3 Other Factors that Affect the CICS Main TCB   17
  2.4 CICS/ESA TCB Structure   19
  2.5 Database TCBS in CICS Regions   20
  2.6 CICS Virtual Storage Management   21
    2.6.1 Virtual Storage Management in CICS/VS and CICS/MVS   23
    2.6.2 Virtual Storage Management in CICS/ESA (Releases 3.1.1 and 3.2.1)   25
    2.6.3 Virtual Storage Management in CICS/ESA (Release 3.3)   27
    2.6.4 Storage Shortage Solutions   28
    2.6.5 Virtual Storage Constraint Today   31
  2.7 Summary   31
  Selected Reading   32

Chapter 3. Analyzing CICS Workloads   33

  3.1 Overview   33
    3.1.1 Primary Audience   33
  3.2 What Is a Workload?   34

viii   Contents

3.3 Workload Classification and Characterization	35
3.3.1 Classifying Work Using Transactions IDs	36
3.3.2 Homogeneity in Workloads	37
3.3.3 Classifying Workloads by Resource Utilization	38
3.3.4 A Comparison of Classification Techniques	39
3.4 The Use of Historical Data	41
3.4.1 Dangers with the Use of Historical Data	41
3.5 Growth Bias	44
3.6 Three Components of Workload Growth	45
3.6.1 How to Calculate the Components of Growth	48
3.6.2 Accounting for Negative Growth	50
3.6.3 Automation of the Calculation Process	50
3.6.4 Accounting for Processor Differences	51
3.6.5 Exceptional Situations	52
3.7 Peak Periods	53
3.7.1 Types of Peak Periods	53
3.7.2 Planning for Peak Periods	54
3.8 Length of Peak Periods	56
3.9 Performance Databases	57
3.9.1 CICS PDBs	58
3.9.2 Commercial PDB Products	59
3.9.3 Operating System PDBs	61
3.10 Service Level Agreements	61
3.11 Summary	62
Selected Reading	62
Chapter 4. Forecasting Changes in Workloads	**63**
4.1 Overview	63
4.1.1 Primary Audience	63
4.2 Changes in the Three Components of Workload Growth	64
4.3 Changes Associated with Volume	65
4.3.1 Variations in Business Activity	65
4.3.2 Converting NFUs into Numbers of Transactions	66
4.3.3 The Relationship Between Business Activity and Peak Transaction Processing	69
4.3.4 Translating Business Activity into Workload Peaks	72
4.3.5 Volume-Related Changes Associated with Staffing	74
4.3.6 Other Factors Influencing Total Transactions	77
4.3.7 Gathering Information	78
4.4 Changes in Complexity/Overhead	78
4.4.1 A Method for Projecting Changes in Complexity/Overhead	78
4.4.2 Another View of Complexity/Overhead	81
4.4.3 Projections for the Entire System	83
4.5 Changes Associated with New Systems	83
4.5.1 Projecting Resources for New Systems	83
4.5.2 New Systems That Replace Old Systems—Estimating Total Transactions	84
4.5.3 New Systems that Replace Manual Systems—Estimating Total Transactions	85
4.5.4 New Systems That Do Not Replace Existing Functions—Estimating Total Transactions	85
4.5.5 Transaction Profiles for New Systems	85

Contents   ix

4.6 Periodic Review of Performance Data	87
4.6.1 Three Steps in the Review Process	87
4.6.2 Scan Performance Data for Anything Unusual	87
4.6.3 Comparing Current Data to Forecasts	88
4.6.4 Comparing Current Data to Previous Periods	88
4.7 Types of Change	89
4.7.1 Time-Related Variance	89
4.7.2 Random Variance	90
4.7.3 Institutional Changes	92
4.8 Reasons to Review Data Periodically	92
4.8.1 The Frequency of Performance Reviews	93
4.9 Summary	94
Selected Reading	94

Chapter 5. The Mathematics of Performance Planning   95

5.1 Overview	95
5.1.1 Primary Audience	96
5.2 Resource Utilization, Bottlenecks, and Rules of Thumb	96
5.2.1 Resource Utilization	96
5.2.2 Workload Growth and Utilization	100
5.2.3 Distortions to the Utilization Relationship	102
5.2.4 Bottleneck Analysis	103
5.2.5 Bottleneck Analysis and Performance Debugging	105
5.3 Queueing Theory	106
5.3.1 What Is a Queueing Theory?	106
5.3.2 Definition of Basic Terms	106
5.3.3 Open Versus Closed Queueing Systems	110
5.3.4 Service Multipliers—The Key to Simplified Performance Estimation	111
5.3.5 Open Single-Server Systems	112
5.3.6 Closed Single-Server Systems	114
5.3.7 Multiserver Systems	119
5.3.8 Selecting the Correct Type of Queueing System	120
5.3.9 Little's Law	121
5.4 Queueing Theory—A Set of Estimation Techniques	121
5.5 Assumptions Behind Queueing Theory	122
5.5.1 Assumption 1: Work Will Arrive Randomly	122
5.5.2 Assumption 2: Average Service Time Will Form a Random Pattern	123
5.5.3 Assumption 3: Average Service Time Will Not Vary With the Work Arrival Rate	124
5.6 The Significance of Random Patterns	125
5.7 An Example of the Application of Queueing Theory	126
5.8 Summary	128
Selected Reading	128

Chapter 6. Estimating the Effect of CPU Demand on CICS Performance   131

6.1 Overview	131
6.1.1 Primary Audience	131
6.2 CPU Processing in CICS	132

6.2.1 CICS TCB Structure	132
6.2.2 An Example of CICS Task Processing	133
6.3 Methods of Measuring CPU Utilization	135
6.3.1 Measuring CPU Utilization Using RMF	135
6.3.2 Measuring CPU Activity Using CMF—CICS/VS and CICS/MVS	136
6.3.3 Measuring CPU Activity Using CMF—CICS/ESA	138
6.3.4 CPU Data in CICS/ESA End-of-Day Statistics	139
6.4 CPU Demand—The Proper Measure of Processor Usage for CICS Systems	139
6.4.1 Dispatch Time as a Measure of CPU Demand	140
6.5 CICS as a Queueing System	141
6.5.1 Estimating CPU-Related Delays—Simple Illustration	143
6.5.2 Why This Estimation Technique Works	150
6.5.3 Estimating CPU-Related Delays—More Complex Illustration	152
6.6 Estimating the Effect of Tuning—Simple Example	156
6.6.1 The Interaction Between Queueing Systems	157
6.7 Transactions that Use Large Amounts of CPU Time	158
6.8 CPU Delays for Other TCBS in a CICS Region	159
6.9 CICS Internal Dispatching Priorities	160
6.10 Summary	162
Selected Reading	162

Chapter 7. Paging, MVS Priority, Processor Speed, and Their Effect on CICS Performance — 165

7.1 Overview	165
7.1.1 Primary Audience	166
7.2 Differences in Queueing Systems	166
7.3 How Paging from Exteranl Storage Affects CICS Performance	170
7.4 How Paging from Expanded Storage Affects CICS Performance	173
7.5 How File OPEN and CLOSE Commands Affect Dispatch Service in CICS Regions	175
7.6 How CI and CA Splits Affect Dispatch Service in CICS Regions	176
7.7 How Total Processor Usage Affects CICS Performance	176
7.7.1 How to Estimate the Effect of Processor Utilization on CICS Performance	177
7.7.2 CPU Time Used by Competing MVS Tasks	178
7.7.3 The Processor Complex as a Queueing System	179
7.7.4 The Effect of Priority Queueing	180
7.7.5 Calculating the Effects of CPU Contention—Approach 1	184
7.7.6 Calculating the Effects of CPU Contention—Approach 2	188
7.7.7 Illustrations of Real-World Queueing Data	190
7.8 Notes on Calibrating Dispatch and CPU Demand Calculations	194
7.9 Estimating CPU Related Delays—An Example	196
7.10 Evaluating How Applications Perform on Different Processors	200
7.10.1 How to Project CICS Performance on Different Processor Configurations	201
7.10.2 Example—Estimating CICS Performance on an Unknown Processor	207
7.11 Differences in Equivalent Processors	213
7.12 Summary	214
Selected Reading	214

Chapter 8. SPE—Planning Application Performance — 217

- 8.1 Overview — 217
  - 8.1.1 Primary Audience — 218
- 8.2 What Is Software Performance Engineering? — 218
- 8.3 SPE and CICS — 220
  - 8.3.1 CICS Application Development in the Past—Why SPE Was *Not* Necessary — 220
  - 8.3.2 CICS Application Development Today—The Need for SPE — 221
- 8.4 SPE—Overall Strategy — 223
  - 8.4.1 SPE Models — 226
  - 8.4.2 Performance Walk-Throughs — 228
- 8.5 Identifying Performance Goals — 229
- 8.6 Building an SPE Model — 230
  - 8.6.1 Determining Application Workflow (Workload Specifications) — 231
  - 8.6.2 Build a Profile of Application Processing (Software Design) — 232
  - 8.6.3 Building the Software Model — 234
  - 8.6.4 Estimating Transaction Volume — 234
  - 8.6.5 Estimating CPU Usage — 237
  - 8.6.6 Evaluating the Software Model — 238
- 8.7 Summary — 241
- Selected Reading — 242

Chapter 9. SPE—Application Design Example — 243

- 9.1 Overview — 243
  - 9.1.1 Primary Audience — 243
- 9.2 Review of SPE Concepts — 244
  - 9.2.1 Suggested SPE Procedure for Evaluating Sample CICS Application — 245
- 9.3 Evaluating New Application Systems—An Example — 246
  - 9.3.1 Establish Performance Requirements — 247
  - 9.3.2 Develop Workload Specifications — 248
  - 9.3.3 Develop Software Design — 250
  - 9.3.4 Build a Software Model — 254
  - 9.3.5 Estimate Best-Case Performance — 255
  - 9.3.6 Evaluate Performance in the Anticipated Environment — 265
- 9.4 Spreadsheets — 272
- 9.5 Summary — 272

Chapter 10. SPE—Application Design Guidelines — 275

- 10.1 Overview — 275
  - 10.1.1 Primary Audience — 276
- 10.2 Improving CICS Application Performance — 276
  - 10.2.1 Controlling CPU Usage in a CICS Environment — 278
- 10.3 General Principles of Effective and Responsive Software — 279
- 10.4 Principle 1—The Fixing-Point-Principle — 280
- 10.5 Principle 2—Locality Principle — 283
  - 10.5.1 Spatial Locality—Closeness of Distance or Function — 284
  - 10.5.2 Temporal Locality—Closeness in Time — 289
  - 10.5.3 Effectual Locality—Closeness in Purpose — 292
  - 10.5.4 Locality of Degree—Matching Processing to Capacity — 295

10.6 Principle 3—Processing Versus Frequency Principle	296
10.7 Principle 4—The Centering Principle	298
10.8 Principle 5—The Asynchronous Processing Principle	301
10.9 Principle 6—Shared Resources Principle	304
10.10 Principle 7—The Instrumentation Principle	308
10.11 Summary	310
Selected Reading	310

Chapter 11. CICS and the DASD Subsystem — 311

11.1 Overview	311
11.1.1 Primary Audience	311
11.2 The CICS I/O Environment	312
11.3 Major Components of I/O Service Time	312
11.4 Common Measures of DASD Service	314
11.4.1 Data About DASD Volumes (RMF Type 74 Records)	315
11.4.2 Data About Channels (RMF Type 73 Records)	316
11.5 Cache Controllers	317
11.5.1 Cache Controller Operation—Read Requests	317
11.5.2 Cache Controller Operation—Write Requests	318
11.5.3 Common Cache Controller Measurement Data	319
11.6 Queueing Theory and DASD Workloads	320
11.6.1 DASD Queueing Systems	322
11.7 Analysis of I/O Service Time	323
11.7.1 DASD Example 1	323
11.7.2 DASD Example 2	332
11.7.3 DASD Example 3	337
11.8 CICS Internal Caching	338
11.8.1 LSR Access of VSAM Files	338
11.8.2 CICS Temporary Storage	342
11.9 Estimating Effective File Service Time for CICS Applications	345
11.10 Recommendations	346
11.11 DB2 DASD Patterns	348
11.12 Summary	349
Selected Reading	349

Appendix A. Open Queueing Tables	351
Appendix B. Closed Queueing Tables	357
Appendix C. Modified Closed Queueing Tables	377
Appendix D. Miscellaneous Notes on MRO	387
Appendix E. SAS Program to Calculate Open Queueing Delays	397

Index   401

Preface

Several years ago, in a public seminar for CICS systems programmers, I presented a paper on CICS workloads and how their growth affected CICS performance. The material was quite basic, but it was new to most of the individuals in the audience. While most of those in the audience had quite a bit of CICS experience, they had little exposure to the concepts of CICS workloads, components of growth, or queueing theory.

In other experiences, I have observed that many capacity planners are only casually familiar with the internal workings of CICS or the forces causing growth in CICS workloads. Capacity planners are often familiar with the general requirements of CICS systems, but not with the details of CICS internal queueing or the relationship between operating system dispatching and CICS performance. They sometimes are not aware of all the factors that can influence the performance of CICS systems and to what degree.

I have also observed that application developers are not always aware of how much influence they can have on CICS performance. Application developers usually are very busy getting systems written and tested and meeting user deadlines. Their focus tends to be on developing systems that work correctly and on completing work on time. They may not have much time to devote to planning application performance.

Three groups of individuals influence the performance of CICS applications, each with different backgrounds and concerns. Each has its own specialized knowledge and skills, and each has its own responsibilities and priorities.

The purpose of this book is to provide all three groups with information useful for planning performance for CICS systems. The book provides a synergy of material from several diverse disciplines. Material from many sources is blended together, providing a unified approach to CICS performance planning.

Acknowledgments

Many individuals have helped me over the past two years. Three particular individuals, though, have helped me throughout much of the development of this book. They are:

Robert Johnson, who provided a style sheet, helped me learn Ventura Publisher, and answered numerous questions about style and typesetting. Bob also was an excellent sounding board for the material on DASD, and offered much valuable feedback.

Dr. Leilani Allen, who was the primary reviewer for the book. More than just reviewing the material, she offered suggestions on style, content, and direction. Leilani was an inspiration and a good source of ideas.

Dr. Arnold Allen, who helped me many times with the mathematics in this book. Whenever I encountered challenges with some type of procedure, I could always count on Arnie to help me out. He frequently offered his help and even ran programs to help me validate data.

Ted C. Keller

CICS

Chapter 1

Introduction

1.1 OBJECTIVE

CICS: Capacity Planning and Performance Management is a book about Customer Information Control System (CICS) performance. It is designed to be a resource for those concerned about CICS performance, whether they come from a systems programming, capacity planning, performance management, or application development background. This book's goal is to provide a set of tools that can be easily applied to the task of planning performance for CICS systems.

Like other books about CICS performance, this book includes some information about CICS internal processes. However, this book is more than just a book about CICS internal processes. Along with CICS-related technical information, it includes material from other disciplines such as performance management, capacity planning, and software performance engineering. This book marries material from several disciplines to provide a practical guide for planning CICS performance.

This book will discuss how to:

- Analyze the components of CICS response time

- Estimate delays associated with dispatch processing within CICS

- Estimate how paging, competition from other *multiple virtual systems* (MVS) tasks, and other systemwide delays affect CICS transaction response time.

- Recognize differences between the *central processing unit* (CPU) measures produced by various tools and decide which are useful for what purposes
- Estimate the performance of CICS applications early in their design
- Design CICS applications that will perform acceptably
- Identify the types of change that can influence CICS workload growth
- Forecast changes in CICS workload activity
- Analyze *direct access storage device* (DASD) service for CICS applications
- Apply simple mathematical procedures to estimate elements of CICS performance

CICS: Capacity Planning and Performance Management provides the reader with a wealth of information about planning performance. The book includes information about all current MVS versions of CICS (CICS/VS,[1] CICS/MVS, and CICS/ESA through release 3.3) and how structural differences between releases affect CICS processing and response time.

1.2 GENERAL CONTENTS

This book contains several major topics, including:

- **CICS internal architecture**. A large part of CICS performance is influenced by how CICS schedules work and shares resources among competing CICS tasks. We will look at CICS internal dispatching and storage management in CICS/VS, CICS/MVS, and CICS/ESA systems. Similarities as well as differences are discussed.
- **Workload classification and characterization**. One of the more important tasks in performance planning is analyzing current activity and projecting future processing. To do this we must be able to separate CICS transactions and systems into logical groups called

---

[1] Support was dropped for the MVS version of CICS/VS release 1.7 on December 31, 1972. Even though that release is no longer considered current, information is provided about release 1.7 because it is still being used by a significant number of users.

workloads. We will discuss the classification and characterization of workloads, criteria for selecting periods of study, the use of long-term trends, and the three components of workload growth. The idea of *growth bias* is introduced, which is the organizational bias affecting workload growth.

- **Techniques to forecast changes in CICS workloads.** We will show that workload growth normally is driven by three factors: Changes in volume (the number of transactions entered), changes in the complexity of existing systems, and new application systems. This book discusses how to separate workload growth into its components and then shows how to forecast changes in each component. Traditional forecasting techniques are discussed along with factors peculiar to CICS workloads. The discussion includes a summary of different types of variance and how this can affect workload change.

- **Queueing theory.** Queueing theory is the mathematics of standing in line. This book presents practical techniques that can be easily applied to estimate delays associated with queueing. Multiple types of queueing systems are discussed, along with suggestions on how they might be used. Tables are provided to allow the use of more sophisticated queueing techniques without the burden of complex calculations. *Every effort is made to simplify complex relationships and to make formulas as easy-to-use as possible.*

- **Internal processing delays.** Internal dispatching delays can represent a large portion of CICS response time. These delays are not measured by most CICS monitors and are usually hidden in the service times for other components. This book shows how to estimate internal dispatching delays. The techniques developed show how to use existing measurement data and the basics of queueing theory to estimate delays. Tables are used to estimate queueing relationships and simplify procedures.

- **The effect of operating system contention on CICS performance.** Competition from other MVS tasks, paging, operating system overhead, and other delays influence the CPU service received by tasks running in CICS regions. We will look at how these delays affect dispatch processing in CICS regions and how this translates into CICS response time.

- **Software performance engineering (SPE) for CICS applications.** Software performance engineering consists of a set of guidelines to evaluate the performance of application systems early in their design. The reason for using SPE is to ensure that applications have the potential to perform acceptably before all the design and programming work have been completed. The concept of SPE suggests that it is less expensive to adjust application design early in the development process. We will discuss how SPE principles can be applied for CICS applications. A chapter-long illustration also is included showing how an SPE study might be performed.

- **Design principles for responsive CICS applications.** There are seven general design principles, or guidelines, that allow the creation of application systems that are more effective (permit users to perform their work more effectively), more efficient (use fewer resources), and more responsive. We will examine each of seven general principles and see how it can be applied in a CICS environment. The use of these SPE design guidelines can help create CICS applications that are more likely to satisfying users' performance needs.

- **DASD architecture and service.** This book will look at the components of DASD service time and how they affect performance. It will show how to analyze available measures of DASD activity and estimate DASD service for CICS applications.

CICS: Capacity Planning and Performance Management provides a synergy of multiple worlds. The principles of workload analysis, growth bias, and queueing theory are applied to CICS's internal architecture, providing a unified structure for evaluating and planning CICS performance. SPE principles also are included. Material is included on analyzing and estimating DASD performance. Techniques for evaluating application performance and designing responsive application systems have been tailored to a CICS application environment. Several disciplines are merged to provide a robust methodology for accessing and planning CICS performance.

CICS: Capacity Planning and Performance Management addresses all three MVS versions of CICS that exist at the time of this writing: CICS/VS (release 1.7 only), CICS/MVS (releases 2.1.0 through 2.1.2), and CICS/ESA (through release 3.3). Differences between versions and releases that affect performance and capacity planning are examined in detail.

1.3 CAPACITY PLANNING, PERFORMANCE MANAGEMENT, AND TUNING

Several terms are commonly used to describe tasks related to computer performance and capacity. *Capacity planning* is the process of planning computer resources to provide service required by users. Capacity planning usually focuses on computer equipment – processors, DASD, memory, tape drives, and other types of hardware. Capacity plans generally cover periods 6 to 24 months in the future. The primary emphasis of capacity planning is to forecast requirements for hardware and to help management plan for its acquisition.

Performance management, on the other hand, is the task of monitoring and controlling existing resources. It concentrates on measuring and allocating existing resources to meet the needs of existing applications. The focus of performance management is short-term in nature, concentrating on providing acceptable service at the present time and several months into the future.

The object of *tuning* is to improve the performance of specific applications, control bottlenecks, or optimize the use of resources. Tuning often involves adjusting system parameters. It also may include modifications to applications or the use of specialized software. Tuning often involves substituting the use of a resource that is in plentiful supply for one that is constrained.

Tuning is a necessary part of performance management. Most capacity plans assume that the environment is running efficiently and that there are no major bottlenecks preventing effective use of resources.

While capacity planning, performance management, and tuning are all important aspects of performance, this book will not focus on any one of the three. Instead, it will attempt to provide a unified approach to planning performance for CICS systems.

1.4 WHY DO PERFORMANCE PLANNING?

It is easy to ask, "Why do performance planning?" The obvious answer to this question is, "To ensure that users will receive the service they need to get their jobs done." This is the primary goal of performance planning. Without question, the primary goal of any kind of performance or capacity planning is to ensure that service requirements can be met.

Another reason to do performance planning is to provide service in a cost-effective manner. Planning helps eliminate waste and allows us to plan systems that are adequate but not overconfigured.

A third reason is to prevent surprises. In today's dynamic, changing CICS environment a number of factors can cause response time to degrade rapidly. Application performance can change very suddenly with the installation of new systems or major changes to existing systems. Surprises may not be pleasant and can be disruptive. However, surprises can be minimized through planning.

A fourth reason to do performance planning is that it takes time to respond to performance problems once they occur. Performance problems commonly are related either to hardware or software bottlenecks and sometimes to both. Some software bottlenecks can be corrected fairly easily. It usually is not that difficult to create a new CICS region or split application systems if applications use the standard command-level interface. In today's environment, these are minor tasks compared to what they might have been ten years ago. Some software bottlenecks can be tricky, though, and may take a considerable amount of time and effort to resolve.

Hardware bottlenecks can take longer to correct. Hardware acquisition usually requires budget and environmental planning. Most organizations require justification and planning before hardware is purchased or leased. When hardware upgrades are needed outside the normal budget process, special action and approval from high-level management may be required. All of this takes time and coordination.

A fifth and very important reason for planning performance is to ensure that new application systems have a good chance of performing acceptably. Many years ago when systems were simpler and application requirements were much less demanding, application design required less attention. Simpler systems typically had a high probability of delivering acceptable performance. Even if performance was not acceptable, minor tuning or relatively inexpensive hardware upgrades would overcome most problems.

In today's environment, however, users require massive systems that address complex business issues. New systems commonly perform a tremendous amount of work. Transactions tend to be larger and use more CPU time, input/output (I/O), memory, and other resources. Today, it is possible to design large, complex systems that do not perform acceptably when installed and defy tuning. Proper planning can help screen application designs before a substantial investment is made in application development.

> **Key Point:** There are five reasons to do performance planning: To provide users the service they need; to control hardware and software costs; to prevent surprises; to allow lead time for hardware and software positioning; and to ensure that new applications can perform adequately.

1.5 WHY LARGE CICS SYSTEMS FACE CONSTRAINTS

In the 1990s, typical large CICS environments contain many CICS regions running together on one or more processor complexes. Typically, there will be one or more terminal-owning regions (TORs), multiple application-owning regions (AORs), and some file- or resource-owning regions (FORs or RORs). It is not uncommon to find as many as 20 or more production CICS regions on a single processor. Some large organizations run hundreds of production CICS systems on a series of processors at a single location.

Despite the fact that most large CICS configurations run many CICS regions, work usually is not divided evenly among the regions. It is not uncommon to find many CICS regions tailored to specific functions or users. Some CICS regions may have been created for security, stability, convenience, or other special purposes. In most environments there will be many CICS regions with low to moderate activity and a few with heavy transaction loads.

This author is aware of one CICS complex containing over 300 production CICS regions. In this complex many regions are quite specialized, processing only a few hundred transactions per day. In this same complex, at least one region is used very heavily and processes several million transactions each day.

> **Key Point:** Normally, CICS workloads are not evenly balanced between CICS regions. Some specialized regions will process very few transactions. Other CICS regions will process large numbers of transactions. In most CICS environments, a relatively small number of CICS regions will process the majority of the transactions. Even when many regions are defined, some will do little processing.

Typically, those regions that process few transactions are not constrained. On the other hand, regions processing large numbers of transactions are the ones likely to face various internal CICS constraints. Thus, the CICS regions that are constrained tend to be the ones processing the most transactions. Perhaps only a few CICS regions are constrained, but they may account for a large percent of all CICS transactions.

1.6 HOW TO USE THIS BOOK

This book has been designed for three specific audiences: Systems programmers, application developers, and capacity planners. A few paragraphs at the beginning of each chapter will suggest what each group should expect from the chapter. Although the three groups come from different backgrounds, there should be new material in each chapter for each audience.

The material in this book was developed in a logical progression. Topics in each chapter build on material from previous chapters. To obtain the maximum benefit from this book, it would be best to read all of the chapters in order.

In today's busy world, many individuals cannot afford to take the time to study an entire book, however useful it may be. To satisfy the needs of those with limited time, the following chapters are suggested for those who have some background and would like to investigate only selected material. It is strongly suggested that the reader become familiar with Chapter 5 before reading Chapters 6, 7, 8, 9, or 11. Much of the material and special terminology introduced in Chapter 5 is very important to understanding this more advanced material. Chapters 5 and 6 discuss how to use Appendixes A and B and Chapter 7 discusses Appendix C.

Table 1.1 identifies many of the general topics covered in this book and the chapters in which they are discussed. A designation of **T** (text) indicates that the chapter discusses the topic. A designation of **P** indicates that the chapter contains material that is a prerequisiste for understanding the topic.

Table 1.1 Location of Selected Topics by Chapter

Topic	\multicolumn{11}{c}{Chapter}

Topic	1	2	3	4	5	6	7	8	9	10	11
Analyze components of CICS response time		P			P	T	T				
Estimate delays associated with dispatch processing within CICS		P			P	T	T				
Estimate how paging, competition from other MVS tasks, and other systemwide delays affect transaction response time		P			P	P	T				
Estimate the performance of CICS applications early in their design		P			P			T	T		
Design CICS applications that will perform acceptably								P		T	
Identify the components of CICS workload growth			T								
Forecast changes in CICS workload activity			P	T							
Analyze DASD service for CICS applications					P						T
Apply simple mathematical procedures to estimate elements of CICS performance						T	T				
Understand differences between and uses of CPU measures produced by various tools		P				T					

Chapter 2

CICS Architecture and Performance Characteristics

2.1 OVERVIEW

Two aspects of CICS internal architecture have traditionally required special planning. When CICS applications stress these architectural features, CICS performance can suffer, and special action may be required. Both of these factors tend to be more global in nature than most other performance concerns and tend to require specific software planning and positioning.

The first of these is *CICS internal dispatching*. As we will see, most processing in a CICS region (even under CICS/ESA) is performed by a single MVS task. This task is limited by several factors, including the power of processor engines, competition from other operating system tasks, paging, and other less obvious delays. Internal queueing for dispatch service can account for many direct and hidden delays and can be an important factor in configuring CICS regions. In this chapter we will look at how dispatching is performed in CICS/VS, CICS/MVS, and CICS/ESA systems. Later, in Chapters 6 and 7, we will show how dispatch-related delays affect CICS performance.

The second topic is how CICS manages *virtual storage*. Historically, virtual addressing limitations (commonly called virtual storage constraint (VSC)) have been a plague to CICS performance. For years, systems programmers spent much time fighting VSC and restructuring CICS regions to provide relief. Today, VSC should no longer be a significant problem for those installations exploiting the latest releases of CICS/MVS or, to an even larger extent, CICS/ESA. However, until installations take advantage of features provided by new software, VSC will still require some planning. Today, VSC is more of a technical issue than one requiring much long-term planning. However, when VSC problems occur, they may force the creation of new CICS regions.

2.1.1 Primary Audience

The material in this chapter is basic architectural information about CICS/VS, CICS/MVS, and CICS/ESA. *CICS systems programmers* probably will be familiar with most of the concepts presented in this chapter, especially if they have been involved with both CICS/MVS and CICS/ESA. It is recommended that experienced CICS systems programmers at least scan the material since this will provide background for several chapters that follow.

Capacity planners who do not have a strong background in CICS should find this chapter valuable. This chapter will present information about how CICS's internal structure can influence performance and processor capacity.

Application developers should find the material in this chapter interesting. While the material might not be applied directly by application developers, it does provide useful background for the design of CICS applications.

2.2 CICS BACKGROUND AND HISTORY

CICS's internal architecture is unique in many ways. Conceptually, CICS is like a mini operating system designed to serve the needs of transaction processing applications. CICS applications are supposed to rely on CICS for all external services.

2.2.1 A Short History of CICS Systems

As shown in Figure 2.1, the earliest release of CICS was simply called "CICS." Most individuals working on CICS systems today do not remember the pre-CICS/VS version of the product. When CICS was first introduced, all applications had to be written in assembler, and *macro-level* was the only programming interface. CICS was designed to run on the

CICS Architecture   13

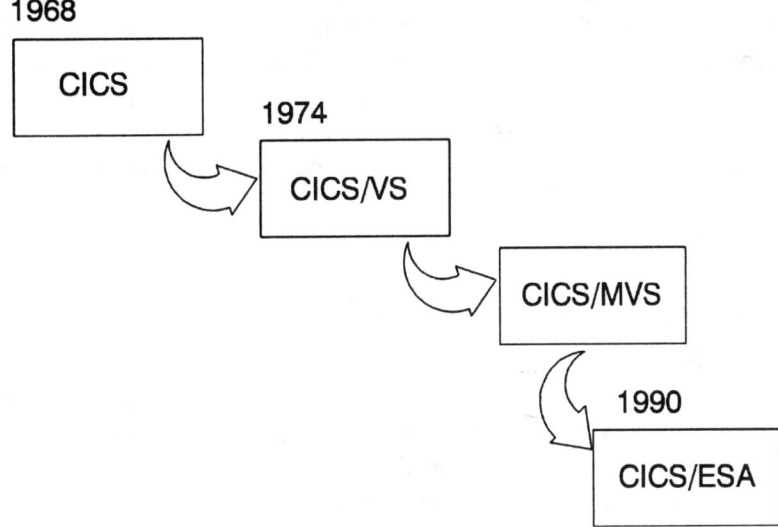

Figure 2.1 Brief history of CICS host-based systems.

old OS operating system and faced the same restrictions of other MVT and MFT applications. There was no virtual storage and real storage was very expensive. Application programs needed to be both small and simple and were constrained by both software and hardware limitations.

In time, COBOL (macro-level) and basic mapping support (BMS) were added. CICS had its limitations, but it was becoming popular.

The next version of CICS was CICS/VS. It eliminated many restrictions of the original version of CICS and provided a wealth of functionality for applications. CICS/VS defined an architecture that remained substantially the same from its initial release through the latest releases of CICS/MVS. The product grew and matured, but the basic architecture survived with little change for almost two decades.

As customers became more sophisticated and their requirements expanded, CICS/VS grew to fit their needs. A series of releases provided continuous improvements in performance and functionality. Some of the more significant performance-related enhancements included *multiple region option* (MRO), *intersystem communication* (ISC), and access to storage above the 16-megabyte line. As CICS/VS grew as a product, it was often among the first systems to take advantage of new services provided by operating systems or other software.

CICS/MVS further expanded the migration of CICS/VS architecture with the addition of the *extended recovery facility* (XRF). When CICS/ESA was released in 1990, a new era began. CICS was completely restructured. CICS functions were broken into *domains* with individual interfaces and well-defined rules for communicating between domains. Much was done to improve existing services and to lay the groundwork for future releases.

2.3 CICS/VS AND CICS/MVS INTERNAL DISPATCHING

One significant bottleneck in CICS architecture today is the way CICS tasks are dispatched. In this chapter, we will describe how CICS dispatches work in the different versions of CICS and why this causes processing bottlenecks. Chapter 6 will discuss how to estimate delays associated with CICS dispatch processing.

2.3.1 MVS Task Scheduling

In MVS systems, the operating system schedules processing using control blocks called *task control blocks* (TCBs). Each TCB represents one operating system task. MVS tasks are dispatched by assigning processor engines to TCBs. Tasks compete for processor resources based on their MVS dispatching priority.

Each TCB can use only a single processor engine at any time. On a multiengine processor (like an IBM 3090-600J, which has six processor engines), the operating system can dispatch a task on any processor engine. However, a task cannot use more than one processor engine at any given time. This limits the amount of processing that can be performed by a single TCB.

> **Key Point:** A single MVS task (TCB) can use no more than the equivalent power of a single processor engine.

For applications that do not perform a large amount of CPU processing, this restriction is almost trivial. However, when MVS tasks, such as CICS regions, have a large demand for CPU service, TCB limitations can have a significant effect on performance.

2.3.2 CICS/VS and CICS/MVS Use of MVS TCBs

CICS/VS and CICS/MVS architecture both use a single TCB for most processing. Virtually all application-related processing, all transaction scheduling, and most CICS services are performed under the control of a singe MVS TCB.

Almost all services (with the possible exception of some *virtual storage access method* (VSAM) processing) needed by any application program will be performed under the control of a single TCB. This TCB is called the *CICS main TCB*.

Since all application processing and most CICS processing must share the same TCB, when application code is processing, CICS cannot schedule other work, recognize the completion of external requests, or handle requests for other CICS services. When the CICS main TCB is busy servicing one CICS task, other CICS tasks will wait.

> **Key Point:** In CICS/VS and CICS/MVS, the *CICS main TCB* will perform virtually all application-related services.

The optional *VSAM subtask* (VSP) is a separate TCB that runs in the CICS address space. It is designed to process selected VSAM requests. When VSP is active, some VSAM processing normally performed by the CICS main TCB is performed by the VSAM subtask. This permits CICS to offload some processing to a second TCB.

The main purpose of the VSAM subtask is to perform VSAM processing under the control of a separate TCB. The CICS main TCB still processes the CICS management portion of application file requests. Only the portion of file requests actually performed by the VSAM access method may be performed by the VSAM subtask.

If VSP is active, CICS will send selected requests to the VSAM subtask. The VSAM subtask then performs access method commands to request I/O service from VSAM. Meanwhile, the main TCB can continue to process work for other CICS tasks. This allows CICS to use up to two processor engines simultaneously in a single address space.

It takes a considerable amount of overhead to pass file requests between the two TCBs. To reduce overhead, a selective scheduling algorithm was implemented in CICS/MVS release 2.1.1. When VSP is active, CICS will send VSAM update-type requests to the VSAM subtask. VSAM browse (GETNEXT) requests are never sent to the subtask. The overhead of communicating between TCBs is usually higher than the cost of actually browsing VSAM data.

Other VSAM requests (read requests) will be sent to the VSAM subtask only when CICS CPU demand exceeds a predefined threshold. When the CICS main TCB is "active" below this threshold, VSAM read requests are processed by the CICS main TCB. Table 2.1 summarizes how processing for VSAM files is accomplished under CICS/MVS 2.1.1 or later.

In CICS/MVS, the subtask threshold is *70 percent CPU usage for the past one-half second*. In other words, if the CICS main TCB was using the CPU more than 70 percent of the time over the past one-half second, VSAM read requests would be passed to the VSAM subtask. Otherwise, VSAM read requests would be processed by the CICS main TCB, and the VSAM subtask would not become involved. This is summarized in Table 2.1.

It is important to remember that the VSAM subtask does not remove a large amount of processing from the CICS main TCB. Normally, VSP will shift *no more than 10 to 15 percent* of CPU processing (usually much less) to the VSAM TCB. The only processing actually moved to the subtask is

Table 2.1 VSAM Events Processed by CICS/MVS (Release 2.1.1 or Later) TCBs

Event	Conditons	TCB that Performs Processing (Assuming VSAM subtask is active)
File request processed	Always	CICS main TCB
VSAM write commands (access method calls)	Always	VSAM subtask
VSAM browse commands (access method calls)	Always	CICS main TCB
VSAM read commands (access method calls)	CICS main TCB using CPU less than or equal to 70 percent	CICS main TCB
VSAM read commands (access method calls)	CICS main TCB using CPU more than 70 percent of time	VSAM subtask

VSAM access method processing. This simply does not account for that much CPU consumption in a typical CICS environment.

> **Key Point:** The optional VSAM subtask can be used to service VSAM access method processing. Normally this will shift no more than 10 to 15 percent of the CPU activity in a CICS region to a second TCB.

By invoking VSP VSAM read requests only when CPU demand is high, CICS avoids the processing overhead of most inter-TCB communication at lower levels of processing and only uses the VSAM subtask fully when there is a potential performance benefit. A primary benefit of using the VSAM subtask for write requests when CPU usage is not that high is that write requests will cause physical I/Os and may cause control interval or control area splits.

It is interesting that the VSAM subtask will process VSAM read requests when the CICS main TCB is *more than 70 percent busy for one-half second*. Even when longer averages (such as minute-long or hour-long averages) are much lower than 70 percent, random spikes in activity can cause the CICS main TCB to be more than 70 percent busy. Thus, even when CPU activity is not that high overall, the VSAM subtask can be fully active for brief periods when it is needed.

Beginning with CICS/MVS release 2.1.1, the VSAM subtask will process only selected VSAM requests. When the subtask is active, write requests will always be processed by the subtask. Browse requests will never be processed by the subtask. Read requests will be processed by the subtask only when the CICS main TCB is more than 70 percent busy.

2.3.3 Other Factors that Affect the CICS Main TCB

We indicated above that TCBs are limited to the equivalent capacity of single-processor engines. That statement is not completely true. TCBs are also limited by any delays that restrict access to processors. Some of the more significant delays include:

Competition from other operating system tasks. Since most CICS work is performed by a single TCB, when that TCB cannot be dispatched, many CICS tasks may have to wait for dispatch service. Any time that the CICS main TCB spends waiting for MVS dispatch because all processors are committed to other, higher-priority work limits the amount of processing that can be performed on the CICS main TCB.

Competition from higher-priority MVS tasks has an indirect effect on CICS response time. In Chapter 7, we will examine how to estimate the effect this contention has on CICS response time.

MVS paging. MVS paging also can restrict access to the CICS main TCB. When a task (TCB) experiences a page fault, an interrupt occurs and processing is suspended until the page fault is resolved. When page faults are resolved from expanded storage, processing can be resumed quickly. When page faults must be resolved from external storage, the TCB will be delayed until the page can be retrieved from DASD.

Paging from external media can have a devastating effect on CICS performance. It normally should take about 15 to 30 ms to retrieve a page from DASD. This can represent a significant portion of the life of transactions running in a CICS region. As few as 5 page-ins per second from external storage can significantly affect a CICS region's ability to perform useful work. Chapter 7 will discuss how to estimate the effect of paging delays on CICS performance.

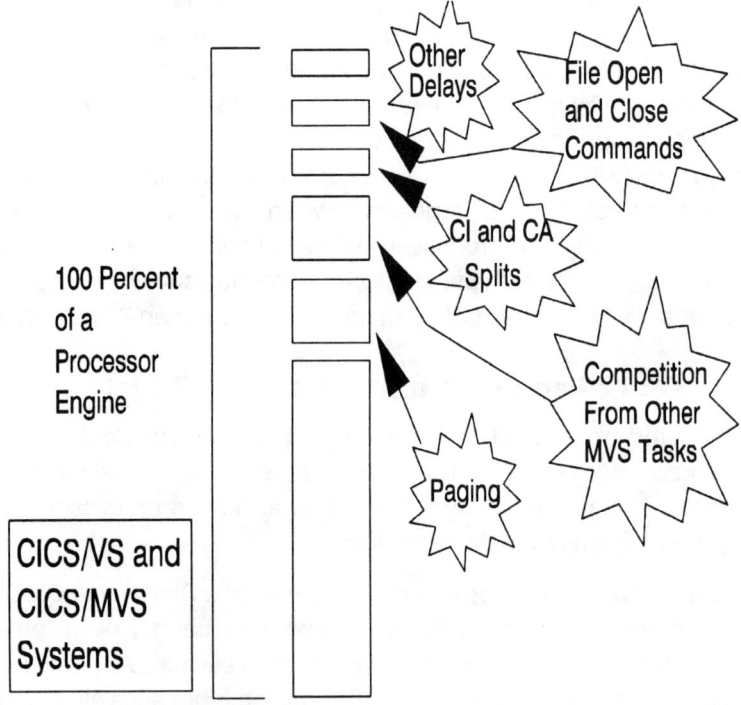

Figure 2.2 Items that restrict access to processors.

File open and close commands (in CICS/VS and CICS/MVS). In CICS/VS and CICS/MVS, file open and close commands are processed by the CICS main TCB. Once an open or close command is issued, CICS processing will be suspended on the task until the command completes.

A number of other less significant factors restrict processing on the CICS main TCB. These will be discussed in detail in Chapters 6 and 7 along with techniques to estimate their effect on transaction response time.

2.4 CICS/ESA TCB STRUCTURE

CICS/ESA is quite different in structure than either CICS/VS or CICS/MVS. Most of the old familiar management modules have been replaced by new *domains* – functionally independent service modules. In connection with this restructuring, CICS/ESA now uses additional TCBs for specialized CICS processing.

The *quasi-reentrant* (QR) TCB is the most significant TCB in CICS/ESA. This TCB is responsible for performing most control functions and application processing. All application processing, most CICS control and service functions, and most services requested by applications occur under the control of the QR TCB. In many ways it is similar to the CICS main TCB in CICS/VS and CICS/MVS.

The *resource-owning* (RO) TCB is new with CICS/ESA. It is designed to isolate the quasi-reentrant TCB from the affects of long waits associated with certain operating system commands. The primary use of the resource-owning TCB is to process file open and close commands and program loads. It also processes external security (RACF) commands that are likely to result in accesses to external storage.

CICS/VS and CICS/MVS treated the program library as a random data set and loaded programs as a series of blocks, one at a time. This allowed CICS to overlap program load activity with processing for other CICS tasks. The program load facility was both cumbersome and inefficient and was a significant cause of delays following storage shortages.

In CICS/ESA, the program load facility has been totally redesigned. Instead of using its own load logic, CICS/ESA makes use of the operating system program loader. The RO TCB issues operating system load commands and waits while programs are being loaded. Processing will continue on other CICS/ESA TCBs while program loads are being processed.

Since CICS/ESA uses MVS load facilities, it can take advantage of the MVS *library look-aside facility* (LLA). By keeping modules in a separate *virtual look-aside facility* (VLF) data space, CICS can retrieve frequently used modules directly from memory. When a request is made to load a module that is already in memory, LLA will transfer the module immediately to the CICS address space.

The resource-owning TCB normally will not do much processing. It does little to remove processing from the quasi-reentrant task. Its primary function is to isolate other CICS TCBs from the potentially long waits associated with operating system services, such as program loads, file opens, and external security.

The third TCB is the *concurrent* (CO) TCB. This TCB is optional and is similar in function to the VSAM subtask in CICS/MVS. Like the VSAM subtask, the CO TCB normally will absorb no more than about 10 to 15 percent of the processing from the QR TCB, and it will add processing overhead.

The rules for dispatching the CO TCB are very similar to those for dispatching the VSAM subtask in CICS/MVS 2.1.1 and later. When the CO TCB is active, VSAM writes are always processed by the subtask. Browse requests are always processed by the QR TCB. VSAM read requests are forwarded to the CO TCB only when CPU usage on the QR TCB is more than 70 percent for about one-half second.

In CICS/ESA release 3.3, a fourth TCB, the SZ TCB, was added. It is used only to support the *front end programming interface* (FEPI) introduced in release 3.3.

Despite a major restructuring in the way CICS processes and schedules tasks, CICS/ESA does little to change the breakdown of work processed under different TCBs. Most CICS processing will still be performed by a single TCB – the quasi-reentrant TCB.

2.5 DATABASE TCBS IN CICS REGIONS

Database 2 (DB2) support was introduced in CICS/VS release 1.7 and IMS/DBCTL support in CICS/ESA release 3.1.1. Each of these products can create separate TCBs in CICS regions. These database TCBs actually process requests for database services *in the CICS address space*.

When a CICS application issues a call for DB2 or IMS/DBCTL services, the request is forwarded to a database TCB in the CICS address space. Database services are actually performed by database TCBs running in the CICS address space. A set of threads controls communication and processing between CICS and the database subtasks.

CICS regions that use either DB2 or IMS/DBCTL should be able to exploit multiple-engine processors. Multiple TCBs can be dispatched simultaneously, each performing different database processing.

When DB2 or IMS/DBCTL TCBs are present in a CICS region, they can be responsible for much of the CPU activity in the region. Depending on how much database processing is required, database TCBs can use more CPU time than CICS itself.

> **Key Point:** Old rules of thumb about how much CPU time a CICS region should use have little meaning when DB2 or IMS/DBCTL are present.

2.6 CICS VIRTUAL STORAGE MANAGEMENT

CICS storage management can have a significant effect on CICS performance. CICS/VS and, to a lesser extent, CICS/MVS architectures have been structured around a set of control areas defined below the 16-megabyte line. This has restricted the amount of storage available to CICS system functions and applications and has been a cause of *virtual storage constraint* (VSC). The term *virtual storage constraint* (VSC) describes the performance and operational limitations of CICS's management of virtual storage.

VSC was one of the first major limitations faced by most large CICS systems. In the early releases of CICS/VS, VSC was a very real limitation. CICS/VS originally was designed to run under the MVS operating system. Then, all resources used by CICS were located in the MVS *private area*. In early releases of MVS, applications were allowed to address only 16 megabytes of storage (their *address space*). Low-storage addresses were reserved for MVS modules and control information. High-storage addresses were reserved for other MVS areas such as the *link pack area* (LPA), the *common system area* (CSA), and the *system queue area* (SQA). The remaining addressable area in the middle of the address space was called the private area.

When CICS/VS first was introduced under MVS, it seemed that a 16-megabyte address space represented more storage than anyone could possibly use. Before long, though, the 16-megabyte limitation became a serious constraint. Application systems became more sophisticated, transaction volume increased, more terminals, files, and programs were defined in each CICS region, and MVS itself consumed more storage above and below the private area. It seemed that CICS systems were being "squeezed" between a constantly increasing demand for virtual storage and a decreasing private area size.

Early CICS/VS releases were limited by the size of the MVS private area. All application programs, file buffers, CICS tables, and most CICS management modules needed to reside within an ever-shrinking private area. Furthermore, prior to the introduction of the *multiple region option* (MRO) and *intersystem communication* (ISC) facilities, applications needing to share resources had to reside in the same CICS region. In essence, VSC implied there was more demand for addressable CICS storage than was available.

Over the last few years, VSC has become much less of an issue. Each successive release of CICS has included facilities to reduced reliance on virtual storage in the private area. With the introduction of CICS/ESA (especially release 3.2.1), most CICS modules and control data have moved above the 16-megabyte line. Similarly, applications can run in and use storage above the line. On the whole, VSC should not be much of an issue for installations running CICS applications capable of exploiting 31-bit addressing in CICS/ESA 3.2.1 (or later).

It is easy to say that VSC is no longer a planning issue, especially since CICS/ESA 3.2.1. However, many shops still have modules that either need to run or reside below the 16-megabyte line. Some shops have found that it is not convenient to convert a large number of modules to run above the line. Many shops have a large investment in VS/COBOL and have not yet converted to COBOL II or COBOL/370[1]. Others have assembler applications that are not always easy to convert. Numerous legitimate reasons prevent installations from exploiting extended addressing.

The current state of VSC is that technology exists to overcome most VSC problems. Whether or not an installation suffers storage constraint problems depends on its ability to take advantage of available software solutions. Most current VSC problems are a factor of an installation's ability to invest resources to exploit existing technology.

---

[1] Support will be dropped for VS/COBOL in June, 1994. After VS/COBOL has been eliminated, there should be very few reasons to keep COBOL modules below the 16-megabyte line.

As we look to the future, the 2-gigabyte limitation will someday become almost as significant as the 16-megabyte limitation once was. Even though 2 billion bytes seems like a large amount of addressable storage, more and more of it is being used. MVS/ESA, CICS/ESA, and other products continue to exploit high addressable storage in each new release. Large buffer pools and large program inventories can consume large amounts of addressable storage. The next frontier may be expanding addressable storage by taking advantage of hiperspaces and other MVS/ESA features.

2.6.1 Virtual Storage Management in CICS/VS and CICS/MVS

The following discussion applies only to CICS/VS and CICS/MVS systems. It describes CICS storage management and how VSC can affect CICS transaction performance.

When CICS/VS and CICS/MVS regions are started, they load CICS management modules, create CICS control blocks, open some files, reserve space for operating system services, and perform other initialization functions. By the end of the initialization process, CICS/VS and CICS/MVS will have created an area called the *dynamic storage area* (DSA). The DSA resides in the private area below the 16-megabyte line and consists of the single large block of storage left after CICS has established all other resident areas. Any dynamically acquired storage requiring 24-bit addressing will reside in the DSA. This storage includes nonresident programs, program work areas, and most dynamic CICS tables.

CICS manages the DSA using a control block called the *page allocation map* (PAM). There is 1 byte in the PAM for each page in the DSA. Storage in the DSA is allocated by page. Storage requests for nonresident programs are allocated from the high end of the DSA. Requests for other types of storage are allocated from the low end of the DSA. Whenever CICS's storage management function either cannot satisfy a request for storage, has fewer pages free in the pool than the size of its storage cushion, or finds program storage holding a page in the DSA below other storage types, CICS will perform a *storage compression*.

When a storage compression occurs, CICS flags all nonresident programs for deletion. Those that are not currently in use are freed immediately; those that are being used are freed once their use count returns to zero. A few discretionary storage areas are also freed, but these usually do not amount to much.

Programs are loaded into the high end of the DSA as they are referenced. Eventually a storage compression occurs, and nonresident programs are deleted. Shortly after the storage compression, a flurry of program loads will reload frequently used modules. Then lesser-used modules will be loaded as they are needed.

If a request for storage cannot be satisfied after a storage compression, or there are still fewer free pages in the DSA than required for the storage cushion, CICS will enter a *short-on-storage* (SOS) condition and issue a console message ("System Under Stress").

During an SOS condition, CICS takes some rather drastic measures to attempt to resolve the storage shortage. Of greatest significance, it will not allow new tasks to begin in the region. Additionally, when an existing task frees storage, CICS will continually attempt to satisfy pending storage requests. This can add a significant amount of processing overhead.

If the SOS condition cannot be resolved, eventually all tasks in a CICS region will be waiting for storage requests. Once that happens, unless some tasks are eligible for purging, CICS will hang. Operators will not even be able to start CEMT commands to cancel transactions. Only cancel commands from external monitors will be of any help, and then not all the time

SOS conditions are extreme symptoms of storage constraint. Typically, before storage becomes constrained enough to cause SOS conditions, storage compression will affect performance. After nonresident programs are deleted by storage compression, many program load requests will follow shortly. As we mentioned above, the program load facility used in CICS/VS and CICS/MVS is notoriously slow. Programs are loaded one at a time, a single block at a time.

> **Key Point:** Usually, one of the first signs of storage shortage in CICS/VS and CICS/MVS systems is high activity on the CICS program library (DFHRPL). A large amount of program load activity is probably an indication of frequent program compressions caused by storage shortages.

It is worth mentioning that the most severe storage shortages usually are caused by large application programs. Whenever CICS needs to load a program or obtain storage for a work area, it must obtain all of the storage in one contiguous area. Very often, storage usage patterns cause storage fragmentation, and available storage is not typically together in one area.

In many cases, when CICS regions experience severe SOS conditions, it is not the absolute lack of storage that causes problems. Instead, they are caused by requests for large blocks of storage that cannot be satisfied because of fragmentation. While there may be quite a bit of free storage in the DSA, there may not be a large enough block of contiguous storage to load a very large nonresident program. It is possible that storage and programs already held by the requesting task may be scattered enough that even when all other tasks end, contiguous storage will not be available to load a very large module.

When storage compression occurs infrequently, its effect on performance will be minor. When storage compression occurs more than a few times per hour, program load delays can have a noticeable effect on performance in CICS/VS and CICS/MVS regions.

Although most CICS installations no longer face serious VSC problems or frequent storage compressions, many still do face challenges with VSC, especially if they are still running CICS/VS. Those who have not been able to exploit MRO or who have a large inventory of VS-COBOL programs may still be struggling with VSC, frequent storage compressions, and even with SOS conditions.

2.6.2 Virtual Storage Management in CICS/ESA (Releases 3.1.1 and 3.2.1)

In CICS/ESA, storage is managed differently than in CICS/VS or CICS/MVS. Instead of a single DSA, two dynamic system areas are maintained in CICS/ESA 3.1.1 and 3.2.1. (CICS/ESA 3.3 is discussed later in this chapter.) The first, the DSA, contains a block of storage below the 16-megabyte line. The second DSA, the *extended dynamic storage area* (EDSA), contains storage above the line. In releases 3.1.1 and 3.2.1, CICS programs will be loaded into the DSA or EDSA by the *loader domain* (LD) based on whether they need to reside above or below the 16-megabyte line.

Instead of waiting until a storage shortage is encountered, CICS/ESA's LD domain will perform what is called *dynamic program storage compression* (DPSC). The LD maintains a target for free storage in both the DSA and EDSA. Periodically, the *storage manager* (SM) domain will notify the LD of the amount of free storage in both DSAs. Whenever the amount of free space in either the DSA or EDSA is less than its respective target, the

SM domain will delete modules not currently in use (those with a use count of zero). Module deletion will done using a *least recently used* (LRU) algorithm. The number of modules deleted is a factor of the amount of free storage available.

CICS/ESA takes a proactive, versus reactive, approach to storage management. Instead of waiting for a storage shortage to occur, CICS/ESA periodically takes action to ensure that storage is available when needed. There are several advantages to this approach. To begin with, modules are periodically removed from DSA areas. This will tend to smooth program reload activity. Instead of the sharp spikes that followed storage compression in CICS/VS and CICS/MVS, program load activity will be more gradual and less of a bottleneck.

A second benefit of DPSC is that the LRU deletion algorithm will tend to keep the more frequently used modules resident in the DSAs. This will reduce the effect of deleting modules. The modules deleted will be those that have been least recently used. In normal situations these modules will have a lower probability of immediate reuse. In other words, instead of deleting all modules when a shortage occurs, DPSC allows the deletion of infrequently used modules periodically.

Another benefit of CICS/ESA's approach to storage management is that it helps control total working set size. When modules are loaded above the 16-megabyte line in pre-CICS/ESA systems, they are placed in operating system storage (storage not managed by CICS). They remain there as long as CICS is up.[2] As modules are loaded above the 16-megabyte line, more storage is mapped to hold modules. CICS/VS and CICS/MVS do not manage this storage.

In CICS/VS and CICS/MVS, modules loaded above the line that are not used frequently can cause page faults and MVS page-ins when they are executed. With DPSC in CICS/ESA, infrequently used programs are removed from storage, and the storage is reused for other programs. This tends to keep the total working set size smaller and can reduce the number of page-ins.

Key Point: With *dynamic program storage compression* (DPSC), CICS/ESA takes a proactive approach to managing program storage in DSAs. DPSC should reduce the chances

---

[2] Modules can be deleted when NEWCOPY requests are issued.

of storage shortage conditions, smooth program load activity, ensure that the most commonly used modules stay in memory, and control CICS working set size.

2.6.3 Virtual Storage Management in CICS/ESA (Release 3.3)

CICS/ESA release 3.3 introduces one of the most significant features since the introduction of CICS. Ever since its inception, CICS has been vulnerable to application programs overlaying CICS modules or control information. All storage in the DSA(s) always contained the same storage protect key, and there was no way to prevent any application from accidentally overwriting memory belonging to other applications or to CICS itself.

CICS/ESA release 3.3 takes the first major step in resolving this problem. Using the subsystem storage protection feature available on selected ES/9000 class machines, release 3.3 protects CICS storage and programs from application programs. Hardware protection can now keep application programs from overlaying CICS control information or modules. This has the potential to eliminate some major causes of CICS system failures.

Although CICS/ESA 3.3 does not eliminate all possible failures nor protect CICS transactions from one another, it is a very important first step in the right direction. This author expects to see additional protection features in future releases of CICS.

CICS/ESA 3.3 has five separate dynamic storage areas. The CDSA and ECDSA are DSAs dedicated to CICS system storage below and above the 16-megabyte line, respectively. These areas contain CICS systems data and modules. Only programs with a CICS execution key can modify storage in these areas.

The UDSA and EUDSA are the DSAs in which user application storage and programs will reside. All CICS programs can modify storage in these areas. Programs with *user* execution key will be placed in the UDSA or EUDSA. All program storage and work areas in the user areas can be accessed by any CICS or application programs.

The ERDSA is a special DSA in which reentrant 31-bit modules will be loaded, regardless of their execution key. Storage in the ERDSA is read-only storage that cannot be modified by either CICS or user class programs. Programs placed in the ERDSA must be truly reentrant and must be link-edited with the RENT and RMODE(ANY). The advantage of loading programs in the ERDSA is that there is almost absolute protection that they will not be overlaid accidentally.[3]

The discussion so far has assumed that the subsystem storage protection feature is available on the processor. If it is not, or if storage protection is not activated (a system initialization option), all storage in the CICS and user class DSAs will have the same storage protection key. The five DSAs will still be maintained, and the ERDSA can still provide read-only protection for reentrant modules.

Even if hardware storage protection is not available, CICS/ESA provides added protection against storage overlays of CICS class programs and storage. Because classes of storage are physically separated from one another, the chance of an accidental storage overlay is reduced.

Along with the added benefit of improved storage protection, CICS/ESA 3.3 provides all the benefits of storage management contained in previous releases of CICS/ESA. DPSC is performed on all five DSAs as needed. Program loads are accomplished by operating system load commands issued by the RO TCB.

2.6.4 Storage Shortage Solutions

Changes in both the operating system (particularly the introduction of MVS/XA and MVS/ESA) and in CICS itself have combined to provide substantial *virtual storage constraint relief* (VSCR) for CICS systems.

CICS's earliest contributions to VSCR were the *intersystem communications* (ISC) and *multiple region option* (MRO) features. With MRO (and, to a lesser extent, with ISC), CICS applications could be split to run in multiple regions.

MRO and ISC *transaction routing* allowed CICS to automatically forward transactions from a CICS region owning terminal definitions [a *terminal-owning region* (TOR)] to one owning application programs and resources [an *application-owning region* (AOR)]. With the advent of transaction routing, most large shops created one or more TORs that

---

[3] The ERDSA is designed to provide read-only protection for eligible CICS modules. This means that the modules absolutely cannot be changed. Unfortunately, some vendor test tools must modify code in application programs to set application break points in testing. To accommodate this requirement, ERDSA read-only protection can be turned off by specifying the RENTPGM system initialization parameter to NOPROTECT. It is this author's assumption that the NOPROTECT option would be used only in test environments. It is probably worth noting that if NOPROTECT is used during testing, modules could conceivably fail in production (with the PROTECT option) that had been tested successfully with the NOPROTECT option.

contained only terminal definitions. This allowed users to separate large terminal control tables from regions in which transactions were processed. A network with several thousand terminals could almost entirely consume the largest CICS/VS or CICS/MVS regions. In many environments, multiple TORs were required just to support large numbers of terminal definitions.

MRO and ISC *function shipping* also contributed to VSCR. Applications written using the *command-level* interface could access resources (such as files and temporary storage) controlled by other CICS regions. This allowed applications to be placed in separate CICS regions even if they accessed common files. Function shipping also allowed the creation of *file-owning regions* (FORs) that contained only file definitions. Since VSAM buffers used to reside below the 16-megabyte line (prior to MVS/XA), FORs could provide substantial virtual storage constraint relief.

In all currently supported releases of CICS, VSAM buffer pools and most VSAM control information are located in storage about the 16-megabyte line. Moving files to FORs does little to relieve VSCR. In current technology, FORs are not created for VSCR. Instead, they are created to improve availability or relieve other constraints. This is discussed in more detail in Appendix D, which discusses MRO strategies.

VSAM *local shared resources* (LSR) also provided significant relief to storage constraint. In the early days of CICS, most VSAM files were defined using *nonshared resources* (NSR). With NSR, each file required its own set of buffers and control blocks, and these all needed to reside in the MVS private area. LSR allowed several files to share a common set of buffers and some common control blocks. Because the shared pool of buffers normally would be significantly smaller than the combined size of all the NSR buffers it replaced, LSR became a favorite means of achieving VSCR.

In modern systems, VSAM buffers will reside above the 16-megabyte line and the use of LSR no longer is a factor in VSCR. LSR, though, is still the preferred method for accessing VSAM data, but for different reasons. When LSR is used, VSAM will invoke a feature called *look-aside* before retrieving data from external storage. If a control interval (CI) is already in an LSR buffer, it will be reused without being reread from DASD.

Most users have found that LSR not only reduces the amount of storage needed for buffer pools, it also reduces DASD activity, improves response time, and even reduces total CPU utilization. (LSR reduces CPU usage by reducing the CPU overhead associated with scheduling

I/Os to DASD.) In older releases of MVS/DFP, LSR scanned the buffer pool, and large buffer pools were not effective. In current releases of MVS/DFP, LSR uses a hashing algorithm that provides consistent, rapid access to data in buffer pools. LSR should provide improved service and lower CPU usage than NSR for most VSAM files used in modern CICS systems.

MVS/XA, along with several releases of CICS that exploited extended architecture features, provided the next quantum jump in VSCR. File buffers moved above the 16-megabyte line. Command-level programs could reside above the 16-megabyte line. Other types of storage, such as main temporary storage, also moved above the line. Each release of CICS had more modules that could either reside above the line or move to the MVS link pack area.

Two popular packages, *Quick Fetch* from Legent Corporation and *Fetch* from Axios, also helped relieve the symptoms of VSC by providing facilities to load CICS programs rapidly. Quick Fetch created a separate address space in which the most commonly loaded modules were stored. Whenever CICS would load a module, if it was in memory, it simply would be transferred from the Quick Fetch address space to the CICS DSA. Fetch improved the efficiency of the load process by storing modules in a special dataset that could be retrieved rapidly. Both Fetch and Quick Fetch improved the speed by which CICS programs could be loaded and reduced the delays following storage compression. A later package, *XA-RELO*, relieved storage constraint by storing load modules above the 16-megabyte line and retrieving them as needed. XA-RELO also attempts to improve DSA storage management by freeing modules when they are not needed.

With MVS/ESA and CICS/ESA release 3.2.1, the process of virtual storage constraint relief is effectively complete. CICS/ESA release 3.2.1 allows most CICS management modules to reside above the line. It moves most remaining control areas above the line, especially the terminal control table. Most of the storage below the line is reserved for application use. If applications are using versions of compilers that support 32-bit addressing, the programs and most of the storage they use can reside above the line. In essence, the CICS product has provided a set of features that should allow installations to address most virtual storage addressability problems.

Key Point: By CICS/ESA release 3.2.1, CICS architecture has removed most of the restrictions that have caused virtual storage constraint. Most remaining virtual storage constraints are related to application systems that require access to storage below the 16 megabyte line.

2.6.5 Virtual Storage Constraint Today

Over time, the developers of CICS have gradually eliminated most sources of VSC. At this time, VSC is no longer as much of a concern as it once was. In many ways, VSC has become primarily a technical issue with only minor effects on performance and capacity planning.

It is not uncommon today to see systems running dozens, if not hundreds, of CICS regions on one or more large processors. Over the years, many of these regions were originally created to relieve VSC. There is a cost associated with running CICS regions and passing data between them. Often, the CPU overhead associated with function shipping requests is greater than the cost of actually accessing the resources.

Since the introduction of CICS/ESA, there has been a movement to recombine some regions previously split to overcome VSC problems. Sometimes, there is no longer need to bear the overhead of running as many regions or communicating requests between CICS regions. It may be cost-effective to recombine resources that were once split to overcome VSC.

The primary reason for discussing VSC is that it has traditionally caused a need for special software planning. As regions became constrained, they would need to be split, and this was not always easy. Additional CICS regions generated more overhead, and when applications are split across multiple CICS regions, MRO services, such as function shipping and transaction routing, can further increase overhead. When VSC ceases to be a problem and some existing regions are recombined, CICS overhead can be reduced.

2.7 SUMMARY

In many ways, CICS is like a miniature operating system to support processing of transaction-based systems. CICS transactions are (or at least should be) dependent on the CICS infrastructure to provide all of their processing needs. CICS applications are also sensitive to internal CICS restrictions that affect performance and service.

Two major architectural considerations require special planning in most CICS environments. The first is the way most CICS processing is dispatched on a single TCB in each CICS region. The second is limitations caused by virtual storage constraint.

Those installations running CICS/ESA or CICS/MVS along with versions of compilers that support processing above the 16-megabyte line probably will find VSC to be little more than an inconvenience. With CICS/ESA 3.2.1 and 3.3, all of the more significant architectural causes of VSC have been eliminated. At the present time, only those installations that are still running older releases of CICS or that have not taken advantage of newer compilers should face serious VSC problems. Others should find VSC to be a manageable technical concern, if an issue at all.

While VSC is becoming less of an issue, dispatching limitations have, if anything, become more acute. With the potential to run more application systems in a single CICS region, the possibility of overloading the primary TCB is a real concern. While it is not measured by most CICS monitors, internal queueing for dispatch service can represent a significant part of CICS response time.

Virtual storage concerns may only have an indirect effect on hardware planning, but CICS CPU limitations have significant influence both software and hardware plans. Performance planning for CICS systems must account for CICS internal processing peculiarities.

SELECTED READING

[BARN91] Barnes, Steve, "CICS/ESA Dispatcher Operation," *CMG Transactions*, Summer, 1991.

[IBM001] IBM Technical Information Search items Q492048, Q543758, Q544379, and Q563137.

[IBM92] CICS/ESA Release Guide, Version 3 Release 3, IBM manual GC33-0792-00, 1992.

Chapter 3

Analyzing CICS Workloads

3.1 OVERVIEW

This chapter introduces several fundamental concepts that will be used throughout the remainder of this book. In this chapter we will look at how to segregate CICS work into meaningful components called *workloads*. We will discuss methods used to characterize workloads, techniques for analyzing change and growth, the value of historical data, and many of the basic steps necessary to establish a workable CICS performance planning process. In this chapter we will also define several basic terms and concepts.

3.1.1 Primary Audience

Systems programmers probably will find much of the material in this chapter new and different. Terms and concepts developed in this chapter will be used in later chapters when we discuss how to project workload growth, assess the impact of resource degradation, and evaluate CICS system performance. If systems programmers anticipate becoming involved in CICS performance planning, it is strongly recommended that they be familiar with most of the material presented in this chapter.

Capacity planners should already be familiar with many of the concepts introduced in this chapter. However, much of the material in this chapter is unique to a CICS environment. It is suggested that experienced capacity planners read at least the sections on growth bias, the components of workload growth, and the analysis of individual CICS regions.

Application developers will probably find much of the material in this chapter to be new and interesting. Though it may not be directly applicable to application development, the concepts are necessary for material introduced in later chapters. It is suggested that application developers become familiar with the major concepts in this chapter.

3.2 WHAT IS A WORKLOAD?

The term *workload* has special meaning to performance or capacity planners. It refers to ways different types of data processing work are combined into meaningful groupings that can be analyzed and studied.

Workloads are logical groupings of work described in terms of either the type or nature of work. Workloads can be defined in terms of CICS transactions, batch work, started tasks, or other measures of activity. When we refer to workloads, we may be speaking in terms of the total number of units (e.g., transactions), the resources used by the workload (e.g., CPU time, DASD, ETC.), or the service (response time) provided by the workload.

In this book we will study workloads associated with CICS systems. Even though other workloads are important and can influence the overall performance of CICS systems, the scope of this book does not allow more than a cursory treatment of non-CICS workloads.[1]

Workloads can be described in a number of ways. They can be described in terms of volume, resources, or service:

- *Volume profiles* identify the number and type of transactions processed.

- *Resource profiles* describe the resources consumed by the workload. They include measures of CPU time used, file requests, DASD I/Os performed, memory used, and other resources consumed.

---

[1] Chapter 7 will examine how non-CICS workloads can affect dispatch processing and performance in CICS regions. Chapter 11 will discuss how non-CICS workloads can affect DASD performance. These are the primary references to non-CICS workloads in this book.

- *Service profiles* describe performance characteristics such as transaction response time.

Workloads are the key to understanding capacity and performance. Before we can project future activity or plan software or hardware configurations, we need to understand the nature of current workloads and their patterns of growth. A large part of the performance and capacity planning processes involves studying workloads, how they are changing, and how they are likely to change.

3.3 WORKLOAD CLASSIFICATION AND CHARACTERIZATION

An important part of working with workloads is to define and describe them. The process of defining workloads is called *workload classification*. In a CICS environment, workload classification involves gathering selected CICS transactions into meaningful groups, or workloads. They may be gathered by transaction identifier (ID), system ID, user, terminal name, or processing characteristics.

The process of describing workloads is called *workload characterization*. Workload characterization involves describing groups of transactions in terms of transaction volume, the resources used by transactions, and the service they receive.

Workloads may be classified in different ways for different purposes. Sometimes we may want to look at transaction counts, resource consumption, or response time for specific application systems. Here, we would probably group transactions by transaction ID or some kind of system ID.

At other times we might be interested in analyzing workloads in terms of processing characteristics. We might need to know how many "small," "medium," or "large" transactions were processed for statistical purposes. We might be interested in the relationship between file requests and CPU usage. We may need specialized groupings to build models of computer systems. Each of these differing needs would require that workloads be classified in different ways.

Part of the challenge in classifying workloads is to group work into a *manageable number of categories*. For most kinds of planning or modeling, it is usually best to group work into no more than 10 to 12 workloads. In complex CICS systems, this may seem impossible at first, but it is not as difficult as it might appear. A relatively small number of transaction types usually are responsible for a large percentage of the transactions received and/or resources utilized. Transactions that are executed infrequently, or that use few resources, can be collected into "miscellaneous" workloads. It is common to define miscellaneous workloads of differing sizes (small, medium, and large) for many types of analysis.

> **Key Point:** Workload characterization is the process of differentiating data processing work into meaningful groupings called workloads. One of the challenges in workload characterization is to define a manageable number of categories.

3.3.1 Classifying Work Using Transactions IDs

In a typical CICS environment, workloads are most often defined in terms of transaction IDs. In most large CICS systems, there will be hundreds or even thousands of different transaction IDs executed each day. The logistics of doing any kind of meaningful analysis for that many transaction types can be staggering. To facilitate analysis and planning, transaction IDs need to be grouped into a manageable number of workloads.

Most installations have naming conventions for CICS transaction IDs. Typically, the first two or three characters of the transaction ID identify specific application systems. For example, all the transactions whose names start with the letters "AR" might belong to the accounts receivable system. Ideally, all accounts receivable transactions and only accounts receivable transactions would start with the letters AR.

When we study the CICS processing being done by the accounts receivable system, we could simply summarize data for the AR transactions, as illustrated in Figure 3.1. The advantage of summarizing transactions this way is that it is an easy way to relate transaction activity and resource consumption with specific business functions.

This approach may be meaningful to the business organization and can be easily communicated to management. It is easy for management to understand, for example, that 15 percent of the processor is devoted to running the accounts receivable application. As business levels increase or new functions or services are added, the cost of added work can be easily associated with services management understands. Workload classification of this type also lends itself to billing and charge-back systems.

Transaction ID

```
┌──┬──┐
│AR│xx│
└──┴──┘
```
→ Accounts Receivable Transactions

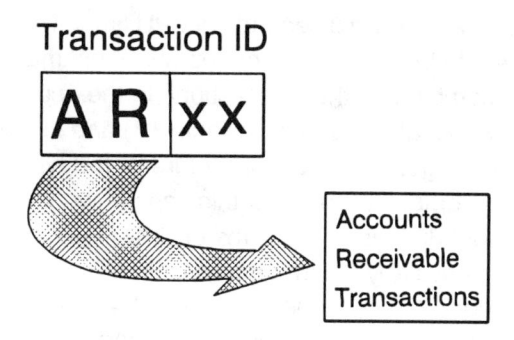

Figure 3.1 Transaction IDs can identify workloads.

3.3.2 Homogeneity in Workloads

It is not always practical to group workloads by transaction or system IDs – the work might not be homogeneous. That is, the individual transactions within a system might have vastly differing performance and resource utilization patterns.

For example, our sample accounts receivable system may consist of 30 different transaction IDs. Of those 30, it is likely that 20 or more would be used infrequently and represent a small portion of both total transactions entered and resources consumed. For planning purposes, these transactions can almost be ignored because of their insignificant effect on the overall system.

Of the remaining 10 transactions, 7 or 8 would be moderate- to high-volume transactions with modest appetites for resources such as CPU time, I/Os, and memory. The remaining two or three transactions, though, might be executed infrequently but consume large amounts of CPU time or perform very high numbers of I/O requests.

Let us suppose that about 95 percent of the AR transactions processed were relatively commonplace. Designed to accomplish some specific function, they would perform a modest amount of processing and return information to the user fairly quickly. For the purpose of illustration, each of these transactions would request about 10 I/Os and use an average of 50 milliseconds (ms) of CPU time. Typical CICS response time would be less than 1 second most of the time.

Continuing the illustration, the remaining 5 percent of the transactions would be considerably more resource-intensive, each performing about

1,000 random I/Os and using 3 seconds of CPU time. Their internal CICS response time would be about 30 seconds under optimal conditions.

If we were to combine all the transactions in the accounts receivable system into one workload (as shown in Table 3.1) and develop a composite profile, we would get a very unfair picture of the type of processing being done. The combined profile of this sample workload would show an average of about 60 I/Os and 200 ms of CPU time per transaction. In fact, we might not have any "average" transactions or even any that were close to the average. The average for the workload would not be a good indicator of the type transactions being processed.

The difficulty with nonhomogeneous workloads is that they limit our ability to perform statistical analysis or do any kind of mathematical modeling. If we were to model workloads containing dissimilar transaction profiles, many of the formulas used by modeling packages would not work correctly. Most modeling systems assume that transactions in a workload are reasonably similar with randomly distributed patterns of resource usage. This would not be the case with nonhomogeneous workloads, and the results produced by modeling and other kinds of statistical analysis could be erroneous.

3.3.3 Classifying Workloads by Resource Utilization

When logically grouped workloads tend to be nonhomogeneous, it may be necessary to use other approaches grouping transactions. One technique is to segregate work into *clusters*. Clusters are groupings of transactions with similar resource utilization patterns. The purpose of developing clusters is to identify groupings of transactions with homogeneous workload profiles.

Table 3.1 Example of a Nonhomogenous Workload

Transaction Type	Percentage of Transactions	Average CPU	Average I/Os
Normal	95%	50 ms	10
Resource intensive	5%	3000 ms	1000
Composite	100%	197.5 ms	59.5

The relationships between resources such as CPU time, I/O requests, or memory can be used to differentiate transactions into separate workloads. Even with a wide range of transactions, it is likely that a few dominant workload patterns will evolve. Applying natural relationships, it is not too hard to devise a set of rules to define workloads suitable for statistical analysis or modeling.

Figures 3.2 and 3.3 illustrate a technique that may be used to group transactions by workload content. Both figures show the relationship between CPU usage and logical I/O requests for transactions in a single CICS region. Figure 3.2 has a larger scale and summarizes most of the transactions running in the region. Figure 3.3 reduces the scale to provide a better picture of the smaller tasks which account for the greatest number of transactions. Notice that the relationships tend to form clusters of natural groupings even though there are a large number of transaction types executing in the region.

The technique of characterizing workloads based on workload content is called *clustering*. Figures 3.2 and 3.3 represent a crude, intuitive method of clustering. Sophisticated mathematical procedures are available which can automatically build clusters. Better groupings can be accomplished by including additional variables such as memory usage. Statistical products, such as SAS, contain procedures to automatically define cluster groups.

3.3.4 A Comparison of Classification Techniques

The process of grouping transactions into workloads is almost more of an art than a science. Workload definitions need to balance logical identity and homogeneity. Unless workloads can be named and associated with some kind of business element, it will be difficult to anticipate changes in the nature or volume of work. Nonetheless, unless workloads are internally consistent and reasonably homogeneous, many types of analysis will not be possible.

Workloads defined strictly on the basis of resource utilization patterns usually cannot be identified intuitively. Unless workloads can be tied to business elements, it may not be possible to forecast changes associated with business activity. Without a way of associating workloads with meaningful system identifiers, there will be no way to measure response time for specific applications or determine whether specific service requirements have been satisfied.

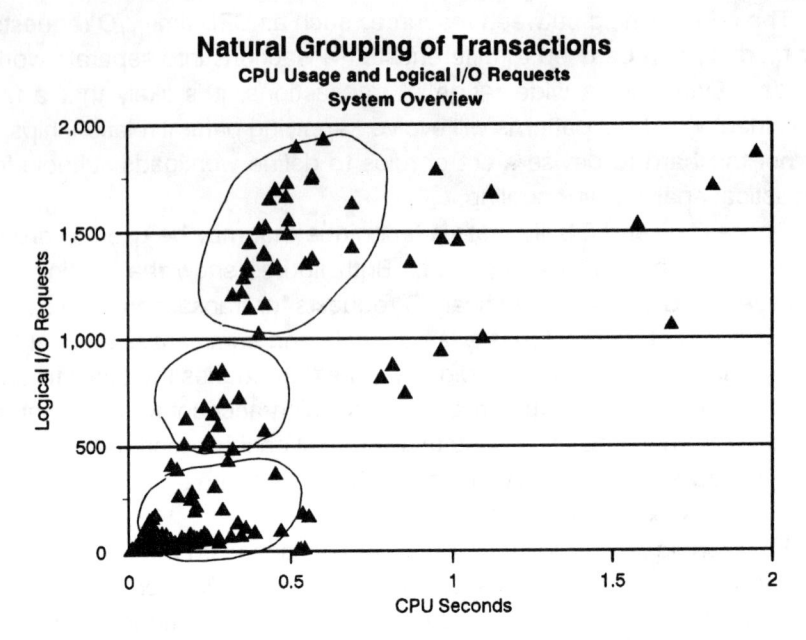

Figure 3.2 CPU - I/O clusters for CICS transactions.

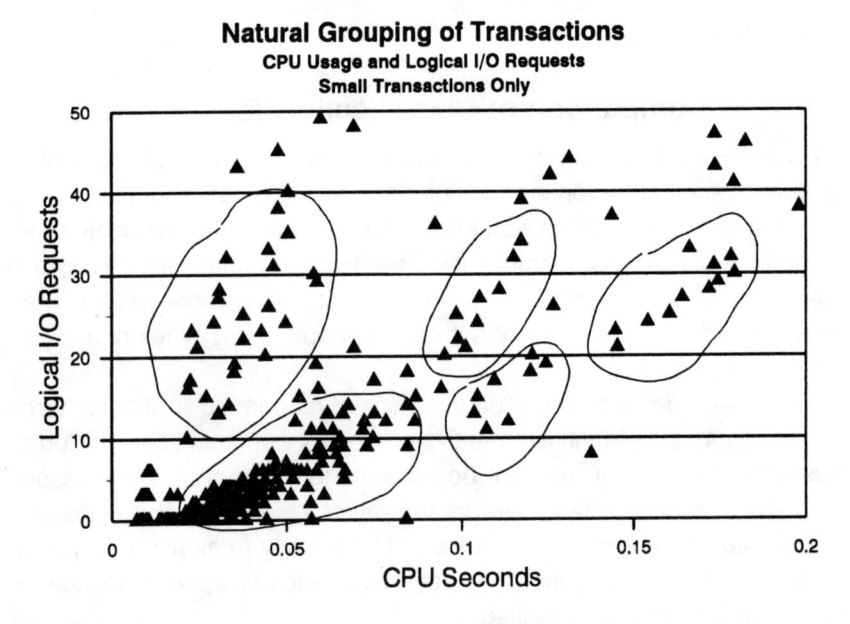

Figure 3.3 CPU - I/O profile for small transactions.

When groupings based on transaction or system identifiers are not homogeneous, it may make sense to subdivide major systems into separate workloads based on workload characteristics. The difficulty in doing this is that this might lead to the definition of numerous workload types. Unless we can keep the number of workloads at a manageable number, it can be difficult to perform many kinds of study.

3.4 THE USE OF HISTORICAL DATA

The use of historical data is an important part of the capacity planning process. As we will see, historical data can help us understand current activity as well as the forces driving changes in workloads. Historical data can be valuable in reviewing what has happened over time.

In the early days of capacity planning, the sophisticated tools and procedures used today were not available to capacity planners. Many of the techniques that we take for granted today were not yet developed.

Graphs and trends became popular quickly. It was easy to plot data and observe trends and relationships between different elements. Some frequently tracked trends included the number of transactions, average CPU utilization, peak CPU utilization, and average response time. This type of data seemed useful back then and is often tracked today.

Data about trends and historical information can give us a good picture of *what has occurred* in the past. This information can provide insight into the nature of change and can be useful for planning. However, *the use of trend data by itself can be misleading and even dangerous.*

> **Key Point:** The use of historical or trend data by itself can be misleading.

3.4.1 Dangers with the Use of Historical Data

When used wisely, historical data can improve the process of performance and capacity planning. However, when used unwisely, historical and trend data can present several hazards. Just because a graph or correlation analysis appears to demonstrate a relationship, it does not mean that the relationship actually exists.

Some of the problems present in the use of historical data include:

- **Past activity is not a guarantee of the future.** The fact that peak CPU usage has grown by 2 to 3 percent each month for the past several months does not necessarily imply that the growth will continue over the next several months. Unless we know the cause of growth in CPU usage, it is not reasonable to assume it will continue.

- **Some relationships that appear to be straight lines are actually nonlinear.** Although some relationships appear to be linear over a small range of values, they may become exponential or parabolic when extended over a wider range of values.

For example, the relationship between the number of transactions and response time is nonlinear (Figure 3.4). At some level of activity, increases in the number of transactions will produce progressively larger increases in response time.

At lower ranges of activity, graph of response times versus transaction volume will often appear linear in nature. For some range of transaction volume, it might appear that response time was increasing proportionately with transaction volume. However, beyond a given level of activity, response time could turn up sharply. It might

Response Time Versus Total Transactions

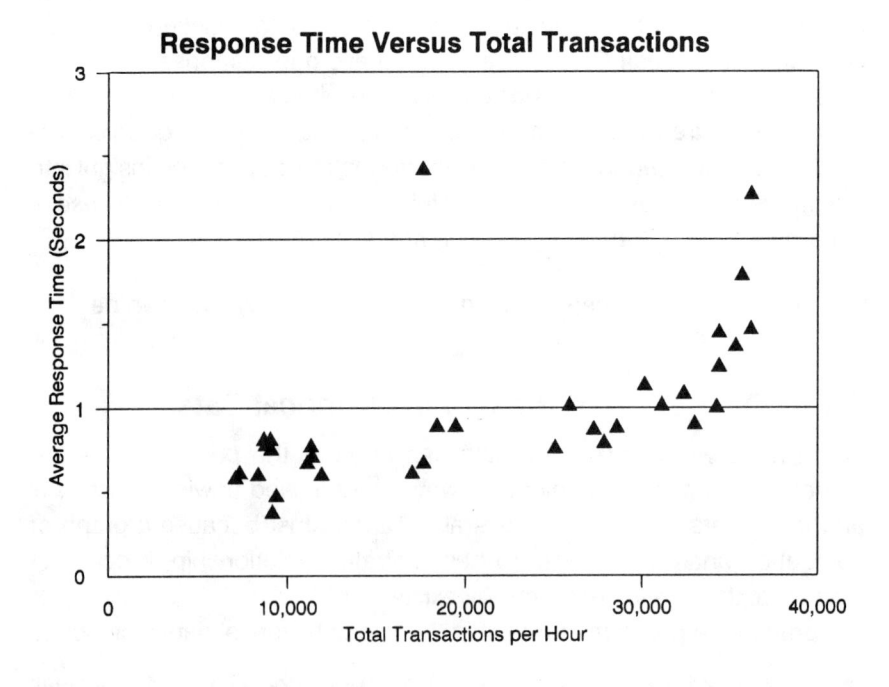

Figure 3.4 Example of a nonlinear relationship.

even pass "the knee of the curve." We will examine the reasons for this effect in Chapter 5.

Figure 3.4 illustrates this principle with real data from a production system. The graph presents data for one week (Monday through Friday). Each observation corresponds to a 1-hour period from the prime shift. The horizontal axis represents the total number of transactions processed in a selected CICS region. The vertical axis represents average CICS response time for those periods.

Notice that the relationship appears to be almost linear for the range of 8,000 to 34,000 transactions per hour. It is fairly obvious that one or more resources hit a bottleneck at about 34,000 transactions per hour, causing response time to degrade almost instantaneously. Data for transaction rates below 33,000 transactions per hour provide little indication of response times for higher levels of activity.

Key Point: One difficulty with the use of trend data is that some relationships that appear to be linear over one range of values are nonlinear above that range.

- **Outliers can distort averages and obscure trends.** *Outliers* are observations that seem inconsistent with other data in a graph. They are common in most kinds of workload analysis. Periods that contain system outages, CICS initiation or shutdown, transaction lockouts, or other abnormalities can cause observations that do not match normal statistical patterns. If there are few outliers and we understand what caused them, they may be ignored or discarded. If there are a large number of outliers, it is probably a good idea to investigate their cause.

  Figure 3.4 shows one *outlier* at about 18,000 transactions per hour. Response time seems out of line for the number of transactions processed. This was caused by a system lockout during that hour.

- **Projections have validity only within the range of values for which we have data.** Beyond that range, we must use caution. Using the preceding example (Figure 3.4), if we had response time data only for transaction arrival rates below 30,000 transactions per hour, we could not safely project response times for higher workload levels using trending techniques. The true nature of the relationship would not be apparent within this limited range.

Key Point: The use of trend or regression data is valid only within the ranges for which we already have data.

- **Trends show correlations between the elements without necessarily implying a cause-and-effect relationship.** Two items may vary with one another, but both may be driven by a third element. It is important to understand the logical relationship between elements before attempting to use data about their relationships.

Key Point: Unless we understand the relationship between two variables, there is danger in using simple correlation techniques to forecast future values.

3.5 GROWTH BIAS

Growth bias is an organization's predisposition to change. A number of common forces are responsible for most changes in computer workloads. Changes in business activity will influence the number of transactions processed. Changes in user staffing can affect the number of transactions entered. The program development staff will be creating and modifying systems. These and other factors are responsible for much of the change in workloads at many organizations.

Growth bias is a reflection of change that is structural in nature. Under normal circumstances, some types of change will continue to influence workload growth over a period of time. Certain underlying forces are causing change and driving growth patterns. As long as these forces remain unchanged, historical patterns of growth are likely to influence growth in the future.

Key Point: Growth bias is a reflection of the structural forces within an organization that influence workload change. It represents an organization's tendency to change.

Before we can determine if past trends will continue, we must identify the factors behind growth. An analysis of growth bias can help identify the forces driving change. It is only when we understand the forces behind change that we can decide if they will continue in the future.

3.6 THREE COMPONENTS OF WORKLOAD GROWTH

There are three distinct components of workload growth. The first component is *volume*. The volume component represents growth related to the number of transactions entered. It is a measure of changes in the use of transactions or systems. Volume-related growth may be caused by increased business activity, new users, additional staffing, or even new functionality. *Any growth associated with the additional use of application systems will be part of the volume component of growth.*

> **Key Point:** The three components of workload growth are *volume*, *new systems*, and *complexity/overhead*.

The second component of growth is *new systems*. When new systems are installed, additional processing will be required to support them. In some shops, new systems will represent a large portion of total workload growth; in others this kind of growth may be inconsequential.

The final component is one that is often overlooked. It is called *complexity/overhead*. In every installation, the nature of the environment and the processing complexity of applications is constantly changing. New releases of software change the amount of processing requirements. Program modifications usually change the program path lengths, even if only slightly.

It may not be obvious, but most program changes do increase the CPU time required to execute a program. It is rare to see program changes actually reduce the number of instructions executed. Very few changes result in the removal of code. Instead, new functions and services are added to existing programs. Even when new code is executed only a small percentage of the time, statements will be executed to decide whether to invoke new code.

Almost all modifications to application programs increase the amount of CPU utilized, but few modifications cause increases large enough to measure. Overall, there is a cumulative increase in the average amount of CPU time required per transaction executed. This is part of the *complexity/overhead* component of growth.

Complexity/overhead can be a major cause of processor growth in some CICS environments. In many organizations, a large part of the programming staff spends most of its time performing maintenance and developing enhancements for strategic or mission-critical applications.

Some systems are modified continually, and there is even backlog of requests for enhancements.

The result is a pattern of growth driven by a steady flow of enhancements to existing applications. Figures 3.5 and 3.6 illustrate this effect with two different applications. Notice in Figure 3.5 that, over a 3-year period, the CPU usage attributed to changes in complexity/overhead accounts for almost one-half of the total CPU time used by this application. Even though the vast of majority of the application alterations were too small to be measured individually, they had a very significant cumulative effect over time.

> **Key Point:** Applications that are modified regularly will probably demonstrate a tendency to increase the amount of CPU time used per transaction.

Complexity/overhead is driven not only by application changes, but also by changes in the software environment. Just as changes to applications tend to generate small, unmeasurable increases in CPU utilization, enhancements to software will tend to do the same thing. Most new releases of software use a slightly larger amount of CPU time. (The introduction of CICS/ESA was a notable exception to this.) As maintenance is applied, software continues to grow in complexity.

New software tools (such as database systems and fourth-generation languages) also tend to increase the amount of processing and memory used by a typical transaction. Software tools with improved functionality commonly are more resource-intensive than older, simpler tools. There is normally a price for functionality and convenience. Together, these factors cause a constantly upward bias in the amount of CPU time and other resources consumed by a typical transaction.

Almost all environments will experience growth in all three components: volume, new systems, and complexity/overhead. Your pattern of growth will be unique to your environment. A key task in analyzing growth is to separate growth into its three components.

Figures 3.5 and 3.6 show the components of growth over a fairly long period (a little over 3 years). Institutional patterns can be identified more easily over longer periods. However, even if we have only a few months of data, it can be worthwhile to track the components of growth. When we understand the components of growth, we will have better information to project changes for the future.

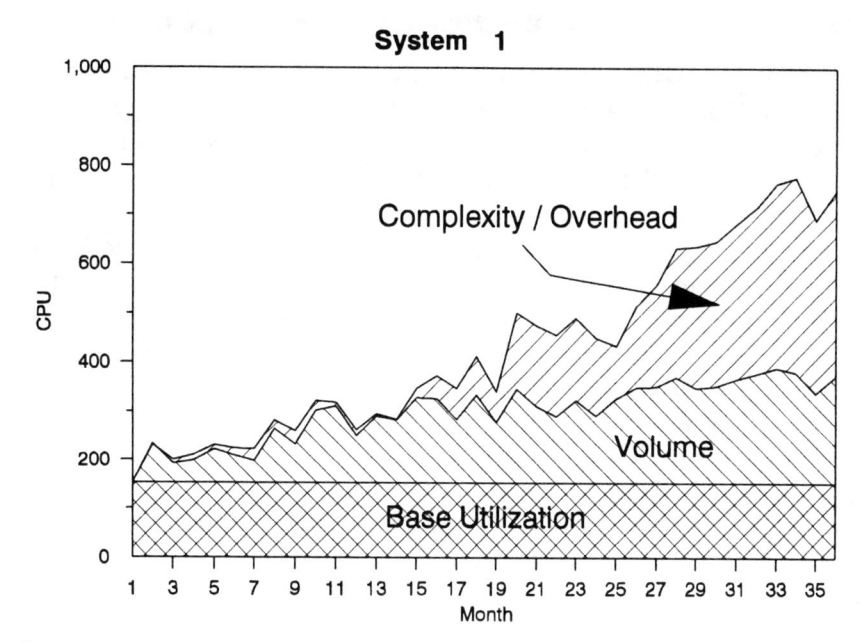

Figure 3.5 Example of components of workload growth.

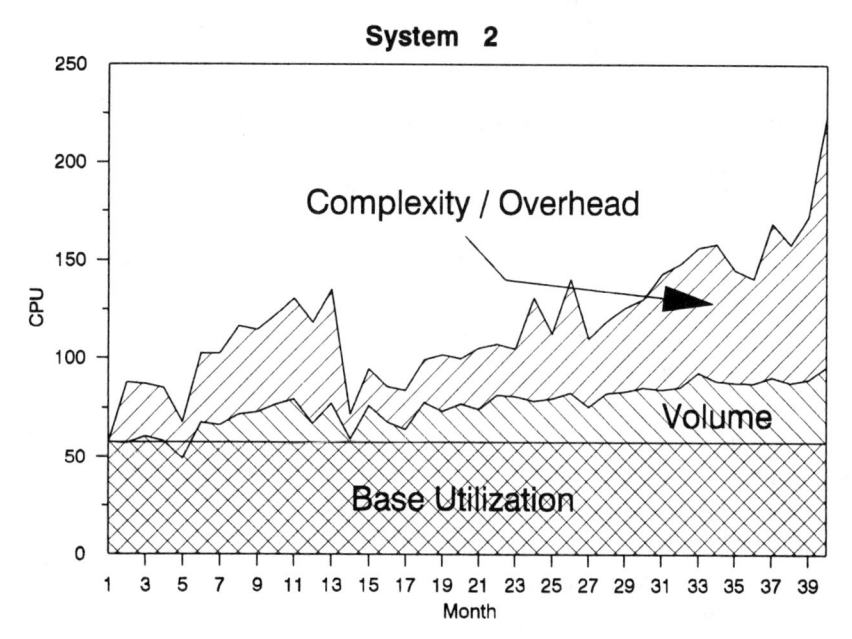

Figure 3.6 Example of components of workload growth.

3.6.1 How to Calculate the Components of Growth

In theory, it is quite simple to calculate the three components of growth. However, the complexity of modern CICS systems tends to make the process quite complicated. We will first look at the mechanics of growth calculations and then review factors that can make them more complicated.

For the purposes of this discussion we will define the *base period* as the point in time to which we will compare measurements from other periods. Each of several successive periods (months, weeks, etc.) will be compared to one base period. To simplify calculations, it is can be helpful to select a base period with a low level of activity.

The calculation of the *new systems component* is fairly simple. It is simply the transactions or systems that did not exist in the base period. With data from a performance data base (we will discuss performance data bases later in this chapter) and a high-level statistical language (such as SAS), we can easily compare current data to data in the base period.

> **Key Point:** When separating the components of workload growth, transactions or systems in the current period that did not exist in the base period will usually be treated as new systems.

It may not always be desirable to categorize all new transaction IDs with the new systems component. Some new transactions IDs might simply be extensions of existing applications or functions. For example, we may choose to associate new AR transactions with the complexity/overhead component of the accounts receivable system. This author's approach has been to treat new transaction IDs that are clearly related to existing systems as complexity/overhead. Other transactions will be numbered with new systems.

The *volume component* of growth is the growth related to changes in transaction volume. It is calculated by multiplying the difference between the number of transactions in the new and base periods by the amount of resource used per transaction in the base period. In essence, the volume component is the product of the original CPU time used per transaction and the change in the number of transactions.

Let us assume that during a one-hour period in the base period, 1,000 AR01 transactions used a total of 50 CPU seconds. Each transaction used an average of 50 ms of CPU time (50 seconds / 1,000 transactions).

In the second month, there were 1,500 AR01 transactions in the corresponding 1-hour period using a total of 90 CPU seconds. Each transaction used an average of 60 ms of CPU time.

The calculation of the volume component of growth is shown in Figure 3.7. The 25 CPU seconds of volume-related growth represents changes in the workload associated with increased transaction volume. It reflects the cost of running 500 additional transactions at 50 ms per transaction (from the base period).

The *complexity/overhead component* is any growth not associated with either new systems or volume. After adjusting for new systems and volume-related changes, the remaining difference can be attributed to the increased cost of executing programs. Continuing with the previous example, the complexity/overhead component would be calculated as shown in the latter part of Figure 3.7. There were 40 CPU seconds of total change in resource utilization. Volume-related growth accounted for 25 CPU seconds. The remaining 15 seconds of CPU time represent growth associated with changes in complexity or overhead.

In this example, we did not have any new systems. If we did, we would have subtracted the amount of CPU time used for new systems first. Then we would have determined the amount of growth related to volume.

Calculation of Volume Component of Growth

```
  Month 2   50 ms * 1,500 trans.   =   75 CPU secs.
- Month 1   50 ms * 1,000 trans.   =   50 CPU secs.
                                        _____
  Volume Component                 =   25 CPU secs.
```

Calculation of Complexity / Overhead Component

```
    Month 2 ........................... 90 CPU secs.
  - Month 1 ........................... 50 CPU secs.
                                        _____
    Total Change ....................40 CPU secs.
  - Volume Component ......... 25 CPU secs.
                                        _____
    Complexity/Overhead ...... 15 CPU secs.
```

Figure 3.7 Calculation of the components of growth.

Finally we would have calculated the changes associated with complexity and/or overhead.

3.6.2 Accounting for Negative Growth

In the example above, both components of growth were positive. That is, there were more transactions in the new period than in the base period, and average CPU time per transaction was higher in the second period than in the base period. When either the number of transactions or CPU usage per transaction decreases, one of the components of growth will have a negative value. The technique illustrated above will still work with negative values as long as the calculations are performed in the correct order (new systems, volume, and, finally, complexity/overhead). Decreases in volume or complexity/overhead will simply show up as negative growth.

3.6.3 Automation of the Calculation Process

The example above was fairly basic and could be performed manually with little difficulty. However, when we are performing longer, more complex studies, it is usually better to automate the calculations. The manual calculations illustrated could easily be coded in a high-level language such as SAS. This would be particularly helpful if multiple systems were to be analyzed over a long period of time.

If you do write a program to calculate the components of growth, you will probably need to be aware of one additional factor. Transactions that existed in the base period may have been discontinued. These discontinued transactions will effectively "shrink" the data from the base period. Depending on how many transactions fall in this category, you may want to include it as a special class in your analysis. Each subsequent month would then have five components: The original base workload, discontinued transactions (always shown as negative growth), new systems, volume-related growth, and growth related to complexity/overhead. This is illustrated in Table 3.2.

In addition to tracing CPU growth, the same principles could be applied to other resources, such as file requests. Values would be compared to those from a base period.

Table 3.2 Components of Growth

Component	Description	Type Growth
Base period	Processing present in the base period	n/a
Discontinued transactions or systems	Transactions or systems running in the base period that have been discontinued	Always negative
New transactions or systems	Transactions or systems that did not exist in the base period	Always positive
Volume-related growth	Changes in the number of tranactions	Positive (increases) or negative (decreases)
Complexity/overhead	Change in the cost of running each transaction	Positive (more resource used) or negative (less resource used)

3.6.4 Accounting for Processor Differences

The calculations illustrated above assumed that the same type of processor was used in both periods. If the two periods ran on different types of processors, adjustments probably would be needed to account for differences in processor speed.

When CICS workloads run on different processors in the same processor class, processor engine speeds should be the same. In theory, the same amount of processing would be charged to similar transactions on either machine, and no adjustment would be necessary. For example, CPU engines on IBM 3090 models 300J, 400J, 600J, etc., should all be the same. In theory, if a CICS application used 50 ms on one of these processors, it would use 50 ms on each of the others.

However, if the *type* of processor changed, an adjustment should be made for processor power. If, for example, an IBM 3090 model 400S was upgraded to a model 400J, the power of each CPU engine would be increased. CICS CPU usage for one of the periods would need to be adjusted before comparing CPU values.

In today's environment, the relative power of various processors is heavily dependent on workload mix. At one time, published reference material would provide a reliable measure of processor power. Unfortunately, today there are often wide differences between processor ratings published by various sources, and the power experienced by users can vary considerably from that projected by vendors.

A simple, but *not* reliable, method of comparing processors is to use one of the many rating scales published by various sources. Be wary, though, that different rating sources may suggest widely varying estimates of relative processor performance. Because of these variances, it is normally wise to refer to multiple sources. Be careful to compare relative values within the same scale since there can be considerable differences between different scales.

Since the growth calculation involves the amount of CPU time used in a CICS region, the comparison involves the relative power of individual processor engines. The best way to obtain single-engine processor speeds is to select the relative power of the uni-processor version of each processor from one rating scale. For example, if the CICS system had been run on a 3090-600J, the equivalent uniprocessor would be a 3090-180J. This would give an approximation of the power of each CPU engine. If the ratings were categorized by workload, we would want to use those values associated with CICS workloads.

> **Key Point:** Published processor ratings provide an indication of relative processor power. However, specific workloads often will not experience the same differences suggested by published ratings. The relative power of processors is dependent on workload mix.

Let us suppose that scales showed processor engines in one processor were 1.5 times as fast as those in another processor. To achieve comparability, we would either divide CPU usage on the slower processor by 1.5 or multiply CPU usage on the faster processor by 1.5. Transactions which used 30 ms of CPU time on the less powerful engine could be expected to use about 20 ms on the more powerful processor (30 ms / 1.5).

3.6.5 Exceptional Situations

It is often difficult to identify all the CPU usage related to a particular workload. When transaction flow through a *terminal-owning region* (TOR) to an *application-owning region* (AOR), we may want to capture resource usage in both the TOR and the AOR. If workloads are identified by transaction IDs, this may be a fairly simple task.

When requests are passed between regions using MRO or ISC *function shipping*, it can be tricky to match resource usage by mirror tasks to requesting CICS transactions. Detail performance records do include a token that allows transactions to be matched, but the process can be quite cumbersome.

When the VSAM subtask feature is active (CICS/VS and CICS/MVS), it is not possible to associate the CPU time used by the VSAM subtask back to specific CICS transactions or systems. Under CICS/ESA, resource usage associated executed under the quasi-reentrant (QR), resource-owning (RO), concurrent (CO), and FEPI (SZ) subtasks will all be collected together in CICS detail transaction statistics.

Database systems further complicate the process. Special action is necessary to associate database activity and resource utilization with CICS transactions.

Even though we may not be able capture all the CPU usage associated with a given system, partial indications may still be useful. As long as we know what data are included in workload studies, that data can be used in planning. Resources that cannot be associated with specific workloads, may be tracked separately. Partial indications of growth patterns can be helpful in tracking workloads.

3.7 PEAK PERIODS

Most performance and capacity plans are built around satisfying the needs of users during processing peaks. If performance is acceptable during peak periods, it will usually be at least that good during periods with lighter processing loads. By configuring a system for the heaviest anticipated workloads, we can normally provide suitable response times for other periods as well.

3.7.1 Types of Peak Periods

For planning purposes, there are two types of processing peaks. The first is the *recurring peak*. Recurring peaks are predictable and repeatable and normally are associated with patterns of business activity. Recurring peaks are commonly associated with a particular time of the day, day of the week, day of the month, or season of the year. Most businesses can identify periods of peak business activity, and these often can be related to recurring processing peaks.

The second type of peak is the *absolute peak*. Most businesses have isolated processing peaks that occur infrequently and/or irregularly. For example, transaction volume could be heavier than normal following a major CICS outage, causing high transaction response times.

> **Key Point:** There are two types of peak periods:
> *Recurring peaks,* which reflect cyclical patterns in business activity and are commonly used in planning capacity, and
> *Absolute peaks,* which reflect exceptional situations that may not be addressed in normal capacity plans.

Figures 3.8 and 3.9 illustrate the difference between absolute and recurring peak periods. Figure 3.8 shows application CPU usage in one CICS region for a one-hour period each workday. Figure 3.9 shows corresponding transaction counts. Both graphs cover the same period (approximately three months).

Figure 3.8 shows that CPU usage regularly peaks at 1,300 to 1,400 CPU seconds per hour each week and that transaction volume peaks at about 55,000 to 60,000 transactions per hour. However, in the fourth week, the region used 1,800 CPU seconds and processed about 72,000 transactions in 1 hour. (This was caused by a CICS outage in the preceding hour. Once the region was restarted, an unusually heavy load of transactions arrived as users attempted to get caught up.)

In this example, the *recurring peak* is about 55,000 to 60,000 transactions and 1,300 to 1,400 CPU seconds per hour. The *absolute peak* is about 72,000 transactions per hour with 1,800 CPU seconds.

3.7.2 Planning for Peak Periods

Each organization must choose whether to base its performance plans on absolute or recurring peaks. The choice will affect the number of transactions and the amount of processing that will be supported.

Most installations do not plan capacity around absolute peak periods. It is more expensive to configure systems to provide normal service during absolute peak periods. Not only could additional processor capacity be required, but other software and hardware requirements could add to the cost of supporting absolute peaks.

If an organization decides to base its plans on recurring peak periods, there may not be sufficient capacity to provide adequate service during absolute peaks. During absolute peak periods, response time will be slow, and users may not be able to accomplish their assigned tasks in a

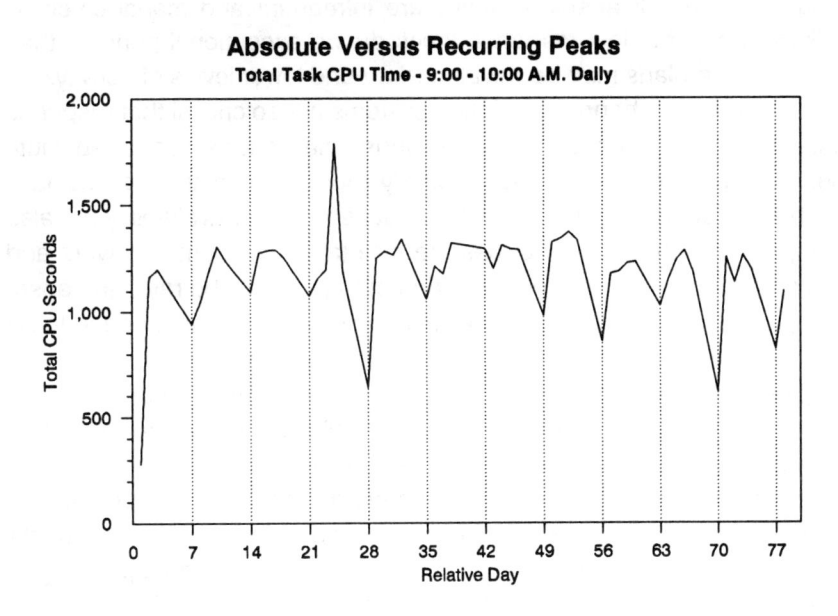

Figure 3.8 Example of absolute and recurring peaks.

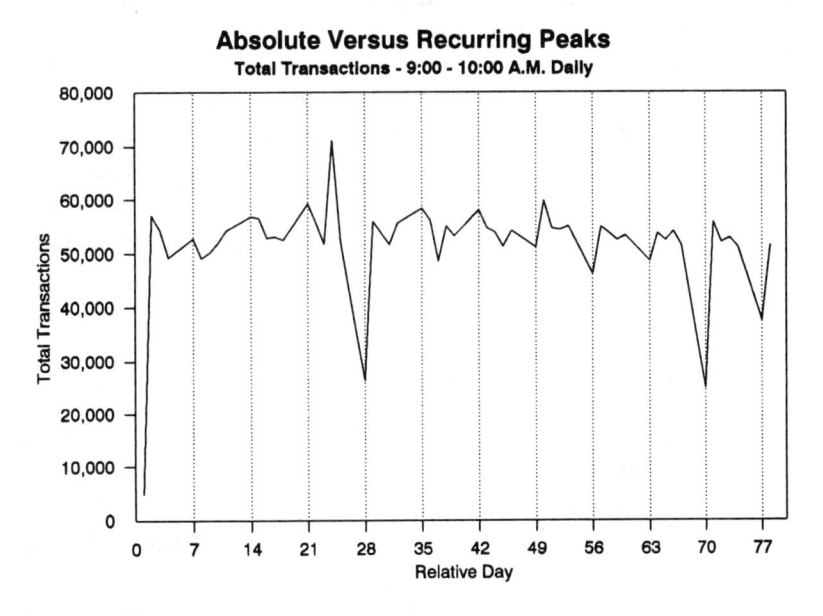

Figure 3.9 Example of absolute and recurring peaks.

timely manner. If absolute peaks are infrequent and management is willing to accept slow response times during exceptional periods, then performance plans may be developed around lower levels of activity.

If, on the other hand, application systems are so critical that response time objectives must be met even under the heaviest loads, absolute peaks will be used in planning. Typically, though, when applications have such an acute need for service, the requirements for availability are also high, and redundant capabilities are maintained for both hardware and software. With such redundancy, long outages could be rare, and absolute peaks would represent peaks in business activity that needed to be serviced quickly.

Processing peaks that occur regularly but infrequently can be treated as absolute peaks. For example, many retail establishments experience unusually high business volume on one or two key business days each year. In a sense, these peaks are recurring in that they are predictable and associated with repeating business conditions. However, we might not choose to configure our environment to meet an extreme processing peak that occurs only once or twice a year. We might make a conscious decision to allow poor response time on the 1 or 2 days each year when business was considerably heavier than normal. (This, of course, would depend on the importance of the application and the economic cost of not providing acceptable service.)

The reason for identifying peak processing periods is to establish the levels of activity used for performance planning. Usually, recurring peaks will be chosen. Most organizations will not choose to spend the additional funds required to support normal service during absolute peak periods. For all intents and purposes, recurring peak periods will be used for most planning, and absolute peaks periods will be discarded or ignored.

3.8 LENGTH OF PEAK PERIODS

How long a period should we use to measure peaks and develop performance plans? There are differences in opinions on this, but a duration of 15 minutes to 2 hours is commonly chosen for on-line systems. This duration tends to be long enough to avoid insignificant spikes, but also focused enough to indicate when users are experiencing problems. *Periods of 15 minutes to 2 hours will reflect the sustained service users are receiving.*

We often speak of resources as being a certain percent busy. However, there is really no such thing as a resource that is, for example, 30 percent busy. Either the resource is being used (in which case it is 100 percent busy) or it is not (then it is 0 percent busy). If we choose short enough periods, we can almost guarantee that we will see utilizations approaching 100 percent. In very short periods, spikes will appear that are not meaningful.

On the other hand, very long periods, such as day-long or shift-long averages, tend to hide high resource utilization and performance problems. It is quite possible that the average response time over an 8-hour period will appear to be acceptable while periods of an hour or more do not meet the users' needs. When long periods are used, it is likely that exceptionally good and exceptionally bad intervals will be averaged together.

> **Key Point:** In performance planning, long periods tend to mask problems while short periods tend to produce meaningless spikes. Both defeat the purpose of performance planning.

It is interesting to note that while very short intervals are seldom used in performance planning, they can be almost essential in debugging specific performance problems. If users report occasional periods with "slow response time," it may be necessary to examine brief intervals in detail. If a problem occurs for only a few minutes, all meaningful data will be lost in hour-long averages.

Similarly, averages covering long periods can also be valuable. Long-term averages can be used to show trends or give a picture of overall resource utilization. However, long-term averages are seldom useful for performance planning.

3.9 PERFORMANCE DATABASES

Performance databases (PDBs) are very useful for developing performance plans. PDBs are libraries or databases used to store statistical information about activity, performance, and resource usage. PDBs may contain data about operating systems (MVS, VM, etc.), CICS, database systems, and/or networks. Optimally, information from different sources in PDBs will be coordinated with one another and be constructed with similar periods and intervals. Several months or years worth of data may be retained in on-line PDBs. Older data usually will either be retained in a more summarized form or stored off-line.

Although it is possible to perform performance planning tasks without a PDB, having a PDB will simplify the task. Even though detailed performance data can be analyzed when needed, it is not likely that data will be available when it is needed unless it is stored in some kind of PDB. In very small installations, it might be hard to justify the costs and efforts of maintaining PDBs. However, in larger environments, PDBs are almost essential.

> **Key Point:** Performance data bases (PDBs) are essential for long-term performance planning, especially for larger systems.

3.9.1 CICS PDBs

The most common source of data for the CICS portion of a PDB is the CICS Monitor Facility (CMF). CMF is a standard component of CICS. It can be activated to capture and record detail performance data. CMF will create a separate record for each transaction, conversational session, or logical mirror transaction. In CICS/VS and CICS/MVS, CMF data can be written either to a CICS journal or to the SMF log. In CICS/ESA, CICS will write CMF data only to the SMF log.

CICS CMF data contains a number of useful statistics including:

- The amount of CPU time used by each transaction (These data have a different meaning in CICS/ESA than they do in CICS/VS or CICS/MVS. This will be discussed in more detail in Chapter 6.)
- The number and type of logical I/Os requested
- Temporary storage and transient data accesses
- Journal service requests
- Wait times for various facilities
- Storage usage

Several vendors have CICS monitors that can be used to collect CICS detail transaction data. Even though the products format data differently and have differing collection techniques, the detail transaction data contains similar information.

Analyzing CICS Workloads   59

In CICS/VS and CICS/MVS, monitors (including CMF) collect CICS detail performance data via hooks in the EMP or trace facilities. Each time any traceable event occurs, monitor logic receives control and checks to see if the event represents anything involving performance data. The process is both cumbersome and resource-intensive.

In CICS/ESA, CMF collects data directly in processing domains. Performance data will be collected whether or not they are written by CMF. Most other monitors now use these data instead of collecting them themselves.

Most medium to large CICS environments can generate a large amount of CICS detail performance data. A separate record is created for each transaction, mirror session, and interactive session. In an MRO environment, there can be several times as many detail records as there are CICS transactions. A large CICS system might create several gigabytes of data each day.

It can take a lot of processing to analyze or study this much detail performance data each day. For this reason, it is common practice to summarize CICS statistical data and use the summarized data for most types of analysis. Typically, CICS statistical data is summarized by CICS region name, transaction ID, hour of the day (or some other interval), and perhaps by some other indicator such as class of transaction. Summarized data will use much less storage, will be easier to use for long-term studies and research, and normally can be kept for a longer period of time. Figure 3.10 illustrates the process of summarizing CICS performance data.

> **Key Point:** CICS PDBs usually contain summarized performance data about CICS transactions and resources consumed.

3.9.2 Commercial PDB Products

Two popular products can be used to summarize CICS detailed statistical data and build CICS PDBs. One product is the CICS component of the Management Information Control System (MICS) from Legent Corporation. MICS contains a comprehensive set of routines to maintain performance data bases. Various components are responsible for maintaining data from different sources (such as CICS, network, MVS, etc.).

The CICS component of MICS includes a program that condenses CICS detail data into summary records. MICS also includes a substantial set of SAS-based programs designed to support a wide range of reporting and analytic functions. MICS is designed to integrate data from multiple sources and accommodate many of the more common analytic functions needed for performance- and capacity-related studies.

Another popular product is Merrill's Expanded Guide (MXG) from Merrill Consultants. MXG can be used to build CICS PDBs. The CICS component of MXG is entirely SAS-based. It provides a shell to read and analyze CICS performance data, and a number of routines to perform various analytical functions. MXG is quite flexible and its greatest strength is the ease with which customized SAS routines can be built for special studies. Its one limitation is that CICS detail data must be read initially via SAS, stored in a SAS work file, and sorted before any summarization can be performed.

In theory, you can write your own routines to summarize CICS detail performance data. Most vendors provide documentation with record formats, and some vendors even provide routines to access or format data. However, record formats can be a bit complex (particularly CMF data), and some research will be needed to determine the meaning and content of data. Once you have overcome these obstacles, though, the task of summarizing the data is not that difficult.

Regardless of how it is done, CICS data should be summarized for performance and capacity planning purposes. We will need a history of

CICS
Detail
Performance
Data

Summarization
Process

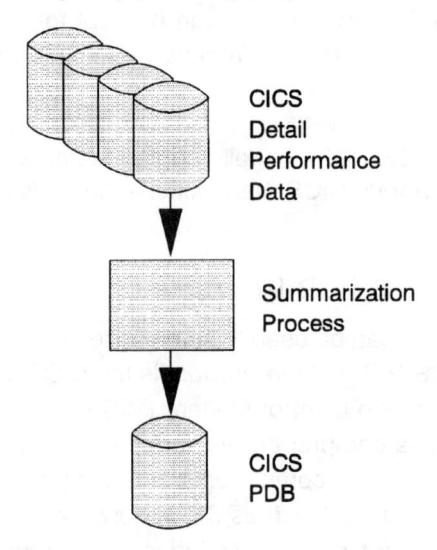

CICS
PDB

Figure 3.10 CICS PDB created from deatil data.

CICS workloads to do any kind of meaningful performance planning. The only practical way to retain this data in most shops is in a summarized form.

3.9.3 Operating System PDBs

In addition to CICS transaction data, operating system data will be needed in planning capacity and performance for CICS systems. Operating system performance data are captured by the *resource management facility* (RMF) (or some equivalent) and stored in the SMF log. Unique SMF record types distinguish different classes of performance data. Most types of RMF data are written to the SMF log at the end of each recording interval (usually 15 minutes to 1 hour).

A few of the more common types of RMF data used in performance planning include:

- **Type 70** - Global information about the system resource utilization such as total CPU busy and total I/O requests

- **Type 72** - Information about each performance group including CPU usage and I/O requests

- **Type 73** - Channel activity

- **Type 74** - I/O activity by device

Both MXG and MICS contain components to build operating system-related PDBs.

3.10 SERVICE LEVEL AGREEMENTS

Earlier in this chapter, we suggested that the purpose of performance planning is to meet our users' needs for service. The term "service," as used in this book, refers to *service level agreement* (SLA). SLAs are prearranged agreements between the data processing department and application users defining expected levels of response time, availability, and other parameters. In most cases, SLAs also include indications of the volume and mix of work anticipated by users.

SLAs serve several important functions. For one thing, users' needs are clearly identified and documented. This gives the performance planner goals and objectives. For another, response time ceases to become a political issue: "Slow" response time is that which does not meet standards defined in the SLA. In essence, SLAs define the structure around which performance plans can be developed. Unless there is an understanding of what service is required, performance planning has little meaning.

3.11 SUMMARY

In this chapter we have reviewed the first steps of the CICS performance-planning process. We have discussed how to characterize workloads, analyze the components of workload growth, and select peak periods. We have also reviewed the value of historical information in the planning process. One of the key concepts introduced in this chapter is that of *growth bias*, or the institutional factors driving change. This is often overlooked in many capacity-planning processes.

SELECTED READING

[GELB91] Gelb, Ivan L., "CICS/ESA Performance and Capacity Management," *CMG '91 Proceedings*, 1991.

[KELL89A] Keller, Ted C., "Estimating CICS Workloads," *CMG '89 Proceedings*, 1989.

[KELL89B] Keller, Ted C., "Workload Trend Analysis: A Capacity Planning Technique for Projecting Resource Requirements in a CICS Environment," *CMG Transactions*, Winder, 1989.

[VONM83] Von Mayrhauser, A. K. and S. L. Biardo, "Performance Management Toolset Consideration for Different Environments," *Proceedings of the 1983 Computer Measurement Group International Conference*, 1983.

Chapter 4

Forecasting Changes in Workloads

4.1 OVERVIEW

In Chapter 3 we discussed how to categorize CICS performance data into meaningful combinations called workloads. We discussed the components of workload growth, recurring and absolute peak periods, and performance databases. Chapter 3 introduced two key ideas – growth bias and the components of workload growth. *Growth bias* is an organization's predisposition to change. As discussed in Chapter 3, workload growth may be categorized in three components: New systems, transaction volume, and complexity/overhead.

Chapter 4 discusses how to estimate changes in CICS workloads. Techniques are suggested to forecast changes in each of the three components of growth. Practical suggestions are offered on how to identify forces driving growth. The chapter also reviews the importance of growth bias and historical data in forecasting future workloads.

4.1.1 Primary Audience

Since Chapter 4 builds on the material presented in Chapter 3, it should have value to the same audiences as Chapter 3. Many *systems programmers* will have little experience analyzing or forecasting CICS workloads.

Much of the material should be new for them. It can help them see some longer-term considerations of planning CICS performance.

Capacity planners commonly use many techniques discussed in this chapter, and, for them, much of the material should be fairly common knowledge. However, some material, such as planning change for three separate components of growth, introduces some techniques not commonly used in many environments. Some material is unique, and all of the material is tailored for CICS workloads. Many capacity planners should find some new techniques worth applying in their own organizations.

Application developers are not normally responsible for planning workload growth. However, some material in this chapter should help them identify the type of information needed by those planning capacity and performance for CICS systems.

4.2 CHANGES IN THE THREE COMPONENTS OF WORKLOAD GROWTH

In this chapter we will discuss the three components of growth and how to develop forecasts for each.

First, we will examine how to estimate changes in *transaction volume*. Changes in transaction volume include any differences in the number of transactions to be executed. The most obvious source of volume changes is variations in levels of business activity. We will see, though, that levels of business activity are not always meaningful in performance or capacity planning. There are many other factors that can have a more direct influence on transaction volume than changes in business volume.

The second component we will examine is changes involving *new systems*. We will examine the dual challenges of estimating transaction volume and workload content. We will discuss the types of information necessary to develop estimates and how historical data can be used to assist in estimating workloads for new systems.

Next, we will look at how institutional factors influence changes in the *complexity/overhead* portion of growth. We will see that the best way to project changes in complexity/overhead is to use historical data. Growth bias is an important tool in forecasting changes in complexity/overhead.

Finally, we will discuss the need to review performance data periodically. It is important to review performance data to ensure that actual performance is in line with projections. We will discuss the types of change we may encounter and the causes of variance.

4.3 CHANGES ASSOCIATED WITH VOLUME

In the material below, we will discuss how to forecast changes in transaction volume. We will look at several different factors that can cause changes in transaction volume. We will see that several of these factors are neither obvious nor easy to estimate.

In our discussion, we will concentrate on how changes will affect peak periods and influence performance planning. It is not only important to know how many transactions will be processed, but we will need to determine when the transactions will be processed and how this will affect peak periods. Estimating the number of transactions running during peak periods is an important part of performance planning. It is the peak processing periods that normally drive performance and capacity plans.

> **Key Point**: Forecasts of volume-related changes should include estimates of both the total number of transactions and how many will occur during peak periods.

4.3.1 Variations in Business Activity

In most organizations, changes in business activity cause direct or indirect changes in data processing workloads. There is often a correlation between business levels and the number of transactions processed. The ratio of total transactions to business units is often both consistent and stable.

Users normally have estimates of how much business activity they anticipate. They typically have plans defining staffing and other budgetary considerations necessary to support anticipated business levels. Their projections of business activity may not be accurate, but they often represent the best information available.

Before business-related information from users can be used, business activity needs to be translated into transaction activity. The challenge is finding units both meaningful to users and useful to the capacity planner.

In the early days of capacity planning, data processing specialists would sometimes ask users how many transactions they expected to process or how much CPU time they planned to use. Some shops even developed elaborate feedback schemes in which users would be told how well they had predicted transaction counts or resource usage. The idea was to make users accountable for the data processing resources consumed by their systems. It was an easy way for capacity planners to get the information they needed without taking responsibility for understanding the data or its basis. If the projections were wrong, it would be the user's fault.

This approach may not be particularly desirable today. Most users of CICS systems do not understand the internal workings of CICS applications and have little idea about how many transactions they will enter. They probably have little control over the way systems are designed or coded and have little influence over how much of any resource their systems use. The user's mission is neither to execute transactions nor to control resource utilization. It is to accomplish business-related services for the organization.

> **Key Point**: In many environments, users will not be familiar enough with CICS internal workings to provide reliable information about resource usage or transaction volume. They are not normally involved in the placement of CICS applications or technical decisions such as whether to use MRO facilities, and they are only indirectly involved in the design and coding of applications. However, users should be able to provide reasonable estimates of the business units they expect to achieve such as total sales, units manufactured, or number of claims.

The term *natural forecasting unit* (NFU) describes measures of business activity in terms that are meaningful to users. NFUs are used to help business planners communicate activity to data processing planners. To be useful, NFUs should be both meaningful to business planners and suitable for estimating workloads. Much of the information commonly generated by the business planning process can become the basis of NFUs.

4.3.2 Converting NFUs into Numbers of Transactions

Later in this chapter we will see that volume-related growth is not always related to business indicators. For some systems other factors, such as staffing and management policies, have more of an influence over transaction volume than absolute measures of business activity. We will discuss how to evaluate those kinds of systems later. At this time, we will look at systems for which there is a relationship between transaction volume and key business indicators.

The first step in forecasting transaction volume is to select the correct NFU. Not all CICS systems in the same environment can be related to the same business indicators. Some systems will hold only an indirect relationship with primary business activity. With the right NFUs, though, there often will be a relatively constant relationship between NFUs and transaction volume. For example, in a system designed to verify credit information, the number of transactions probably will vary directly with the number of credit sales. The number of credit sales will be a better indication of transaction volume than total sales volume.

After selecting the correct NFU, the next step is to translate NFUs into transaction workloads. The key task in this step is to discover the raw relationship between business units and total transactions. Figures 4.1 and 4.2 show the relationship between daily business activity and corresponding transaction volume for two different systems. Both systems support the same primary business activity. However, system 1 has a much stronger relationship with these NFUs than system 2. There is more variance on a day-by-day basis for system 2.

The primary difference between system 1 and system 2 is that transactions for system 1 must be entered on the same business day as the corresponding business activity. In system 2 transactions are normally entered on the same business day but can lag by one or two days if necessary. While both systems are driven by the same business activity, there is less of a day-by-day correlation to business volume for one than the other. Part of the variance in system 2 may be explained by user staffing, and this should be considered when projecting transaction volume.

Some systems that support mainline business activities are only indirectly affected by business volume. Workloads may increase in the same general direction as business volume, but they may not grow proportionately. Activity for these systems may lag mainline business activity by days or weeks. Examples might include systems supporting functions such as sales returns or credit collections. Alternate NFUs will be necessary for such systems. Users usually will have an idea of the relationship between primary business activity and work done in their areas.

Other systems will "stair-step;" that is, they will remain at a given level until business activity crosses some threshold, and then they will jump to the next level. Systems tied primarily to staffing or equipment usage

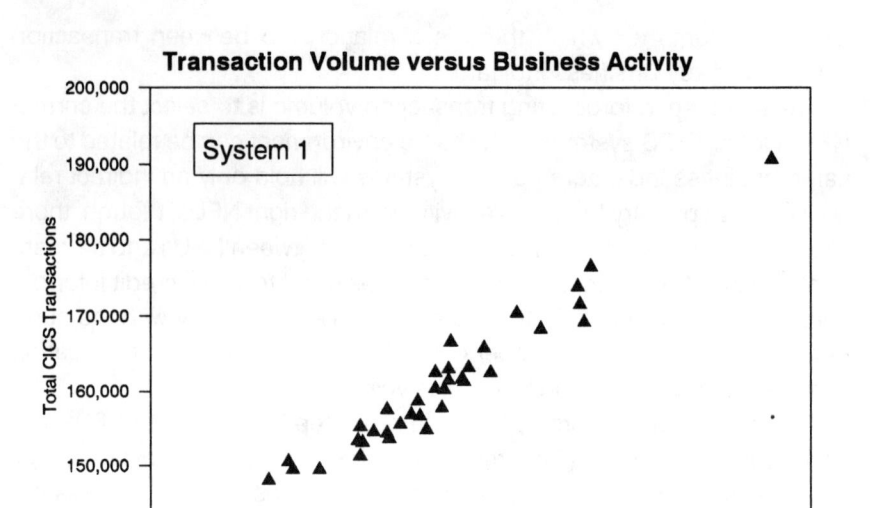

Figure 4.1 NFUs versus total number of transactions.

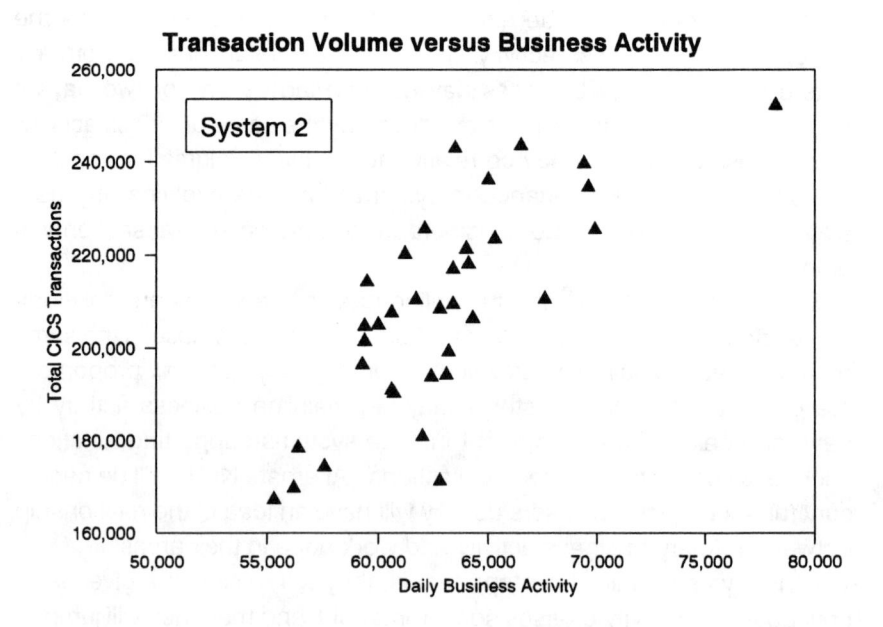

Figure 4.2 NFUs versus total number of transactions.

might function this way. Additional equipment or staffing will be acquired after business reaches a certain plateau.

4.3.3 The Relationship Between Business Activity and Peak Transaction Processing

Projections of the total transaction volume are not very useful for performance planning. It is more important to know how many transactions will run during peak periods. Transaction volume increases that occur during off-peak hours may have little effect on performance plans. Unless the additional transactions cause a shift in processing peaks, they might have little influence on total capacity requirements. Typically, growth in transaction processing during nonpeak periods will simply take advantage of unused capacity.

As we discussed in Chap. 3, performance plans normally are designed to provide acceptable service during recurring peaks. The assumption is made that if facilities are adequate to satisfy service needs during recurring peaks, they should be adequate during offpeaks as well. Consequently, it is important to learn how changes will affect peak periods.

> **Key Point**: The most important task in projecting volume-related growth is to estimate how changes affect peak periods.

Although there may be a strong correlation between total CICS transactions and business activity, peak transaction levels will not necessarily increase correspondingly. This is illustrated in Figures 4.3, 4.4, 4.5, and 4.6. Figures 4.3 and 4.4 show the relationship between average transactions per day and business activity. Clearly, there is a relationship between the number of transactions processed each day and business activity.

In system 1, the peak number of transactions per hour increased along with business volume (see Figure 4.5). Transaction activity during peak periods grew more or less proportionately with business volume. However, total transactions per hour reached a peak for system 2 at 53,000 business units per day and never climbed much above that, despite total business volume. Although the number of transactions per day increased with business volume, the peak number entered in any hour did not.

System 1 was used by many users across a large network. Transactions were entered primarily during a 4- to 5-hour window as work occurred. When business activity was heavy, more transactions were en-

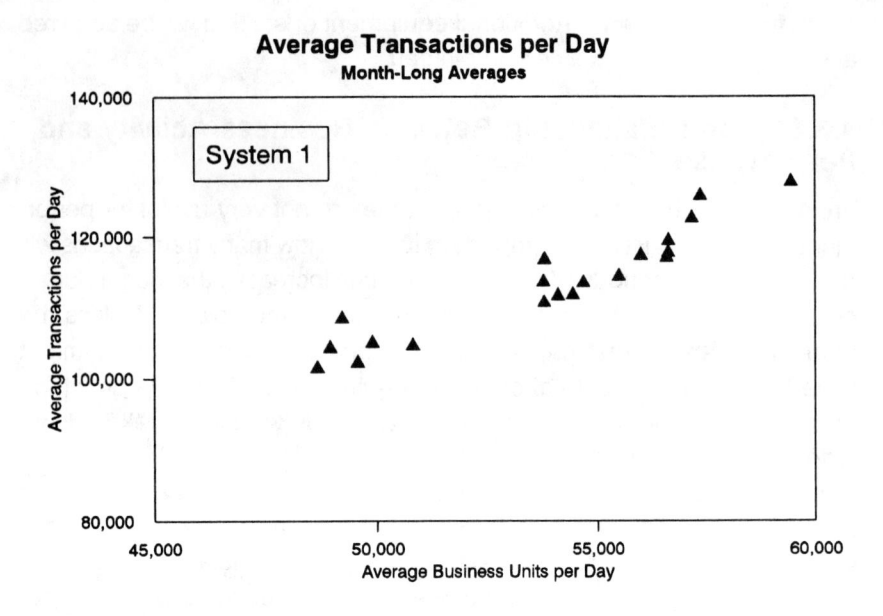

Figure 4.3 Average transactions versus average NFUs.

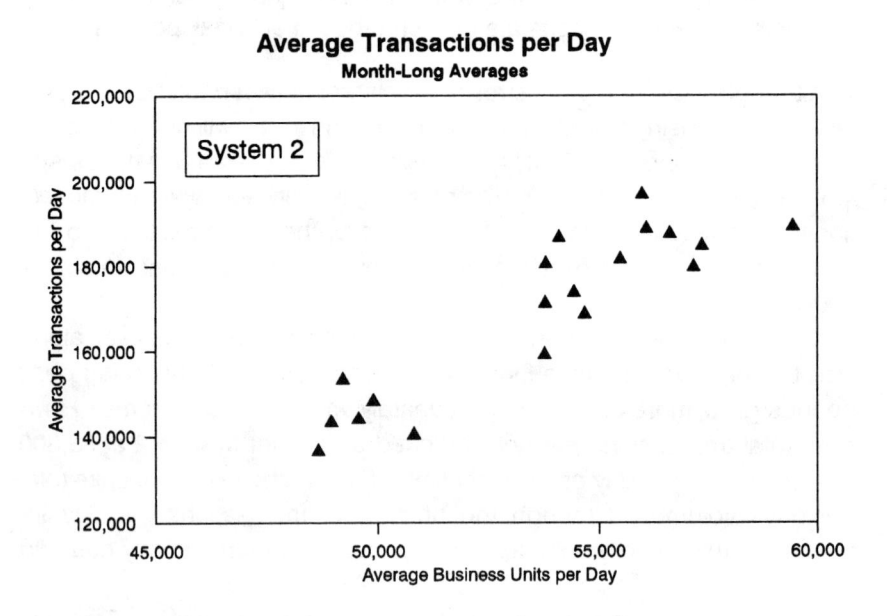

Figure 4.4 Average transactions versus average NFUs.

Peak Transactions versus Business Activity
Month-Long Averages

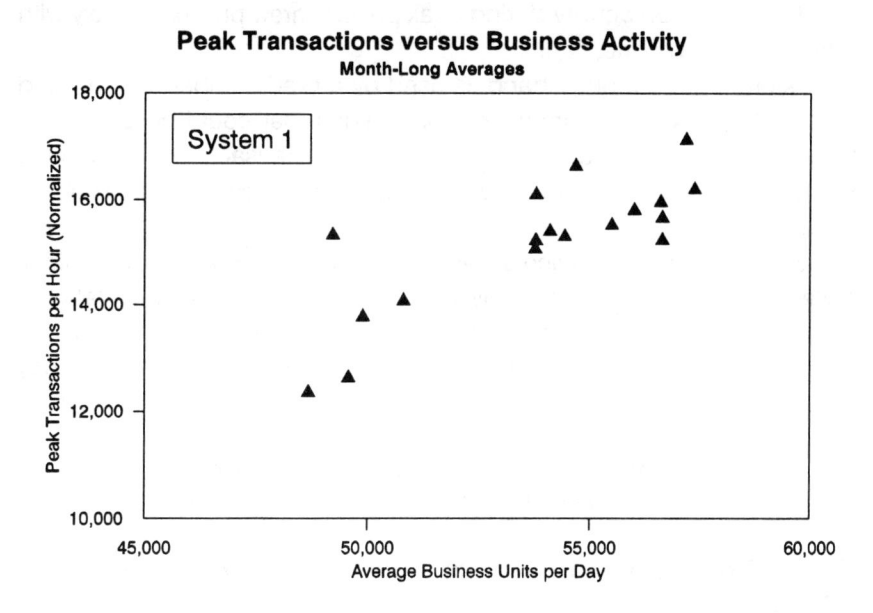

System 1

Figure 4.5 Peak transactions versus average NFUs.

Peak Transactions versus Business Activity
Month-Long Averages

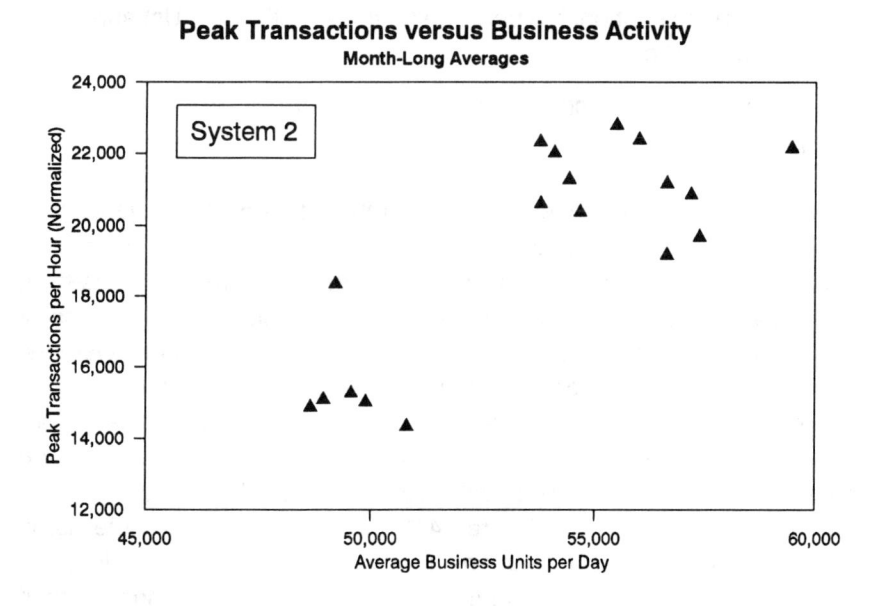

System 2

Figure 4.6 Peak transactions versus average NFUs.

tered. Transaction activity during peak periods grew proportionately with total business volume.

System 2, on the other hand, is used by a fixed number of dedicated users. The maximum number of transactions that could be entered is limited by the number of users that could enter transactions. In systems like this, levels of business activity will not necessarily affect peak transaction activity.

Systems involving service activities with fixed staffing (such as claims, collections, or auditing) probably will have structural limitations that control peak transaction volume. The peak number of transactions that can be entered in any hour is limited by the number of users and the rate they work.

> **Key Point**: Processing peaks for some workloads are more dependent on levels of staffing than on total business activity.

4.3.4 Translating Business Activity into Workload Peaks

We have already discussed the first two steps in converting NFUs into volume-related projections. They are:

1. Research the relationship between business activity (NFUs) and transaction volume.

2. Determine whether structural limitations may cap processing during peak periods.

After we have determined that the number of transactions varies with business activity, the next step is to estimate how many will be entered each hour. In most systems, transaction arrival patterns are consistent from day to day. Typically, they are associated either with patterns of business activity and with shift or work schedules. In many systems, transactions tend to be entered at about the same time each day.

A quick way to review how many transactions are processed each hour (or other period) is to plot activity by time of day. Figures 4.7 and 4.8 show charts of transaction arrival patterns for two different systems. It may not be obvious, but Figures 4.7 and 4.8 both contain the same number of observations (about one month's worth of data). In Figure 4.7, the pattern is so consistent that many points almost overlay one another. In Figure 4.8, the percent of activity varies considerably for each hour.

Forecasting Changes in Workloads 73

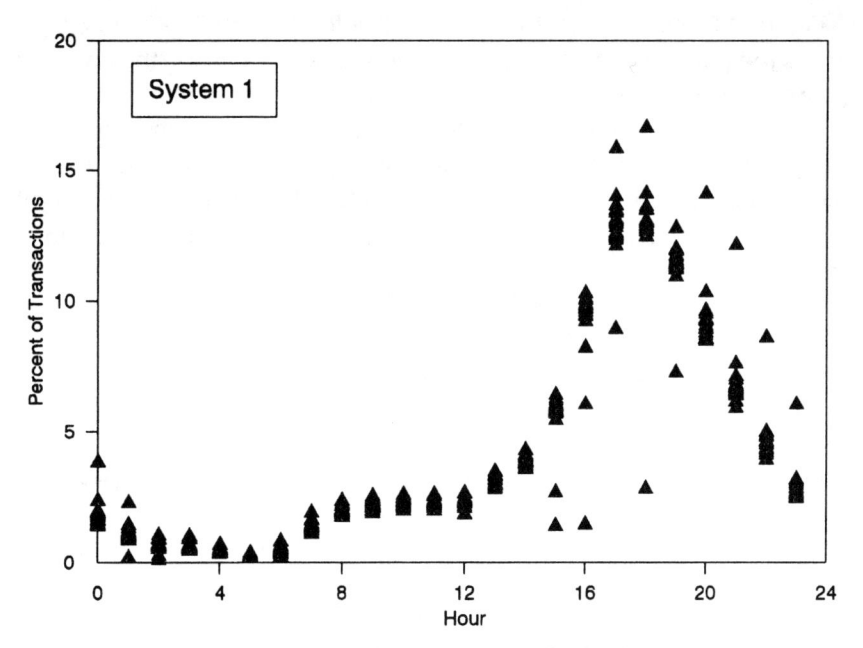

Figure 4.7 Percent of transactions processed each hour, system 1.

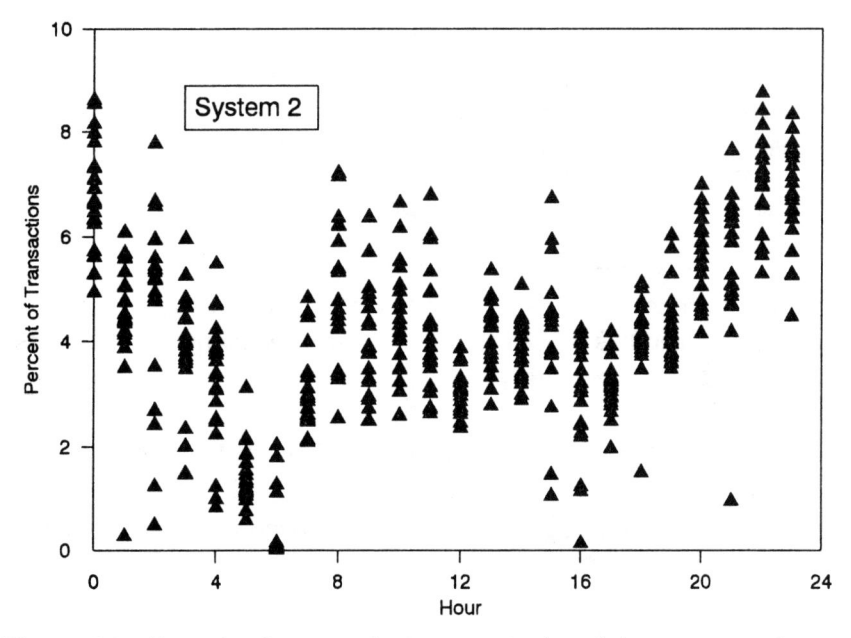

Figure 4.8 Percent of transactions processed each hour, system 2.

Figure 4.9 provides another perspective for the data in Figure 4.8. It shows the percent of system 2 transactions executed during the normally heaviest hour (hour 22) compared to the total number of transactions for that day. We can see that as the total number of transactions entered in a day increased, the percent entered during the peak hour decreases. The reason for this is that system 2 is entered by a limited number of users, which restricts the number of transactions that can be entered in any hour.

The key to projecting peak transaction volume for system 1 will be NFUs associated with business activity. The key for system 2 will be the number of users entering transactions.

The outliers on the graphs were caused primarily by CICS outages. Hours during which outages occurred had significantly less activity than normal while periods following outages usually had higher activity than normal.

In systems restricted by staffing, only so many transactions can be entered in any hour. In some systems, heavier business activity will be met by working more hours (additional shifts or overtime). In others, it may cause a backlog that is serviced over a period of days or weeks. In either case, peak processing levels can be insensitive to changes in total business volume.

> **Key Point**: In many systems, business activity can be a good indicator of transaction volume during peak periods. In other systems, staffing or other internal factors limits the number of transactions that can be entered in any hour. Here, other factors must be used to project peak transaction volume.

Table 4.1 summarizes the major steps involved in estimating volume-related growth associated with changes in business activity. The most significant goal in this process is to establish how changes in business activity affect the number transactions processed during peak periods.

4.3.5 Volume-Related Changes Associated with Staffing

The discussion above suggested that peak transaction volume is sometimes more closely tied to staffing than to levels of business activity. Many CICS systems are designed for specialized users whose primary activity involves use of the system. Since the number of users is limited, the rate

Processing Peaks Compared to Total Transactions

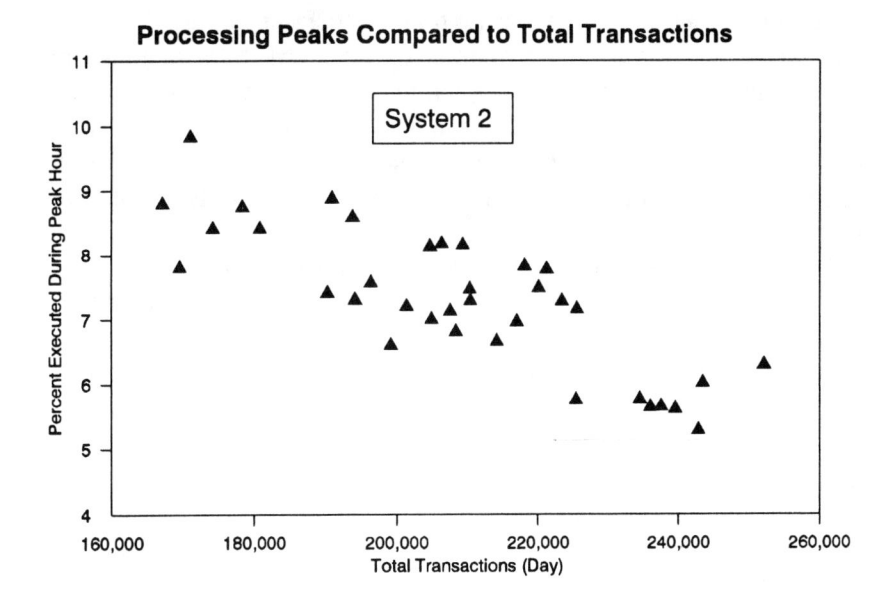

[Scatter plot labeled "System 2" showing Percent Executed During Peak Hour (y-axis, 4 to 11) versus Total Transactions (Day) (x-axis, 160,000 to 260,000)]

Figure 4.9 Percent of transactions during peak hours, system 2.

Table 4.1 Tasks Involved in Estimating Workload Growth Resulting from Increases in Business Activity

Step	Task
1	Select NFUs appropriate for the workload being studied.
2	Establish the relationship between NFUs and total transaction volume.
3	Obtain forecasts of NFUs from users.
4	Determine if there are structural limitations to processing peaks.
5	Research the percentage of transactions processed during peak periods (hour, etc.).
6	Estimate the total number of transactions that will be processing during peak periods for projected levels of business activity.

at which transactions are entered is also limited. Here, peak processing tends to be more a factor of staffing than of business activity.

In some systems a limited number of users switch between assignments, depending on business demands. This causes processing peaks that are more closely tied to business activity. When business activity is heavy, more users will be entering transactions. Transaction peaks for these systems will be dependent on both business activity and the total number of potential users.

For systems whose users spend most of their time entering transactions, peak transaction activity normally is controlled by the number of users. Individuals using this type of system tend to work at a steady, consistent rate. Workload patterns will be closely aligned with user activity, such as shift changes and breaks. Transaction arrival patterns can be consistent from day to day. For these systems, user staffing plans should provide the best indicator of future transaction peaks.

It is also important to consider the way users adjust staffing to adapt for changes in business activity. If higher levels of business automatically trigger additional staffing, peak transaction volume will closely follow business activity. If, on the other hand, there is a reluctance to increase staff until increased business levels prove to be permanent, peak transaction activity will not be affected as quickly. There will be more lead time before transaction volume increases.

Organizational limits also can affect transaction peaks. It may not be possible to push business activity beyond a certain level. Once business reaches the point that all equipment is busy, additional increases in business will not affect peak transaction activity. Over the long term, if higher levels of business activity are sustained, additional facilities and staff may be added. In essence, this will institutionalize the growth and increase potential transaction activity. This is part of *growth bias* — the structural changes within an organization that drive changes in transaction workloads.

> **Key Point**: When transaction volume is controlled primarily by user staffing, workload forecasts should include user plans and behavior. Both temporary and permanent adjustments to staffing levels will affect peak processing. Changes in shift schedules also can affect workload peaks.

4.3.6 Other Factors Influencing Total Transactions

Several other factors can affect the number of transactions processed. One of these is *additional functionality*. When new functions are added to application systems, the systems may be used more frequently. It may not be easy to predict changes in transaction volume associated with new functions. Sometimes the pent-up demand for new features is so strong that transaction volume can increase dramatically.

Another factor affecting transaction volume is when a system is installed in stages. Sometimes, users are introduced to new systems in groups. An initial group of users may run a pilot, and then other users may be allowed to use the system as training and/or other facilities become available. For these systems, additional planning may be required if the system is introduced over a long period.

System response time also may affect the number of transactions entered. If response time is slow (possibly just prior to a processor upgrade), users will not be able to enter transactions as quickly. This will reduce the rate at which transactions enter the system.

When response time is especially slow, users may even elongate the work day, coming in earlier or working later. This will tend to spread peak processing over longer periods. Users may avoid any optional services and perform only necessary functions. Extremely slow response time can affect user behavior in many ways.

> **Key Point**: Slow response time can affect user behavior and reduce the number of transactions entered.

When system response time improves, users will be able to enter transactions more rapidly. This, in itself, can increase the number of transactions entered. Furthermore, user behavior may change as well. If users were working off-hours to take advantage of better response time, they might return to normal working hours. Additionally, they might change work patterns and begin to use optional screens and services.

> **Key Point**: Peak transaction activity normally will increase when response time improves (possibly after a hardware or software upgrade). Some reasons for this include latent demand, changes in user behavior, and changes in the use of optional or discretionary services.

Table 4.2 lists several factors that can cause increases in transaction volume during peak periods. Different factors will be responsible for change in different systems.

4.3.7 Gathering Information

An important part of the planning function is obtaining forecasts of change. Performance planners need to gather information about changes in the business environment. These include projections of business activity, staffing for key systems, and, for large systems, changes in functionality or usage. Unless the planner has access to information about the factors driving growth, it will be hard to develop forecasts or plans.

4.4 CHANGES IN COMPLEXITY / OVERHEAD

Chapter 3 discussed how workload growth could be separated into three major components. One component, the *complexity/overhead* component, defines growth that is driven by changes in and enhances to application programs and systems software. As applications and systems are modified, they grow in complexity and require additional processing resources.

4.4.1 A Method for Projecting Changes in Complexity/Overhead

In most environments, complexity/overhead will increase slightly each month. As a rule, growth will be more or less steady as long as institutional factors remain the same. While growth will vary each week or month, the overall growth rate probably will be more consistent over longer periods, such as quarters or years.

Table 4.2 Causes of Volume-Related Growth in CICS Applications

1	Business volume
2	Number of users
3	New functions or services
4	New users
5	Phased implementation of application systems
6	System response time

Growth bias identifies the effect of numerous smaller, almost unmeasurable changes. It is a measure of the collective effect of program and software modifications and maintenance.

Along with the slow, steady change related to growth bias, occasional spikes in growth usually can be associated with specific identifiable changes. Spikes, or sharp changes, should be isolated from trends or growth bias. These should be planned for and dealt with separately.

The following steps can be used to project changes in complexity/overhead. Here, we will concentrate on changes in CPU usage. Similar techniques could be applied to project growth of other resource usage, such as file requests.

1. **Collect a history of data for key systems during recurring peak periods.** It is important that data represent peak periods — not day-long or month-long averages. In many large, complex systems, CPU per transaction can vary considerably at different times of the day or on different days of the week. It is important to select CICS statistical data from the peak periods driving performance plans. To improve reliability, at least one year of history should be used.

2. **Chart or graph the data from peak periods by month or week.** This should present a picture of growth and point out specific spikes. Large or unusual changes should be identified separately and documented. Obviously, this kind of information is easier to gather if this research is done periodically. The result of this research will be a list of specific events that caused significant growth along with an average growth per month (or other period). This average growth is a major part of growth bias.

    Figure 4.10 shows growth in CPU usage per transaction for a large system. The arrows point to some months experiencing higher than normal growth and one with an unusual decrease in CPU usage. Unusual changes should be identified separately and excluded from growth bias calculations.

3. **Determine what institutional changes might affect growth trends.** The types of activity that can affect growth bias include the number of program developers working on maintenance and the type enhancements they are working on. It is important to look at how many program developers are assigned to maintenance for major applications. If there is little maintenance on a system, average resource use by transaction should not change much.

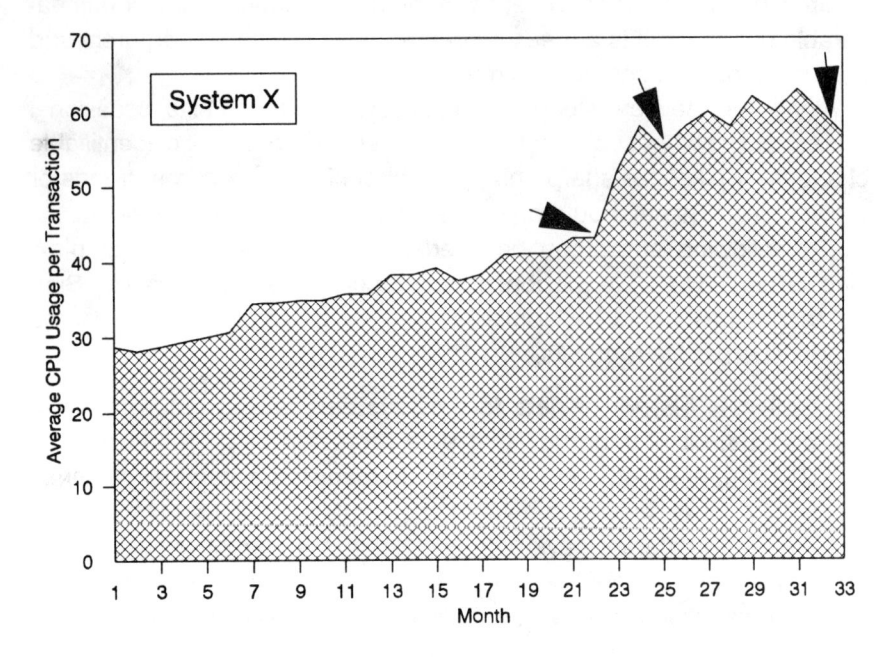

Figure 4.10 Growth in average CPU usage per transaction; this is one factor that affects growth in complexity/overhead.

Although the relationship between programming activity and growth in complexity/overhead is neither consistent nor proportionate over the short term, longer-term growth patterns should be more reliable.

4. **Estimate a growth rate for complexity/overhead.** The growth rate normally will be based upon historical growth and information about future development activity. It may be stated either as an absolute value (e.g., average growth of .5 ms of CPU usage per transaction per month) or as a percentage (e.g., 1% increase per month). *Separate growth rates probably will be needed for different applications.*

5. **Add growth for changes associated with specific projects.** Growth projected for specific, major changes will be added to resource use per transaction. Particular attention should be paid to major file conversions, new technology (such as relational databases), changes in the nature of systems (macro-level to command-level conversions), changes in programming languages, or use of new

Forecasting Changes in Workloads 81

programming techniques. All these can affect transaction profiles dramatically. Also be aware of new releases of software – especially new releases of CICS, CICS monitors, and operating systems.

6. **Multiply the anticipated growth in resource per transaction by the projected number of transactions in peak periods.** This will give the total change in the complexity/overhead component.

So far, this discussion has concentrated on changes in CPU utilization. This is a very important component of change, but other components need to be tracked as well. It is important to trace DASD activity, but this is not as easy to do in a CICS environment. Chapter 11 discusses the peculiarities of CICS file processing and DASD I/Os in more detail.

4.4.2 Another View of Complexity/Overhead

In both Chapter 3 and the discussion above, the complexity/overhead component of growth has been defined as all growth not associated with either new systems or volume. There are times, though, when it might be wise to further divide this component into two parts.

In Figure 4.11 we can see that current resource utilization for any system is composed of four elements. (New and discontinued systems have intentionally been excluded from this chart for simplicity.) The first element is the resource utilization associated with the *base period*. This is, in essence, the product of the total number of transactions in the base period and the average resource per transaction (CPU, in this example) in the base period. These calculations are shown in Table 4.3.

The second element is *volume-related growth*. It is the product of the change in total transactions and the average CPU per transaction from the base period. The remaining CPU utilization can be attributed to changes in *complexity/overhead* – changes to existing applications or software. This corresponds to the definition in Chap. 3.

When developing projections, it is sometimes beneficial to further subdivide the complexity/overhead component. The portion labeled "*pure complexity/overhead*" represents that portion of complexity/overhead associated with base-level workloads. It is the product of total base-level transactions and growth in CPU usage per transaction.

The second portion, labeled "*combined growth*" is a factor of *both* volume-related growth and changes in complexity/overhead. It is the product of the change in total transactions and the growth in CPU usage per transaction. It is, in effect, dependent on two variables.

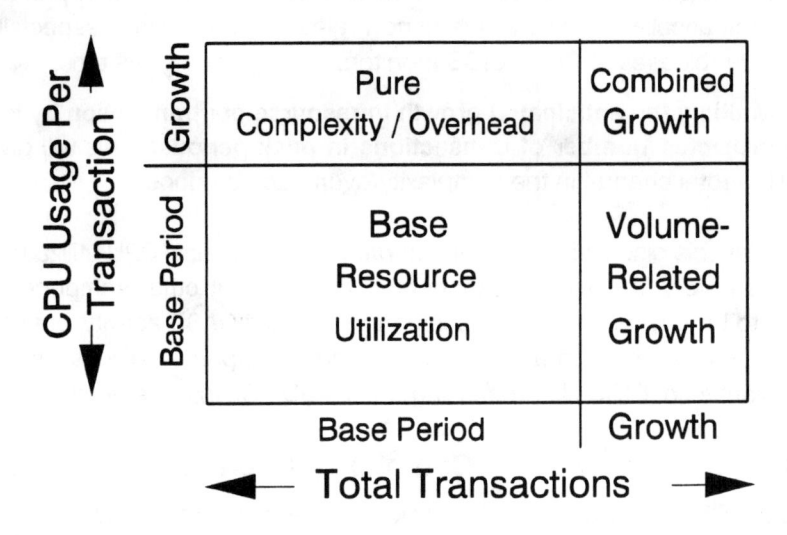

Figure 4.11 Expanded components of workload growth.

It is important to recognize that part of the growth in complexity/overhead is dependent on total transaction volume. When changes in transaction volume are very high, it may be advisable to separate growth into all four basic components.

Table 4.3 Components of Growth for a Single Application System

Component	Calculation		
Base period	CPU usage per tranaction (base period)	x	Number of transactions (base period)
Volume-related growth	CPU usage per tranaction (base period)	x	Change in total transactions
Pure complexity/overhead	Change in CPU usage per transaction	x	Number of transactions (base period)
Combined growth	Change in CPU usage per transaction	x	Change in total transactions

4.4.3 Projections for the Entire System

The procedure outlined above suggested that we look at growth in individual systems. In most large shops, though, there are far too many applications to examine specific growth patterns for each. Nevertheless, a few applications usually account for a large percent of total transaction volume and resource utilization. In most shops, only a few application systems will be examined by themselves. Other workloads can be studied as a group with coarser levels of precision.

> **Key Point**: The key to projecting growth in complexity/overhead is to have a good history of transaction profiles along with a log identifying major changes. Once we identify significant known changes and separate them from other growth, we can establish an average growth rate for complexity/overhead. As long as the programming staff continues to modify the same set of applications in similar ways, there should be long-term consistency in the growth rate.

4.5 CHANGES ASSOCIATED WITH NEW SYSTEMS

Perhaps the most challenging growth to forecast is that associated with totally new systems. In existing systems, we have a history of past activity and patterns of use. We also may have information about users and plans for application changes.

With new systems, though, it can be quite difficult to obtain reasonable estimates of either activity or resource utilization. Although application analysts and user representatives may understand new systems, there is a good chance that they will underestimate either transaction volume or resource requirements. It can take considerable effort to obtain reliable information about new systems. (We will spend more time in Chapters 8 and 9 discussing how to size new CICS application systems.)

4.5.1 Projecting Resources for New Systems

When planning for new systems, we will need to estimate how many transactions will be entered and how much total resource they will consume during peak periods. To do this, we will normally need to identify three separate pieces of information. They are:

- The number of transactions to be entered

- The time at which the transactions will be processed
- The amount of resource each transaction will consume

In may not be necessary to estimate the total number of transactions as long as we can determine how many will be entered during peak periods. However, it is often easier to estimate total transactions and then derive the number processed each hour than to estimate peak activity directly.

There are a few different techniques that can be used to estimate how many transactions will be entered for new systems. The technique used will depend, to some extent, on whether the new system will replace an existing system, replace a manual process, or provide a totally new function.

4.5.2 New Systems That Replace Old Systems — Estimating Total Transactions

Usually, if users were satisfied with existing systems, new systems would not be developed to replace the old. It normally is too expensive to reengineer old systems unless some additional functionality is added. New systems usually can do more than systems they replace, and this may cause an increase in the number of transactions processed.

When a new system replaces an existing system, the old system may provide an indication of transaction volume for the new system. It is likely, though, that the new system will generate *at least as many transactions* as the system it replaces. New systems usually have new features and conveniences. They typically include better panel navigation, more menus, and improved help facilities. All these features can generate additional transactions.

New systems often provide services that make users' jobs easier. Once available, these services may receive considerably more use than anticipated. As users learn to exploit new features, activity may increase even further.

New systems commonly provide more powerful transactions, each accomplishing the work of several transactions from the old system. It would appear at first that this would reduce the total number of transactions processed. It is possible, though, that more powerful transactions will not decrease transaction volume at all. Users may end up entering about the same number of transactions, but they can get more work done in the same amount of time.

4.5.3 New Systems that Replace Manual Systems — Estimating Total Transactions

When a new system is designed to replace a manual process, it may be very difficult to anticipate transaction volume. Processes that had been performed manually may be performed more often once they have been automated. If a manual system is used to search for information, the number of retrievals may be limited by the time it takes to look up data. Once the process is automated, considerably more retrievals may be done.

Typically, if estimates of transaction volume are based on the replacement of existing manual work, the estimates will be low. Once a new system is installed, it should will be easier to use than the manual system it replaces, and probably will be used more heavily.

> **Key Point**: It is usually better to assume that estimates of transaction volume for new systems will be low. There are many factors that can cause transaction volume to be underestimated.

4.5.4 New Systems That Do Not Replace Existing Functions — Estimating Total Transactions

When there is no history of how a process has been used, estimates of transaction volume will be a function of the user's impression of how the system will be used. There will be a number of challenges in projecting transaction volume for these systems.

Some new systems are designed to enter and store information. Here, transaction volume can be estimated from projections of the amount of information to be entered. However, most systems include more than just information entry — they also include transactions that retrieve information and perform queries. It is often the volume of query processing that is most difficult to predict. Sometimes, there is almost no way to estimate the way users will take advantage of new information. It is often safe to assume that user estimates of transaction system usage will be low.

4.5.5 Transaction Profiles for New Systems

There are several techniques that may be used to estimate resource usage for new systems. We will quickly review a few techniques here, but will explore this topic in greater detail in Chapters 8 and 9.

Small (low-volume) systems normally will not require as much planning as major applications. Such systems are normally placed in existing CICS regions and seldom have much effect on the performance of either the individual CICS region or system as a whole. Unless transactions use excessive amounts of resources, rough estimates of transaction profiles will normally suffice for most types of planning. Systems that are small enough may even be included with complexity/overhead trends.

One way to estimate transaction profiles for small systems is to copy them from known, existing systems. If a new system will perform about the same type of processing as an existing system, it may use about the same amount of resources. Of course, to use this technique, the systems should be written in the same language, use the same technology, run in a similar environment (similar region structure, MRO functions, etc.), and use similar CICS resources. Unless the two systems are functionally similar, it may not be wise to copy resource profiles

Another technique that can help estimate CPU utilization is *logical I/O density*. Logical I/O density is the measure of how much CPU time is expended, on the average, for each logical I/O requested by an application. Logical I/O density tends to be consistent for similar applications in the same environment. It also tends to be consistent over time, changing along with the complexity/overhead component of growth. It is possible to calculate approximate CPU usage using logical I/O density.

It is worth noting that *logical* I/O density — not *physical* I/O density — is the suggested measure of I/O activity. Logical I/Os are those requested by applications; physical I/Os are requests that actually result in physical I/O requests. With caching techniques such as LSR and CICS data tables, many I/O requests will be satisfied internally without requiring physical I/Os. Thus, logical I/O density probably is a better predictor of processor usage.

It is worth noting that logical I/O density normally is a measure of the amount of transaction CPU usage associated with each logical I/O. This CPU measure is, in essence, the direct amount of CPU time consumed within CICS to perform a logical I/O. It does not include either CICS region overhead or uncaptured system CPU time. As a rule, the total load for running a transaction will be 1.2 to 1.4 times that predicted by logical I/O density (more about this in Chapters 6 and 7).

A more accurate (and more difficult) method of estimating resource usage is detailed analysis and modeling. For large, complex systems this may be the only method of projecting resource usage that will produce acceptable results. The major challenges with modeling are the amount of work involved and the difficulty calibrating results. Chapters 8 and 9 will show how to analyze and model new CICS applications early in their design stage.

4.6 PERIODIC REVIEW OF PERFORMANCE DATA

Periodic reviews of performance data are an important part of performance and capacity planning. There is no way to know whether forecasts are on target unless we review performance data regularly. Forecasts of business or transaction volumes could be inaccurate; application modifications can cause unexpected changes in transaction profiles; and environmental changes can cause surprises. By reviewing performance data regularly, we can detect unanticipated changes and refine and improve performance and capacity plans.

4.6.1 Three Steps in the Review Process

This author recommends a three-step approach for reviewing performance data. As illustrated in Figure 4.12, the three steps are:

- Scan performance data looking for anything unusual.
- Compare workload profiles in the current peak periods (usually recurring periods) to forecast values.
- Compare current workload profiles to profiles from similar periods in a previous month or quarter.

Each of these steps is discussed in detail below.

4.6.2 Scan Performance Data for Anything Unusual

The first step in reviewing performance data is to scan for anything unusual. This is done to ensure that nothing exceptional has occurred that might invalidate other types of analysis. For example, a major CICS outage would skew normal performance measures. After an outage, transaction volume will usually be higher than normal as users attempt to get caught up.

Periods during which something exceptional occurred often can be spotted by unusual resource usage or performance profiles. Periods displaying unusually high or low transaction volume or unusually slow

```
Periodic Review        Scan data for
of                     Exceptional
Performance Data       Conditions

                       Compare current
                       Data to forecasts

                       Compare current
                       data to previous
                       data.
```

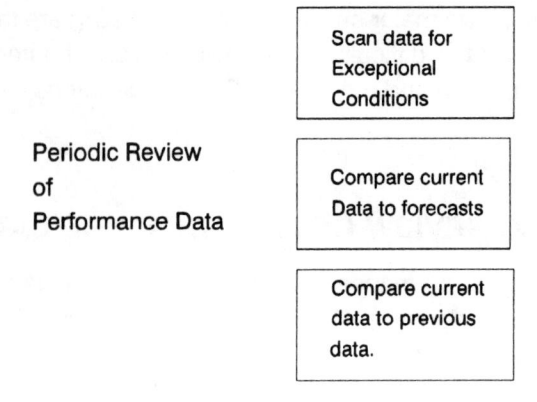

Figure 4.12 The performance review process.

response time should be researched closely. Data from unusual periods normally will be dropped and not used in performance planning.

4.6.3 Comparing Current Data to Forecasts

After determining that data are reasonable, the next step would be to compare major workloads with forecasts. The primary reason for comparing current data to forecasts is to discern if performance and capacity plans are on target. Major differences between actual activity and projections could require adjustments in long-term projections and plans.

The data compared to forecasts will be high-level in nature including transaction volume and response times for major systems, resource usage for CICS regions or for the system as a whole, and the utilization of significant resources.

Significant inconsistencies between actual data and forecasts will suggest changes in the assumptions underlying plans and forecasts. These should be investigated in more detail.

Performance data for new systems also should be compared to forecasts once the new systems are implemented.

4.6.4 Comparing Current Data to Previous Periods

The third activity is a comparison of workload profiles for major systems from the current period with comparable data from a previous period (month, quarter, etc.).

The purpose of comparing current performance data to data from a previous period is to *detect specific workload changes that might be significant but not visible globally.* Normally, only medium- to high-volume transaction types would be examined. Significant changes in workload profiles should be researched and compared to forecasts. This is just another step that can help keep performance and capacity plans current.

With a performance database and a statistical language such as SAS, it is not difficult to compare selected data from two different months (or other periods). Characteristics that might be compared would include the peak number of transactions, response times, and average CPU usage, memory, and I/Os per transaction. Differences greater than some predefined threshold (e.g., 10 or 15 percent) can be listed for further investigation.

4.7 TYPES OF CHANGE

Changes in performance data normally are driven by one of three general causes. It is important to know which of the three causes were involved, since this will affect the way we interpret the change and apply information.

The three causes of change are:

- Time-related variance
- Random variance
- Institutional changes

4.7.1 Time-Related Variance

Time-related variance consists of changes in workload activity that recur regularly. Time-related variance is usually related to business activity and/or institutional functions that occur at regular intervals. Variations that are sensitive to time of day, day of the week or month, or different times of the year are time-related.

The most obvious and most commonly used time-related variance is for *transaction volume*. In most systems, the number of transactions processed varies considerably by time of day and day of week. Recurring peak periods are good examples of identifiable time-related variance in transaction volume.

However, time-related variance also applies to workload profiles. For some transactions, average resource utilization and workload content can vary consistently at different times. Users may use systems differently at different times, and this can cause differences in workload profiles.

One cause of time-related variance in transactions profiles would be screens on which variable amounts of data might be entered. The amount of processing in a transaction might vary depending on the number of fields entered. If the number of fields entered tends to vary at different times of the day or week, processing profiles will be different. For example, if an application allowed users to enter up to 20 items per order, the amount of processing would depend on the number of items entered. If larger orders were received on certain days of the week, processing profiles would reflect these differences.

Some applications perform multiple services under the same transaction ID. When the mix of services is time-dependent, the transaction profile will vary. System usage may vary with patterns in business activity. This can be another cause of time-related variance.

An example of time-related variance can be seen in Figure 4.13. Average CPU usage per transaction for this transaction varies by day of the week and is higher later in the week. Something about the way the application system is used requires more processing on Fridays than Mondays.

4.7.2 Random Variance

Random variance is caused by incidental changes in workload activity that occur from hour to hour and day to day. Random variance may reflect minor variations in the level of business activity, the rate at which users are entering transactions, the number of users active, the type of functions being used, or any number of other factors. Random variance is normal and occurs in all systems. Most systems will exhibit a range of random variation for both transaction volume and profiles.

> **Key Point**: Random variance is normal and should be expected. Transaction volume and resource profiles both will vary depending on random circumstances.

Figures 4.14 shows a transaction with noticeable random variance in average CPU time per transaction. It also shows a pattern of time-related variance similar to that shown in Figure 4.13. However, the data seem to vary widely from week to week and is less consistent than that shown in Figure 4.13. Transactions in Figure 4.14 are more heavily influenced by random variance than those in Figure 4.13.

Forecasting Changes in Workloads 91

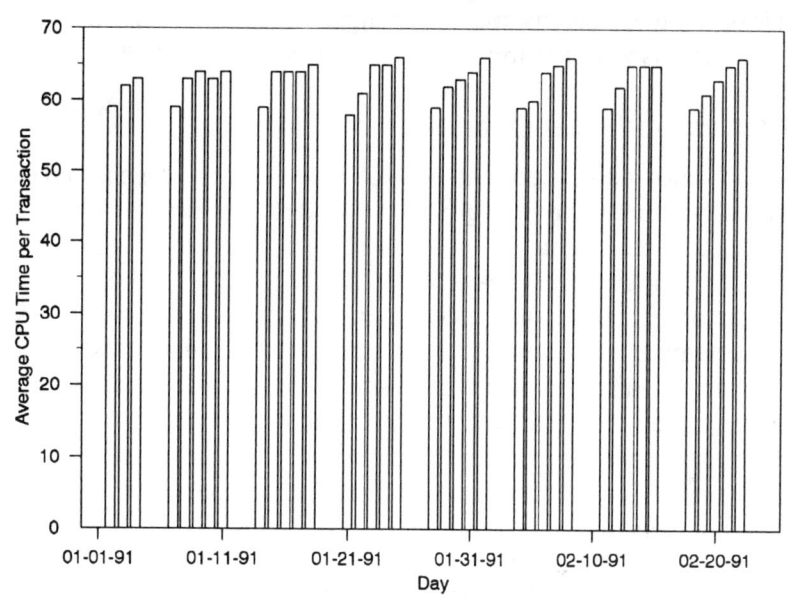

Figure 4.13 An example of time-related variance in CPU usage per transaction.

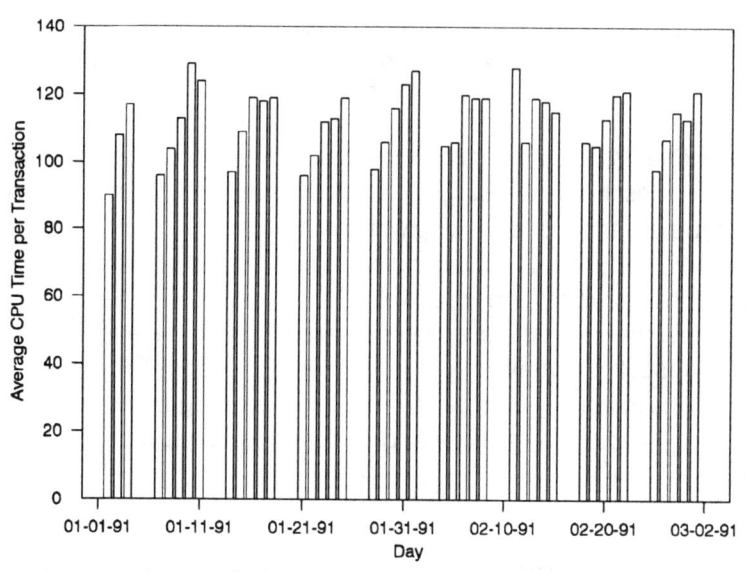

Figure 4.14 An example of random variance in CPU usage per transaction.

It is easier to isolate institutional changes (which we will discuss below) for the systems with less random variance in workload profiles.

4.7.3 Institutional Changes

The final and most important type of change is *institutional change*. Institutional change is part of growth bias and reflects events that alter the basic content of workloads. These changes are *permanent in nature* and *affect long-range capacity plans*.

Institutional changes may affect either complexity/overhead or transaction volume. Sustained changes in transaction volume probably reflect new users. Changes in resources used per transaction normally represent application modifications or enhancements. In both cases, it is likely that the total resource usage will be affected in future periods.

When institutional changes are identified, it is good to document them and adjust workload forecasts if necessary. If institutional changes are consistent with forecast values, this will reinforce forecasts and plans. If they are unexpected or inconsistent with forecasts, some adjustment to forecasts and plans may be in order.

> **Key Point**: Institutional changes are variations in workloads that are likely to remain in future periods. Unanticipated institutional changes may require adjustments to performance plans.

Sometimes random variance may be greater than either time-related variance or institutional changes. This can make it difficult to determine which type of variance is causing workload changes. It can be hard to tell whether the variance observed indicates changes in workload profiles or is simply the result of random activity.

The best way to handle extremes of random variance is to compare long-term (such as week-long or month-long) averages. Even with drastic variations in activity from day to day, longer averages will tend to show less variance and may allow the identification of seasonal patterns and institutional changes.

4.8 REASONS TO REVIEW DATA PERIODICALLY

There are many reasons to review performance data periodically. A few of these are summarized below:

- **To identify institutional changes and their effect on forecasts.** Large changes that had not been anticipated could require revisions of forecasts.

- **To stay familiar with current performance and capacity data.** There is no better way to prevent surprises than to be familiar with current activity.

- **To develop a history of workload changes and their causes.** Significant changes in resource utilization, transaction volume, or response time should be documented. This information can help us account for the factors driving resource growth. In some systems, changes in the complexity/overhead component represent a large percent of processor growth. A record of identifiable changes can help explain overall growth in processor demand. Such a record can be useful when documenting the need for increased capacity to management. In some environments, workload growth may be caused primarily by dozens (or hundreds) or small changes, none of which would be visible to management. A list of the most significant changes can help explain why additional equipment is required.

- **To help us improve our forecasting skills.** It is often difficult to develop accurate projections of resource utilization or transaction volume before systems are implemented. We probably will never perfect the art of projecting changes in workloads. However, with practice, our ability to forecast workload changes can improve.

- **Tuning opportunities.** Occasionally the review process will uncover increases in resource usage that seem unreasonable based on our understanding of the changes involved. This may point out opportunities for tuning. When this situation occurs, though, it should be approached with tact.

4.8.1 The Frequency of Performance Reviews

The frequency at which performance data is reviewed will vary from organization to organization. In many larger shops with permanent performance and capacity planning staff, performance plans might be reviewed monthly or even weekly. In other shops, staffing may allow only quarterly or less frequent reviews of capacity data.

While it is good to review performance data on a weekly or even daily basis, the primary reason to perform such frequent reviews would be to detect short-term performance problems. The emphasis of daily or weekly reviews is managing performance – monitoring and tuning a changing environment. It is usually neither practical nor necessary to review or revise performance plans more frequently than once a month.

On the other hand, it is usually good to review capacity plans at least once a quarter. Unless the environment is extremely static with few changes in either transaction volume or program function, workloads could change dramatically and affect the validity of long-term plans. It is important to review data frequently enough to adjust plans on a timely basis.

4.9 SUMMARY

In this chapter we presented an approach to developing workload forecasts. We looked at how to develop growth projections for each component of workload growth (volume, complexity/overhead, and new systems). We discussed many factors that could affect workload growth and how to estimate their impact. We examined types of variance and how these affect the way we deal with change. Finally, we discussed the periodic review of performance data and how they can be used to refine workload forecasts.

SELECTED READING

[MILL91] Mills, Terry L., "Capacity Planning: An Implementation Architecture," *Proceedings of the Twelfth Annual IS Performance/Capacity Management Conference*, 1991.

Chapter 5

The Mathematics of Performance Planning

5.1 OVERVIEW

This chapter will present several basic mathematical techniques that can be used in performance and capacity planning. While a certain amount of mathematics is involved, every effort has been made to keep the material as simple and to the point as possible. *The emphasis in this and subsequent chapters has been to provide simple, easy-to-use techniques that can be applied to evaluate the performance of CICS systems.*

The formulas used in this chapter are simple and involve only basic mathematical functions. In most cases, formulas have been reduced to simple charts and tables for ease of use. Several limited set of tables are included in this chapter for illustration purposes. Three sets of more complete table data have been included in Appendixes A, B, and C. These tables are provided to allow the reader to estimate service delays for various situations.

Several subsequent chapters will use the principles developed in this chapter. Over a series of chapters we will explore how to estimate components of performance and response time. We will see how to estimate processor constraint, evaluate the impact of other MVS workloads on CICS performance, evaluate how CICS applications will perform on different processors, and estimate the performance of new CICS applications. All of these topics will use the material developed in Chapter 5.

5.1.1 Primary Audience

Systems programmers and *application developers* probably will not be familiar with much of the material in this chapter. Although the principles discussed are commonly used by performance analysts and capacity planners, they are not widely used in other areas of data processing. Both systems programmers and application developers are encouraged to become familiar with the principles discussed in this chapter, especially those dealing with queueing delays.

Experienced *capacity planners* probably will be familiar with many principles discussed. They are encouraged to scan the material, though, and to familiarize themselves with the author's terminology and approach to queueing delays.

5.2 RESOURCE UTILIZATION, BOTTLENECKS, AND RULES OF THUMB

A *bottleneck* occurs when a resource becomes overworked and restricts processing flow. Depending on the nature of the workflow, bottlenecks can exist in either hardware or software. In a CICS environment, processor speed, DASD, channels, virtual storage, maximum tasks, journals, temporary storage, and database systems all can be bottlenecks. Each of these can limit the potential amount of work processed by CICS application systems.

The identification of bottlenecks is important in both long- and short-term performance planning. When we are debugging performance problems, we try to identify bottlenecks and tune them. In long-term performance planning, we try to project which resources will become bottlenecks, then appropriate hardware and software can be proposed to support anticipated levels of activity.

5.2.1 Resource Utilization

Resource utilization is a measure of how busy the resource is. It is usually expressed in terms of *percent busy*. Some common measures of resource utilization include CPU busy and device busy. For example, when we state that a DASD device is 20 percent busy, this is a measure of resource utilization.

Arrival rate is a measure of how much work is requested per unit of time. A common measure of arrival rate is the number of I/O requests processed per second at a DASD device. As a rule, resource utilization should increase approximately proportionately with the work arrival rate.

Figure 5.1 illustrates this principle in theory. Assuming the average time it takes to perform an event remains constant, the relationship between arrival rate and resource utilization should approximate a straight line. In this example, we have assumed that it takes an average of 15 ms to perform an I/O, once the I/O request is communicated to the device. As long as this value remains constant, the relationship between work arrivals and device utilization should be similar to the line shown in Figure 5.1.

Figure 5.1 shows that the device should be about 15 percent busy when there are 10 I/O requests per second. This would be calculated as follows:

$$10 \text{ I/Os per second} \times 15 \text{ ms per I/O} = 150 \text{ ms per second}$$
$$= \frac{150 \text{ ms}}{1000 \text{ ms}} = .15 = 15\%$$

Similarly, the device would be 30 percent busy with 20 requests per second, and 45 percent busy with 30 requests per second.

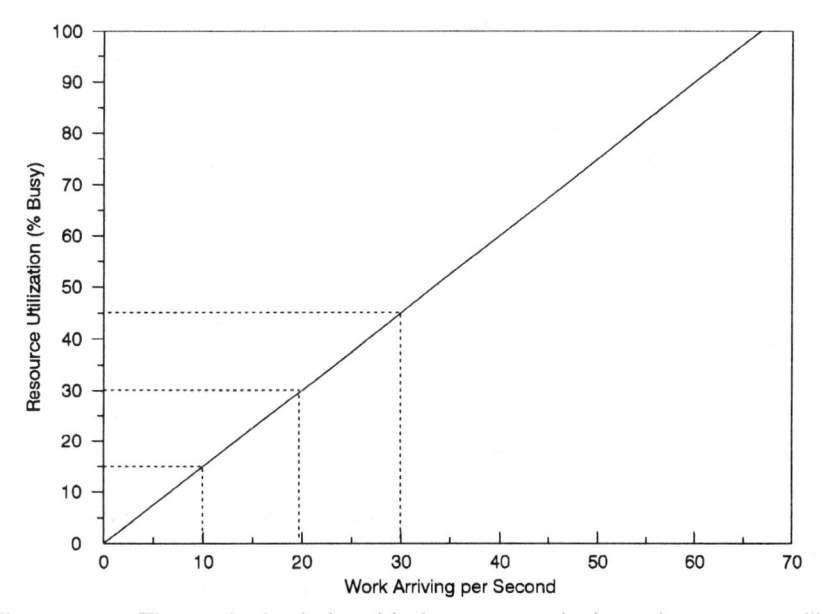

Figure 5.1 Theoretical relationship between arrivals and resource utilization.

98   Chapter Five

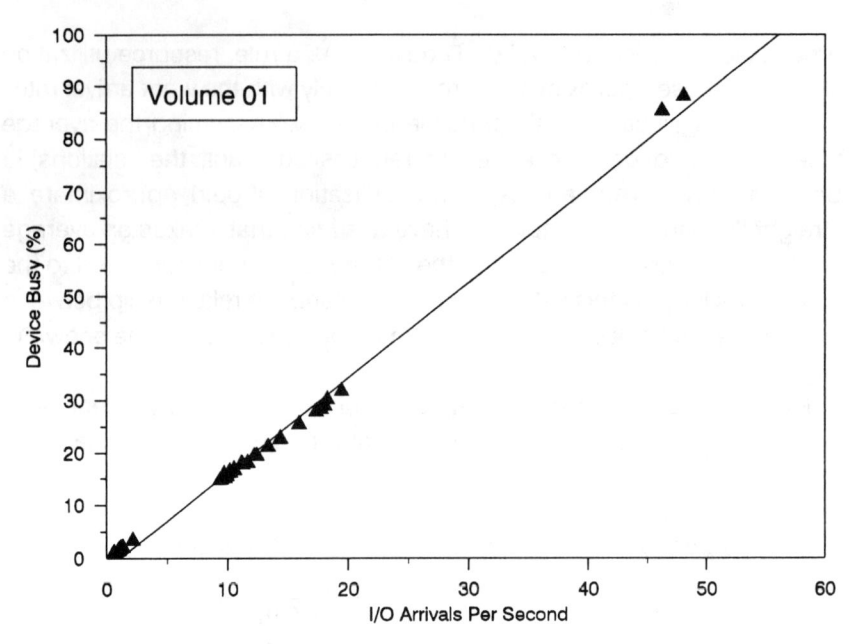

Figure 5.2 Example of a consistent relationship between device busy and I/O arrival rate.

Figures 5.2, 5.3, and 5.4 demonstrate sample relationships between I/O arrival rate and resource utilization. All three DASD volumes (01, 02, and 03) contain only VSAM files used almost exclusively by CICS applications. Performance data was collected from the same period each day for several weeks. Each point on the graphs represents one hour of data.

Volume 01, illustrated in Figure 5.2, shows the classical relationship between work arrivals and resource utilization. The ratio is very consistent over a wide range of activity. The volume contains a single data set used almost exclusively for a single CICS application.

Volume 02, illustrated in Figure 5.3, contains many VSAM files used by multiple CICS applications. There is a correlation between I/O arrivals and device busy, but there is more variance than there is for volume 01. The large number of files and variety of applications on volume 02 can cause variations in data access patterns. This graph suggests that there are differences in access patterns (such as average seek time, the amount of data transferred, etc.) when different files are used by different applications.

Volume 03 presents an interesting pattern. As shown in Figure 5.4, it seems that as access becomes more intense, the volume becomes

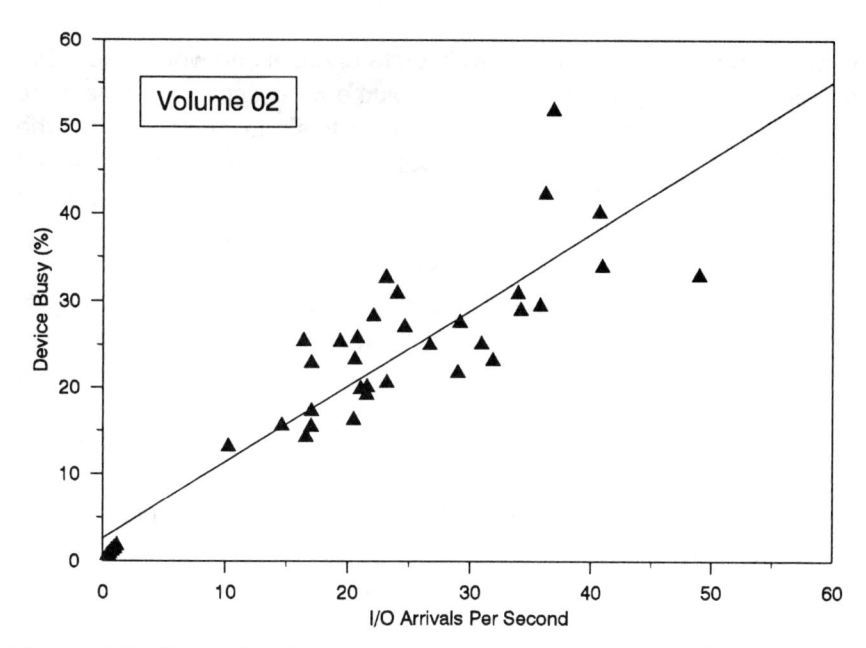

Figure 5.3 Example of a usable relationship between device busy and I/O arrival rate.

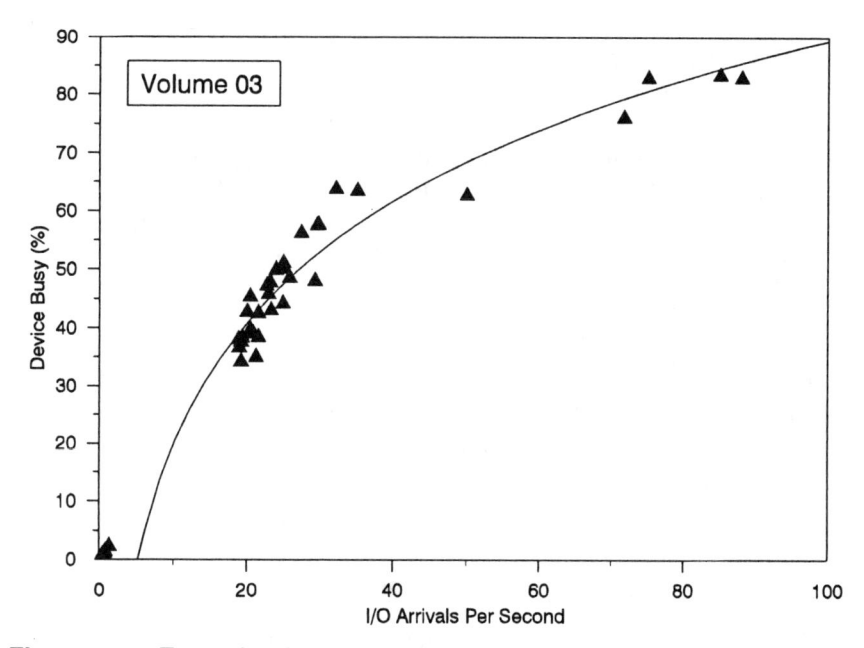

Figure 5.4 Example of a logarithmic relationship between device busy and I/O arrival rate.

busier at a decreasing rate. This is quite unusual and would imply that server time actually improved for this volume when activity became more intense. The most probable explanation for this phenomenon is that the type of workload changed as the arrival rate increased. It is possible that files with good cache-hit ratios represented a larger portion of the work at higher levels of activity. DASD performance will be discussed in more detail in Chapter 11.

Resources such as the volumes shown in Figures 5.2 and 5.3 simplify performance and capacity planning. It is fairly easy to estimate resource utilization when there is stable linear relationship between the arrival of work and resource utilization.

The only reason data for volume 03 are presented is to suggest that in the real world data do not always match theory. Theory and common sense would suggest that, if anything, service times should become longer at higher levels of utilization. However, there is often more behind the nature of data than linear relationships and projections might imply. It is often necessary to understand the background behind data before making assumptions or projections.

The volumes in these examples were accessed primarily by CICS workloads. When other workloads, such as TSO or batch work, share volumes with CICS data, access patterns often become uncertain and more difficult to predict.

> **Key Point:** Most performance modeling software assumes that as work arrival rates increase, resource utilization will increase proportionately. The assumption is that the *same mix of workloads* will be be present at different levels of activity and be responsible for increased workloads. This should normally be a reasonable assumption, but workload growth sometimes does not follow ideal patterns.

In the discussion above, DASD devices were used in the illustrations. Unfortunately, though, DASD is often a good example of a poor relationship between the work arrival rate and resource utilization. DASD service times will commonly elongate as total activity and channel paths become more heavily utilized. This will be discussed in more detail in Chapter 11.

5.2.2 Workload Growth and Utilization

There is a second important assumption in performance and capacity planning. We normally must assume that the amount of resource used per transaction will remain constant despite the rate at which transactions arrive. For example, if a particular transaction used 40 ms of CPU time per transaction at one level of activity, it would use about the same amount of CPU time at higher levels. This is normally a safe assumption as long as comparable periods are used. While there are exceptions, this assumption is usually valid for most kinds of planning.

In our discussion of the types of variance in Chapter 4, we noted that transaction profiles can vary on different days or at different times. Not only will the number and types of transactions vary, but the resources used by specific transactions will vary as well. Therefore, it is important to account for *time-related variance* when analyzing workload growth. We should be certain that recurring patterns are considered when projecting workloads from month to month. We would not want to use data from one time of day to project workload growth for another.

The significance of these first two principles is that as transaction arrival rate increases, resource activity and utilization also should increase proportionately. In other words, the amount of CPU consumed, the number of I/Os requested, and, to a lesser extent, the time-weighted demand for memory should vary directly with transaction arrival rate. Figure 5.5 illustrates how this would work in theory.

As noted, we can usually expect resource utilization to increase proportionately with transaction volume. The average amount of CPU used, I/Os requested, and other resources used per transaction will commonly

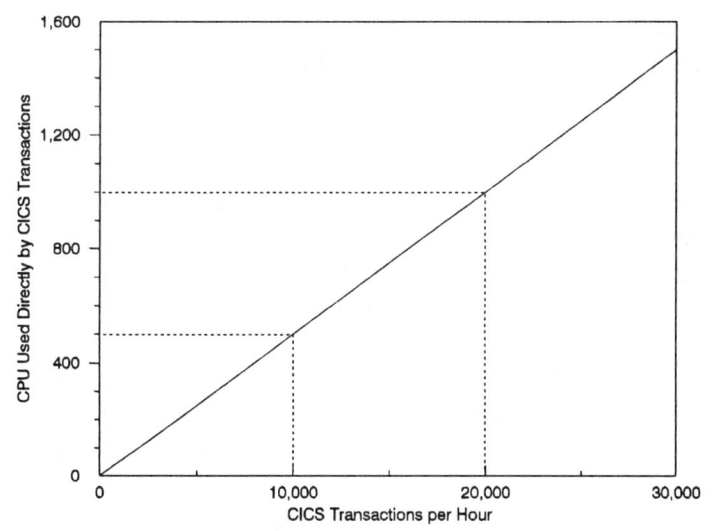

Figure 5.5 Resource utilization versus total transactions.

remain stable regardless of transaction volume. There will be exceptions, and these should be addressed when developing projections and performance plans.

5.2.3 Distortions to the Utilization Relationship

In a CICS environment, several factors can obscure the relationship between the number of transactions processed and the utilization of resources. One factor, commonly called the *low utilization effect*, relates to the way CICS schedules work. When all CICS tasks in a region are waiting (for I/O, etc.), CICS performs overhead functions, searches for possible work, and then issues an operating system wait. When there are few transactions running, CICS will wait more frequently, and the amount of CPU time spent looking for work will increase.

Consequently, total CICS CPU utilization will be proportionately higher when activity is very light. The low utilization effect will not affect the amount of CPU time used directly by each transaction. It will, however, affect the total amount of CPU time used by a CICS region. The amount of CPU time reported by CMF or similar monitors for individual transactions should remain stable, but the total CPU usage accumulated by RMF for the address space (performance group) will reflect the differences.

Hit ratios of buffer pools also can distort the relationship between transaction activity and resource utilization. Various CICS facilities use internal caching techniques to reduce the number of I/Os performed by DASD. For example, VSAM *local shared resources* (LSR) will reuse data already in buffers without reaccessing DASD.

When data are cached in memory, the percent of accesses satisfied from memory may decrease as transaction activity increases. More users (CICS tasks) will compete for access to data. This may cause the number of physical I/O events to increase more rapidly than the arrival rate of transactions.

Some transactions may be used differently depending on the level of transaction activity. Transaction types that include multiple functions might have differing usage patterns. These, in turn, could cause variations in workload profiles. For example, discretionary services might be used less frequently during periods of heavier business activity. Users might choose to bypass nonessential options when business activity is the heaviest.

There is seldom a pure linear relationship between transaction activity and total resource utilization. In most situations, though, the relationship will be close enough to linear to be useful for planning. It is important, though, to recognize that there can be significant exceptions that may distort projections.

5.2.4 Bottleneck Analysis

Bottleneck analysis can be useful both in short-term performance analysis and long-term performance planning. When researching short-term performance problems, we commonly look for resources that are "too busy" or overworked. Performance planning also requires that we recognize potential hardware and software bottlenecks so that we may develop appropriate plans.

> **Key Point:** One of the keys to successful performance planning is learning how to avoid future bottlenecks.

As we will see later in this chapter, service or performance deteriorates at an ever-increasing rate as resources become busier. The delays associated with receiving service increase exponentially with increased activity. When servers are very busy, small increases in activity can produce large increases in service time.

This effect is often called the *knee of the curve*. The knee of the curve is the point at which small increases in utilization cause service to become rapidly unacceptable. However, as we will see later, there is no absolute knee of the curve. Service degradation is relative, depending on several factors.

Rules of thumb (ROTs) are simply well-known knee-of-the-curve values (actually, values just slightly less than the knee-of-the-curve) that can be applied to specific hardware and software systems. Although somewhat folklorish in nature, ROTs usually are practical statements of the effect of queueing delays (which we will discuss later in this chapter) on real-world situations. When resources such as CPU time, DASD devices, or channels are operated above ROT values, performance normally will be degraded or erratic.

> **Key Point:** Rules of thumb attempt to define target levels of utilization for various types of resources. When resources utilization is higher than the ROT, performance commonly will become unacceptable.

If we know the amount of CPU time, number of I/O requests, and other resources used directly by each transaction, we can use *bottleneck analysis* to estimate resource limitations. Using information about resources, we can estimate the level of transaction activity at which each resource will become a bottleneck. ROTs can be used to determine the order in which resources will become bottlenecks.

Table 5.1 and Figure 5.6 illustrate how these concepts might be applied for a very simple system. Transaction A will run in its own CICS region. Each transaction will use an average of 50 ms of CPU and perform 2 I/Os to file 1 and 5 I/Os to file 2. Transaction profiles are not expected to vary at different transaction arrival rates. Resource utilization is assumed to be proportionate with device activity. Device service times and activity rates are shown in Table 5.1.

For purposes of the example, it is assumed that the CICS region will use about 5 percent CPU even when there are no transactions running. File 1 and file 2 will be placed on volume 1 and volume 2, respectively, and no other files will reside on these volumes. Volume 2 is cached and will receive better service time than volume 1. Transaction A will be the only application using these files.

In this example, we have assumed that uncached DASD volumes should not be more than 35 percent busy and cached volumes, 50 percent busy, when used for random accesses. We also have assumed that a CICS region should not use more than 60 percent of a processor engine. There is nothing magic about these numbers. Other values could have been used in different circumstances. The values used in this example are simply guidelines for hypothetical devices representing points at which individual service will begin to become a bottleneck.

Figure 5.6 shows that file 1 will be the first resource to reach its threshold. File 1 will become about 35 percent busy at about 30,000 transactions per hour. If device service becomes unacceptable above

Table 5.1 Resource Utilization by Transaction

Resource Name	Resources Used Per Transaction	Service Time Per Unit	Resource Load at 1 Trans. / Sec	Equivalent Resource Busy
CPU	50 ms		50 ms / sec.	5%
File 1	2 random I/Os	20 ms	40 ms / sec.	4%
File 2	5 cached I/Os	6 ms	30 ms / sec.	3%

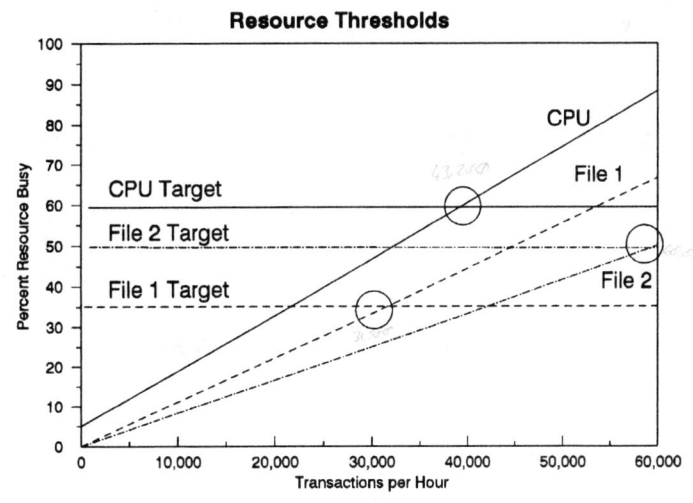

Figure 5.6 Utilization of three resources based on transaction volume.

this point, some action would be needed to process more than 30,000 transactions per hour. The figure also shows that CPU usage in the CICS region will reach a ROT threshold at about 40,000 transactions per hour, and file 2 at 60,000.

We never established what level of service was actually needed by the application in this example. We simply estimated the point at which each system resource would reach an "out-of-capacity" condition. This analysis provides no indication of whether the application will have acceptable response time or if resources could have operated acceptably at higher levels. It simply shows the range of transaction activity that will allow resources to operate in their "normal" service range.

5.2.5 Bottleneck Analysis and Performance Debugging

Bottleneck analysis is commonly used in debugging performance problems. When application systems experience performance problems, analysts almost intuitively look for resources that are overworked. It usually does not take much time to spot resource bottlenecks with the aid of a good resource monitor.

Using published ROT values [see ZIMM91], performance analysts can look for resources that are more heavily used than ROT recommendations. There is a good chance that unacceptable response time will caused by overworked resources. When resources are used too heavily, applications will receive less than acceptable service.

5.3 QUEUEING THEORY

5.3.1 What Is a Queueing Theory?

Each of us will find ourselves waiting in line from time to time. Whether in a bank, supermarket, or doctor's office, we will need to wait for goods or services. And, when it takes a long time to get something done, it seems that we spend more time waiting in line than receiving service.

Queueing theory is a set of principles and formulas that can be used to estimate how long customers will wait to receive a service. It is simply the mathematics of waiting in line.

> **Key Point:** Queueing theory is the mathematics of waiting in line.

Based on statistical functions, queueing theory is rich in formulas that can be useful in estimating almost any aspect of delays (e.g., average wait time, number of customers waiting, 90th percentile wait time, etc.). Although queueing theory is heavily based in statistics and can involve many complex mathematical formulas, we will demonstrate ways of estimating queueing delays without becoming bogged down in complex calculations.

In this chapter, we will look at the basics of queueing theory and how to apply fundamental concepts without the use of complex formulas. Tables and charts will be presented where possible to summarize principles and formulas. The reader will *not* need to use complex formulas to take advantage of the concepts presented in this chapter.

This chapter will discuss how to use easy-to-obtain information to estimate queueing delays. The emphasis will be on applying simple, easy-to-use procedures.

5.3.2 Definition of Basic Terms

We will begin our discussion of queueing theory by defining a few terms. The first term is *server*. A server is any person or thing that provides a service. Tellers in a bank, checkout clerks in a supermarket, and doctors are all servers with which you are familiar. If servers are busy when you need to use them, you must wait. You will enter some kind of formal or informal line and wait until a server becomes available.

Servers also exist in computer systems. CPUs, DASD devices, memory, and channels can all be viewed as servers. When a program needs to accomplish work, it will request the use of various servers and wait for their availability. If a task needs to do some processing and a processor is available, the task will be dispatched. If not, it will wait until a processor becomes available. If a program requests an I/O, it will have to wait if the device is already busy.

> **Key Point:** A *queueing system* or *system* is simply a server or group of servers and a line (or queue) in which customers wait when the server is busy.

Figure 5.7 illustrates a simple queueing system. This bank has a single drive-up automatic teller machine (ATM). Customers enter the system (*arrive* in their vehicles), wait in a *queue* (line) if necessary, receive *service* from the machine, and eventually leave the system.

This type of system is called a *single-server system* because there is only one server. Other examples of single-server systems include a barber shop with one barber, the CPU in a uniprocessor, or a DASD device containing specific data needed by an application. In these systems, there is only one server and a single line of customers waiting to get the server.

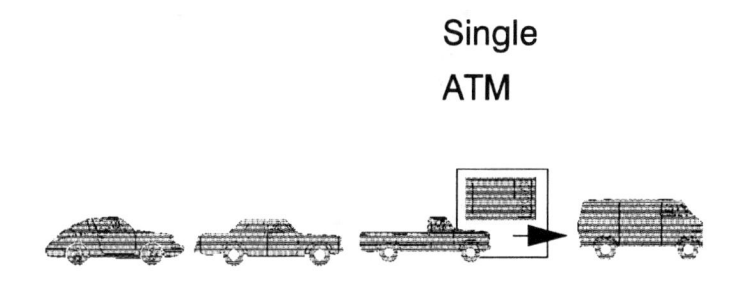

Single
ATM

Figure 5.7 Single-server queueing system.

Figure 5.8 illustrates a *multiserver system*. Multiserver systems are characterized by multiple interchangeable servers. When customers enter a multiserver system, they will use any available server. There is only one line (queue) and customers will wait only if all servers are busy.

The key element of a multiserver system is the single line or queue for multiple servers. When customers enter a system and must select and wait for a particular server, this is not a multiserver system. It is, instead, a collection of single-server systems.

Key Point: True multiserver systems can be distinguished by the single queue shared by multiple servers.

There are considerable differences in performance between single- and multiserver systems. Customers will be serviced more quickly in a true multi-server system than in a collection of single-server systems. That is why most airlines and many banks now use a single line (queue) for multiple servers.

Average arrival rate is the rate at which customers enter the system. It is usually expressed in terms of arrivals per unit of time, such as customers per hour or transactions per second. The Greek letter lambda (λ) is commonly used to represent average arrival rate.

Average service time is the average time it takes for a server to service a customer. It is the average (mean) time it takes for the server actually to perform service. The terms *E[s]* or *Ws* are commonly used to represent

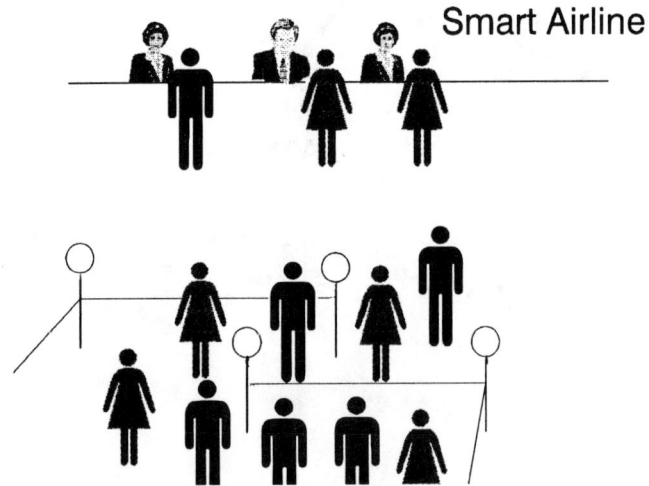

Figure 5.8 Multiserver queueing system.

average service time. An example of average service time would be the time it takes a bank teller to complete a transaction once the customer reaches the window.

Average service time should be expressed in the same time units as average arrival rate. If average arrival rate is stated in terms of customers per hour, average service time should be stated as hours (or fractions of hours) service per customer.

Traffic intensity is the rate at which work arrives in the system. It is the *product* of *average arrival rate* and *average service time*. The expression *u* is commonly used to represent traffic intensity. If 45 customers arrive in a bank per hour and each customer requires an average of 2 minutes (.0333 hours) service, 90 minutes or 1.5 hours of work will arrive in the bank each hour. Traffic intensity would be 1.5; that is, 1.5 hours of work will arrive at the bank each hour.

$$u = \frac{45 \text{ customers}}{\text{hour}} \times \frac{0.0333 \text{ hours service}}{\text{customer}}$$

$$= \frac{1.5 \text{ hours of work}}{\text{hour}}$$

Server utilization is a measure of system busy. It is a measure of both how busy the system is as a whole and how busy each server is on the average. It is calculated by *dividing traffic intensity by the number of servers*. If 1.5 hours of work arrive each hour and there are three servers (*c*) to perform the work, server utilization would be .50. Each server would be busy 30 minutes per hour or 50 percent of the time. The Greek letter rho (ρ) is used for server utilization.

$$\text{Server utilization} = \rho = \frac{u}{c} = \frac{1.5}{3} = .5$$

Total service time or *total wait time* are terms used for the total amount of time a customer must wait to receive service. Total service or wait time is the sum of *average service time* (time actually spent receiving service) and *queue time* (time spent waiting in a line or queue while the server is busy). Total wait or service times reflect total customer delays. The symbol *W* is commonly used to represent total service or wait time.

Total service time = queue time + average server time
$$W = W_q + W_s$$

5.3.3 Open Versus Closed Queueing Systems

Many specialized types of queueing system exist to estimate performance. Different sets of queueing formulas have various degrees of accuracy, depending on the properties of data. When real-world data match the assumptions upon which queueing formulas were built, the queueing formulas can provide a good estimate of performance. When real world does not match basic assumptions, the results of queueing formulas can be inaccurate or inconsistent.

Few real-world systems match any theoretical queueing system perfectly. However, many real-world situations match general-purpose formulas closely enough to be useful. In some cases, more specialized queueing systems can be more precise. However, the mathematics for specialized systems can be quite cumbersome, and specialized systems often require information that is difficult to obtain.

In this book, we will discuss how to apply two types of general-purpose queueing systems. The first type, commonly called *open queueing*, describes a system in which the emphasis is on a random flow of customers. The second type, *closed queueing*, is used to describe the interaction between a fixed number of customers who repeatedly return to a set of servers.

Open queueing systems assume an *unlimited population of customers* arriving in a system at a specified average rate. Since the number of customers is theoretically unlimited, open queueing formulas tend to exaggerate both the number of customers waiting in the system and average response times. Open queueing systems can be inaccurate when real-world systems contain a small number of customers. The smaller the number of potential customers, the more open queueing formulas can distort performance.

Open queueing formulas can closely approximate actual performance for systems with large numbers of customers (several thousand or more). The larger the number of customers, the more likely open queueing theory will approximate actual performance. Open queueing systems can produce reasonable estimates of some specialized systems with smaller numbers of customers; this will be discussed later in this chapter.

Although open queueing systems tend to overstate delays, they are popular because of their ease of use. For systems with a single server, open queueing formulas are very simple and easy to apply.

Closed queueing systems are so named because they are defined with a fixed number of customers. Closed queueing formulas describe how servers will respond to a set of customers that return to servers at regular intervals. Because they deal with a limited number of customers, closed queueing systems commonly will be more accurate and more reflective of reality than are open systems.

The major challenges with closed queueing systems are that the mathematics can be quite involved, and it is not always easy to gather all of the information needed. In this chapter, we will provide a simplified method of using closed queueing systems that does not require either complex mathematics and uses data that can be easily obtained.

5.3.4 Service Multipliers — the Key to Simplified Performance Estimation

In most types of queueing system, there is a relationship between resource utilization and total service time. In some queueing systems, total service or wait time can be calculated directly from resource utilization (how busy the resource is) and average service time (how long it takes the server to service a customer). In other queueing systems, additional information will be required to calculate total service time.

We will use the term *service multiplier* to define the relationship between average service time (time actually at the server) and total service time [1] (including queueing). In some situations, we will need only average resource utilization to determine the service multiplier. In more complex systems (such as closed queueing systems), we will need additional information.

> **Key Point:** *Service multipliers* define the relationship between *average service time* (time spent receiving service from a server) and *total wait time* (including queueing).

The approach taken in this book is to use service multipliers to calculate service or wait time. To simplify calculations, tables are provided with service multipliers for open and closed queueing systems. We will use the symbol M_{table} to represent the service multiplier.

The general formula for calculating total service (wait) time will be:

---

[1] The terms total service time and total wait time are used interchangeably in this text.

Total service time = average service time [at the server]
 × service multiplier [from a table]

Let us assume that you would like to estimate how long it will take to complete a transaction in a bank. It takes a teller an average of 5 minutes to process a customer. There are four tellers working, and they, as a group, are busy about 80 percent of the time. We look up the service multiplier in a table (we discuss how to determine which table to use later in this chapter) and find it to be 1.75. That means that total wait time will be 1.75 times the average time it takes one of the servers (tellers) to process a customer (5 minutes).

Customer wait time = 1.75 × 5 minutes = 8.75 minutes

In this example, it will take an average of 8.75 minutes for a customer to receive service. Five minutes will be spent actually receiving service and 3.75 minutes will be spent waiting in line.

5.3.5 Open Single-Server Systems

The mathematics of open single-server systems is quite simple. The service multiplier can be calculated directly from server utilization.

In open systems, total wait time is determined by the probability the server will be busy when the customer arrives. The busier the resource, the greater the chance a customer will need to wait for service, and the longer the customer will wait. If a single server (such as a barber shop with one barber) is 50 percent busy, there is a 50 percent chance that customers will need to wait some amount of time. Similarly, if the barber is busy 90 percent of the time, there is a 90 percent chance that the barber will be working on someone else whenever a customer arrives. Customers will need to wait for one or more other customers 90 percent of the time.

The length of time it will take a customer to receive service from an open single-server system can be estimated from the following open queueing formula:

$$\text{Total wait time} = W = \frac{\text{average service time}}{1 - \text{server utilization}} = \frac{W_s}{1 - \rho}$$

This formula can be restated as:

W = service multiplier × average service time = $M_{table} \times W_s$

For open single-server systems, the service multiplier can be calculated as

$$\text{Service multiplier} = M_{table} = \frac{1}{1 - \text{server utilization}} = \frac{1}{1 - \rho}$$

The formulas for service multipliers (M_{table}) for other types of queueing systems is more complex and have not been included in this book. Service multiplier tables have been provided for the queueing systems we will be using.

Table 5.2 contains a selected group of service multipliers for *open single-server systems*. A more complete table is provided in Appendix A. Table 5.2 shows us that when a server is 50 percent busy, the service multiplier is 2. This means that customers will wait twice as long as the average service time to receive service. If it takes an average of 3 minutes to perform a transaction at an ATM and the machine is busy 50 percent of the time, it will take an average of 6 minutes to complete a transaction.

W = service multiplier × average service time = 2 × 3 min. = 6 min.

Of the 6 minutes total wait time, an average of 3 minutes will be spent receiving service at the ATM, and 3 minutes will be spent waiting in line. If the ATM was 75 percent busy, the service multiplier would be 4, and total wait time would be 12 minutes.

Table 5.2 Sample Service Multipliers for Open Single-Server Systems

Resource Utilization	Service Multiplier
.10	1.1
.25	1.3
.33	1.5
.50	2
.67	3
.75	4
.80	5
.90	10
.95	20

$W = 4 \times 3$ min. $= 12$ min.

It will still take only 3 minutes to perform the transaction, but the customer will wait about 9 minutes to get to the machine.

When the population of potential customers is fairly large, the delays predicted by open queueing formulas can be reasonably accurate. However, when the population is small, open queueing formulas will tend to overstate delays, sometimes significantly.

5.3.6 Closed Single-Server Systems

In contrast to open queueing systems, closed queueing systems are defined by a fixed set of customers. Closed queueing systems were first developed to describe a system called the *machine repair model*.

In the machine repair model, machines will break down periodically, be repaired, return to service, and then break down again. The goal of the model was to determine how long it will take to repair a machine (including queueing for the repairer). The significant parameters in the machine repair model are:

- The mean-time-to-failure
- The average time it takes a repairer to repair a machine
- The number of repairers
- The number of machines in the system

Mean time to failure is defined as the length of time after a machine is returned to service before it needs service again. Figure 5.9 illustrates the machine repair model.

Closed queueing systems are common in data processing applications. In a CICS system, users commonly enter transactions, wait for a response, review their output, and then enter another transaction. The time between when the user receives a response and enters another transaction is called *think time*. Think time is the equivalent of mean time to failure.

Most internal components in CICS systems can be modeled as closed systems. We will discuss this in more detail in chapters that follow.

In closed queueing systems, the *total number of customers* and *the relative frequency at which customers return to the server* are the primary factors controlling the service multiplier. Unlike open queueing systems,

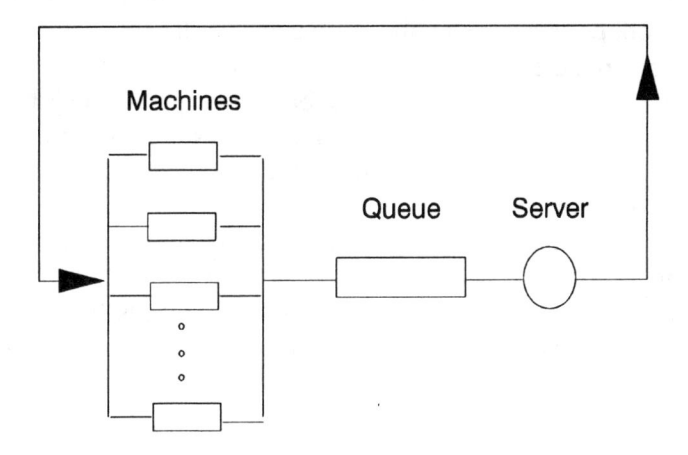

Figure 5.9 The machine repair model.

the service multiplier cannot be calculated directly from server utilization. Server utilization is actually a derived value.

In closed queueing systems, many different scenarios can result in the same server utilization. For example, a single server that is 50 percent busy could be serving a group of 10 customers that returned to the server very frequently. Or, it could be serving 50 customers that returned less frequently, or 500 customers returning even less frequently. The average time a customer would wait for service will be different in each of these three situations. Each scenario has differing performance characteristics and differing sets of service multiplier values.

Server utilization is the most readily available measure of data processing activity. Server utilization measures are usually easy to obtain and frequently referenced. The main challenge to using server utilization with closed queueing systems is that it cannot be easily used with standard formulas. In this book, though, we will examine how to use closed queueing systems to estimate performance — using resource utilization and other available information. Tables have been included to allow performance estimates based on server utilization and other easy-to-obtain data.

There are really two different kinds of closed queueing systems. In some systems, the number of customers does not change very much but the rate at which they request service varies. This controls server utilization. In other systems, the number of customers in the system can vary, but their work profiles remain about the same. In this case, the number of customers in the system tends to control server utilization.

Table 5.3 shows service multipliers for closed queueing system with more or less steady workload profiles. In these systems, the rate at which customers return to servers is stable, but the number of customers varies to control server utilization.

The *return ratio* shown in Table 5.3 is the ratio of *think time* or *mean-time to failure* to *average server time*. If customer think time is 20 seconds and average service time is 2 seconds, then the return ratio is 10. Customers will spend 10 times as long away from the server as they will actually using the server. Conceptually, the return ratio is the ratio of "up time" to "repair time" (excluding queueing).

$$\text{Return ratio} = \frac{\text{think time}}{\text{average service time}} = \frac{20 \text{ sec.}}{2 \text{ sec.}} = 10$$

To create Table 5.3, the number of customers was varied while holding the return ratio steady. For any given return ratio, only whole numbers of

Table 5.3 Sample Service Multiplier for Closed Queueing Systems

Average Server Utilization	Service Multiplier					
	Closed Queueing					Open Queueing
	Return Ratio					
	10	20	40	100	500	
.10	1.0	1.0	1.1	1.1	1.1	1.1
.25	1.2	1.2	1.3	1.3	1.3	1.3
.33	1.2	1.4	1.4	1.4	1.5	1.5
.50	1.6	1.8	1.8	1.9	2.0	2
.67	2.1	2.4	2.7	2.8	3.0	3
.75	2.4	2.8	3.1	3.6	3.9	4
.80	2.7	3.4	3.8	4.2	4.8	5
.90	4.2	4.6	5.7	6.9	8.8	10
.95	4.8	6.3	8.2	10.3	14.6	20

Note: In this table, the time between visits to the server remains steady and the number of customers varies. Open queueing values are shown for comparison.

customers can be used. This means that the server utilizations listed in the table are approximate.

Figure 5.10 presents information similar to that shown in Table 5.3. It shows service multipliers for a closed queueing system and an open system. Notice that the open queueing system always has a higher service time.

Another way of looking at closed systems is to consider what happens when *the number of customers does not change but the average time between trips to the customer varies*. In a processor configuration dedicated to CICS workloads, the number of regions and active TCBs might remain fairly constant much of the day. However, total processor utilization could vary significantly at different times. The variance would be caused primarily by changes in the processing intensity of CICS and other higher-priority regions. In other words, the number of customers requesting service (MVS TCBs) would remain constant, but the intensity at which they demanded CPU service would vary.

Table 5.4 summarizes the relationship between resource utilization and the service multiplier when the number of customers does not change but the rate at which they return to the server (return ratio) is varied. Open queueing figures are shown for comparison. Similar data are shown in Figure 5.11 for 10 and 100 customers.

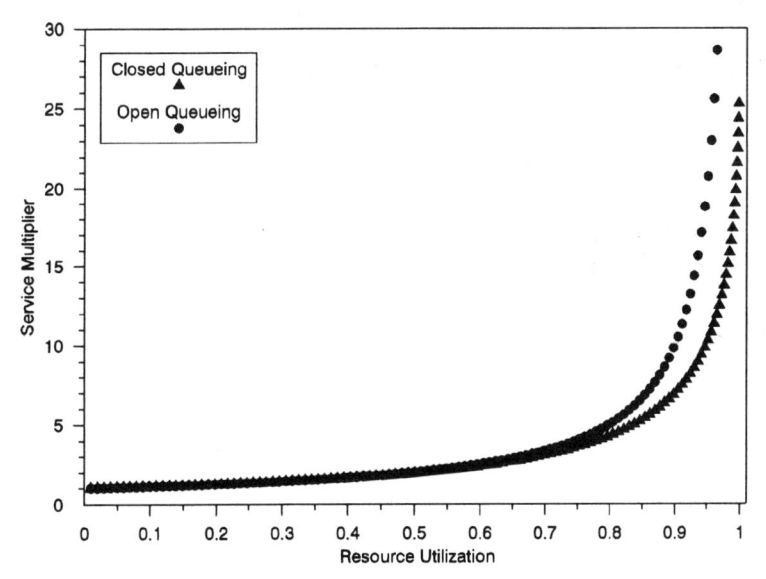

Figure 5.10 Comparison of service multipliers in open and closed queueing systems.

Table 5.4 Sample Service Multiplier for Closed Queueing Systems

Average Resource Utilization	Service Multiplier					
	Closed Queueing Number of Customers					Open Queueing
	10	20	30	50	90	
.10	1.1	1.1	1.1	1.1	1.1	1.1
.25	1.3	1.3	1.3	1.3	1.3	1.3
.33	1.4	1.4	1.5	1.5	1.5	1.5
.50	1.7	1.8	1.9	1.9	2.0	2
.67	2.2	2.5	2.6	2.8	2.9	3
.75	2.6	3.0	3.2	3.4	3.6	4
.80	2.8	3.4	3.7	4.0	4.3	5
.90	3.6	4.6	5.2	6.0	6.9	10
.95	4.3	5.8	6.8	8.1	9.8	20

Note: In this table the number of customers remains steady and the time between visits to the server varies. Open queueing values are shown for comparison.

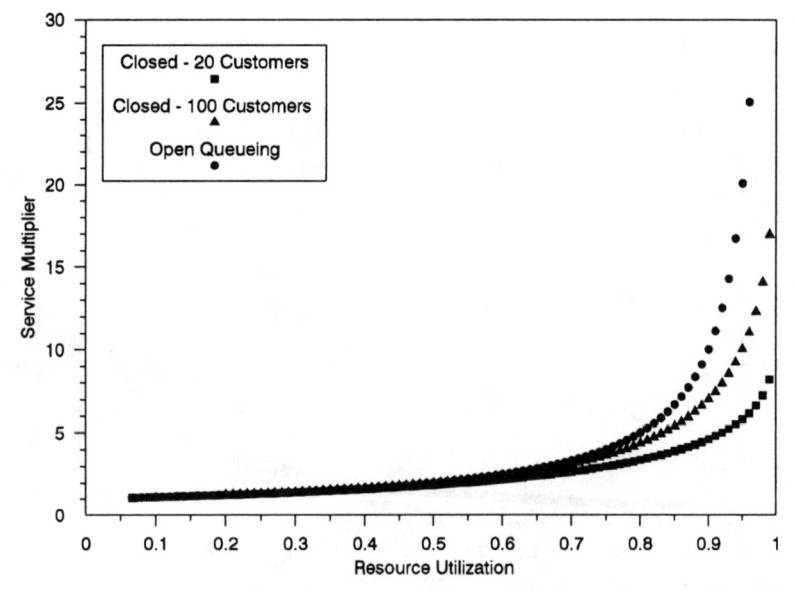

Figure 5.11 Comparison of service multipliers in open and closed queueing systems.

Figures 5.10 and 5.11 both show that open queueing formulas will predict higher service times than closed systems. We can see that open systems can overstate the service multiplier, especially at higher levels of server utilization. Even when systems have as many as 100 customers, open queueing formulas can overstate service times.

In the real world, many systems have large numbers of customers. ATMs, barber shops, and doctors' offices are all examples of systems with large enough customer bases to approximate open queueing systems.

In contrast, open queueing systems usually are less appropriate when estimating performance for computer systems. Most servers have a small enough number of potential customers so open queueing formulas can overstate total wait times, especially at higher levels of server utilization. Later in this chapter when we discuss assumptions behind queueing theory, we will see that open queueing systems can provide reasonable estimates of some types of data processing work. In general, though, closed queueing systems provide better estimates of data processing service.

5.3.7 Multiserver Systems

So far we have discussed single-server systems – systems with a single server. We will now look at *multiserver systems* – systems with multiple servers, each capable of providing the same service. As we mentioned earlier, the key to multiserver systems is a single queue. Formulas for multiserver queueing systems assume that customers will wait in a single queue and use the first available server.

The formulas for both open and closed multiserver systems are more complex than their single-server equivalents and are not discussed in this book. Service multipliers for these formulas have been included in Appendixes A and B. The formulas themselves are not provided but can be found in [ALLE90].

Multiserver systems provide better service than single-server systems. In a single-server system, customers must wait if the server is busy. When there are multiple servers, customers will wait only if all servers are busy. The probability that a customer will wait is less when there are more servers.

Table 5.5 provides sample service multipliers for closed systems with 2, 4, and 6 servers. This table reflects systems with a constant return ratio and a varying number of customers. Table 5.5 shows that service at any

Table 5.5 Service Multipliers for Multiserver Systems

	Service Multiplier										
	Closed Systems								Open Systems		
Utilization	Return ratio = 10			Return ratio = 50			Return ratio = 100				
	Servers			Servers			Servers			Servers		
	2	4	6	2	4	6	2	4	6	2	4	6
.10	1.0	1.0	1.0	1.0	1.0	1.0	1.0	1.0	1.0	1.0	1.0	1.0
.25	1.0	1.0	1.0	1.0	1.0	1.0	1.1	1.0	1.0	1.1	1.0	1.0
.33	1.1	1.0	1.0	1.1	1.0	1.0	1.1	1.0	1.0	1.1	1.0	1.0
.50	1.2	1.1	1.0	1.3	1.1	1.0	1.3	1.1	1.0	1.3	1.1	1.0
.67	1.5	1.2	1.1	1.7	1.3	1.1	1.7	1.3	1.1	1.8	1.3	1.1
.75	1.7	1.3	1.2	2.1	1.5	1.3	2.2	1.5	1.3	2.3	1.5	1.3
.80	1.9	1.4	1.3	2.4	1.6	1.4	2.6	1.7	1.4	2.8	1.7	1.4
.90	2.7	1.9	1.6	3.7	2.4	1.9	4.1	2.5	1.9	5.3	3.0	2.2
.95	3.5	2.5	2.0	5.3	3.3	2.4	5.9	3.2	2.3	10.3	5.5	3.9

level of utilization is better when there are more servers. For example, a system with two servers that are 50 percent busy will provide better service than two single-server systems that are each 50 percent busy.[2]

5.3.8 Selecting the Correct Type of Queueing System

When estimating service, it is important to choose the correct type of queueing system. We must decide whether the system is a single- or multiserver system, whether to use open or closed queueing tables, and when we are using closed queueing systems, whether the number of customers or the server return ratio should be used to obtain service multipliers. Unless the correct tables and techniques are selected, queueing formulas will not correspond to real world results.

In Chapters 6, 7, and 11, we will discuss how to select appropriate queueing tables in different circumstances, and how apply them to CICS performance.

---

[2] This, of course, assumes that average server time is the same in both systems.

5.3.9 Little's Law

A fairly simple formula, commonly called *Little's law* (after J.D.C. Little who developed the mathematics behind it), provides additional insight into the nature of queueing systems. Little's law allows us to relate the number of customers in a system to average wait time and arrival rate. The formula is simply

L = average arrival rate × average wait time = $\lambda \times W$

L (for Little, of course) stands for the number of customers in the system. Lambda (λ), as we mentioned earlier, represents the average rate at which customers arrive. W is the average wait time — the sum of time spent in the queue and at the server.

Let us assume that 20 customers arrive at an ATM each hour, and that they spend an average of 6 minutes (.1 hours) in the system (using or waiting to use the ATM). From Little's law, we can see that there would be an average of 2 customers in the system at any given time.

L = average arrival rate × average wait time = 20 × .1 = 2

Similarly, if we knew the customer arrival rate and the average number of customers in the system, Little's law would allow us to calculate average wait time.

5.4 QUEUEING THEORY — A SET OF ESTIMATION TECHNIQUES

As we discuss ways to apply queueing theory, we need to remember that the best any queueing formula can do is approximate service and performance information. All queueing theory is built on the application of statistical principles to a series of random events. Every time a series of random events occurs, the results will be slightly different. Even with similar input, performance for similar periods will be different because of random arrival patterns. Random events in the real world are seldom repeated identically.

Since queueing theory deals with random events, its purpose is to provide approximate indicators of performance. Regardless of how perfectly real-world patterns match theoretical patterns, there will be differences between real and predicted results. The most we can hope to achieve with queueing theory or any modeling technique is to produce estimates that resemble the real world.

> **Key Point:** It is important to remember that queueing theory deals with random events and only can provide *estimates* of real world performance.

5.5 ASSUMPTIONS BEHIND QUEUEING THEORY

The formulas used in open and closed queueing theory are based upon a few assumptions. If the system being studied conforms to these assumptions, then queueing formulas can provide a reasonable estimate of expected wait times. When systems deviate significantly from the assumptions, then results will be neither accurate nor reliable.

Unfortunately, the real world seldom meets the assumptions of any queueing system precisely. Something in the real world will be different, causing queueing formulas to be less than perfect. Despite the imperfections, many real-world systems are close enough to the assumptions that queueing formulas can provide reasonable approximations of service.

5.5.1 Assumption 1: Work Will Arrive Randomly

A key assumption of both open and closed queueing systems is that *work will arrive randomly*. The mathematics used to develop queueing formulas depends on a random distribution of customer arrivals. In open queueing systems this implies that there is an equal chance of a customer arriving at any instant. In closed systems, user think times (mean time to failure) must exhibit a random pattern.

Interarrival time is the average time between the arrival of customers. Customer arrivals can be stated either in terms of average arrival rates (such as the number of customers per minute) or interarrival time (the average time between customer arrivals). In essence, interarrival time is the inverse of the average arrival rate.

To illustrate the concept of random arrival patterns, let us suppose that customers arrive at a rate of 30 customers per hour. This translates into an average interarrival time of 2 minutes (60 minutes / 30 arrivals); customers should arrive an average of 2 minutes apart. If arrivals demonstrated a "random" pattern, we would expect the majority of interarrival times to be around 2 minutes.[3] Some interarrival times would be about 4, 5, and 10 minutes (customers would arrive 4, 5, or 10 minutes apart), but the number of interarrivals would become smaller as values became more distant from 2 minutes.

The importance of this assumption can be illustrated with a CICS region experiencing frequent *short-on-storage* (SOS) conditions. Since CICS will not start new tasks during a SOS condition, transactions that arrive during an SOS will accumulate until the SOS is cleared. When the SOS is cleared, CICS will then attempt to start new tasks (subject, of course, to max-task and other constraints).

This would cause a bunching effect. After SOS conditions, a larger number of tasks would start than normal. If SOS conditions occurred frequently, the system would perform as if activity were heavier than the average would indicate. Response time would be slower, not only because of the direct effect of SOS conditions, but also because of the additional queueing delays associated with the bunching of transaction processing following SOS conditions.

5.5.2 Assumption 2: Average Service Time Will Form a Random Pattern

Another assumption made for both open and closed queueing systems is that *average service time will be randomly distributed*. The length of time spent at the server will not be a constant, but will form a random pattern with a constant average. Queueing formulas assume that service times can be mapped into what is called a Poisson distribution; that is, most of service times will be close to the average. Some service times will be higher than the average, but there will be fewer service times as values become higher than the average.

Many types of service have a distribution that is reasonably close to Poisson. For example, Figure 5.12 shows the distribution of CPU use for transactions in a CICS region. Although the pattern is not perfectly Poisson in nature, it has the general shape of a Poisson distribution. This distribution type would lend itself to the use of open and closed queueing formulas.

When service times are not random, but relatively constant, both open and closed queueing formulas will overstate total service times. In many

---

[3] This pattern is commonly called a Poisson distribution.

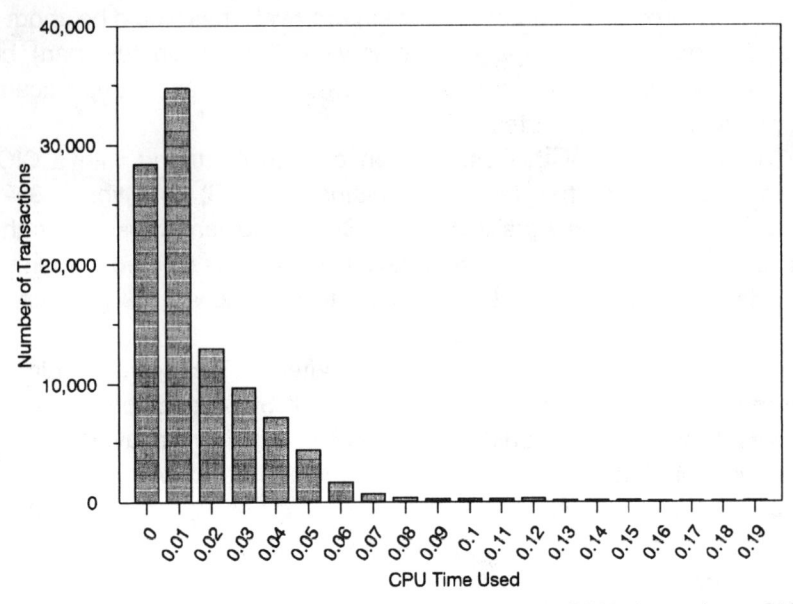

Figure 5.12 Sample distribution of transaction CPU times in a CICS region.

data processing applications, a server will perform almost the same service for each customer. When this happens, average queueing delays will be reduced, and both open and closed formulas will overstate service.

5.5.3 Assumption 3: Average Service Time Will Not Vary With the Work Arrival Rate

Another assumption is that *the average service time will not vary with the arrival rate of work*. Regardless of how many customers are waiting in line or how long the server has worked, the server will continue to serve customers at the same *average* rate. In the real world, as lines become longer, servers might either work more quickly or perhaps become tired or frustrated, and work more slowly. In data processing systems, others types of contention may come into play as servers become busier. Basic queueing theory ignores these factors. If the server works at different rates for different levels of server utilization, queueing projections will be inaccurate.

5.6 THE SIGNIFICANCE OF RANDOM PATTERNS

Several times in the preceding discussion we referred to random patterns. We suggested that in order for the queueing systems discussed in this book to be useful, both the average arrival rate and average server times should have random patterns. A random pattern implies that interarrival times and service times are neither fixed nor bunched.

Sometimes workload characteristics are not random but, more or less, fixed. For example, average CPU time for some transactions may be almost always the same value. Whenever the transaction executes, it will take about the same amount of CPU. (This tends to be the exception more than the rule for complex application systems.)

When either interarrival rates (workload arrival patterns) or server times are close to constant, total service time (including queueing) will be lower than that predicted by open or closed queueing formulas. The more consistent these times are, the better the service produced by the system.

When average server time is randomly distributed, most customers will receive service close to average service time. However, some customers will receive very quick service, and some will receive very long service, perhaps several times the average. Average server time will be the average (mean) of all service times.

Although the average (mean) of both randomly distributed and fixed service times would be the same, the fixed service time would provide better service − sometimes much better service. This is because the server with fixed service times would not have to deal with theoretical extremes in service.

Similarly, random distribution implies that there is no bunching in interarrival rates. This was discussed previously in this chapter. Bunching of arrivals tends to increase average queueing times.

The point of this discussion is that both open and closed queueing systems can either overstate or understate performance. If there is a bunching of arrivals, then both systems can understate service. If service times or interarrival times are fixed (instead of random), then both open and closed queueing systems will overstate service.

In many cases, computer workloads will exhibit patterns close enough to random that closed queueing formulas will do a reasonable job forecasting service and performance. It is important to understand, though, that not all activities are truly random, and this can affect the accuracy of queueing formulas.

Key Point: When computer workloads exhibit random arrival patterns and random server times, then queueing formulas and tables can provide a reasonable approximation of total service time.

As a rule, when interarrival and service patterns are both random, closed queueing formulas will be more accurate than open queueing formulas for data processing work. Because open queueing formulas assume an unlimited number of customers, they will tend to overstate service, especially at higher levels of utilization.

When real-world service times are significantly lower than those predicted by closed queueing formulas (or tables), it is likely that average server time is more constant than random. When real-world service times exceed those predicted by *closed* queueing systems, it is likely that there is some kind of bunching present or that the distribution is bimodal. And, when real-world service times exceed those predicted by open queueing systems, you can be sure that some kind of extreme bunching or skewing is present. When real-world service times for a limited number of customers is higher than open queueing systems, then it is likely that there is severe bunching of interarrival or service times.

5.7 AN EXAMPLE OF THE APPLICATION OF QUEUEING THEORY

Let us assume there is a single ATM in a small town. About 3,000 customers can access the ATM. In the evening hours, the ATM is the only source of cash in town. On Friday evenings, customers arrive at the ATM about once every 3 minutes. This would mean that the average arrival rate would be .33 customers per minute. A customer will spend about 2 minutes using the machine.

We have been asked to determine the average time it will take a customer to receive service and the average number of customers that will be using or waiting to use the ATM. We have been told that the bank does not want its customers to wait more than 5 minutes. They would like to know if adding a second ATM would allow them to achieve their service goal if a single machine does not meet the service goal.

The first task is to calculate *traffic intensity* – how much work is arriving at the ATM each minute. This is the product of the rate at which customers arrive (.33 per minute) and the amount of service each customer needs (2 minutes). Traffic intensity is .66.

u = .33 customers per minute × 2 minutes per customer = .66

Server utilization is the portion of time that the server is busy. Since there is only one server (ATM), server utilization will be the same as traffic intensity. Server utilization is .66.

In a system with 3,000 customers, open and closed queueing systems should produce similar results unless server utilization is very high. Therefore, it should be safe to use open queueing formulas to predict service time.

We can use the *service multiplier* from Table 5.2. When the server utilization is .67, the service multiplier should be about 3. A service multiplier of 3 indicates that total customer wait time (waiting in line plus receiving service) should be 3 times the time spent at the server. Since the average service time is 2 minutes, the total customer wait time should be about 6 minutes.

W = 3 (service multiplier) × 2 min (average server time) = 6 min

About 4 minutes will be spent waiting in line and 2 minutes actually performing the transaction at the ATM.

Since the 6-minute time is higher than our target, our next step will be to evaluate the impact of adding a second ATM. Assuming that two machines can be connected in a *multiserver system* with a single queue, we will reassess potential service.

To begin with, *traffic intensity* would remain unchanged – the same .66 minutes of work will arrive in the system each minute. However, since there are two ATMs (servers), *average server utilization* would be one-half the traffic intensity or .33.

$$\text{Average server utilization} = \rho = \frac{.66 \text{ mins. of work each minute}}{2 \text{ servers}} = .33$$

The *service multiplier* for an *open* queueing system with 2 servers that is 33 percent busy is 1.1 (from Table 5.5).

Total service time would be about 2.2 minutes with two servers. This should satisfy the bank's requirements.

$W = 1.1$ (service multiplier) × 2 min (avg. service time) = 2.2 min

The result of adding a second ATM would be dramatic. This is because the service multiplier for the single server was high. Unless server utilization and the corresponding service multiplier are high, additional servers will have only a minimal effect on performance.

In this example, we assumed that we could add a second ATM, and that both machines would have the same average service time as the original machine. If the machines were stand-alone entities that were not serviced by a common host, this would be possible. In many cases, though, adding another server (such as additional DASD volumes on a string) will cause contention and an increase in service times for other servers. We have ignored this effect in this example and have assumed that we could add a second server without degrading service on the first server.

5.8 SUMMARY

In this chapter, we have reviewed some fundamental principles of performance measurement and evaluation. We have introduced concepts of servers, resource utilization, bottleneck analysis, and queueing systems.

We have explored two types of queueing system. Open queueing systems are the easiest to use but tend to overstate service. Closed queueing systems are more complex but provide more accurate estimates of performance, especially for data processing applications.

In chapters that follow, we will show how to apply open and closed queueing to CICS performance and capacity planning. In Chap. 6, we will discuss how to estimate delays associated with receiving CPU service in CICS. In Chap. 7 we will analyze the impact of operating system contention on CICS performance and how to compare the performance of different types of processors. In Chap. 11, we will see how queueing systems can be used to estimate DASD service. The material introduced in this chapter will be used in several of the following chapters.

SELECTED READING

[ALLE83] Allen, Arnold O., "Modeling of Computer Systems," *Proceedings of the 1983 Computer Measurement Group International Conference*, 1983.

[ALLE90] Allen, Arnold O., *Probability, Statistics, and Queueing Theory with Computer Science Applications*, 2d ed., Academic Press, San Diego, 1990.

[ALLE91] Allen, Arnold O. and Gary Hynes, "Approximate MVA Solutions with Fixed Throughput Classes," *CMG Transactions*, Winter 1991.

[ZIMM91] Zimmer, Harry, "Rules of Thumb '91," *CMG Transactions*, Summer 1991.

Chapter 6

Estimating the Effect of CPU Demand on CICS Performance

6.1 OVERVIEW

Although most CICS transactions use a modest amount of CPU time (typically between 10 and 100 ms), delays associated with receiving CPU service can account for a large portion of a transaction's response time. In this chapter, we will discuss how to quantify CPU-related delays for CICS transactions.

This chapter will show you:

- How to estimate the delays associated with receiving CPU service in a CICS region.
- How to determine the extent of CPU constraint in CICS regions.

This chapter will present techniques that can be used to estimate delays in existing CICS systems for which some performance data are available. More advanced topics will be discussed in Chapters 7, 8, and 9.

6.1.1 Primary Audience

CICS systems programmers and *capacity planners* should find the material in this chapter useful. It will discuss how to quantify the effect of CPU degradation on CICS performance. This chapter will discuss different measures of CPU activity and how they can be used to estimate total CPU-related delays.

Application developers may not have occasion to apply this material directly. Nevertheless, it is recommended that they at least scan this material. Many ideas from this chapter will be used in later chapters when application design and performance are discussed.

6.2 CPU PROCESSING IN CICS

6.2.1 CICS TCB Structure

In Chapter 2, we introduced the concept of *CPU demand*. CPU demand is the time the *CICS main TCB* (in CICS/VS and CICS/MVS) or the *quasireentrant (QR) TCB* (in CICS/ESA) is using or trying to use a processor.

In this book, we will use the term *primary TCB* to refer to either the *QR TCB* (CICS/ESA) or *CICS main TCB* (pre-CICS/ESA). In both CICS/ESA and pre-CICS/ESA systems, most application processing occurs under control of the primary TCB. Although other TCBs are available to off-load some processing and operating system waits, the largest amount of application processing occurs under control of the primary TCB. This is true for all versions of CICS that exist at the time of this writing, including CICS/ESA release 3.3.

All transactions running in a CICS region must share a single TCB (the primary TCB) to perform all application processing and most CICS services. In Chapter 2 we mentioned that other TCBs can be active in CICS regions. The optional *VSAM subtask* (in CICS/VS and CICS/MVS) and the optional *concurrent* (CO) *TCB* (in MVS/ESA) allow a second TCB to handle some CICS processing. When these subtasks are active, they can perform VSAM processing for selected I/O requests. As much as 10 to 15 percent of the processing in a CICS region may be handled by these TCBs.

The major objection to the use of the VSAM subtask or CO TCB is added overhead. It will take additional CPU processing to support the extra TCB and intertask communication. To limit this overhead, only selected requests are passed to the subtask in CICS/MVS and CICS/ESA.

There is also a *resource-owning* (RO) TCB in CICS/ESA and a journal subtask in CICS/VS and CICS/MVS. The primary function of these subtasks is not to off-load CPU processing. It is rather to isolate application processing from long operating system waits. The RO TCB will handle program loads, external security, and file open and close commands. The journal subtask will process journal open and close requests. While only a small amount of processing is shifted to these TCBs, they help shield the primary TCBs from long waits.

6.2.2 An Example of CICS Task Processing

To better illustrate the effect of CPU delays in a CICS region, let us examine what happens during the execution of a typical transaction. This illustration is very general and, except where noted, might apply to either CICS/ESA or previous versions of CICS.

After a task is started, CICS will perform processing in several management modules or domains and eventually pass control to the application. Once the application receives control, it will usually do some processing and then request a CICS service (such as obtaining storage or reading a file). Several CICS management modules or domains will be executed to service the request. In some cases, the task may need to wait for an event to complete before control is returned to the task. Eventually CICS will attempt to redispatch the task

Most of the processing done for the CICS application is performed under control of the primary TCB. Except for selected VSAM I/O accesses (which could be performed under the CO or VSAM subtask) and program load requests (CICS/ESA), nearly all of the processing directly or indirectly required by CICS tasks is performed using the primary TCB.

When a CICS task issues a file control request, the primary TCB performs most of the CICS processing for the request. If the VSAM or CO subtask is active, *selected* VSAM access method requests are passed to the subtask. The subtask then perform the actual VSAM access method calls.

CICS dispatch logic will control which CICS task is dispatched, and all CICS tasks will compete for dispatch service. All CICS tasks require service from a single MVS TCB, and only one can be dispatched on that TCB at a time.

When a TCB experiences a page fault, no further processing will occur on the TCB until the page fault is resolved. When a page fault occurs on the primary TCB, most application processing will be suspended for the duration of the page fault. When the required page is in expanded storage, the page fault will be resolved very quickly. When the page resides on external storage, the task waits until the page is read from external storage. Access times for pages read from DASD will commonly be between 15 and 30 ms.[1]

> **Key Point:** Since most transaction processing is preformed under control of the primary TCB (the main or QR), when it experiences a page fault, nearly all application processing will be suspended. Until the page has been retrieved from expanded or external storage, application processing will be delayed.

When the VSAM subtask or CO TCB experiences a page fault, only those tasks requiring selected VSAM services will be affected. Page faults in the RO TCB have little impact on overall CICS performance because of the limited amount of processing done under that TCB. Only page faults on the primary TCB have a significant effect on CICS performance. This will be discussed in more detail in Chapter 7.

In CICS/VS and CICS/MVS systems, file open and close commands will delay processing for the main TCB. Since open and close SVCs[2] are issued by the main TCB, all task processing will wait until the open completes.

In CICS/ESA, open and close commands are processed by the RO task. When an open or close command is issued, the RO task waits, allowing processing to continue on the QR TCB.

> **Key Point:** In CICS/VS and CICS/MVS, commands to open and close files are processed under the control of the CICS main TCB. When open or close commands are issued, application processing is suspended. In CICS/ESA, file open and close commands are processed by the RO TCB, isolating the QR TCB from these delays.

---

1   Service times for external page faults can be much lower if the volume is cached or if solid-state DASD is used. If a page is located in cache or transferred from solid-state storage, page service time can be as low as 1 to 2 ms.
2   SVCs (supervisor calls) are the instructions used to initiate operating system services.

The primary TCB must compete with other operating system tasks for the availability of processors. Processors are not always available when the primary TCB is ready to be dispatched. When the primary TCB is waiting for a processor, application processing in the region will be delayed.

In summary, nearly all application processing occurs under control of the primary TCB (the CICS main TCB in CICS/VS and CICS/MVS or the QR TCB in CICS/ESA). Other TCBs in the region are responsible for limited amounts of processing. Paging, file opens, and competition from other MVS tasks limit the amount of processing that can occur on the primary TCB.

6.3 METHODS OF MEASURING CPU UTILIZATION

Several different sources may be used to measure CPU usage for CICS applications. Each source has its own meaning. In the material below, we will look at several sources of information about CPU usage and what each measures.

6.3.1 Measuring CPU Utilization Using RMF

RMF is commonly used to measure the CPU time used by CICS regions and by the system as a whole. RMF Type 70 records contain information about systemwide activity. Type 72 records contain information about the resources used by individual MVS performance groups. Type 70 and Type 72 records are recorded once each RMF interval (typically between 10 minutes and one hour).

Performance groups are collections of work defined for MVS. Operating system workloads (such as batch jobs, CICS regions, or started tasks) are commonly mapped into *control performance groups* based on their MVS job name or started task name. Each control performance group represents a unique group of workloads.

Typically, separate control performance groups are defined for significant workloads. CICS regions, especially CICS regions with high CPU usage or high transaction volume, are commonly assigned to their own performance groups. When specific CICS regions are mapped into their own performance groups, Type 72 records can be used to obtain information about CPU usage for those regions.

Note: Important CICS regions commonly are mapped into their own control performance groups. When this is done, separate RMF Type 72 data will be collected for each significant CICS address space. To simplify the discussion that follows, the assumption will be made that important CICS address spaces have been mapped into their own control performance groups.

Type 72 records contain two primary measures of CPU time.[3] One is *TCB time*. TCB time is the amount of CPU time used directly by all MVS tasks (TCBs) processing in the address space. The other is *SRB time*, which is the time accumulated for *service request block* (SRB) processing. SRBs are scheduled asynchronously by MVS to perform special services. SRB time will be much lower than TCB time in most CICS regions.

Since Type 72 records include CPU time for the entire address space (actually, performance group), measures of CPU time will not reflect how much time was used by any particular TCB. Type 72 records provide no indication of how much CPU time was used by any specific TCB.

> **Key Point:** RMF Type 72 data includes CPU time for all tasks (TCBs) running in an address space (performance group). It does not indicate which tasks were responsible for CPU usage.

RMF Type 72 data can provide a good indication of of how much total capacity will be needed to support a CICS region. Type 72 records provide the best information about how much CPU time was used by an address space. However, CPU data in Type 72 records do not indicate how much processing occurred on each TCB.

6.3.2 Measuring CPU Activity Using CMF — CICS/VS and CICS/MVS

The *CICS monitor facility* (CMF) and other similar monitors are the primary source of information about CPU usage in CICS transactions. In *CICS/VS* and *CICS/MVS*, CMF is designed to capture CPU data and other resources used by the primary (main) CICS TCB. CPU times in individual transaction records include *only* the CPU time used by the main TCB.

---

[3] With CICS/ESA 4.2, additional CPU data are captured. In addition to TCB and SRB CPU times, Type 72 records also include CPU usage associated with task initiation and swapping, hiperspace activity, and a portion of I/O interrupt time. Of these three, only the I/O interrupt time will be of much significance in most CICS environments.

Effect of CPU Demand on CICS Performance 137

CMF logic in CICS releases before 2.1.1 (and similar logic in older versions of most other CICS monitors) used the MVS *dispatch* SVC to capture CPU usage. Each time CICS switched control between tasks, CMF would issue the dispatch SVC. This caused MVS to update CPU statistics for the address space. CMF would then associate all newly accumulated CPU time with the CICS task that had been executing.

This worked well when there was only one TCB active in a CICS region. When additional TCBs became common, the "dispatch" technique caused erroneous results. CPU time used by other TCBs in the region would be charged to whatever CICS task happened to be active at the time. CPU time used by the VSAM subtask or DB2 TCBs would be randomly charged to CICS tasks.

If you are running a release of CICS earlier than 2.1.1 or are using an older release of other CICS monitors, CICS detail transaction statistics could contain erroneous CPU information.

To correct this problem, CMF was changed in CICS/MVS release 2.1.1 to use the *timer* facility instead of the dispatch SVC to capture CPU time. Monitors still issue an SVC each time a CICS task switch occurs, but CPU data are collected only for the task that was executing. The timer facility captures CPU usage only for the primary TCB. Most other CICS monitors have also switched to this technique.

There is considerable overhead associated with capturing CPU usage when either of these CPU collection techniques is used. Considering how frequently CICS task switching takes place and the relative expense of performing either the dispatch or timer SVC, a considerable portion of CICS's active time can be spent collecting CPU usage.

An easy way to reduce CICS CPU demand and CPU utilization in CICS/MVS and CICS/VS systems is to turn off the collection of CPU statistics in CMF. It is interesting that a significant user of CPU time is the logic to capture CPU usage data.

If CPU statistics are turned off, CMF will collect only dispatch time. As we will see later, transaction dispatch time can be more useful than CPU time in estimating CICS performance anyway. CPU dispatch time is a better measure of software capacity and can even be used to approximate CPU time.[4]

---

[4] In Chapter 7, we will discuss the relationship between CPU time and dispatch time.

6.3.3 Measuring CPU Activity Using CMF — CICS/ESA

In CICS/ESA, CMF was redesigned to be both more comprehensive and less resource-intensive. In CICS/VS and CICS/MVS, CMF and other CICS monitors[5] received control as part of the EMP/Trace facility. In essence, at the numerous points at which trace could receive control, monitors would be activated so they could check if any data needed to be collected. The process was both cumbersome and CPU-intensive.

In CICS/ESA, transaction statistics are collected directly in CICS domains. When information changes, the appropriate domain simply updates relevant CMF statistical information. The process is both more efficient and more comprehensive than that used in CICS/VS and CICS/MVS.

Additionally, CICS/ESA takes advantage of the MVS/ESA "timeused" facility to collect CPU data. Instead of using an SVC to collect CPU data, the timeused facility invokes MVS/ESA logic directly. This saves a considerable amount of CPU overhead and allows CPU data to be collected more efficiently.

> **Key Point:** CMF processing is more efficient in CICS/ESA than in CICS/MVS or CICS/VS. It takes considerably less overhead to collect transaction statistics (particularly transaction CPU utilization) than it does in previous versions of CICS.

In CICS/ESA, CMF was changed to record information for all four CICS TCBs (the QR, RO, CO, and SZ TCBs).[6] Information about resources used by any of the four TCBS is included in CMF transaction detail records. Each detail record contains a more complete profile of transaction activity.

However, with only a single field for each element, CMF will not show which TCB was responsible for which activity. With only one CPU data field, CPU time used by any of the four TCBs will be collected as a single entity for each transaction.

The approach taken by CICS/ESA provides a more complete profile of how much CPU time is used by each transaction. CMF statistics include

---

[5] In this context, we are referring only to those monitors that collect detailed transaction data.
[6] The SZ TCB was added in CICS/ESA 3.3 to support the FEPI interface. It was not present in CICS/ESA 3.1.1 or 3.2.1.

Effect of CPU Demand on CICS Performance

all CPU time used by each of the CICS TCBs This provides better information for analyzing workload growth and planning total capacity. However, since CPU data from all four CICS TCBs are collected in a single element, this makes it more difficult to estimate CPU degradation within CICS.

> **Key Point:** In CICS/ESA, CMF CPU time includes CPU time accumulated by any of four CICS TCBs (the QR, RO, CO, and SZ TCBs). In CICS/MVS, CMF CPU time includes only time accumulated by the CICS main TCB.

6.3.4 CPU Data in CICS/ESA End-of-Day Statistics

In CICS/ESA, *end-of-day* statistics provide the best source of information about how much CPU time was used by the QR TCB. Written only to SMF, end-of-day statistics provide both CPU time and dispatch time for each of the four CICS TCBs.

End-of-day statistics will be recorded automatically every 3 hours, at midnight each day, and during normal CICS shutdown. The frequency at which these statistics are recorded can be modified. An interval of once each hour is suggested.

CICS end-of-day statistics contain CPU and dispatch times for each CICS TCB. These data can be used to prorate transaction CPU usage among the CICS TCBs. While it will not produce perfect results, end-of-day statistics provide the only means of estimating how much transaction CPU time is associated with each of the CICS TCBs. Such estimates are useful for an entire region, but may not be valid for specific transactions or classes of transactions.

6.4 CPU DEMAND — THE PROPER MEASURE OF PROCESSOR USAGE FOR CICS SYSTEMS

As mentioned earlier, most application processing in a CICS region takes place on the primary (main or QR) TCB. When this TCB cannot be dispatched, most application processing will be suspended. While the primary TCB is waiting, no CICS tasks are being dispatched. Anything that can prevent the primary TCB from being dispatched will limit the amount of processing that can be done in the CICS region.

We have defined *CPU demand* as the total time the primary CICS TCB is using or trying to use a processor. It represents the time that tasks within CICS are being dispatched. If the availability of the primary TCB were to be viewed as a queueing system, CPU demand would represent the time a TCB was in use.

6.4.1 Dispatch Time as a Measure of CPU Demand

The time called *dispatch time* is closely related to *CPU demand*. Dispatch time is the elapsed time that occurs while CICS tasks are dispatched and trying to use the processor. In theory, the sum of dispatch times for all CICS transactions and system tasks should represent all the time CICS was using or trying to use a processor. In essence, the sum of dispatch times for the primary TCB is the definition of CPU demand.

As we mentioned earlier, dispatch time starts when CICS passes control to a task. It ends when control is returned to CICS (the task issues another request for a CICS service).

If there were no delays, dispatch time would be the same as CPU time. The major differences between dispatch time and CPU time are delays for page faults, competition from other operating system tasks, and file opens (in CICS/VS or CICS/MVS). Any delays that prevent the primary TCB from processing will be reflected in the difference between dispatch time and CPU time.

In CICS/VS and CICS/MVS, total dispatch time can be calculated by adding dispatch times from all CICS transactions and dispatch times for CICS system tasks such as task control (KCP) and terminal control (TCP). Transaction dispatch times can be located in detail transaction statistics collected by CMF or other monitors. Dispatch times for KCP, TCP, and other system tasks can be obtained from periodic statistics.

In CICS/ESA, end-of-day statistics provide the best measure of dispatch time for the QR TCB. The dispatcher portion of these statistics contains information about how much CPU time and dispatch time was accumulated for each of the four CICS TCBs (QR, RO, CO, and SZ). For performance planning, these stats should be recorded at least once per hour. Without this information, it may be difficult to estimate either CPU demand or dispatch time per transaction in CICS/ESA.

> **Key Point:** End-of-day statistics provide the best measure of CPU demand in CICS/ESA. CPU demand for each CICS TCB can be obtained by using the dispatch time recorded in dispatcher portion of end-of-day statistics.

Table 6.1 summarizes common measures of CICS CPU usage in an MVS environment.

6.5 CICS AS A QUEUEING SYSTEM

Conceptually, the CICS dispatcher can be viewed as a queueing system. Transactions arrive in CICS, are dispatched by CICS, do some processing, request CICS services, and again compete for the chance to be

Table 6.1 Common Measures of CPU Usage

Source	What Is Measured	Advantages	Disadvantages
RMF Type 72 records	5 classes of CPU for each performance group (address space).	Can show total captured CPU for an address space.	Does not show how much CPU was used by each TCB.
CMF CPU and dispatch data (CICS/VS and CICS/MVS)	CPU and dispatch times for the CICS main TCB for each transaction and system task.	Shows CPU and dispatch times for the CICS main TCB; excellent for performance planning.	Does not reflect CPU used by other TCBs; this limits usefulness in estimating total resources used by workloads.
CMF CPU and dispatch data (CICS/ESA)	CPU and dispatch times accumulated by all four CICS TCBs for each CICS transaction.	Good for estimating total resource usage for CICS workloads.	Does not reflect CPU or disptach times for individual TCBs; has limited value in performance planning.
CPU and dispatch data in end-of-day statistics (CICS/ESA)	CPU and dispatch times for each of the four CICS TCBs.	If collected on a regular basis, can provide good information about CPU usage and CPU demand.	Unless these data are collected frequently (at least once per hour), they may not be useful for performance planning.

dispatched. In many ways this process resembles the machine repair model or closed queueing systems discussed in Chapter 5.

Figure 6.1 presents CICS as a closed, or machine-repair, queueing system. The round circles represent servers such as CPU or DASD. The rectangles represent queues for the servers.

Transactions enter the system at point A. After a task has started, it will alternate between dispatch queueing, dispatch processing, and waiting for other CICS services. Once CICS dispatches the task, the task will use or attempt to the CPU until it requests another CICS service. After the CICS service is complete, the task will again need to be dispatched. Eventually the task will complete processing and leave the system at point B.

At any point in time, a task can be in one of three states:

- Queued for dispatch service
- Dispatched, trying to use a processor
- Waiting for some other event

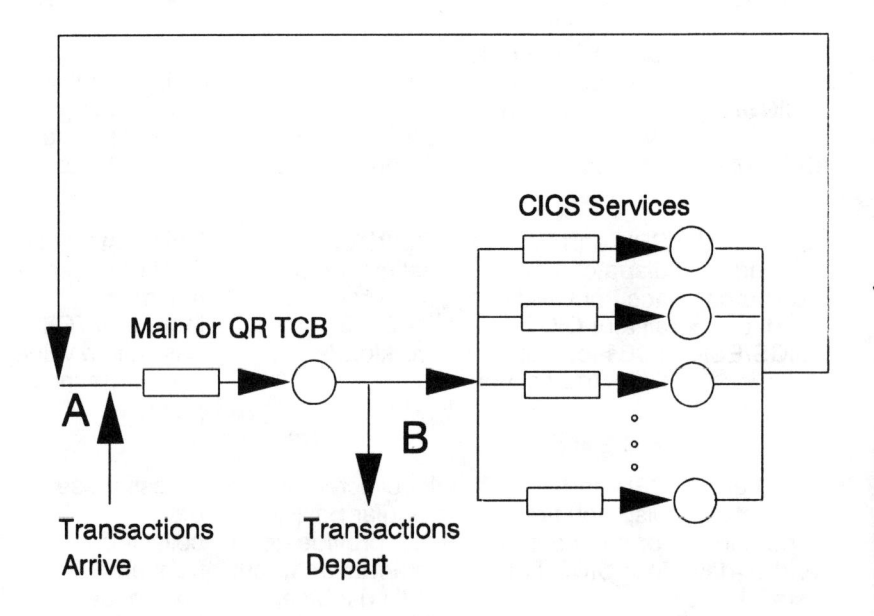

Figure 6.1 CICS as a closed queueing system.

The length of time tasks spend waiting for other events controls the frequency at which they return to be dispatched.

Basically, CICS systems can be seen as a collection of closed queueing systems. The primary TCB is a closed queueing system. DASD volumes are also closed queueing systems, each being fed by tasks in one or more CICS regions (or by other workloads). The CICS system, itself is a closed queueing system with users supplying transactions, waiting for a response, "thinking," and then entering additional transactions.

6.5.1 Estimating CPU-Related Delays — Simple Illustration

In the previous discussion, we indicated that CICS processing could be viewed as a queueing system. In the material that follows, we will examine how to apply queueing concepts and estimate CPU-related delays in CICS systems.

- First, we will present a simple example involving a CICS system with light CPU activity.

- Next, we will discuss the rationale behind the technique illustrated in the example.

- Finally, we will present a slightly more advanced example.

In Chapter 7, we will continue this discussion and look at how to quantify the effects of other delays on dispatch time and CICS performance.

> **Note:** The material in this section assumes that the reader is familiar with the basic concepts of queueing theory (presented in Chapter 5), the author's approach to estimating queueing parameters (also presented in Chapter 5), and the concepts of CICS dispatch processing discussed in this chapter and in Chapter 2.

Description of CICS Region. During a period of light activity, the following measurements were observed for a CICS region:

- Average CPU time per transaction was 45 ms.

- Average dispatch time per transaction was 50 ms.

- Total CPU demand in the CICS region was about 10 percent.
- Average transaction response time was 1 second.

For the purpose of this illustration, we will assume that all CICS tasks run at the same CICS dispatching priority. For simplicity, we will also assume that all (or virtually all) of the CPU time consumed in this region was used by a single TCB – the primary TCB.

Our goal is to determine the average amount of CPU-related delay per transaction in the region.

Review of Basic Queueing Concepts. In the queueing model shown in Figure 6.1, we used the primary (main or QR) TCB as the primary server. The model depicts a closed (machine-repair) model with a limited number of customers. Customers, in this model, are the CICS tasks competing for CPU (dispatch) service.

In Chapter 5, we suggested that we would use both open and closed (machine-repair) models in this book. In this chapter, we will use the closed (machine repair) model because it is more representative of the dispatching delays occurring in most CICS regions.

In Chapter 5 we stated that we could estimate total wait time (total service time) for closed queueing systems if we knew a few simple pieces of information. They are:

- **The number of servers.** There is only one server – the CICS main or QR TCB. Even when multiple CICS TCBs are active, they each have their own special purpose and are not interchangeable. CICS tasks waiting for one TCB cannot be dispatched on any other TCB.

- **Average time spent at the server (average server time).** This is average dispatch time per CICS task.

- **Average server utilization (how busy the server is).** CPU demand or total dispatch time for the QR TCB is used as the measure of server utilization.

- **Either the number of customers *or* the frequency customers return to the server (server return ratio).** We will need to know or estimate one of the two parameters.

Dispatch time per task and CPU demand are either measured or derived from measurement data. In this example, they were given; in later examples, we will show how they can be obtained from measurement data. One of the two remaining items can be easily derived, as we will see later in this chapter. We can use this information with the appropriate tables (Appendix B), to estimate queueing delays and wait times.

Basic Queueing Parameters. In a closed queueing system, the activities driving resource utilization are more important than the resource utilization itself. If a closed queueing system is 100 percent busy but has only two customers, each customer would wait only for the other customer. Total queueing delay could not exceed average server time. On the other hand, when the server is 100 percent busy and there are 75 customers in the system, each customer could, in theory, wait for as many as 74 other customers to receive service.

In this illustration, *server utilization* is represented by *CPU demand*. Server utilization (CPU demand) will be controlled by:

- **Average server time.** This is the average time the server spends with each customer or *average dispatch time per transaction*.

- **The number of customers.** This is the *average number of active CICS tasks*.

- **The rate at which customers (CICS tasks) return to the server.** This is the *rate at which tasks complete other services and are eligible for redispatch by CICS*.

All three of these elements influence both server utilization (CPU demand) and total service time (total dispatch time per task including queueing).

The purpose of this illustration is to show how to estimate CPU (dispatch)-related delays. We have been given CPU demand, average dispatch time per transaction, and average transaction response time. We will use this information and the queueing tables in Appendixes B to estimate total CPU-related time per transaction.

Service Multipliers. In Chapter 5, we introduced the concept of service multipliers. Service multipliers are factors that can be used to estimate queueing delays. Total service time (including queueing) is the product of average server time and the appropriate service multiplier.

We will use service multipliers to calculate CPU-related time per transaction. We will multiply average dispatch time by an appropriate service multiplier to obtain total CPU-related delay.

Total CPU-related time = average dispatch time × service multiplier

Appendix B contains service multipliers for closed queueing systems. Two sets of tables are provided. The first set (Tables B.1 through B.8) was calculated by keeping the the rate customers returned to the server(s) steady while the number of customers varied. Eight tables are provided in this set, corresponding to one through eight servers. The second set of tables (B.9) was calculated holding the number of customers steady and varying the rate they returned to the server(s). The second set of tables contain data only for single-server systems.

In closed queueing systems, there are a range of service multipliers for each level of server utilization. The key to estimating service is knowing which service multiplier to use. Most of the remainder of this illustration will show how to determine which service multiplier to select. The technique shown is not difficult to use and can be applied fairly easily.

Using Tables to Estimate Total CPU-Related Time per Task. In this illustration, we will use Table B.1 to estimate CPU-related queueing. Table B.1 was built by holding each of 10 server return ratios constant and varying the number of customers. Since there can only be whole numbers of customers (we cannot have a partial customer), server utilization values shown are approximate. It is not possible to calculate exact server utilizations for each possible return ratio.

Each column in Table B.1 shows the closest possible server utilization for each level of utilization and return ratio. For example, on the first page of Table B.1, the column labeled "Return ratio = 20," shows a server utilization of .506 in the ".50" row. This means that .506 is the closest utilization possible for that exact return ratio/server utilization combination.

Even though the tables in Appendix B contain only selected utilization values, there should be enough entries to estimate performance delays for most situations. Mathematical models only can be expected to create reasonable estimates of real-world events. These tables should contain enough information for these purposes

Table B.1 contains data for single-server systems. Each CICS TCB in a CICS region represents its own single-server system. Even when multiple CICS TCBs are active, each has its own function, and none are interchangeable. Work required of the main or QR TCB can be performed only by that TCB.

To use Table B.1, we will need to estimate the server return ratio. This is the rate customers return to the server or, in this example, the ratio of other delays to dispatch time. It is fairly easy to estimate this using the steps that follow.

As shown in Figure 6.2, CICS tasks can be in only one of three states. Tasks can be *dispatched by CICS, waiting to be dispatched*, or *waiting for other services*. The *server return ratio* (Return$_{ratio}$) *is the ratio of the time tasks spend waiting for all other services to the time they are dispatched on the primary TCB*.

$$\text{Return}_{ratio} = \frac{\text{Time waiting for other services}}{\text{Dispatch time}}$$

$$= \frac{\text{Response time} - (\text{Dispatch time} + \text{Dispatch queueing})}{\text{Dispatch time}}$$

In Chapter 5, we stated that the service predicted by open queueing formulas would always exceed that predicted by closed queueing systems for the same level of utilization. As the number of customers increases, service suggested by closed queueing formulas will approach that predicted by open formulas. For this reason, we can use the service

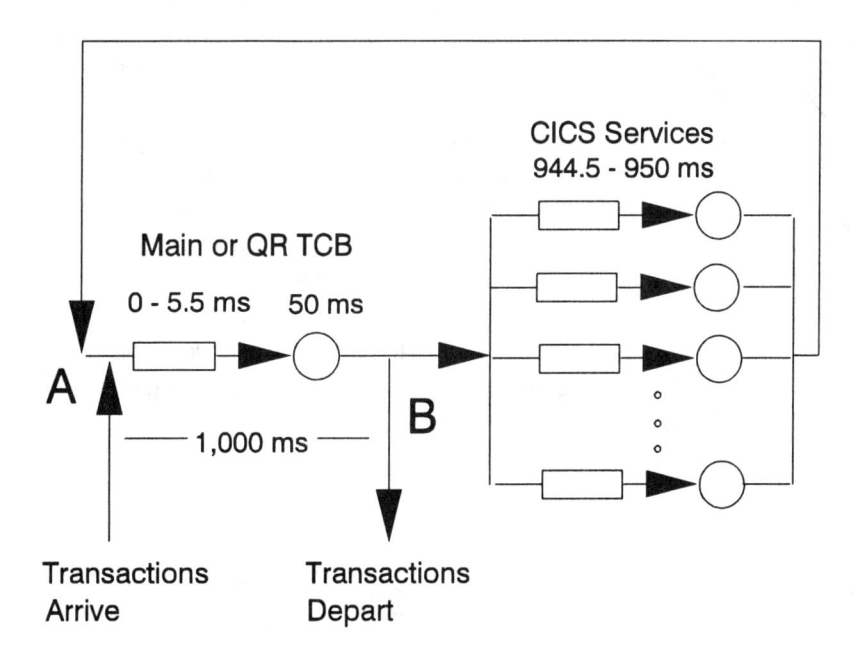

Figure 6.2 Where time is spent in a typical CICS transaction.

multiplier for open queueing systems as a limit of service multipliers possible for closed systems.

We stated that CPU demand for this region was about 10 percent. Using Table A.1 (open queueing systems), we can obtain the maximum service multiplier for a closed queueing system. Table A.1 shows a service multiplier of 1.11 for single-server systems that are 10 percent busy. Thus, the maximum service multiplier for a closed system that is 10 percent busy should be about 1.11.

Since we know that the CICS main TCB was about 10 percent busy and that the service multiplier should be no more than 1.11, we can determine that it should take no longer than 55.5 ms (50 ms x 1.11), including queueing, to receive 50 ms of CPU dispatch-related service.

Maximum dispatch-related service = 1.11 × 50 ms = 55.5 ms

We were told that average transaction response time is 1 second or 1,000 ms. It consists of the sum of dispatch time, queueing within CICS for dispatch, and all other delays. Dispatch time plus queueing should be between 50 ms and 55.5 ms (50 ms of service would include no queueing time). Therefore, all other delays must account for 944.5 ms (1,000 ms - 55.5 ms) to 950 ms (1,000 ms - 50 ms) of the response time. This can be seen in Figure 6.2.

The next step in this illustration is to develop a better estimate of the server return ratio. Using the maximum and minimum "other delay" values we just calculated, we can see that the maximum and minimum server return ratios are 19 and 18.9, respectively. Note that the denominator in the minimum return ratio calculation is 50 ms, *not 55 ms*. The Return$_{ratio}$ is the ratio of time away from the server to the time actually spent at the server. Tasks will spend an average of 18.9 to 19 times as long waiting for other events as they will be dispatched on the primary TCB. This information is summarized in Table 6.2.

$$\text{Maximum Return}_{ratio} = \frac{\text{Other delays}}{\text{Average dispatch time}} =$$

$$= \frac{1{,}000 \text{ ms} - 50 \text{ ms}}{50 \text{ ms}} = \frac{950 \text{ ms}}{50 \text{ ms}} = 19$$

$$\text{Minimum Return}_{ratio} = \frac{1{,}000 \text{ ms} - 55.5 \text{ ms}}{50 \text{ ms}} = \frac{944.5 \text{ ms}}{50 \text{ ms}} = 18.9$$

Table 6.2 Derivation of Server Return Ratios for First Illustration

	Minimum Service Multiplier = 1.00	Maximum Service Multiplier = 1.11
Average dispatch time	50 ms	50 ms
Dispatch Queueing	0 ms	5.5 ms
Other Delays	950 ms	944.5 ms
Total transaction response time	1000 ms	1000 ms
Server return ratio (Return$_{ratio}$)	19	18.9

We have now determined that tasks in this region spent 18.9 to 19 times longer waiting for other events (such as I/O) than dispatched for CPU service within CICS.

Table B.1 shows us that the service multiplier for a Return$_{ratio}$ of 20 is approximately 1.05. (Remember, data in Table B.1 is approximate.) Using this service multiplier, we can see that total dispatch-related time should be about 52.5 ms.

Total CPU-related time = average dispatch time × service multiplier
= 50 ms × 1.05 = 52.5 ms

In this illustration, very little time was spent queued for dispatch within CICS. Dispatch service time including queueing was about 52.5 ms, and dispatch time was 50 ms. Thus, only about 2.5 ms of an average transaction's response would be spent waiting for dispatch within CICS.[7]

In summary, this exercise shows that transactions in this CICS region should take about 52.5 ms to receive CPU service. Forty-five milliseconds per transaction would be spent actually using the CPU (this was stated); 5 ms (the difference between CPU time and dispatch time) would be spent waiting for CPU service at the operating system level (waiting for

---

[7] It is worth noting that CPU queueing is not necessarily reported correctly by all CICS monitors. When an event such as a file I/O request completes, the QR TCB will not recognize the completion of that event until it receives control. This recognition can be delayed when another task is processing at the time the event completes. Theoretically, once an event completes, the CICS task is waiting for a chance to be redispatched. Monitors that are driven by internal facilities will not be able to recognize the time events complete as dispatch or CPU queueing but will assign this time to the service time for the event. Thus, some monitors may overstate event wait time and understate CPU queueing.

paging, competition from other MVS tasks, etc.); 2.5 ms would be queued within CICS for dispatch service. Table 6.3 summarizes the components of CPU-related service for the CICS region in this illustration.

> **Key Point:** Only three pieces of information are needed to estimate CPU-related delays for CICS transactions. They are *average dispatch time per transaction, total dispatch time for the region (CPU demand)*, and *average transaction response time*. Other information can be estimated from these three key elements.

Observations about CPU Demand. It is obvious that the 50 ms of CPU dispatch per task in this illustration is not accumulated all at one time. Tasks will receive control many times and alternately wait for the completion of various CICS services. The 50 ms probably represents the accumulation of many small events each of which took 2 ms or less. Each task would be dispatched several times, and each time it was dispatched, it competed with other CICS tasks for dispatch service.

In is not necessary to know the details of dispatch activity within each transaction to estimate dispatch queueing. Since total dispatch time and total dispatch queueing are merely the sum of dispatch times of individual tasks, average dispatch time per task for the region and total dispatch time (CPU demand) are the key elements used in estimating dispatch queueing delays.

6.5.2 Why This Estimation Technique Works

In the illustration above, the server return ratio was the key to estimating CPU-related delays. This technique may seem confusing and is not at all intuitive. Nevertheless, there are good reasons for its working the way it does.

The time tasks spend waiting for other events and the time they are dispatched for CPU form a transaction-profile for the CICS region. The

Table 6.3 Components of CPU-Related Service Time

CPU time per task	45 ms
Operating system delays	5 ms
Dispatch time per task	50 ms
Queueing within CICS for dispatch	2.5 ms
Total CPU-related time (per transaction)	52.5 ms

key of the profile is the ratio of other waits to dispatch time. This ratio, the server return ratio, defines the portion of CICS response time required for CPU time and for other waits. Once the server return ratio is known, total dispatch-related time can be estimated easily.

When CICS tasks access most of their resources from memory (such as data tables or large LSR pools) or from high-speed external devices, the portion of task response time associated with other waits will be low. Tasks of this kind tend to be CPU-intensive, requiring dispatch service a large percent of their task life.

When tasks spend most of their time waiting for slower resources (such as uncached DASD), the ratio of other waits to dispatch time will be higher. Tasks of this kind tend to require CPU service less frequently.

Transactions that are CPU-intensive (i.e., transactions that spend a large portion of their response time dispatched for CPU) will contribute more heavily to total dispatch time. Transactions that are wait-intensive (i.e., spend much of their response time waiting for external events or internal locks), contribute less to total dispatch time. Fewer CPU-intensive transactions will need to be active than wait-intensive to generate the same level of CPU demand.

> **Key Point:** It will take fewer active CPU-intensive tasks to generate the same amount of CPU demand as a larger number of wait-intensive tasks.

The number of active CICS tasks it will take to obtain a given level of CPU demand is dependant on the portion of task response time (excluding dispatch queueing) represented by CPU dispatch time. If tasks in a CICS region spend 40 percent of their response time (excluding queueing) dispatched by CICS, it would take an average of a little more two active tasks to drive CPU demand to 80 percent. Tasks waiting for dispatch service will normally wait for only one other task.[8]

On the other hand, when transactions spend more time waiting for other services (such as file I/Os), a smaller percent of their active time will be spent trying to use the CPU. For this reason, a larger number of wait-intensive tasks will be active to generate the same amount of CPU

---

[8] It is worth noting that workloads which spend such an exaggerated percent of their response time using the CPU may hold the CPU for longer periods of time and restrict the dispatching of other CICS transactions. Such CPU domination could skew the performance of other workloads.

demand. If tasks in a CICS region spend 5 percent of their active time dispatched for CPU, it will take at least 21 active tasks to generate CPU demand of 80 percent. When tasks need to wait for dispatch service, they probably will wait for a larger number of other tasks.

Since a task's life can be spent in one of three states (dispatched, queued for dispatch, and waiting for other CICS services), the total number of tasks required to generate a given level of CPU demand will be higher than what would be calculated by simply dividing utilization by CPU time per task. CPU queueing must be considered.

The *less* time tasks spend dispatched compared to the time they spend waiting for other events, the *higher* the return ratio. Higher server return ratios imply a large number of customers (CICS tasks) to achieve the same level of server utilization. This is why Table B.1 in Appendix B shows higher service multipliers for higher return ratios at most levels of utilization.

The key is that when the ratio of other waits to task dispatch time is lower, tasks will spend a larger percentage of their response time dispatched for CPU. This will reduce the number of tasks that need to be active to drive CPU demand to the same level of activity. And this will cause less dispatch queueing as service multipliers become lower.

The technique used in this chapter to estimate CPU-related service times takes advantage of queueing formulas and their relationship to task profiles. It should be possible to estimate the average amount of dispatch queueing per task based on CPU demand, task dispatch time, and average task response time. Together, these form a profile that identifies the queueing characteristics of a system.

> **Key Point:** In closed queueing systems, a limited range of service multipliers exist for any given level of utilization. This range limits how much dispatch-related queueing is possible for specific transaction profiles.

6.5.3 Estimating CPU-Related Delays — More Complex Illustration

In the illustration above, we estimated dispatch-related queueing for a very simple system with light activity. In this illustration, we will expand on this technique and develop a more sophisticated example.

Description of the CICS Region. Let us assume that the following conditions were observed:

Effect of CPU Demand on CICS Performance

- Average dispatch time is 60 ms per transaction.
- Average CPU time is 45 ms per transaction.
- Total CPU demand in the CICS region is about 75 percent.
- Average transaction response time is 1.7 seconds.

We will assume that all CICS tasks run at the same CICS dispatching priority and that virtually all CPU time in this region is consumed by a single TCB.

Estimating Maximum and Minimum Dispatch-Related Time. We will follow a procedure similar to the one used in the previous illustration. The first step will be to estimate minimum and maximum dispatch time including internal queueing.

The minimum service multiplier shown in Table B.1 for a utilization of 75 percent is 2.38. We will use this as the minimum service multiplier. The maximum service multiplier is the equivalent service multiplier from the open queueing tables. (Queueing delays predicted by open queueing systems should be higher than closed queueing multipliers.) A value of 4.0 was obtained from Table A.1 (open queueing systems).

Together these numbers tell us that when CPU demand is 75 percent, total dispatch time including queueing should be between 2.38 and 4.0 times average dispatch time per transaction.

We calculate minimum dispatch-related time by multiplying average dispatch time (60 ms) by the minimum service multiplier (2.38). The maximum time would be the product of average dispatch time (60 ms) and the maximum service multiplier (4.0). Dispatch-related service time including queueing should be between 142.8 ms and 240 ms.

Minimum dispatch-related time = 2.38 × 60 ms = 142.8 ms

Maximum dispatch-related time = 4.0 × 60 ms = 240 ms

Narrowing the Range of Dispatch-Related Time. The minimum and maximum dispatch-related times will be used to establish the *maximum* and *minimum* server return ratios. These are ratios of other CICS waits to average dispatch time. Other CICS waits consist of the portion of response time not associated with dispatch time or dispatch queueing.

Chapter Six

$$\text{Maximum Return}_{ratio} = \frac{(1{,}700\text{ ms} - 142.8\text{ ms})}{60\text{ ms}} = \frac{1{,}557.2\text{ ms}}{60\text{ ms}} = 26.0$$

$$\text{Minimum Return}_{ratio} = \frac{(1{,}700\text{ ms} - 240\text{ ms})}{60\text{ ms}} = \frac{1{,}460\text{ ms}}{60\text{ ms}} = 24.3$$

Since the return ratio should be between 24.3 and 26.0, we can use the service multipliers from Table B.1 for return ratios of 20 and 30 to narrow the estimate of dispatch time and queueing. The table shows service multipliers of 2.84 and 3.13 for return ratios of 20 and 30, respectively. Dispatch-related delays per task should be between 170.4 ms and 187.8 ms.

Low dispatch–related time
 = low service multiplier × average dispatch time
 = 2.84 × 60 ms = 170.4 ms

High dispatch–related time
 = high service multiplier × average dispatch time
 = 3.13 × 60 ms = 187.8 ms

We can now calculate new server return ratios:

$$\text{Maximum Return}_{ratio} = \frac{(1{,}700\text{ ms} - 170.4\text{ ms})}{60\text{ ms}} = \frac{1{,}529.6\text{ ms}}{60\text{ ms}} = 25.5$$

$$\text{Minimum Return}_{ratio} = \frac{(1{,}700\text{ ms} - 187.8\text{ ms})}{60\text{ ms}} = \frac{1{,}512.2\text{ ms}}{60\text{ ms}} = 25.2$$

Since the return ratio has been narrowed to such a small range, we can use Table B.1 to more closely approximate the service multiplier. The service multiplier for a return ratio of 25 is 3.00. Total dispatch-related delays for the task should be about 180 ms.

(approximate value) $W = W_s \times M_{Table} = 60\text{ ms} \times 3.00 = 180\text{ ms}$

Reviewing What We Did. We have used an iterative process to estimate CICS internal dispatch-related delays including queueing. Let us pause for a minute and look at what we have actually done. We started knowing that total transaction response time was 1.7 seconds (1700 ms), average dispatch time was 60 ms, and CPU demand was 75 percent. Of the 1,700 ms total response time, 60 ms would be spend dispatched for CPU, and 1,640 ms (1,700 ms – 60 ms) would be spent either queued (waiting) to be dispatched or waiting for some other kind of event (for I/Os, etc.). The goal of this process is to determine how much of the 1,640 ms falls into each of these two categories.

When CPU demand is 75 percent, we know that total dispatch-related time (including queueing) should not be more than 240 ms (4 * 60 ms). As long as that this system does not violate the assumptions behind closed queueing systems, then the service multiplier should be less than that for open queueing systems. In other words, when a server in a closed system is 75 percent busy, total service time (including queueing) should be less than 4.0 times average server time. The service multiplier was obtained from Table A.1. That means that at least 1,460 ms (1,700 ms – 240 ms) of the response should be associated with other waits.

We used the lowest service multiplier shown in Table B.1 (a value of 2.38 for server utilization of .75) to establish a minimum value for dispatch-related time. From this we established that dispatch-related time would be between 142.8 ms (2.38 * 60 ms) and 240 ms and that other waits would be between 1,460 and 1,557.2 ms.

Instead of using the minimum service multiplier suggested in Table B.1, we could have used an absolute minimum service multiplier of 1.0. Strangely enough, the final results would have been the same regardless of which minimum was used. When the real service multiplier is lower than that shown in Table B.1, this will show up in the initial calculation of minimum and maximum server return ratios.

Using this information, we then refined the transaction profile. We knew that the ratio of other work to dispatch time should be between 24.3 (1,557.2 ms / 60 ms) and 26.0 (1,460 ms / 60 ms). Using the "20" and "30" columns in Table B.1, we see that the service multiplier for work with this type of profile should be between 2.84 and 3.13.

Using the more restrictive range of service multipliers, we further refined the range of possible dispatch times. The result was that total dispatch-related delays (including queueing) should be about 180 ms in this example.

Table 6.4 Components of CPU-Related Service Time

CPU time per task	45 ms
Operating system delays	15 ms
Dispatch time (CPU demand) per task	60 ms
Queueing within CICS for dispatch	120 ms
Total CPU-related time (per transaction)	180 ms

Summary of illustration results. The process above illustrated how to estimate delays related to dispatch queueing for CICS transactions. Eventually we determined that total CPU dispatch time including queueing should be about 180 ms.

As summarized in Table 6.4, about 1,520 ms of the 1,700 ms average transaction response time probably was spent waiting for miscellaneous services such as file I/Os. CPU time per transaction was stated to be 45 ms. Another 15 ms of each transaction's response was spent queued in the operating system for delays such as paging or higher-priority MVS tasks. This is the difference between average dispatch and CPU time per transaction. Finally, 120 ms was spent queued in CICS waiting for dispatch on the primary TCB. Total CPU-related (dispatch-related) time should be about 180 ms per transaction.

The technique presented above allows us to estimate total CPU-related delays (dispatch service and queueing) in a CICS region based on CPU dispatch time per task and CPU demand for the region. The technique offers only an approximation of dispatch service and queueing, but is close enough for most types of analysis.

6.6 ESTIMATING THE EFFECT OF TUNING – SIMPLE EXAMPLE

Having shown how to estimate current delays, we will now look at how to estimate the effect of simple changes within a CICS region. We will build upon the example above to illustrate the effect of operating system tuning.

Let us assume the CICS region was given a higher MVS dispatching priority. As a result of this, average dispatch time per transaction was reduced from 60 to 55 ms.

CPU demand would also be reduced by this tuning. Since CPU demand is defined as the sum of transaction dispatch times, changes to average dispatch time per transaction should also affect CPU demand. Total CPU demand would be reduced proportionately from 75 percent to 68.7 percent.

$$\text{New CPU demand} = \frac{55 \text{ ms}}{60 \text{ ms}} \times .75 = 68.7$$

Assuming that there were no changes in any of the other delays experienced by the transaction, the server return ratio would increase to 27.6.

$$\text{New server return ratio} = \frac{\text{other delays}}{\text{dispatch time per tran.}} = \frac{1520 \text{ ms}}{55 \text{ ms}} = 27.6$$

Using the values for 70 percent server utilization and return ratios for 25 and 30, we can estimate the new service multiplier to be between 2.57 and 2.73. Thus total dispatch time including internal queueing should average between 141 ms and 150 ms. Reducing dispatch time by only 5 ms per transaction, in this situation, would reduce dispatch queueing and total response by at least 30 ms.

Although the largest component of CPU-related delay was internal queueing within CICS for dispatch, this value is controlled by dispatch time per transaction and CPU demand. Both of these factors are influenced by operating system delays.

Although queueing for dispatch within CICS usually represents the largest portion of CPU-related service, changes that affect average dispatch time and CPU demand can have a significant influence over queueing. Remember that any changes in average transaction dispatch time will produce similar changes in CPU demand.

6.6.1 The Interaction Between Queueing Systems

It should be obvious that as the number of active CICS tasks increases, CPU demand in the CICS region should also increase. What may not be obvious, though, is that as activity increases, other delays normally increase as well. Increases in CPU usage typically coincide with increases in activity at other servers, such as DASD devices. This will increase queueing delays and lengthen the time it takes to receive service at other servers. The percent of response time associated with CPU time will decrease.

As total activity increases, individual CICS tasks will require dispatch service less frequently. Delays at other servers (such as DASD devices) will increase, and this will slow the rate at which transactions consume CPU and dispatch service. Although transactions may use the same amount of CPU and dispatch service, they will use it over a longer period when other delays increase.

As we saw in Chapter 5, activity will grow at different rates for different resources. If delays for other services increase more rapidly than CICS dispatch time, the Return$_{ratio}$ for the CPU dispatch server will increase. If CICS dispatch time increases because of additional paging or competition from other operating system tasks, the Return$_{ratio}$ can decrease.

In a CICS environment, the average number of active transactions is the primary factor driving increases in CPU utilization. However, increases in the number of active transactions should increase activity at other servers. VSAM files, DASD volumes, and channel activity will all become busier as transaction activity increases. Consequently, CICS tasks normally will wait longer for external services as transaction activity increases.

The point of these comments is that changes at any server in a closed queueing system can affect performance at other servers. In simple examples, like the one above, it is probably safe to extrapolate the effect of changes to a single element. However, when more complex changes are made, it would be wise to examine how the change affects other servers. This could be a fairly cumbersome task if done manually. In most cases, the use of modeling software would be quite helpful to evaluate the effect of complex changes.

6.7 TRANSACTIONS THAT USE LARGE AMOUNTS OF CPU TIME

In most CICS environments, tasks will spend most of their time waiting for other servers, such as VSAM files or database systems. Typically, tasks will spend at least 10 to 20 times as long at other servers as they spend dispatched within CICS. For this reason, we have used a minimum server return ratio of 10 to estimate total CICS dispatch-related time in the previous examples.

However, in some cases, CPU processing is a much larger portion of transaction response time. In some CICS regions, transactions may access a large percentage of their file requests from large LSR buffer pools or data spaces. In this case, the ratio of other waits to dispatch time will be much smaller.

When most of the transactions in a CICS region spend a large portion of their response time using the CPU, the ratio of other waits to dispatch time will be lower than the minimum value shown in the table. In these cases, we might want to start with a minimum service multiplier of 1.0 in the iterative process of estimating total dispatch-related time. As it turns out, though, it does not make that much difference which minimum value you start with. The initial calculation of other waits and service multipliers will place the return ratio in the correct range anyway.

For example, if the following conditions existed in a CICS region:

- CPU demand on the primary TCB is .75.
- Average dispatch time is 50 ms.
- Average transaction response time is .4 seconds (400 ms).

Using the iterative procedure outlined earlier in this chapter, we would select a minimum service multiplier of 2.38 (from Table B.1) and a maximum service multiplier of 4.0 (from Table A.1). This would suggest that total dispatch-related time (including queueing) should be between 119 ms and 200 ms.

From this, we calculate that other waits should be between 200 ms (400 − 200 ms) and 281 ms (400 − 119 ms). These values suggest server return ratios in the range of 4.0 and 5.6.

Since both calculated the server return ratios (4.0 and 5.6) are lower than the lowest entry shown in Table B.1 (the lowest return ratio in the table is "10"), we cannot further refine our estimate. The best we can do is estimate that the service multiplier for total dispatch time should be less than 2.38. Total CPU-related delays should be less than 119 ms.

6.8 CPU DELAYS FOR OTHER TCBS IN A CICS REGION

In the examples presented so far, we have assumed that virtually all processing occurred on the primary TCB. If additional CICS TCBs are active in a region, similar procedures could have been used to evaluate those delays.

In CICS/ESA, CMF data includes information about all four CICS TCBS. This can be divided between the TCBs using end-of-day statistics, which provide information about CPU time and dispatch time for each of the four CICS TCBs. Similar information is hard to obtain in pre-CICS/ESA systems.

Using techniques outlined in this chapter, individual delays also can be calculated for the RO, CO, and SZ TCBs. However, these TCBs will normally be dispatched less than 10 to 15 percent of the time (usually much less than 10 to 15 percent), and the corresponding service multipliers will usually be minimal (1.1 or less). Usually, it is not necessary to evaluate CPU delays on these other CICS TCBs, but this can be done if there is reason to do so.

When DB2 or IMS/DBCTL are running in a CICS region, separate TCBs are created for each thread between CICS and DB2. While the total amount of CPU time used by database TCBs can be substantial, each TCB services only one transaction at a time. For this reason, the internal queueing for CPU dispatch that affects the CICS TCBs is not a factor for database TCBs. Instead, database TCBs compete for CPU time at the operating system level. This type of CPU queueing will be discussed in more detail in Chapter 7.

6.9 CICS INTERNAL DISPATCHING PRIORITIES

In CICS/VS and CICS/MVS, CICS tasks are controlled by a chain or list of *dispatch control areas*(DCAs). There are separate chains for active and suspended DCAs. Tasks are dispatched from the active DCA chain based on their internal dispatching priority. When multiple tasks have the same dispatching priority, the earliest task on the list is given preference over other tasks.

When a CICS task requests a CICS service that requires it to wait, other CICS tasks can then be dispatched. However, when a task requests a service that can be satisfied without waiting, the task will be eligible for immediate redispatch. If all tasks have the same dispatching priority and one task performs a large number of services that do not require waiting, the task can dominate the CPU, and other tasks will wait for dispatch service.

CICS/ESA replaced the DCA chain with a chain of *dispatch task areas*(DTAs). This provided a new dispatching scheme that corrects the problem to a certain extent. When tasks return to the dispatcher function, they are placed at the end of the list of tasks with the same dispatching priority (this is called round-robin dispatching). This prevents a single task from gaining unfair advantage due to its position on the queue. Furthermore, when CICS tasks are queued for dispatch for a long time, their dispatching priority can be adjusted automatically to ensure that they eventually will be dispatched. The result is a smoother, less disruptive flow of transaction processing.

However, even under CICS/ESA, it still is possible for one task to dominate processing. When a CICS task issues requests for certain services that do not require waiting, the task can be redispatched continually without entering in the normal round-robin priority scheme. Some common commands that allow a CICS task to retain control include ASKTIME, HANDLE, FREEMAIN, ENQ, and DEQ. File control read and browse commands for which records are found in VSAM buffers also will bypass CICS dispatch functions in CICS/ESA and can therefore allow a task to dominate processing. (See the IBM reference guides listed at the end of this chapter.) In fact, if a task were to dominate CICS dispatching for a prolonged period of time (e.g., several seconds) and it was not just in a loop, it would probably be because it was reading a large number of VSAM records for which all CIs could be located in buffer pools.

In many installations, the majority of CICS tasks run at the same dispatching priority. In these environments, priority considerations can be ignored unless CICS tasks commonly or frequently dominate the processor. Particularly in a CICS/ESA environment, if most tasks run at the same priority, the effects of priorities will be minor and should not materially affect average service times.

When some CICS transactions dominate CICS dispatching, they are disruptive and will alter the nature of dispatch queueing. As will be discussed in Chapter 7, disruptive workloads cause delays that are longer than those explained by normal queueing parameters. When disruptive forces are present, closed queueing formulas may understate delays. In such cases, open queueing tables (from Appendix A) may need to be used instead of closed queueing tables to account for additional queueing. When it is necessary to use open queueing formulas to predict dispatch service times, it is likely that service will not be smooth, but erratic with periods of lengthy delays.

When multiple CICS priorities are used for a large percent of the transactions in a CICS region, specialized mathematics is necessary to estimate service for each priority class. The procedures are advanced and beyond the scope of this book. Unlike differences in MVS dispatching priorities, which will be discussed in Chapter 7, there is no easy method of estimating the effect of priority-related delays within CICS. Mathematical procedures that can be used to estimate the effect of non-preemptive priorities can be found in [ALLE90].

The material in this chapter has assumed a CICS workload in which the vast majority of the work is processed at the same CICS internal dispatching priority. It has also assumed that no disruptive transactions are present in the environment. These conditions should be true in most CICS environments. It is likely that if either of these two assumptions are not true, total service time will be worse than that predicted by closed queueing formulas and tables.

6.10 SUMMARY

This chapter has examined CICS performance in terms of queueing systems. We have explored a general technique that can be used to estimate the affect of dispatch queueing on CICS performance.

We have not yet discussed the impact of operating system-related delays, showed how to compare CICS performance on different types of processors, or developed models of general situations. These more advanced topics will be discussed in the following chapters.

SELECTED READING

[ALLE84] Allen, Arnold O., "Getting Started in Analytic Modeling," *Conference Proceedings, CMG XV International Conference on the Management and Performance Evaluation of Computer Systems*, 1984.

[ALLE90] Allen, Arnold O., *Probability, Statistics, and Queueing Theory with Computer Science Applications*, 2d ed., Academic Press, San Diego, 1990.

[ALLE83] Allen, Arnold O., "Modeling of Computer Systems," *Proceedings of the 1983 Computer Measurement Group International Conference*, 1983.

[BARN91] Barnes, Steve, "CICS/ESA Dispatcher Operation," *CMG Transactions*, Summer 1991.

Buzen, Jeffrey P., "Queueing Models: Beyond the Basics," *CMG '86 Conference Proceedings*, 1986.

[IBM001] *CICS/ESA Performance Guide, Version 3 Release 2.1*, IBM publication number SC33-0659-01.

[IBM002] *CICS/ESA Problem Determination Guide*, IBM publication number SC33-0678-01.

[IBM003] IBM Technical Information Search items CVD02M7, Q444833, Q446639, Q462492, Q521563, and Q537441.

[MERR91] Merrill, H. W. Barry Merrill, "MVS/ESA Performance, Accounting, and Capacity Data That is Now Captured in MVS/ESA Version 4.2," *CMG '91 Proceedings*, 1991.

[MULL91] Mullen, John William, "MVS/ESA Dataspaces and HIPERSPACES: Measuring and Evaluating the Cost", *CMG Transactions*, Winter, 1991.

Chapter

7

Paging, MVS Priority, and Processor Speed and Their Effect on CICS Performance

7.1 OVERVIEW

In this chapter we will discuss how page faults, competition from other MVS tasks, processor speed, and other environmental factors influence CICS performance. After looking at each factor in detail, the chapter will present a comprehensive procedure for estimating how environmental factors affect CICS performance. The chapter will conclude with a discussion of how to compare CICS performance on different processor configurations.

This chapter will show how to:

- Estimate the effect of paging, page faults satisfied from expanded storage, and competition from other MVS workloads on CICS performance.

- Estimate the effect of processor speed and MVS contention on CICS transaction response time.

- Compare the performance of CICS applications on different types of processors.

7.1.1 Primary Audience

Capacity planners and *systems programmers* will be able to apply ideas from this chapter in planning processor configurations and researching causes of CPU constraint. Some material may be more detailed than would be required for everyday use, but the overall concepts should provide insight into factors influencing CICS performance. *Application developers* probably will have limited use for much of the material in this chapter. They will find most of the information they need in the first and last few pages.

7.2 DIFFERENCES IN QUEUEING SYSTEMS

Before we continue our discussion of CICS processing, it is important to explore some basic relationships. There are major differences in *capacity* (the ability to perform work) and *performance* (the service delivered). While some systems may appear to have similar capacity, they might have dramatically different performance characteristics.

Figure 7.1 illustrates three different queueing systems. The first system, system A, represents a system with two servers. Each server has a separate queue. A customer must select one of the queues and remain in that queue until served. An example of this might be a town with two ATMs several miles from each other. Once customers select a machine, they will probably remain at that machine until they receive service.

The second system, system B, represents a system with two servers and a single queue. Customers will enter the single queue and wait for service by the first available server. This might be represented by two ATMs at the same location with a shared queue.

The third system, system C, represents a system with a single server that can work twice as fast as the servers in either system A and B. In system C, the ATM is customized to allow customers to complete transactions in half the time as the other two systems (perhaps software performance engineering was used in the design of the applications).

In system A, each server represents a single-server system. In system B, the servers form a multiserver queueing system. In system C, the server is a single-server system (as is system A), but the server works twice as quickly.

Table 7.1 shows the difference between total service time for several levels of server utilization. The table contains values for open queueing

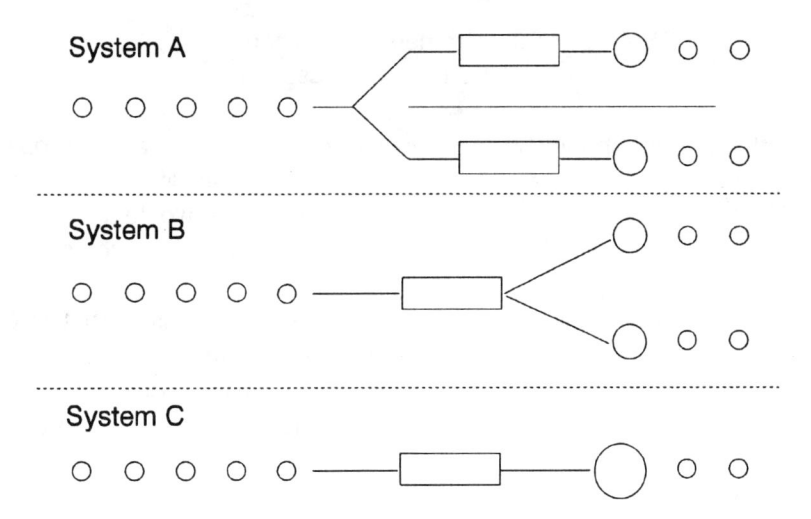

Figure 7.1 Three different queueing systems.

systems and four varieties of closed queueing systems. An average server time of 1.0 was used for systems A and B, and 0.5 for system C.

The slowest of the three systems will be the system with two independent servers. Throughout the range of data shown in Table 7.1, the best performer is the single, "twice-as-fast" server. It is this author's understanding that the single "twice-as-fast" server should always be the best performer for most standard queueing disciplines.

It is easiest to explain the differences in performance if we treat the three systems as open queueing systems. systems A and C are both single-server systems. The same amount of work arrives at both A and C each period. If an average of 20 customers arrive each hour for both servers in system A, each server would process an average of 10 customers. In system C, all customers would be processed by the single server but the server would work twice as quickly. If average service time was 3 minutes (.05 hours) per customer in system A, server utilization for system A would be

$$\text{Server utilization A} = \frac{10 \text{ customers}}{\text{hour}} \times \frac{.05 \text{ hours}}{\text{customer}} = .50$$

Similarly, average server time for system C would be 1.5 minutes (.025 hours) per customer, and server utilization would be

$$\text{Server utilization C} = \frac{20 \text{ customers}}{\text{hour}} \times \frac{.025 \text{ hours}}{\text{customer}} = .50$$

Both systems should have the *same server utilization* and, as open queueing systems, the *same service multiplier*. The difference is that customers spend half as much time at server C as they would at server A. Service time for server C always will be one-half what it is for the servers in system A.

The service multiplier for an open single-server system that is 50 percent busy is 2.0. In this example, customers will spend 6 minutes in system A (2.0 x 3 minutes) and 3 minutes in system C (2.0 x 1.5 minutes).

System B is a two-server system. The service multiplier for an open two-server system that is 50 percent busy is 1.33. Customers in system B would wait 3.99 minutes (1.33 x 3 minutes). Three minutes would be spent receiving service and .99 minutes waiting in the queue.

Table 7.1 Comparison of Queueing Systems with Theoretically Identical Capacities

		System		
		A	B	C
Type of Queueing System	Server Utilization	Two Single Servers	Multi-server	Twice-as-Fast Server
Open Queueing Systems				
	.50	2.0	1.33	1.0
	.75	4.0	2.29	2.0
	.90	10.0	5.26	5.0
Closed Queueing Systems				
Return ratio of 20 (systems A, B) and 40 (system C)	.50	1.8	1.2	0.9
	.75	2.8	1.9	1.6
	.90	4.6	3.2	2.8
Return ratio of 40 (systems A, B) and 80 (system C)	.50	1.9	1.3	1.0
	.75	3.1	2.0	1.7
	.90	5.7	3.5	3.3
10 customers for system A and 20 for systems B and C	.50	1.7	1.3	0.9
	.75	2.6	1.8	1.5
	.90	3.6	2.6	2.3

In Table 7.1, we used average server times of 1.0 for Systems A and B and 0.5 for system C. Using the service multipliers above, Table 7.1 shows total service times of 2.00, 1.33, and 1.00 for systems A, B, and C, respectively, for servers that are 50 percent busy.

Closed (machine-repair) systems are more complex than open systems. In closed systems, customer profiles must be considered. As mentioned in Chapters 5 and 6, server utilization in closed queueing systems is a factor of average server time, the number of customers, and the frequency at which they return to the server. If average server time remains constant, server utilization will be controlled by the number of customers and the rate at which they return to the server.

If the customers in systems A, B, and C all have similar "think" times, the ratio of "think" time (time between visits) to server time will be twice as high in system C as it is in systems A and B. This is because average server time for system C is one-half what it is for systems A and B. Therefore, system C will have a *server return ratio* twice as large as either systems A and B.

From Table 7.1, we can see that system C will be a little faster than system B, and that both systems will be substantially faster than system A. As suggested above, systems B and C will always outperform system A, and system C should perform better than system B. Figure 7.2 illustrates the relationship between systems A, B, and C.

> **Key Point:** Queueing systems that appear to have the same capacity may have differing performance characteristics. Systems with two servers will not normally perform as well as systems with a single more powerful server.

It is important to remember that closed queueing systems normally represent a series of interrelated machine-repair systems. When any element changes, it will cause changes in other interrelated systems as well. When service improves for one server, other servers in a system will be visited more frequently. This will increase their level of utilization, which in turn will cause increased queueing, and so on.

When service time decreases at any server in a closed system, activity should increase at other servers. When the cause of a bottleneck is removed, utilization should increase for other resources.

This is one of the reasons why upgrading a processor frequently uncovers performance problems in other areas, such as DASD. Once CPU queueing is reduced, other resources will be used more heavily and

Comparison of Queueing Systems

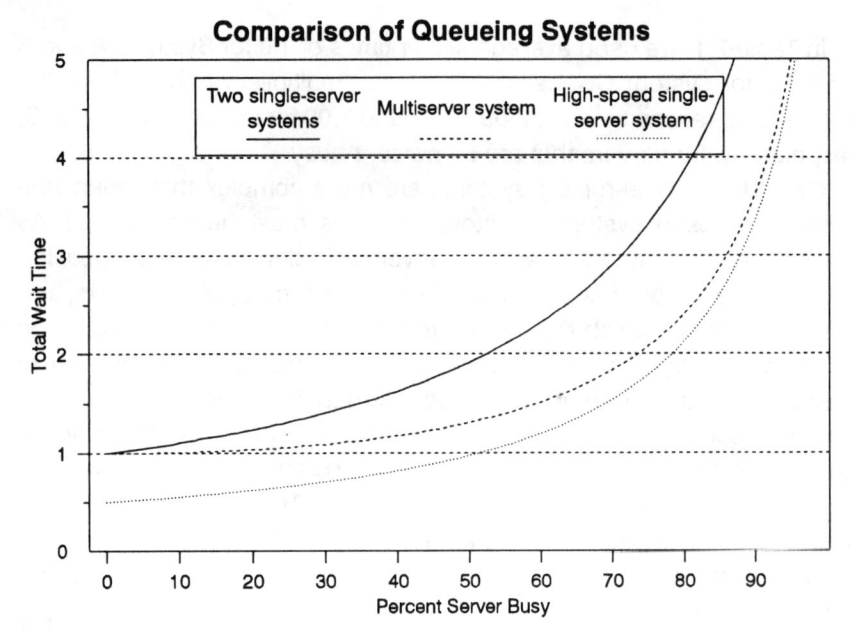

[Graph: Total Wait Time vs Percent Server Busy (0-90), comparing Two single-server systems, Multiserver system, and High-speed single-server system]

Figure 7.2 A comparison of unlike queueing systems.

new bottlenecks may appear. Performance planning for interrelated machine-repair systems requires that all servers be reviewed.

Furthermore, if there was a constant "think time" between transactions, servers could enter transactions more frequently when response time improved. Overall, an improvement in service at any server can cause increased resource utilization at other servers and an increase in the work entered by users.[1]

7.3 HOW PAGING FROM EXTERNAL STORAGE AFFECTS CICS PERFORMANCE

When an MVS task experiences a page fault, it will wait until the appropriate page is located and moved to real storage. If the required page resides in expanded storage, it will simply be moved to real storage. Processing will resume very quickly. If the page must be retrieved from

---

[1] Various studies have shown that changes in response time will affect user behavior. Some studies suggest that user think time will decrease when response time improves. Changes of this type are beyond the scope of this illustration.

external storage (DASD), the task (TCB) will wait until an I/O is completed and the page is loaded into memory.

In a CICS environment, paging will affect performance in two ways. Not only will transactions be delayed by page faults, but the TCB which had the page fault will not be able to dispatch other work until the page fault is resolved.

The following illustration demonstrates the effect of paging from external storage. Let us assume the following:

- CPU demand for the primary CICS TCB is 75 percent.

- Average dispatch time per transaction (on the primary TCB) is 60 ms.

- CICS tasks spend 1.5 seconds (1500 ms) waiting for other servers (such as VSAM files and temporary storage). This is about 25 times as much as they are dispatched for CPU (1500 ms/60 ms). This implies that the return ratio is 25.

- The primary TCB is experiencing about two page-ins from external storage per second.

- Page service time is 25 ms.

We would like to determine the effect of paging on CICS performance. The first step is to estimate total dispatch-related time including queueing. Total dispatch time will the product of average dispatch time and a service multiplier selected from Table B.1 (Appendix B). The service multiplier is about 3.00 for a server that is 75 percent busy with a return ratio of 25. It should take about 180 ms (including queueing) to receive dispatch service:

Total dispatch time = service multiplier × average dispatch time
= 3.00 × 60 ms = 180 ms

We know that the primary TCB is experiencing two page-ins per second and that average page service time is 25 ms. Paging delays will contribute 50 ms per second to CPU demand. (Remember that CPU demand represents the total time the primary TCB was using or trying to use a processor. It is, in essence, the sum of dispatch times for a CICS TCB.)

CPU demand of 75 percent means that the primary TCB is attempting to use a processor 750 ms each second. Here, 50 ms of that 750 ms is spent waiting for page-ins from external storage. CPU demand without paging would be about 700 ms per second.

Since CPU demand is, by definition, dispatch time for the primary TCB, a reduction in CPU demand also should cause a reduction in average dispatch time. When CPU demand is reduced by 7 percent (.75 to .70), average dispatch time should similarly be reduced. Average dispatch time per transaction would be reduced to 56 ms if paging were eliminated.

Using the revised CPU demand and dispatch times, we can calculate dispatch-related time without paging.[2]

$$\text{Total dispatch time} = \text{service multiplier} \times \text{average dispatch time}$$
$$= 2.57 \times 56 \text{ ms} = 143.9 \text{ ms}$$

Total dispatch-related service time would be reduced to 143.9 ms if paging were eliminated. This represents a reduction of 36.1 ms per transaction (180.0 ms - 143.9 ms).

In Chapter 6, we developed a model that showed response time as the sum of dispatch time, internal dispatch queueing, and all other waits. Therefore, total response time (with paging) should be about 1680 ms including paging.

$$\text{Total task life} = \text{CPU dispatch time} + \text{queueing for dispatch}$$
$$+ \text{ All other delays}$$
$$\text{Total task life} = 60 \text{ ms} + 120 \text{ ms} + 1500 \text{ ms} = 1680 \text{ ms} = 1.68 \text{ secs.}$$

During the 1.68 seconds of average task life, the task would have been affected in one way or another by about 3.4 page-in requests (2 page-ins per second times 1.68 seconds). This means that an average of 3.4 times in a transaction's life, processing would have been specifically delayed by page-in activity. Tasks may have been processing, queued for dispatch or waiting for other events when page faults occurred. If tasks waited an average of one-half the page-service time, they would experience additional delays of 42.5 ms per transaction.

---

[2] To be completely rigorous, we should have adjusted the server return ratio for the lower dispatch time (without paging). Here, it would be 26.8 (1500 ms/56 ms). Due to the coarseness of Table B.1, we could use server return ratios of 25 and 30 to establish a range of service multipliers. The resulting range of service multiplier would be between 2.57 and 2.73.

$$\text{Direct paging-related delays} = \frac{25 \text{ ms} \times 3.4}{2} = 42.5 \text{ ms}$$

In this example, CICS tasks running in this region would pay an average penalty of about 78.6 ms for paging delays. This includes 36.1 ms of dispatch queueing and 42.5 ms of direct delays.

$$\text{Total paging effect} = \text{dispatch queueing} + \text{direct paging delays}$$
$$= 36.1 \text{ ms} + 42.5 \text{ ms} = 78.6 \text{ ms}$$

It is easy to see the negative effect that paging can have on CICS performance. In this example, two page-ins per second made a difference of 78.6 ms in transaction response time. When CPU demand is lower or average transaction life is shorter, paging will have less of an impact on performance. The old rule of thumb of limiting external paging to 2 to 5 page-ins per second per CICS region appears to be quite reasonable.

As external paging increases, CPU demand will increase a bit less than proportionately. As mentioned earlier in this chapter, when any element changes in a closed queueing system, it will affect other servers. In this example, the impact on other servers should be trivial. When the number of page-ins per second is higher, adjustments should be made for delays at other servers.

7.4 HOW PAGING FROM EXPANDED STORAGE AFFECTS CICS PERFORMANCE

In contrast to page-ins from external storage, page faults satisfied from expanded storage are usually both acceptable and, in some senses, desirable. When a page fault can be satisfied by a page in expanded storage, it will be moved to real storage and processing can resume almost immediately. In most situations, a moderate rate of page movement between real and expanded storage reflects a good balance of main and expanded storage usage.

An old rule of thumb is that it takes about 75 microseconds to retrieve a page from expanded storage. The source of this is that on an IBM 3090-600S, the instruction to move a single page from expanded to real storage requires about 75 microseconds. On faster processors, page movement times are usually faster, with some as low as about 30 microseconds. That is just the cost of moving a single page from expanded storage to real storage.

Resolving a page fault from expanded storage requires more processing than simply retrieving a page. The operating system must process the page fault interrupt, locate the page, move the page, and return control to the application. The total CPU time to service a page fault typically will be three to five times the cost of moving a single page from expanded storage.

> **Key Point:** The total CPU time required to satisfy a page fault from expanded storage is usually *three* to *five* times the processing time it takes to move a single page to main storage from expanded storage.

The CPU time spent servicing page faults and moving pages from expanded storage will not be included in address space or transaction statistics. Neither RMF Type 72 data (performance group statistics) nor CICS CMF statistics include the CPU time spent servicing page faults. This CPU usage will be included only in total system-wide CPU usage.[3]

Unless CPU usage is extremely high, limited paging from expanded storage will have a minor effect on CICS performance. If a CICS region experienced as many as 200 page-ins per second from expanded storage and each took 250 microseconds to resolve, the total cost would be about 50 ms. This would add only 5 percent to CPU demand.

In the example in Section 7.3, we saw that only 2 page-ins per second from external storage could cause a 5 percent increase in CPU demand. On a 3090 S-class processor, it would take about 200 page-ins from expanded storage to cause the same affect on CPU demand. Using the same data as Section 7.3, there would be a similar queueing cost of 36.1 ms per transaction.

However, unlike external paging delays, paging from expanded storage takes such a short time (relative to other delays, such as I/Os) that the effect of direct paging delays will be much less. Transactions experiencing page faults or queued for dispatch service will wait for the page movement delays, but transactions waiting for file I/Os probably will not be affected materially by these delays. The length of a page movement

---

[3] The CPU time spent processing page faults is commonly called uncaptured time – system overhead that is not specifically associated with any particular address space.

is so small compared to the length of an I/O or other external wait that the chance of the other event completing while the page movement is occurring is very small. The direct affect of page movements will be limited, for the most part, to the portion of response time that a transaction is dispatched or queued for dispatch.

Starting in MVS/ESA release 4.2, RMF provides information that can be used to estimate delays associated with page-ins from expanded storage. RMF Type 72 statistics include the number of page-ins from expanded storage. Unfortunately, no information is captured about CPU time – only the number of page-ins is captured. We can estimate page-in time using a value of about 225 to 375 microseconds per page-in for a 3090 S-class processor. This value would be adjusted for other processors based on their relative engine speed. Although this estimate is not perfect, it should provide an indication of the cost of satisfying page faults from expanded storage.

7.5 HOW FILE OPEN AND CLOSE COMMANDS AFFECT DISPATCH SERVICE IN CICS REGIONS

In CICS/VS and CICS/MVS, file open commands are performed by the main CICS TCB. Whenever an open command is issued, the main TCB will wait until the open has completed. Since open commands can be lengthy (sometimes over a second), processing many file opens can restrict dispatch service.

For all intents and purposes, file open commands can be treated similarly to page-ins from external storage. The main CICS TCB cannot be dispatched while open processing is occurring. Time that file opens are being processed contributes to CPU demand.

In CICS/ESA, file opens are performed by the concurrent (CO) TCB. When the CO TCB issues a file open, it will wait. However, the QR TCB can continue to dispatch applications while the CO TCB waits for open processing. The CICS task requesting the open will wait, but most other application processing can continue uninterrupted.

Since the CO TCB processes both file opens and program loads, it can become a minor bottleneck when both open and load activity are heavy. The CO TCB may be constrained shortly after CICS startup when many CICS programs are being loaded and most files are being opened. After this period, the CO TCB normally will not be very busy.

7.6 HOW CI AND CA SPLITS AFFECT DISPATCH SERVICE IN CICS REGIONS

In CICS, VSAM files can be accessed either by *local shared resources* (LSR) or *nonshared resources* (NSR). When files are accessed via NSR, CI and CA splits can affect CPU demand. With NSR, when a control interval (CI) or control area (CA) split occurs, the TCB issuing the update (or add) request will not be dispatched until the split completes.

When the primary TCB issues a VSAM update that results in an NSR split, most application processing will be suspended until the split is completed. However, if the VSAM subtask or the CO TCB is being used, the subtask TCB will be nondispatchable during the split, and other processing can continue on the primary (main or QR) TCB.

Strategically, it is best to avoid VSAM splits if possible. If splits must occur, CI splits are less damaging than CA splits (CI splits may take up to 100 ms while CA splits can last over a second). When a large number of splits cannot be avoided, it is normally better to use *local shared resources* (LSR), unless there is some compelling reason to use NSR.

When a CI or CA split occurs under LSR, only the entity being split will be unavailable. LSR does process CI and CA splits less efficiently than NSR, but it does not restrict TCB processing while the split is being processed. Other portions of the file will remain available, and the TCB can continue processing.

The use of LSR and NSR to control the effects of CI and CA splits is discussed in more detail in Chapter 10.

7.7 HOW TOTAL PROCESSOR USAGE AFFECTS CICS PERFORMANCE

In a CICS environment, total CPU utilization is not nearly as important as CPU demand in each CICS region. In a processor with multiple engines, CICS TCBs can be dispatched as long as a processor engine is available. The more engines, the greater the chance one will be available when it is needed.

Furthermore, the amount of CPU time used by higher- or equal-priority MVS tasks is more significant than the total amount of CPU time used. MVS is designed to run efficiently, even with processor usage approaching 100 percent. If MVS dispatching parameters are set up correctly, favored tasks can process almost as if there was no other work in the system. When total CPU utilization becomes intense, lower-priority MVS tasks will receive less CPU service and will suffer the most degradation.

In most environments with moderate to heavy CICS activity, CICS will be considered a favored workload. As a rule, heavily used CICS regions will be assigned a higher dispatching priority than batch work and most TSO processing.

7.7.1 How to Estimate the Effect of Processor Utilization on CICS Performance

MVS tasks with the same or higher dispatching priorities as CICS regions will influence performance in those regions. Competition from MVS tasks will affect CICS dispatch service. When all processor engines are doing work for higher- or equal-priority MVS tasks, CICS TCBs may need to wait for service. This will affect CPU demand, which will affect internal queueing for dispatch service, and this will be reflected in CICS transaction response time.

There are several challenges in estimating the effect of processor competition on CICS performance. The first is to determine the amount of CPU time used by MVS tasks with the same or higher dispatching priority as the CICS region being examined. This should not be too difficult if your installation maintains a good performance data base (PDB) and you have information about MVS dispatching priorities. One caution, though: Not all MVS tasks in a performance group will necessarily run at the same dispatching priority.

A second challenge is that not all MVS dispatching algorithms are based solely on workload type. For purposes of this discussion, it will be assumed that fixed dispatching priorities are used for MVS tasks with the same or higher dispatching priority as CICS workloads. Minor deviations to this will have little effect on the techniques we will discuss. However, when certain esoteric priority techniques are used for CICS or other major workloads, it will be difficult to estimate delays.

A final challenge is in the mathematical processes themselves. The calculations used to estimate preemptive priority classes is quite complex and too advanced to be included in this book. However, two simple techniques will be suggested to estimate the effect of MVS priority queueing in the type of MVS environments in which CICS systems commonly run. Although these techniques are not precise, they should provide a reasonable approximation of how operating system delays affect CICS dispatching.

7.7.2 CPU Time Used by Competing MVS Tasks

Two pieces of information are needed to estimate CPU queueing caused by contention with other MVS tasks. The first is the amount of CPU time used by all workloads with a higher dispatching priority than the CICS task being evaluated. The second is the amount of CPU time used by workloads with the same dispatching priority.

RMF Type 72 records contain information about how much CPU time is used by each MVS performance group.[4] This is probably the best source of information about CPU time used by specific workloads. Unfortunately, not all tasks in the same performance group necessarily run at the same MVS dispatching priority. Additionally, database tasks in CICS address spaces may execute at a lower dispatching priority than CICS TCBs. Furthermore, dispatching priorities in some performance groups may vary dynamically depending on processor and performance group loads. It may not be easy to separate CPU times into priority-based groups mechanically. Some analysis of data and assumptions may be necessary to estimate CPU usage for different MVS priority classes.

When calculating CPU usage for higher-priority MVS tasks, it is important to include CPU usage associated with operating system overhead. This CPU time is commonly called *uncaptured* time. Uncaptured CPU time is the time that accrues while the system is handling interrupts, services page faults, and performs other overhead functions that cannot be associated with specific address spaces. The significance of uncaptured CPU time is that most of it is executed at the highest MVS dispatching priority.

The easiest way to calculate uncaptured time is to subtract the sum of CPU times shown in *all* RMF Type 72 records[5] from total CPU usage in the Type 70 record for that period. The easiest way to do this is to convert the percent CPU busy in the Type 70 record into total CPU seconds for the period,[6] and then subtract CPU times in each of the Type 72 records. The CPU overhead thus calculated can be then added into the total CPU time used by higher-priority tasks.

---

[4] As noted earlier, we will assume that each important CICS region and most significant MVS workloads are mapped into their own MVS control performance group.
[5] This, of course, assumes that important MVS workloads have been mapped into control performance groups.
[6] Remember to account for the number of CPU engines in the conversion. A four-engine processor that was 50 percent busy for an hour would have used 120 seconds of CPU time, not 30 seconds.

7.7.3 The Processor Complex as a Queueing System

Figure 7.3 presents the processor complex as a queueing system. In this figure, the set of processor engines forms a multiserver queueing system in which MVS tasks can be dispatched on any available processor. The other servers shown in Figure 7.3 represent delays (such as waiting for I/O events or user input) that control the rate at which MVS tasks need CPU service.

Production CICS regions are normally given a relatively high MVS dispatching priority. As a rule, the types of tasks that have the same or higher dispatching priorities than CICS regions run more-or-less continuously. Normally, these would include system and service tasks such as VTAM, JES, and DB2 and other CICS regions. The types of workload that compete with CICS regions are commonly resident most of the time.

Variable workloads, such as batch jobs and TSO users, are usually assigned lower dispatching priorities than highly used CICS regions. Workloads that enter and leave the system frequently are typically assigned lower dispatching priorities.

Conceptually, queueing for dispatch in the operating system is different from dispatch queueing within CICS. CPU demand and queueing

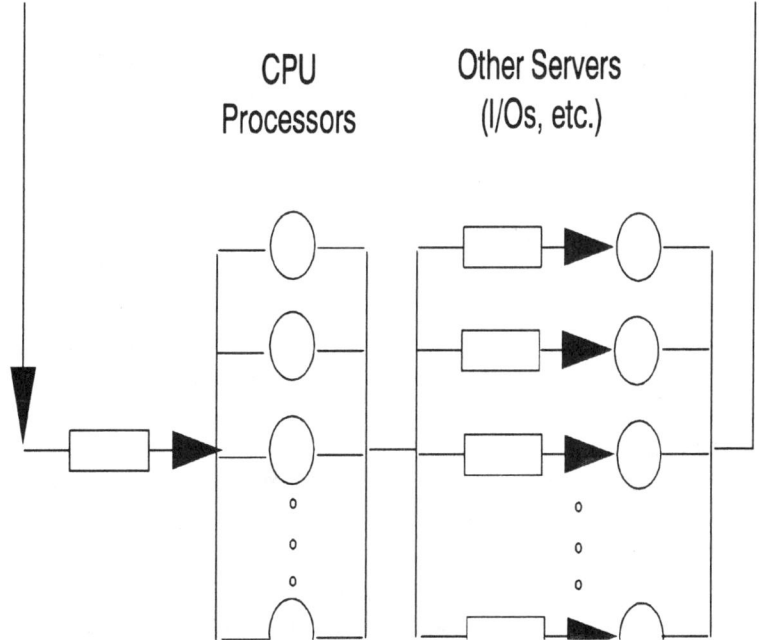

Figure 7.3 The processor as a queueing system.

inside a CICS region are driven primarily by the number of active tasks. Normally, the number of tasks running in a CICS region has the most direct effect over how much CPU time is used in that region.

At the operating system level, CICS TCBs face processor competition primarily from other CICS regions, system tasks, and operating system overhead. For the most part, these tasks run constantly and usually do not vary considerably in number. Thus, the processor complex can be viewed as a queueing system in which the number of customers (MVS tasks) is more or less stable.

Although the amount of processing done by system and service tasks may be driven by transaction activity, the *actual number of MVS tasks with the same or higher dispatching priority* typically does not vary very significantly. When transaction activity is low, these tasks require less processor service. As activity rises, these tasks request processor service more frequently. Conceptually, a limited number of customers (MVS tasks) compete for access to a fixed number of servers (processor engines).

7.7.4 The Effect of Priority Queueing

The mathematics to resolve multiple levels of priority and differing priority schemes for multiserver systems (e.g., multiprocessors), is complex, and beyond the scope of this book. *However, there are some simple techniques that can provide reasonable estimates of the effects of priority queueing without the use of complex mathematical formulas.* While these techniques do not represent a perfect theoretical fit, they usually provide a reasonably close estimate of service for systems with multiple priorities.

This chapter presents two approaches to estimating how MVS dispatching priorities affect CICS dispatch time and service. Both techniques work reasonably well, and both should provide usable results for typical MVS environments running production CICS systems.

Both approaches described below are designed only for what is called *preemptive resume* priority systems. In preemptive resume systems, whenever a higher-priority task needs service, work for lower-priority workloads can be suspended. When service is completed by a higher-priority task, lower priority work can be resumed. This happens to be a model of *fixed-priority dispatching* in MVS.

One key assumption applies to both approaches. It is that any workload will perform as if no lower-priority work existed in the system. For all practical purposes, it is possible to ignore workloads with lower priorities. All workloads, including low-priority batch processing, generate a certain amount of system overhead that executes at the highest dispatching priority. In the discussion and examples in this chapter, high-priority overhead will be considered, but the CPU time used directly by lower-priority tasks will not.

> **Note:** The techniques presented in this chapter apply to preemptive resume priority systems, such are commonly represented by MVS fixed-priority dispatching algorithms. This material addresses the affect of MVS workloads on CICS dispatch service. The techniques discussed in this chapter should not be applied to CICS internal dispatching priorities.

Approach 1. Adjust server times to account for interruptions by higher priority work. This first approach was adapted from a technique suggested by King [KING90] for preemptive resume systems. This approach recognizes that it takes lower priority tasks longer to receive service when higher-priority tasks are active. Since lower-priority tasks are interrupted by higher-priority tasks, it takes them longer to receive service than it would if higher priority work did not exist.

> **Approach 1.** The first method of estimating the effect of higher-priority workloads on CICS dispatch processing is to adjust average server time to account for the time servers are interrupted by higher priority tasks.

In this approach, we adjust average server time to account for interruptions by higher-priority tasks. We do this by multiplying average server time by a service multiplier based on how much CPU time is being used by higher-priority workloads. This *effective server time* is then used to calculate total service time. This would be shown as

Effective server time = average service time (at the server)
× service multiplier (for higher priority workloads)

To calculate total service time, we multiply the effective server time by a service multiplier for all competing CPU usage. This service multiplier would be based on the sum of all CPU time used by higher and equal priority tasks:

Total service time =
    effective service time
    × service multiplier (for higher + equal priority tasks)

In a CICS environment, the total service time shown above is then used to calculate both CPU demand and average dispatch time per transaction. We will discuss several specific applications of this approach later in this chapter.

It is worth mentioning that this author's research has shown that approach 1 is very reliable for systems with a single preemptive resume server. This approach is usable, but not quite as accurate, for priority systems with multiple servers.

Approach 2. Separate average service time by priority classes. The second approach involves estimating the effect of separate priority classes on total service. This approach relies on two premises. The first is that average service time for the entire workload is equal to the sum of *weighted* service times for all priority classes. The second is that average service time for a workload can be estimated using a service multiplier based on the server utilization of the entire workload.

> **Approach 2.** The second method of estimating the effect of higher-priority workloads on CICS dispatch processing is to estimate the effect of separate priority classes on total service.

The first premise is that the whole is equal to the sum of its parts. Service time for a workload containing several priority classes will be the sum of service times for each priority class *weighted by* the percentage of work represented by each class. *Lambda* (λ) represents the arrival rate of all work in a system, lambda$_1$ (λ_1) the arrival rate for the highest-priority workload, lambda$_2$ (λ_2), the second-highest-priority workload, and so on. W represents service time for the workload as a whole and W_1 for the highest priority class of work. Thus, the formula for total service time would be

$$W = (\frac{\lambda_1}{\lambda} \times W_1) + (\frac{\lambda_2}{\lambda} \times W_2) + \cdots + (\frac{\lambda_n}{\lambda} \times W_n)$$

λ_1/λ represents the portion of work arriving in the system associated with priority class 1.

In projections of CPU service, it is difficult to obtain true arrival rates for workloads. We normally have information about the amount of CPU time used by workloads but not about the rate at which requests for CPU service are received. CPU usage can be transformed into percent utilization, but not necessarily into arrival rates. In theory, resource utilization varies with workload arrival rate, but the relationship is not quite linear for closed queueing systems.[7] However, even though this relationship is not precise, it is close enough to linear to allow us to substitute resource utilization in the formula above.

Subject to the limitations just mentioned, the formula above can be restated as

$$\text{Service multiplier}_{overall} = (\frac{\% \text{ busy}_1}{\% \text{ busy}_{overall}} \times \text{service multiplier}_1)$$
$$+ (\frac{\% \text{ busy}_2}{\% \text{ busy}_{overall}} \times \text{service multiplier}_2)$$
$$+ \cdots$$

The *second premise* is that average service time for the entire system will be approximately equal to that predicted by queueing formulas for the system as a whole.[8] Using the formula presented in previous chapters, total service time will be the product of the average server time and an appropriate service multiplier.

$$W = \text{average server time} \times \text{service multiplier}$$

In the second approach, only two pieces of information are needed to estimate service time for any priority class. They are the amount of CPU time used by workloads with higher priorities and the amount of CPU time used by workloads with higher and equal priorities. (This is essentially the same information required for Approach 1.)

Combining the formulas above and on the previous page, we get

---

[7] If the world could be viewed as an open queueing system, resource utilization would vary directly with workload arrival rate as long as average server time remained constant. However, in closed queueing formulas, arrival rate, service time, and queue time together control resource utilization. At lower to moderate levels of resource utilization, there is an almost linear relationship between work arrival and resource utilization. At higher levels of server utilization (especially above 90 percent), the relationship will be less reliable.

[8] This assumption is valid only when the entire workload is somewhat homogeneous as a whole.

Service multiplier$_{high+equal}$ =
$$\frac{\% \text{busy}_{high}}{\% \text{busy}_{high+equal}} \times \text{service multiplier}_{high}$$
$$+ \frac{\% \text{busy}_{equal}}{\% \text{busy}_{high+equal}} \times \text{service multiplier}_{equal}$$

In this equation, "equal" refers to workloads with the same dispatching priority as the CICS region being analyzed. "High" refers to all workloads with a higher dispatching priority. "High+equal" represents the combination of "high"-priority workloads and "equal"-priority workloads.

We can easily estimate both the overall service multiplier and the service multiplier for the high-priority work. The only unknown in the equation is the service multiplier for work with the same dispatching priority as the CICS region. (Remember that we are ignoring any workloads with dispatching priorities lower than the CICS region we are evaluating.)

We can obtain the service multiplier for the CICS region by rearranging the equation on the previous page as follows:

service multiplier =

$$\frac{\text{service multiplier}_{high+equal} - \frac{\% \text{busy}_{high}}{\% \text{busy}_{high+equal}} \times \text{service multiplier}_{high}}{\frac{\% \text{busy}_{equal}}{\% \text{busy}_{high+equal}}}$$

Once this service multiplier has been calculated, it can be used to estimate both dispatch time and CPU demand. It has been the author's experience that this approach provides close estimates of CPU contention for multiprocessor configurations.

7.7.5 Calculating the Effects of CPU Contention — Approach 1

In this section, we will define a series of specific steps that can be used to estimate CPU contention using approach 1. These steps show how to estimate CICS CPU demand and dispatch time per transaction. These two factors can then be used to estimate total CPU-related delays using techniques suggested in Chapter 6.

After outlining both approaches, an example will follow demonstrating how they can be applied.

1. **Determine the amount of CPU time used by higher-priority MVS tasks.** RMF Type 72 data are the best source of information about how much CPU time is used by each performance group. (Of course, this assumes that control performance groups have been defined.) The ICS/IPS members of SYS1.PARMLIB identify workloads and their dispatching priorities. Be aware, though, that not all tasks in a performance group necessarily execute at the same MVS dispatching priority.

   It is very important to include MVS overhead with higher-priority CPU usage. Most MVS overhead operates at the highest dispatching priority, and MVS overhead represents a significant portion of total CPU time used. As mentioned earlier, MVS overhead can be calculated by subtracting the sum of CPU times shown in all RMF Type 72 records from processor utilization shown in the RMF Type 70 record. (This will work only when workloads are mapped into control performance groups.) Be sure to include *all classes of CPU time* contained in the Type 72 records in the calculation of MVS overhead.

   Along with higher-priority workloads and MVS overhead, other CPU usage should be included with higher-priority CPU usage. SRB time (time accumulated for SRB processing) is dispatched ahead of normal TCB processing in an address space. Interrupt processing (MVS/ESA 4.2 and later) executes at the highest dispatching priority. For workloads with the same dispatching priority as the CICS region being studied, SRB time should be counted as part of higher-priority CPU usage. Interrupt processing for all performance groups also should be counted as part of higher-priority CPU usage.

   It is usually easiest to calculate the total number of CPU seconds associated with higher-priority work and translate that into a percent busy. The goal of this first step is to calculate the percent of time (relative to 100 percent) the processor was busy executing higher priority work.

2. **Estimate degradation associated with higher priority MVS tasks.** The equations for the standard machine repair model tend to overstate MVS dispatch contention for many CICS environments. The tables in Appendix C are based on a special version of the machine-repair model. They contain service multipliers that more closely approximate the delays associated with MVS dispatch queueing.

It has been this author's experience that the standard machine-repair model tends to overstate contention for MVS dispatch at higher levels of utilization. The author's research also has indicated that pure deterministic (constant) service times tend to understate contention. What is needed is an M/G/C/K/K queueing system. Since I could not locate a set of formulas for this type of queueing system, I developed a simulation model of a closed (machine-repair) system with a controlled, but not fixed, variance on service time.

The model was used to develop the equivalent of a M/G/C/K/K queueing system. Th results of this simulation are shown in Appendix C. The tables in Appendix C provide a more realistic estimate of MVS dispatch contention than conventional closed and open queueing disciplines. The tables in Appendix C are appropriate for the type environments in which production CICS workloads are commonly run.

Chapter 5 suggested that queueing formulas would provide good estimates of service only when real-world conditions were consistent with the assumptions behind the formulas. In general, closed (machine-repair) queueing formulas are based on the assumption that service times and think times have random patterns. When either service times or think times are almost constant with little variance, real-world systems will provide better service than queueing formulas predict. When service times or think times are bunched around multiple values, real-world service will be worse than that predicted by those formulas.

Key Point: When real-world systems violate the assumptions upon which queueing formulas are built, the formulas will either overstate or understate true service.

On systems dedicated to CICS workloads, contention for MVS dispatch service tends to be less intense than that predicted by closed queueing systems. Tables C.1 through C.8 in Appendix C were developed to account for these differences and provide estimates of MVS dispatch service in such environments.

We can use service multipliers from Tables C.1 through C.8 to estimate contention by higher-priority tasks. The eight tables contain data for different numbers of servers. We choose which table to use based on the number of processor engines and the column in the table based on the number of higher-priority MVS tasks. In most cases, we would assume the number of customers is lower than the actual number of MVS tasks. This is because some MVS tasks seldom do much processing. We then select the row (server utilization) using the percent of the processor used by higher priority work.

The tables in Appendix C can be used to estimate systemwide processor contention for the type MVS environments used to run production CICS systems. In some cases, though, special situations may require that we use tables in Appendixes A or B instead. Later in this chapter, in the section on calibrating CPU dispatch times (see page 194), we will discuss how to determine which of the three sets of tables to use.

3. **Determine the amount of CPU time used by all equal- and higher-priority MVS tasks**. This calculation is similar to that performed in step 1. Here, we also will include CPU time used by tasks with the same dispatching priority as the CICS region we are evaluating. In theory, if any workload running at the same priority is using DB2, and the DB2 subtasks run at a lower priority, these DB2 CPU times should be excluded from this calculation. If DB2 CPU usage is insignificant or if DB2 work is executed at the same priority as CICS, then this adjustment will not be necessary.

4. **Estimate the effect of competition from equal- and higher-priority MVS workloads**. A service multiplier will be selected from the same table used in step 2. The number of tasks (customers) will be adjusted to include equal-priority tasks. The preliminary dispatch time and CPU demand values calculated in step 2 both will be multiplied by this service multiplier. These products reflect the portion of dispatch time and CPU demand associated with receiving CPU service from MVS.

5. **Adjust for hidden delays**. In most environments, it will be hard to isolate or measure some factors that affect the relationship between CPU time and dispatch time. These factors might include uncaptured CPU usage (such as from resolving page faults), routines that request operating services, and unusual situations. This author's experience has been that a constant multiplier of 1.03 to 1.08 should be appropriate most of the time. We will discuss how to estimate this multiplier later in this chapter when we discuss the calibration of dispatch time.

6. **Adjust for other delays, such as paging, CI and CA splits, and file opens.** The next step is to add estimates of other delays such as paging, page faults from expanded storage, CI and CA splits for NSR files, and file open and close commands (pre-CICS/ESA). Both CPU demand and average dispatch time per transaction are adjusted by the same factors.

    Paging information is obtained from RMF data. However, paging statistics are collected at the performance group (address space) level and are not segregated by TCB. When multiple TCBs are active in a CICS region, it is necessary to estimate how many page faults are associated with each TCB.

    Information about CI and CA splits can be found in transaction statistics available in some CICS monitors, but this type of data is not always precise. If specific CICS transactions are known to perform file open and close commands, information from these transactions might be included.

> **Key Point:** Steps 1 to 6 above show how to calculate CPU demand and dispatch time per transaction in a CICS region. CPU demand and dispatch time can then be used to estimate the amount of CPU contention or dispatch queueing within the CICS region.

Dispatch time is measured by CMF, and CPU demand usually can be calculated more directly. Normally, one would not go through all this work just to obtain these two measures. However, the steps in approaches 1 and 2 are an important part of the several other processes, such as estimating differences in CICS application performance on different processors, which we will discuss later in this chapter.

7.7.6 Calculating the Effects of CPU Contention — Approach 2

Most of the steps in this approach are very similar to those in approach 1. The narrative that follows will not repeat a discussion of steps that are the same as in approach 1. The reader show refer to the discussion on the previous pages for this material.

The same information will be collected and the same service multipliers selected from Tables C.1 through C.8. The only difference is in the way the information is applied.

1. **Determine the amount of CPU time used by higher-priority MVS tasks.** This step is identical with step 1 in approach 1. See page 185.

2. **Obtain the service multiplier for CPU usage by higher-priority MVS workloads from the appropriate table.** The same service multiplier is selected that would have been selected in step 2 of approach 1. See page 185.

3. **Determine the amount of CPU time used by all equal- and higher-priority MVS tasks.** This step is identical with step 3 in approach 1. See page 187.

4. **Obtain the service multiplier for CPU usage by equal- and higher-priority MVS workloads.** This is the same service multiplier selected in step 4 of approach 1. See page 187.

5. **Use the formula below to calculate the overall service multiplier for dispatch service.** The formula below was derived earlier in this chapter. It will be used to calculate CPU demand and dispatch time in the CICS regions. The percent busy for "high" workloads was calculated in step 1 and the percent busy for "high+equal" workloads in step 3. The "high" service multiplier was selected in step 2, and the "high+equal" service multiplier in step 4. The percent busy for "equal" workloads is simply the difference between the CPU usage identified in steps 3 and 1.

$$\text{service multiplier}_{CICS\ region} = \frac{\text{service multiplier}_{high+equal} - \frac{\%\ busy_{high}}{\%\ busy_{high+equal}} \times \text{service multiplier}_{high}}{\frac{\%\ busy_{equal}}{\%\ busy_{high+equal}}}$$

6. **Multiply both average CPU time per transaction and CPU busy for the primary TCB by the service multiplier calculated in Step 5.** These calculations provide the basis for average dispatch time per transaction and CPU demand, respectively.

7. **Adjust for hidden delays.** This step is identical with step 5 in approach 1. See page 187.

8. **Adjust for other delays, such as paging, CI and CA splits, and file opens.** This step is identical with step 6 of approach 1. As in Approach 1, both CPU demand and average dispatch time per transaction are adjusted for each of these delays. See page 188.

The calculations in both approaches 1 and 2 provide estimates of two important factors: average dispatch time per transaction and total CPU demand for the primary CICS TCB.

7.7.7 Illustrations of Real-World Queueing Data

A few figures have been included to illustrate the effect of operating system contention on dispatch time and CPU demand. Figures 7.4 and 7.5 show the relationship between the dispatch ratio and competing CPU usage for two different CICS regions. The *dispatch ratio* is simply the ratio of average dispatch time to average CPU time per transaction. It is a measure of the contention caused by processor competition, paging, and other delays.

Figures 7.4 and 7.5 show dispatch ratios for two CICS/MVS regions running on a 3090-600J processor. Both figures suggest that there is some relationship between the dispatch ratio and the amount of CPU time consumed by higher- and equal-priority MVS tasks. Region 02 (Figure 7.5) shows quite a bit of variance, indicating that other factors (such as paging and priority contention) account for a significant portion of dispatch time. Region 01 (Figure 7.4) shows less variance, but still shows that factors other than CPU competition contribute to CPU demand and dispatch time.

Figures 7.6 to 7.9 show a comparison of estimated dispatch time to actual values. Each observation in these figures shows actual dispatch ratios divided by calculated ratios. A value of 1.0 indicates that calculated dispatch times match actual dispatch times. Estimates in Figures 7.6 and 7.8 were calculated using approach 1; those in Figures 7.7 and 7.9 were calculated using approach 2. The only factors that were included in these estimates were CPU contention, paging, and hidden delays. Other delays either could not be determined or were insignificant.

Notice that estimated values for both approaches 1 and 2 tend to show a good fit over a wide range of activity, especially in region 01. It appears that many of the factors that caused so much variance in Figures 7.4 and 7.5 have been accounted for in the estimation techniques.

Paging, MVS Priorities, and Processor Speed 191

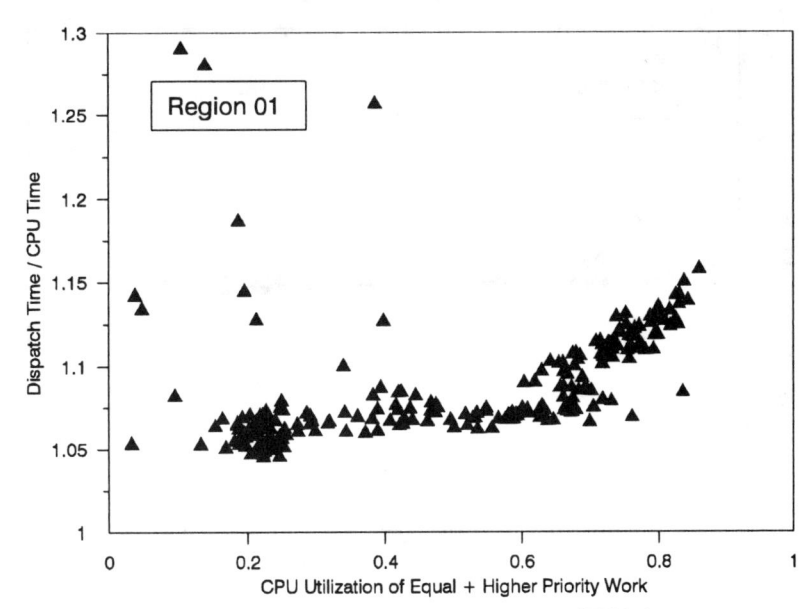

Figure 7.4 Example of ratios of dispatch time to CPU time per transaction mapped against total competing CPU utilization for the processor (region 1).

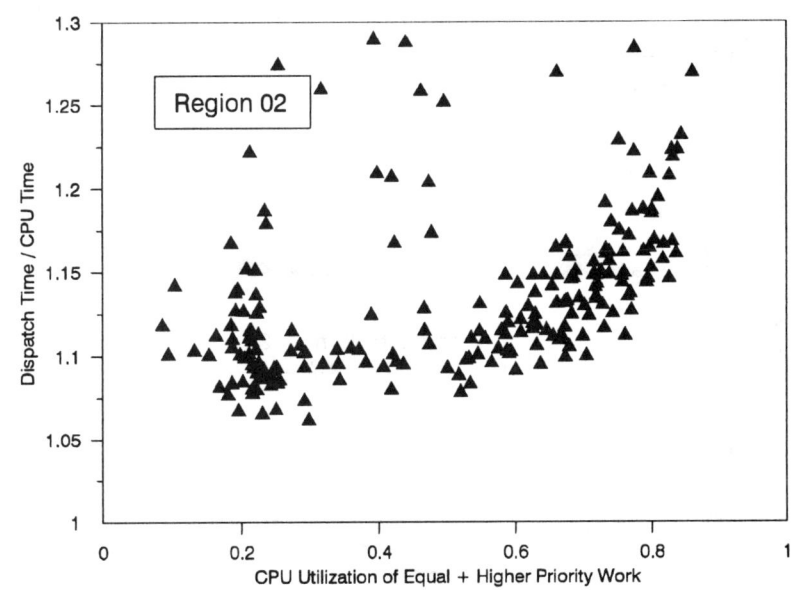

Figure 7.5 Example of ratios of dispatch time to CPU time per transaction mapped against total competing CPU utilization for the processor (region 2).

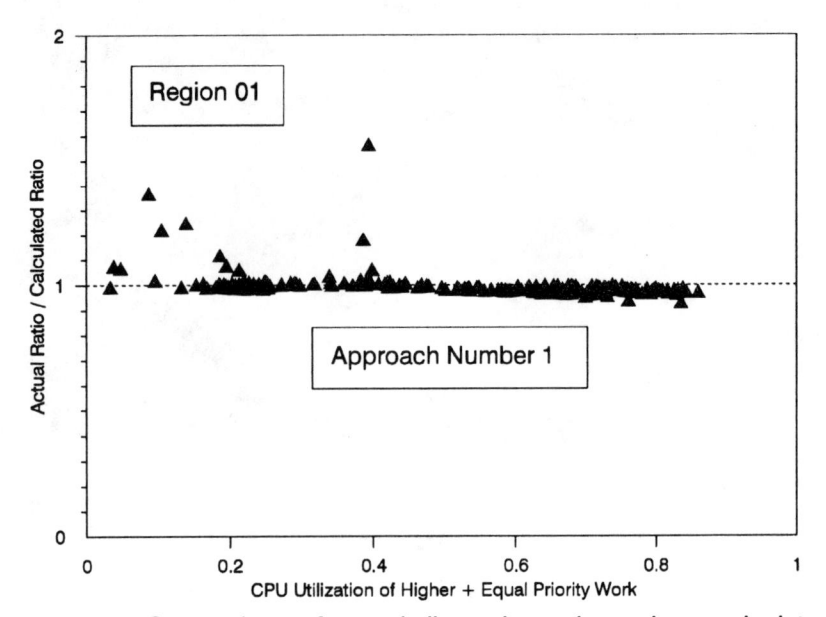

Figure 7.6 Comparison of actual dispatch service ratio to calculated dispatch service ratio. This is a measure of the effectiveness of algortihms to estimate system-wide processor contention.

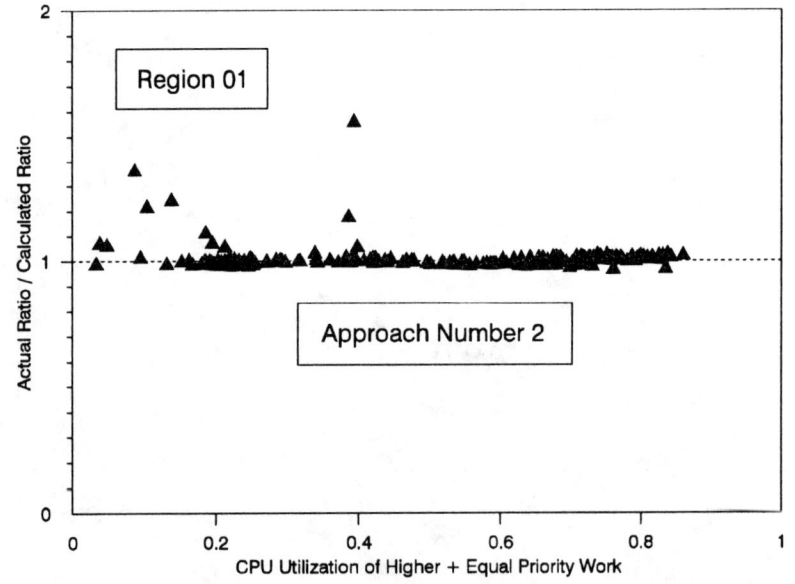

Figure 7.7 Comparison of actual dispatch service ratio to calculated dispatch service ratio. This is a measure of the effectiveness of algortihms to estimate system-wide processor contention.

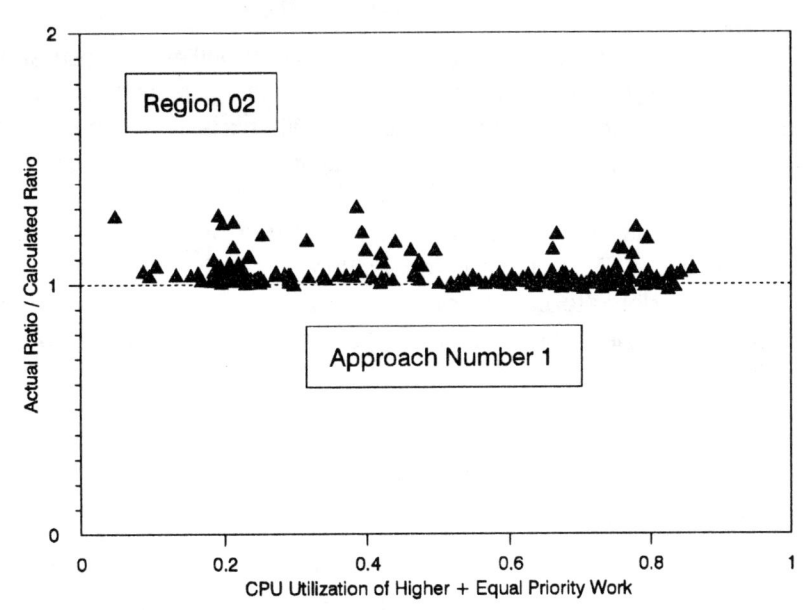

Figure 7.8 Comparison of actual dispatch service ratio to calculated dispatch service ratio. This is a measure of the effectiveness of algortihms to estimate system-wide processor contention.

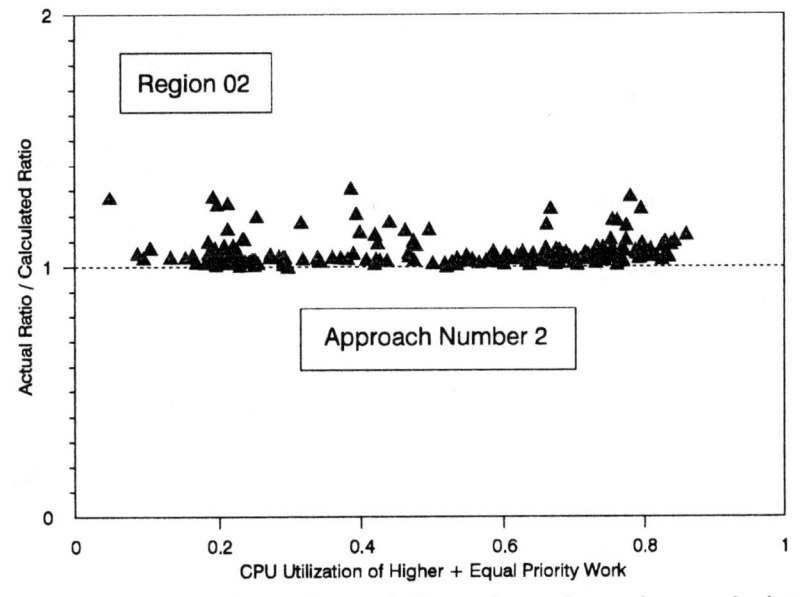

Figure 7.9 Comparison of actual dispatch service ratio to calculated dispatch service ratio. This is a measure of the effectiveness of algortihms to estimate system-wide processor contention.

Figures 7.6 through 7.9 all show a number of outliers. These stray observations represent periods in which something unusual occurred, such as a storage violation or system dump. When a large dump is taken, a significant amount of elapsed time can occur with little CPU usage. This will cause high dispatch time values.

All four charts show a fairly good correlation between actual and predicted values. As a general observation, it appears that approach 1 will slightly understate service at lower levels of utilization and slightly overstate it at higher levels. Approach 2 seems to provide a slightly better overall fit than approach 1.

7.8 NOTES ON CALIBRATING DISPATCH AND CPU DEMAND CALCULATIONS

It is worth noting that estimates developed in Figures 7.6 through 7.9 all used service multipliers from an electronic version of Appendix C. In most environments, CICS will be treated as a favored workload, and most competing workloads will not dominate processors for long periods of time. With this stipulation, the tables in Appendix C should produce reasonably good estimates of competing dispatch service.

In some cases, though, MVS tasks running with a higher priority than CICS will not only use a large amount of CPU time, but will hold a processor for long periods. Depending on the MVS dispatching algorithms used, workloads of this type can be disruptive to tasks with lower priorities. Instead of enjoying a steady, random flow of processing, lower-priority work may be dispatched less frequently. Such delays can cause tasks to wait longer to receive CPU service.

When CICS is running in a nondedicated environment or with disruptive or hostile workloads, it may be necessary to use tables in Appendix B or even in Appendix A to account for the affects of hostile workloads or bunching. When it is necessary to use these latter tables to estimate dispatch contention, average response times may not reflect the true nature of service. It is likely that service will be uneven and inconsistent.

The best way to decide which set of tables to use is to experiment with your own data. When you do, be sure to use many samples from a wide range of activity including both periods with very high and very low utilization. It is easier to spot patterns if data are graphed similar to that shown in Figures 7.6 through 7.9.

You may find that, after accounting for standard delays, the tables in Appendixes C, B, and A all consistently understate dispatch time at higher levels of processor utilization. In this case, you can be sure that the CICS region is competing with some hostile or disruptive workload and is not receiving regular access to processors. Something in your environment is disrupting normal CPU dispatching, causing service to be neither regular nor consistent.

> **Key Point:** The tables in Appendix C normally provide the best indication of MVS dispatch contention for CICS workloads. However, in some environments, the tables in Appendixes A or B may provide better estimates. The choice of which tables to use depends on the type of processing in the MVS tasks that compete with CICS for dispatch service.

One of the steps in both Approaches 1 and 2 is to adjust both dispatch time and CPU demand for hidden delays. This author's experience has been that a value between 3 and 8 percent seems to work for most CICS/MVS regions. In most environments, there are differences between dispatch time and CPU time that cannot be explained solely by queueing or other measurable delays. These differences appear even at very low levels of CPU utilization. The easiest way to estimate this value is to use the ratio of actual to estimated dispatch times for periods when competing CPU utilization is very low. Unexplained differences represent the hidden delays.

A good way to calibrate dispatch processing is to calculate a series of dispatch ratios and plot them in a graph similar to those show in Figures 7.6 through 7.9. If there are many outliers, you either have included data from unusual periods (perhaps including outages) or have not accounted for all the factors influencing dispatch time in your environment. If you are running vendor software that performs operating system services directly, activity in that software may explain some of the variance. A good place to look would be at any vendor products running in the CICS region that have their own SVCs or do nonstandard processing. Chances are that most CICS application packages and optimizers will not be the cause of such outliers.

Once you have accounted for all factors and have eliminated unusual periods, the actual to calculated ratios should approximate either a straight line or a curve. If the graph shows a line parallel to the X-axis with values close to 1.0, then you have accounted for most of the factors affecting MVS dispatch times. If estimated values are consistently low at higher levels of utilization, you may need to switch from the tables in Appendix C to those in Appendix B or Appendix A.

7.9 Estimating CPU Related Delays — An Example

It is not likely that the two approaches outlined above will be used regularly in day-to-day performance analysis. However, these techniques provide the foundation upon which more advanced processes are based. In this example, we will look at how to use these techniques to evaluate CPU constraint. Later, we will look at how these techniques can be used to compare CICS performance on unlike processors.

Let us assume that we have been asked to analyze CPU degradation in a *CICS/MVS* region. We would like to determine what portion of response time is associated with delays receiving CPU service.

We know the following about the CICS region:

- CICS internal response time is 2.5 seconds.

- Average CPU time is 50 ms.

- The region is using a processor about 65 percent of the time.

- The region is experiencing 2 page-ins per second from external storage and 90 page-ins per second from expanded storage. Page service time from external storage is measured at 20 ms. Page service time from expanded storage is estimated to be about 200 microseconds (0.2 ms).

The processor contains four processor engines and is 95 percent busy. An on-line monitor shows that 20 other CICS regions are running at the same dispatching priority as this region. As a group, they are consuming 50 percent of the processor. The monitor also shows that lower priority MVS tasks are using only about 15 percent of the CPU. All other CPU time can be charged to higher-priority tasks or CPU overhead. The region is not running DB2, or IMS/DBCTL, or a VSAM subtask.

Our goal is to estimate what portion of the 2.5-second CICS internal response time is associated with CPU-related delays The steps we follow would include:

1. The first several steps determine *CPU demand* for the *primary TCB*. Since neither VSAM subtasking nor databases are being used in this CICS/MVS region, it is probably safe to assume that the primary

Paging, MVS Priorities, and Processor Speed

(CICS main) TCB is using almost all the CPU time consumed in the region. Thus, the CICS main TCB should be using a CPU 65 percent of the time. It also should be safe to assume that all paging activity is associated with the CICS main TCB.

2. We know that the processor is about 95 percent busy. From the information given, we can see that:
   a. 15 percent of the CPU used is being consumed by lower-priority tasks.
   b. 50 percent is being used by a group of CICS regions that share the same dispatching priority as the region being studied.
   c. 30 percent is associated with higher priority tasks and system overhead.

3. We will use approach 2 to estimate the effect of system-wide processor contention. The first two steps in approach 2 estimate CPU use by higher priority tasks and select an appropriate service multiplier

   We know that higher-priority tasks (including MVS overhead) use 30 percent of the total processor. We have estimated that this CPU activity is associated with the equivalent of about 30 tasks. Table C.4 in Appendix C shows a service multiplier of 1.01 when four servers are 30 percent busy serving 30 customers.

   Therefore, the service multiplier associated with higher-priority workloads is 1.01.

4. The next two steps in Approach 2 determine total CPU usage for all higher- or equal-priority tasks and select an appropriate service multiplier. Table C.4 is used again. The column for 50 customers (30 higher-priority + 20 equal-priority) that are 80 percent busy shows a service multiplier of 1.16.

   Therefore, the service multiplier associated with equal and higher priority workloads is 1.16.

5. The next step is to calculate the service multiplier for dispatch time and CPU demand. As shown earlier in this chapter, the formula is:

$$\text{service multiplier}_{\text{CICS region}} = \frac{\text{service multiplier}_{\text{high}+\text{equal}} - \frac{\%\ \text{busy}_{\text{high}}}{\%\ \text{busy}_{\text{high}+\text{equal}}} \times \text{service multiplier}_{\text{high}}}{\frac{\%\ \text{busy}_{\text{equal}}}{\%\ \text{busy}_{\text{high}+\text{equal}}}}$$

$$\text{service multiplier} = \frac{1.16 - (\frac{.30}{.80} \times 1.01)}{\frac{.50}{.80}} = \frac{1.16 - .379}{.625} = 1.25$$

6. Using the service multiplier calculated above, we can start the calculation of average dispatch time per transaction and CPU demand. Multiplying the 50 ms CPU time per transaction by 1.25, our initial calculation of dispatch time per transaction is 62.5 ms. Similarly, the CICS main TCB should be using or trying to use the CPU 81.3 percent of the time (.65 times 1.25). Dispatch time per transaction should be at least 62.5 ms, and CPU demand should be at least .813.

7. The next step is to adjust CPU demand to account for hidden delays. An estimate of 6 percent is being used in this example. The estimate for CPU demand increases to 86.2 percent (.813 x 1.06).

8. The delays associated with page-ins from external storage are now added to CPU demand. We know that this CICS region is experiencing 2 page-ins per second and that page service time is 20 ms. Paging should contribute 40 ms per second to CPU demand. The estimate of CPU demand increases to 90.2 percent, accounting for the effect of paging.

$$\text{CPU demand} = \frac{862 \text{ ms} + (2 \times 20 \text{ ms})}{1,000 \text{ ms}} = \frac{902 \text{ ms}}{1,000 \text{ ms}} = .902$$

9. We know that this address space is experiencing 90 page-ins per second from expanded storage. We have estimated that it should take about 200 microseconds to resolve a page fault from expanded storage on this class processor. (See page 173 for a discussion of how to estimate the length of time it should take to resolve page faults from expanded storage.) Thus, page-ins from expanded storage would add another 18 ms per second to CPU demand (90 page faults per second times 200 microseconds per page fault). With this, CPU demand should be 920 ms (902 ms + 18 ms) per second or 92 percent. *The primary TCB should be using or trying to use the processor about 920 ms per second, or about 92 percent of the time.*

10. Dispatch time per transaction should be adjusted for the effects of hidden delays and paging in the same way that CPU demand was adjusted above. CPU demand increased 13 percent (.813 to .92);

Paging, MVS Priorities, and Processor Speed 199

average dispatch time also should be adjusted by 13 percent. Total dispatch time per transaction should be about 70.6 ms (62.5 ms x 1.13).

11. In this example we will assume that other delays are minor and can be ignored. Therefore, total CPU demand should be .92 (920 ms per second) and average dispatch time per transaction should be 70.6 ms.

12. Total CPU-related service time is the product of dispatch time per transaction and the appropriate service multiplier. As we did in Chapter 6, we will use an iterative technique to estimate dispatch service time and queueing. Table B.1 (Appendix B) shows a minimum service multiplier of 4.20 for a single server that is 92 percent busy. Table A.1 (Appendix A) shows that the maximum service multiplier should be about 12.50. (Refer to Chapter 6 for a discussion of the rationale behind this approach.) This means that dispatch service time including internal queueing should be between 296.5 and 882.5 ms.

Minimum dispatch related service = 4.20 × 70.6 ms = 296.5 ms

Maximum dispatch related service = 12.50 × 70.6 ms = 882.5 ms

13. The minimum and maximum server return ratios can be estimated using the maximum and minimum dispatch times calculated above. The server return ratio is the ratio of time waiting for other services to time actually dispatched on the primary TCB. (Remember that CICS internal transaction response time consists of dispatch time, queueing for dispatch, and other waits.) Average transaction response time is 2.5 seconds (2,500 ms), and between 296.5 and 882.5 ms of response time should be spent waiting for dispatch service. Therefore, somewhere between 1,617.5 and 2,203.5 ms of response time should be associated with other delays.

$$\text{Maximum return ratio} = \frac{(2{,}500 \text{ ms} - 296.5 \text{ ms})}{70.6 \text{ ms}} = \frac{2{,}203.5 \text{ ms}}{70.6 \text{ ms}} = 31.2$$

$$\text{Minimum return ratio} = \frac{(2{,}500 \text{ ms} - 882.5 \text{ ms})}{70.6 \text{ ms}} = \frac{1{,}617.5 \text{ ms}}{70.6 \text{ ms}} = 22.9$$

14. Using the estimated minimum and maximum return ratios, we narrow the service multiplier and total dispatch service. Using the columns for return ratios "20" and "40" in Table B.1 show service multipliers of 5.13 and 6.53 in the .92 utilization row.

    Repeating steps 12 and 13 with the new range of service multipliers, dispatch-related service should be between 362.2 and 461.0 ms. Therefore, the server return ratio should be between 28.9 and 30.3. Repeating steps 12 and 13 with return ratios of 25 and 40, dispatch-related service should be between 390.4 and 461.0 ms. The new range of return ratios is 28.9 and 29.9.

    The return ratio should be a little less than 30, and the service multiplier should be a bit less than 5.89. Using this service multiplier, we can project that *total dispatch-related delays should be slightly less than 415.8 ms.*

    Transactions running in this CICS region should spend about .42 seconds trying to receive CPU service. This time would be broken down as follows: 50 ms actually receiving CPU service; 20.6 ms in operating system delays (higher-priority tasks, paging, etc.); and 345.2 ms queued within CICS for dispatch service.

    Key Point: The techniques developed so far allow us to analyze the causes of CPU contention within CICS regions. In the following section, we will build on these techniques and look at how to compare CICS processing on different types of processors.

7.10 EVALUATING HOW CICS APPLICATIONS WILL PERFORM ON DIFFERENT PROCESSORS

One of the more difficult decisions facing anyone involved in planning performance is how will existing workloads perform on a new processor. Typically, we might be interested in few processor alternatives, and we probably will not have access to the any of them. We would be faced with the task of evaluating potential performance without being able to run existing workloads on proposed configurations.

We need two types of information to compare CICS performance on different processors. First, we must have *information about existing workloads*. This information is similar to that previously discussed in this chapter. We would need to know about the resources used by CICS and other workloads.

Second, we need estimates of processor differences. For CICS workloads, the *relative speed of the individual processor engines* is very important. In processors with similar processing capacity, the speed of individual processor engines can make a significant difference in transaction response times. The *number of processor engines and total processor power* are also important. Total processor power and the number of CPU engines influence MVS dispatching delays.

We also need information about other hardware features, such as the *amount of real and expanded storage*, the *number of channels*, and *relative channel speeds*. Normally, the amount of memory is important because it affects the number of page faults and the amount of paging. As discussed above, these affect CPU demand and overall CPU utilization.

The number of channels and channel speeds may not be immediate concerns. As a rule, faster channel speeds are a factor only if existing DASD and controllers can take advantage of them. Differences in channels or channel speeds tend to affect long term performance potential and capacity more than specific performance at the time of a conversion. Until existing peripheral equipment can use new features, they will not affect performance differences.

7.10.1 How to Project CICS Performance on Different Processor Configurations

In the material below, we will look at how to compare CICS performance on different processors. First, we will outline a procedure for comparing CICS performance when CICS workloads are moved to a different processor. Following the outline, we will develop an example showing how it can be used.

We will assume that the workload currently exists and can be measured on an existing processor. We also will assume that we do not have access to the second processor. We will refer to the first processor as the *existing* processor. We will refer to the second processor as the *unknown* processor. It is "unknown" in the sense that it is not available upon which to run the CICS workload. We have information about the unknown processor but cannot use it to run our CICS workload. If the workload could be run on the "unknown" processor, the task of estimating performance would be simplified, and we could use the procedures outlined earlier in this chapter to compare processor performance.

Processor comparisons often are associated with the acquisition of new hardware. Consequently, such comparisons usually are performed thoroughly and carefully. When comparing processors, we should evaluate data for multiple CICS regions and multiple periods. Normally, though, we would concentrate on CICS regions experiencing high CPU demand or running high volumes of transactions.

A. Gather data about the current CICS workload and environment. The steps in this section were all discussed earlier in this chapter. The reader is encouraged to review that material for additional detail or clarification.

1. Determine average CPU time and dispatch time per transaction on the existing processor. Our emphasis will be on CPU time and dispatch time for the primary CICS TCB. Chapter 6 discussed sources of this data and where to obtain it in different CICS environments.

2. **Determine the amount of CPU time used by the CICS primary TCB on the existing processor.** Normally we will select performance data from recurring peak periods. (Recurring peak periods were defined and discussed in Chapter 3.) We would want to evaluate periods in which total processing was most intense, and periods when the CICS regions was used most heavily. As a practical matter, we probably will examine several periods to prevent anomalies or quirks in data from skewing our results.

3. **Determine the total amount of CPU time being used by higher and equal priority MVS tasks on the existing processor.** Two pieces of data are needed: The amount of CPU time used by higher-priority MVS workloads and the amount of CPU time used by higher- plus equal-priority workloads. We discussed how to obtain this information earlier in this chapter.

4. **Estimate the portion of dispatch time caused by competition from MVS tasks.** Approach 1 or approach 2, presented earlier in this chapter, can be used to estimate the effect of systemwide CPU use on dispatch processing. Tables C.1 through C.8 normally will be used to estimate processor contention. As was mentioned earlier in this chapter, it might be necessary to use tables in Appendixes B or

A instead of Appendix C if there are hostile or disruptive workloads running at higher priorities than CICS workloads.

5. **Add a factor to account for hidden delays.** A multiplier of 1.03 to 1.08 will be appropriate in most situations.

6. **Determine the effect of paging on the existing processor.** Even if both processor configurations have the same amount of memory, the effect of paging and page faults resolved from expanded storage should be estimated separately for each processor.

7. **Determine the effect of other delays on CPU demand.** These include file open and close commands in CICS/VS and CICS/MVS and VSAM CI and CA splits for files accessed via NSR.

B. **Estimate CPU usage on the unknown processor — average CPU time per transaction and CPU time used by the primary TCB.**

1. **Estimate average CPU time per transaction on the unknown processor.** The only way to know with certainty how much CPU time it will take to run a given workload on a given processor is to run the workload on that processor. Since this is usually not possible ahead of time, the next best approach is to use one or more processor rating scales published by various vendors.

   We start by estimating the *ratio of engine speeds on the two processors*. This is done by comparing processor speeds for the largest uniprocessors in each processor series. For example, an IBM 3090 model 180J is a uniprocessor with the same engine speed other larger J-class processors such as 3090-400J or 3090-600J processors.

   To calculate CPU usage per transaction on the unknown processor, we calculate the ratio of processing power of the unknown to processing power of existing uniprocessors. Then we divide average CPU time per transaction by the ratio. This provides an indication of how much CPU time it will take to execute similar transactions on the unknown processor. If the "unknown" uniprocessor was rated at 20 and the existing uniprocessor at 15, we would divide CPU time per transaction by 1.33 (20 / 15).

   Processor scales are provided by hardware vendors, leasing companies, consulting groups, and software vendors. There is often considerable variety in estimates of relative processor performance in different rating scales. One scale may rate one processor more powerful than another, while another scale may rate them just the opposite. All ratings are workload-dependent, and there are no absolute answers. If major differences exist between rating scales, you may want to consult multiple sources, average the differences, or review differences experienced by others in similar environments. Of course, when comparing processor ratings, *always pick pairs of ratings from the same vendor.*

Key Point: It is important to remember that processor performance is closely related to the nature of workloads. One workload may receive the equivalent of a 15 percent boost in processor power when moved to a different processor while another workload may be almost unaffected. Even CICS workloads at the same installation may receive widely differing performance results when moved to a different processors.

2. **Estimate CPU time used by the primary TCB on the unknown processor.** The ratio developed in Step B.1 above also is applied to CPU utilization for the primary TCB. Processor differences that affect CPU time per transaction also affect the amount of CPU time used by the primary TCB.

3. **Estimate the amount of CPU time that will be used by higher and equal priority tasks on the unknown processor.** We again need to refer to processor rating scales, but this time to look at specific processor models. First we calculate the ratio of total processor power on the two processors. Then we divide the CPU utilization percentages developed in step A.3 by this ratio. This provides an estimate of time the unknown processor will spend servicing higher- and equal-priority MVS workloads.

    Be aware that differences in processor ratings can be more severe for processors as a whole than for individual processor engines. Not only will there be perceived differences in individual processor speeds, but there will be differences in estimates of the multi-processor overhead.

4. **Estimate the effect of paging on the unknown processor.** Even if both processors have the same amount of memory, paging needs to be included in the calculation of CPU demand. Remember that differences in processor speed influence the time it takes to resolve

page faults and move pages from expanded storage. Differences in engine (uniprocessor) speed may be the best indicator of how much time it will take to resolve page faults from expanded storage.

Let us assume that it takes 200 microseconds to resolve a page fault from expanded storage on the existing processor. Let us also assume that engine speed on the "unknown" processor is supposed to be 1.33 times as fast as on the existing processor. It is likely that it should take about 150 microseconds (200 microseconds / 1.33) to resolve page faults from expanded storage on the unknown processor.

C. **Estimate CPU demand for the unknown processor.**

1. **Calculate dispatch delays associated with competition from MVS tasks on the unknown processor.** The same approach (approach 1 or approach 2) should be selected for this step that was used in step A.4. If the number of processor engines is different on the two processors, you will need to select a different table than was used in step A.4.

2. **Account for hidden delays on the unknown processor.** The same multiplier should be used in this step that was used in step A.5.

3. **Calculate the effects of paging on dispatch time and CPU demand for the unknown processor.** If processors have different amounts of real or expanded storage, paging and page migration rates should be adjusted appropriately. Page migration time should be adjusted based on the relative difference of individual processor engine speeds.

4. **Adjust transaction dispatch time and CPU demand on the unknown processor for other factors such as file opens and VSAM CI or CA splits.** These delays should be similar to those obtained in step A.7.

D. **Estimate transaction response time on the unknown processor.**

1. **Calculate total dispatch-related service including CICS internal queueing.** As we did earlier in the chapter, we will use Table B.1 to obtain a service multiplier for CICS internal dispatch processing. In this step, though, we will not need to use an iterative approach. We

already have an estimate of total dispatch time and other delays per transaction. From this, we can calculate a server return ratio. The return ratio is then used to select a service multiplier directly from Table B.1.

Total dispatch-related time is simply the product of the service multiplier and average dispatch time. This would be *the total amount of delay associated with receiving CPU service on the primary CICS TCB.* This time includes internal queueing within CICS for dispatch service.

Some caution may be necessary here since the duration of other CICS delays might change on the unknown processor. If, for example, the unknown processor had faster channel speeds that would be exploited, it may be necessary to revise the return ratio appropriately. If some of the "other delays" include requests shipped to other CICS regions via function shipping, these delays can change on the unknown processor. Such differences can affect the duration of other delays and the server return ratio.

E. **Estimate the delays associated with other MVS TCBs running in the CICS region.**

1. **Estimate the difference in processor-related delays for other subtasks running in the CICS region.** If additional CICS TCBs are being used, it may be worth calculating dispatch queueing delays for each. The same process would be used that was used for the primary TCB. Usually, the amount of CPU demand on the RO, CO, and VSAM TCBs is small enough that it is not significant in comparing processors.

    The main reason other TCBs have been given so little attention in this discussion is that they seldom consume enough CPU time to drive queueing very high. Even if a VSAM or CO TCB were busy as much as 20 to 30 percent of the time (extremely high values for most CICS systems), the internal service multiplier would only be 1.1 to 1.3. Total dispatch service time including queueing would be no more than 1.1 to 1.3 times average dispatch time. A task requiring 5 ms of dispatch service on the CO TCB (again, very high for most CICS environments) would take 5.5 to 6.5 ms to receive that service. In other words, dispatch queueing for the RO, CO, and VSAM subtasks should be insignificant most of the time.

DB2 and IMS/DBCTL TCBs also may be considered, but a slightly different approach will be taken. Database TCBs would be affected only by pure engine speed and MVS-related processor competition. The amount of CPU time per transaction would be adjusted by the same factor used in step B.1. This CPU value would then be subject to contention by higher and competing MVS workloads. Since only one CICS task would be connected to a database TCB at a time, there is no need to calculate internal processor queueing for the database TCBs. Instead, CICS tasks would wait for the opportunity to use database TCBs (actually, threads).

F. Compare the total CPU-related service time on the unknown processor to that on the existing processor.

Each CICS region and period should be analyzed separately when estimating differences between processors. A new processor must satisfy multiple workloads at different times of the day.

So far we have considered only dispatch-related delays within a single CICS region. When CICS applications access resources in other CICS regions, chances are that service times for these resources will change on different processors. To get the complete picture of processor differences, each delay should be analyzed. The sum of all the differences will be the total difference in performance.

7.10.2 Example – Estimating CICS Performance on an Unknown Processor

We will use the same data developed in Section 7.9 (see page 196) to illustrate how to estimate CICS processing on an unknown processor. In that section, we evaluated the components of dispatch queueing for an existing CICS workload. We will restate information from that example and will add information about an unknown processor. The following information applies:

- A CICS/MVS region in which neither DB2 nor VSAM subtasking are running.

- A one hour period is being examined. During that hour, average CICS response time was 2.5 seconds.

- Average CPU time per transaction was 50 ms.

- The CPU contains four processor engines and was 95 percent busy overall.
  - 30 percent of the CPU was consumed by higher-priority workloads and MVS overhead.
  - 50 percent was used by competing workloads – primarily other CICS regions.
  - 15 percent was used by lower-priority workloads.
- The primary TCB was using 65 percent of a processor (65 percent CPU busy).
- In Section 7.9 we calculated average dispatch time per transaction to be 70.6 ms. We will assume that we found measured dispatch time to be 72 ms per second. There will always be some minor differences due to timing, random variance, and other delays we cannot estimate. Since our estimate is close to actual, we will ignore this minor difference. The difference could have been caused by random variance or by hidden dispatching costs. If estimates are consistently lower than actual, it is probably an indication of hidden dispatching costs. We will assume that we were able to determine that the difference was attributable to random variance.
- The CICS region was experiencing 2 page-ins per second from external storage and 90 page-ins from expanded storage. Average page service time from external storage was measured as 20 ms; page service time from expanded storage was estimated to be 200 microseconds. We estimated that external paging was contributing 40 ms per second and paging from expanded storage was contributing 18 ms per second to CPU demand.
- We calculated CPU demand to be 92 percent.
- We estimated it would take a task about 415.8 ms to receive dispatch service:
  - 50 ms actually using the CPU
  - 20.6 ms waiting for the effects of processor contention, hidden delays, and paging delays.
  - 345.2 ms queued within CICS for dispatch service.

We know the following about the *unknown* processor:

- The unknown processor is a three-engine processor.

- The unknown processor is supposed to be 1.03 times as powerful as the existing processor overall. This assessment was derived using several processor rating scales.
- Engine speed on the unknown processor is believed to be 1.3 times as powerful as engine speed on the existing processor.
- The unknown processor will have the same amount of real and expanded storage as existing processor.

Using this information, we will use the steps outlined above to compare CPU-related delays on the two processors.

A. Gather data about the current CICS workload and environment.

All the information that would have been developed in steps A.1 through A.6 was stated above.

B. Estimate CPU usage on the unknown processor – average CPU time per transaction and CPU time used by the primary TCB.

1. **Estimate average CPU per transaction on the unknown processor.** CPU time per transaction in this CICS region is 50 ms on the existing processor. We understand that the unknown processor has an engine speed 1.3 times as fast as the existing processor. (As we mentioned earlier, we cannot be sure exactly how much CPU time the workload will use on the unknown processor.)

    Average CPU time per transaction should be about 38.5 ms on the unknown processor (50 ms / 1.3).

2. **Estimate CPU time used by the primary TCB on the unknown processor.** We will again use the expected difference in engine speeds. The primary TCB was 65 percent busy on the existing processor.

    The same workload should use 50.0 percent (.65 / 1.3) *of a processor engine on the unknown processor.*

3. **Estimate the amount of CPU time that will be used by higher and equal priority tasks on the unknown processor.** Higher-priority MVS workloads (including MVS overhead) used 30 percent of the existing processor; tasks with the same dispatching priority used 50 percent. As a whole, the unknown processor is supposed to be about 1.03 times as powerful as the existing processor.

Higher-priority work should use about 29.1 percent (.30 / 1.03), and higher- plus equal-priority work should use about 77.7 percent (.80 / 1.03) of the unknown processor.

It is worth noting that a different processor ratio was used in Step B.3 than was used in steps B.1 and B.2. The first two steps used the ratio of uni-processor speeds; this third step used the ratio of total processor power. In the first two steps we were looking at CPU usage within a single region; in this step, we are concerned with processor-wide workloads.

4. **Estimate the effect of paging on the unknown processor.** The unknown processor will have the same amount of real and expanded storage as the existing processor. Assuming similar memory reference patterns, the unknown processor should experience about 2 page-ins per second from external storage. We will assume similar page service times on both processors.

Page-ins from external storage should add 40 ms per second to CPU demand on the unknown processor.

The number of page-ins from expanded storage also should be about the same on the unknown processor as it was on the existing processor. However, the processor engine is 1.3 times faster on the unknown machine. It should take less time to service page faults from expanded storage.

Page-ins from expanded storage should add about 13.8 ms per second (18 ms per second / 1.3) *to CPU demand.*

C. **Estimate CPU demand for the unknown processor.**

1. **Calculate dispatch delays associated with competition from MVS tasks on the unknown processor.** Since we used approach 2 in estimating CPU demand for the existing processor, we should use this approach to calculate CPU demand and dispatch time for the unknown processor. We begin by calculating the service multiplier.

In step B.3 we estimated that higher-priority workloads will use 29.1 percent of the unknown processor and that higher- plus equal-priority workloads would use 77.7 percent. The corresponding service multipliers from Table C.3 (the unknown processor has three processor engines) are approximately 1.02 and 1.25. Using the service multiplier formula from approach 2, we can estimate degradation from MVS tasks:

Paging, MVS Priorities, and Processor Speed

$$\text{service multiplier} = \frac{\text{service multiplier}_{high+equal} - \frac{\%\ busy_{high}}{\%\ busy_{high+equal}} \times \text{service multiplier}_{high}}{\frac{\%\ busy_{equal}}{\%\ busy_{high+equal}}}$$

$$\text{service multiplier} = \frac{1.25 - (\frac{.291}{.777} \times 1.02)}{\frac{.486}{.777}} = \frac{1.25 - .382}{.625} = 1.39$$

In step B.2 we estimated that the primary TCB for this CICS region would use about 50.0 percent of a processor. This is multiplied by the service multiplier of 1.39 to estimate the effect of competition from other MVS workloads. *CPU demand would be at least .695* (.50 x 1.39). The CICS/MVS main TCB should be trying to use a processor at least 69.5 percent of the time.

CPU time per transaction should be about 38.5 ms on the unknown processor. Including processor competition, *dispatch time per transaction should be at least 53.5 ms* (38.5 ms x 1.39).

2. **Account for hidden delays on the unknown processor.** We should use the same multiplier of 1.06 that was used for the existing processor. CPU demand should increase to 73.7 percent (.695 x 1.06) and dispatch time to 56.7 ms (53.5 ms x 1.06).

3. **Calculate the effects of paging on dispatch time and CPU demand for the unknown processor.** In step B.4, we estimated paging delays would be 40 and 13.8 ms for external and expanded paging, respectively. With the effect of paging, CPU demand should be about 79.1 percent [(737 + 40 +13.8) ms / second]. Similarly, dispatch time per transaction should increase to 60.9 ms [56.7 ms x (.791 / .737)].

4. **Adjust transaction dispatch time and CPU demand on the unknown processor for other factors such as file opens and VSAM CI or CA splits.** In this example, we have assumed that no other delays except paging and contention from higher priority tasks will contribute to CPU demand. Therefore, CPU demand should be about 79.1 percent. Total dispatch time per transaction should be 60.9 ms on the unknown processor.

D. **Estimate transaction response time on the unknown processor.**

1. **Calculate total dispatch-related service including CICS internal queueing.** We will continue to use Table B.1 to obtain service multipliers for CICS dispatching delays including internal queueing. The selection of a service multiplier is simplified since we already know average dispatch time and the length of other delays.

   Response time on the existing processor was 2.5 seconds (2,500 ms). Of that time, approximately 415.8 ms was related to CPU dispatch time and queueing. Other CICS delays (DASD, etc.) accounted for 2,084.2 ms. We will assume that the duration of other delays does not change materially on the unknown processor. Thus, CICS transactions should wait about 2,084.2 ms for other delays on the unknown processor.

   Average dispatch time was estimated to be 60.9 ms. This means that the ratio of other waits to dispatch time (the server return ratio) should be about 34.2.

$$\text{Server return ratio} = \frac{\text{other delays}}{\text{dispatch time}} = \frac{2{,}084.2 \text{ ms}}{60.9 \text{ ms}} = 34.2$$

   CPU demand for the unknown processor was estimated to be about 79.1 percent. The server return ratio is between 30 and 40. The .80 server utilization row of Table B.1 shows service multipliers of 3.62 and 3.76 for return ratios of 30 and 40, respectively. Using these service multipliers, total dispatch-related delays should be between 220.5 ms (3.62 x 60.9 ms) and 229.0 ms (3.76 x 60.9 ms). *The total time associated with receiving CPU service on the unknown processor should be about 229.0 ms or less.*

E. **Estimate the delays associated with other MVS TCBs running in the CICS region.**

In this example, the CICS main TCB was the only TCB active in the region. If other tasks, such as the VSAM subtask, had been active, we might have attempted to calculate dispatch queueing for each. Usually, the amount of CPU time consumed by such TCBs will be small enough that internal queueing can be ignored. Furthermore, in CICS/MVS systems, it can be difficult to get good measures of CPU activity for the VSAM subtask.

F. **Compare the total CPU-related service time on the unknown processor to that on the existing processor.**

In this example, we estimated that CPU-related service should change from about 415.8 ms to less than 229.0 ms. Transaction response time would have improved by about .2 seconds simply because of reduced internal queueing in the CICS region.

Other CICS regions on the same processor also would benefit from reduced internal queueing. The level of improvement would be a factor of how much CPU time they used and their MVS dispatching priority. CICS regions with high CPU demand and relatively high dispatching priorities (compared to other workloads) will benefit the most from faster processor engines.

When CICS applications use MRO function shipping to access resources in other regions, each request experiences delays associated with dispatch service in the "ship-to" region. Improvements in dispatch service times will reduce function shipping delays. Thus, for transactions using function shipping, transaction response time could be reduced considerably more than the .2 seconds associated with internal dispatching.

To be rigorous, function shipping delays should be evaluated on a region by region basis, and these changes be added to internal changes. The total difference in CICS performance would include both internal improvements and changes in function shipping delays.

7.11 DIFFERENCES IN EQUIVALENT PROCESSORS

In the preceding example we showed that the performance of a CICS application can be influenced by the speed of processor engines. In the example, the two processors had about the same amount of total processing power. We stated that the unknown processor was expected to be about 1.03 times as powerful overall as the processor on which the existing workload had been run.

The most significant difference between the two processors was the difference in the speed of the two processor engines. In the example, it was stated that processor engines were 1.3 times faster on the unknown processor than on the existing one. Nearly all of the performance differences in these CICS workloads could be attributed to differences in processor speed.

> **Key Point:** As a rule, when two different processors have about the same amount of total power, the one with the fewest

number of engines normally should provide better service for CICS applications.

7.12 SUMMARY

This chapter has built slowly on a succession of ideas. It started with a discussion of differences in queueing systems. It then discussed paging (from both real and expanded storage), CI and CA splits, competition from other MVS tasks, and other elements that affect CICS dispatch time. Two approaches were suggested to account for the effect of MVS dispatch contention on CICS CPU service.

Next, the chapter showed how to bring all these factors together and determine their collective effect on transaction response time. A detailed example was provided showing how to estimate the effect of system delays on CICS performance.

Finally, the chapter presented a method of comparing CICS performance on different processors. We discussed how to estimate how an existing CICS workload would perform on a different type of processor. A methodology was presented along with a comprehensive example.

Much of the material in this chapter probably will not be used directly in day-to-day performance analysis or planning. However, the concepts presented in this chapter should be quite valuable for those evaluating or planning processor configurations for CICS workloads.

SELECTED READING

[ALLE84] Allen, Arnold O., "Getting Started in Analytic Modeling," *Conference Proceedings, CMG XV International Conference on the Management and Performance Evaluation of Computer Systems*, 1984.

[ALLE83] Allen, Arnold O., "Modeling of Computer Systems," *Proceedings of the 1983 Computer Measurement Group International Conference*, 1983.

[ALLE90] Allen, Arnold O., *Probability, Statistics, and Queueing Theory with Computer Science Applications*, 2d ed., Academic Press, San Diego, 1990.

[BARN91] Barnes, Steve, "CICS/ESA Dispatcher Operation," *CMG Transactions*, Summer, 1991.

[IBM001] IBM Technical Information Search items Q480337, Q544608.

[KING90] King, Peter J.B., *Computer and Communication Systems Performance Modelling*, Prentice Hall International (UK), Hertfordshire, Great Britain, 1990.

[MULL91] Mullen, John William, "MVS/ESA Dataspaces and HIPERSPACES: Measuring and Evaluating the Cost", *CMG Transactions*, Winter, 1991.

Chapter

8

SPE — Planning Application Performance

8.1 OVERVIEW

Software performance engineering (SPE) is a methodology used to design application software that will perform acceptably. In this chapter, we will look at how we can SPE to ensure that delivered systems have the potential to meet users' needs.

Chapter 8 is a key chapter in this book. The theme for this book is planning performance for CICS systems. In this context, SPE principles provide a structure for planning and controlling performance for CICS applications.

This chapter presents the author's impression of what SPE is and how it can be applied in a CICS environment. There are several pioneers in the field of SPE including Dr. Connie Smith, Dr. Thomas Bell, Dr. Anneliese von Mayrhauser, and others. Chapters 8, 9, and 10 draw from the specific methodology presented by Dr. Connie Smith in her book [SMIT90]. Credit for many of the ideas presented in these chapters must be given to those who developed this science and especially to Dr. Smith whose ideas have been the starting point for these three chapters.

SPE consists of two separate components: one that addresses how to evaluate application performance ahead of time and one that offers design guidelines for responsive application systems. This and the following chapters address the first component, that of helping ensure acceptable application performance when systems are installed. Chapter 10 explores how to design applications that are responsive, efficient, and effective.

8.1.1 Primary Audience

This chapter should be especially valuable for *application developers*. More than anyone else, they have the power to influence application performance through the design of application systems. In this chapter and in Chapter 9, application developers will be shown how to evaluate the consequences of design alternatives. Chapter 10 will provide tools to design efficient, responsive, and effective CICS application systems.

CICS systems programmers also should benefit from this chapter since they often become involved when applications fail to perform. With a knowledge of SPE, systems programmers can help application developers avoid the need for heavy tuning once CICS applications are installed. SPE can help systems programmers as they plan internal capacity for CICS regions.

Capacity planners should find SPE particularly helpful in planning future resource requirements. By becoming involved early in the design of new application systems, they have the opportunity to improve their forecasts of future hardware needs. SPE can help them avoid surprises and provides them better data for planning.

8.2 WHAT IS SOFTWARE PERFORMANCE ENGINEERING?

Software performance engineering is a two-part approach to ensure that applications can deliver acceptable performance. The first part, which we will discuss in this and the following chapter, provides a process for evaluating performance and capacity considerations early in the application life-cycle. The second part is a set of principles that contribute to the design of efficient, responsive application systems.

Over the past several years, many major systems have experienced significant performance-related problems that were not detected until applications were installed in production. The worst stories include applications that took years to develop at costs of tens of million of dollars that could not be used due to unacceptable system response. At some time or another, almost every major shop has had to struggle with poor performance in some large new system.

When application systems do not perform acceptably, several things usually occur:

- First, and most important, users are inconvenienced. If response time is a little "slow," users can do their work, but not as efficiently as they might like. Very slow response, though, may discourage or even prohibit use of the system.

- Systems programmers, performance analysts, and application developers usually have to spend time searching for the cause of unacceptable response time. Additional work is required to analyze performance.

- Normally some effort is made to tune either system resources or application processing. If tuning can solve the problem, no further effort is needed.

- If tuning does not produce acceptable results, it may be necessary to acquire more hardware. Of course, hardware cannot solve all problems, and financial resources may not be available to purchase or lease new hardware.

- When neither tuning nor hardware can provide acceptable solutions, it may be necessary to restructure or reengineer applications. This is usually an expensive, time-intensive process that can delay implementation by months or years.

- At the extreme, systems or portions of systems may be abandoned simply because they cannot be made to perform acceptably. This may not only inconvenience users, but it may affect corporate goals and competitiveness.

- Application systems that do not meet user service requirements usually represent an economic loss to the organization.

The value of SPE is that it provides a methodology for screening application performance throughout the development life-cycle. At various stages in the design process, user requirements and application performance are assessed. Inefficiencies can be identified when they are most easily and inexpensively corrected.

SPE includes *two separate components.* The first, which we will discuss in this chapter and Chapter 9, involves the *review and sizing of application systems.* The second component, which we will discuss in Chapter 10, centers on *design principles* that can help produce applications that perform efficiently and effectively. These design principles can be easily incorporated into existing design methodologies to improve overall application flow and performance.

> **Key Point:** Software Performance Engineering (SPE) consists of two components: (1) methods of assessing application performance; and (2) design principles that result in improved application efficiency and effectiveness.

8.3 SPE AND CICS

8.3.1 CICS Application Development in the Past — Why SPE Was *Not* Necessary

Over the past two decades, hardware has continually become more powerful while the cost per unit of service has declined. At the same time, users have been demanding increasingly sophisticated application systems. Most organizations have a steadily increasing application development backlog as users become ever more dependent on data processing services.

The result has been that application developers have been under pressure to design and implement systems quickly. They often must fight both tight schedules and limited people resources. With all of the challenges of delivering functional products in a timely manner, traditionally, there has been little time to deal with performance issues during application design.

Moreover, CICS applications used to be much simpler than they are today. Before the days of extended addressing and multiple-region environments, designers knew that only the most basic type of systems could perform well enough to run under CICS. The types of systems that would be developed were typically simple, with limited scope and functionality.

Structural limitations in early releases of CICS required many installations to develop rules governing the amount of memory, CPU time, and I/Os applications could use in CICS transactions. The scope of application systems running in CICS was routinely limited and controlled. Unless systems could fit into rigid design criteria, they would not be developed as CICS applications.

When CICS application systems were simpler and more tightly controlled, there was only a small chance of creating a system that could not be made to perform. There was little need to plan for performance when most problems could be easily resolved by tuning or adding hardware.

System programmers typically suggested the standards of what could be done in CICS applications. Then, if application systems had performance problems, it became the responsibility of the system programmer to locate the cause and take corrective action. If VSAM files were on a volume that was "too busy," they could be moved to another, less active volume. If CICS regions were constrained (usually by virtual storage or by CPU demand), additional CICS regions could be created.

If the capacity of the hardware was not adequate, systems developers would look to capacity planners to resolve the problem. Capacity planners were expected to forecast how much hardware capacity would be required.

> **Key Point:** In early CICS systems, systems programmers and capacity planners had more influence over application performance than did application developers. With limited design alternatives, performance was more of a technical issue than a design issue.

In those days, application developers could focus their efforts on application functions and user deadlines. They did not need to worry about performance as long as they used "common sense" (which meant "Don't do anything overly elaborate") and followed the written or implied application design guidelines that were then common.

8.3.2 CICS Application Development Today – The Need for SPE

CICS's architecture has expanded significantly over the past two decades. Features such as extended addressing, expanded storage, large VSAM buffer pools, program execution "above the line," MRO/ISC, and COBOL II have all helped define a powerful processing environment in which transactions can perform massive amounts of work and still deliver reasonable service.

Much more work can be done in CICS transactions while still delivering acceptable service. Large CICS transactions can run without disrupting CICS performance or creating unworkable bottlenecks. The need to set rigid standards for application design has all but disappeared.

For example, all CICS application programs once needed to reside and execute below the 16-megabyte line. Because of limitations in the size of the MVS private area, most installations limited program size. When programs could move above the line, and large amounts of real and expanded storage became affordable, the need to restrict program size diminished. Many CICS application programs today are massive, performing a myriad of functions. The primary restrictions on program size now are maintainability and installation guidelines on modularity.

Another example of how CICS workloads have changed is in the number of file accesses per transaction. Applications that take advantage of data tables or large LSR buffer pools can perform dozens or even hundreds of file requests and still deliver subsecond response time. A tremendous amount of work can be accomplished in CICS systems while still delivering acceptable performance.

With increased performance potential, CICS application systems have become increasingly complex and elaborate. Users expect more of today's systems, and developers are continually creating more complex business applications. There is almost no limit to the type of applications that might be designed. Application boundaries are limited only by the imagination and ambition of system developers.

Most large shops no longer set rigid limits on what is allowed in CICS transactions. Modern hardware and software technology have eliminated the need to restrict CICS applications. It is common to find CICS transactions that run for minutes (or even hours). Transactions that perform thousands of file accesses are common today. System designs considered unreasonable a few years ago are now commonplace.

This is where the risk begins. Since it is possible to design massively complex CICS applications that can perform acceptably, it is no longer obvious what is or is not acceptable application design. With all the advances in hardware and software, there is no clear-cut limit on how much work can be done in CICS applications.

Furthermore, trade-offs between resource usage and cost are not intuitively obvious. It is still expensive to keep large amounts of data in memory. However, with large application systems only a fraction of all data can be kept in processor storage. Most large processors service many applications, and each can only expect to take advantage of a portion of the resources available.

The presence of relational database systems, especially DB2, further complicates matters. There is a strong inverse correlation between the complexity of database design and the level of performance that can be delivered. Simple DB2 systems can perform quite well but do not provide the flexibility application developers require. Complex designs can be made to perform, but frequently only with difficulty.

Single SQL calls can perform so much work that it is hard to get a good handle on what is really being done. It can be hard to tell ahead of time exactly what DB2 will choose to do in any given situation. Many shops are unpleasantly surprised either by the performance or resource costs of their first CICS/DB2 systems.

Thus, while almost anything is "possible" today, many designs are not practical. In reality, there is no way to configure systems powerful enough to provide acceptable response time for some kinds of system design.

Application developers can be expected to take advantage of all the tools and facilities afforded them. There is no reason for them to avoid certain features or facilities just because they are sometimes misused. Every tool has its benefits and its costs. It is only with wisdom that a balance between functionality, performance, and cost can be achieved.

> **Key Point:** SPE helps prevent surprises. Application systems that incorporate performance goals early in the design process are more likely to run acceptably when installed. Although system tuning options are more powerful than ever, there are limits to what tuning can accomplish. The risk of application failure due to unacceptable performance is higher for large, complex application systems, particularly those that exploit newer technology.

8.4 SPE — OVERALL STRATEGY

SPE stresses the use of available data to assess potential application performance. In the early stages of application design, little detailed information is available. However, enough general information is normally available to assess whether a proposal is close to reasonable. If a system requires average CICS response time of 2 seconds but early analysis suggests a range of 10 to 20 seconds, the design will need some work.

As application design matures, additional data will become available. With this information, application performance and capacity projections can be refined. Figure 8.1 depicts some tasks that can be performed in various phases of the project life-cycle.

Requirements definition phase. After a project has been approved and resources allocated, the first steps are to *define and document applica-*

Requirements Definition	Determine performance requirements. Perform preliminary assessment of application requirements, capacity, and potential performance.
Early Design Phase	Determine if design can meet performance requirements or function within the proposed configuration.
Mature Design Phase	Develop more accurate assessment of performance and capacity requirements.
System Test	Measure test results and determine if they match earlier projections.
Implementation	Compare production performance and resource usage with projections.
Maintenance Phase	Evaluate the effect of changes and growth on long term performanc and capacity.

Figure 8.1 SPE activities that occur during different phases of the application development life-cycle.

tion requirements. Application developers work with users to establish the scope of the project and the general characteristics of systems.

The primary SPE objectives in this phase are to discover system performance requirements and the general flow of the system. Although most details are not available at this time, it should be possible to discern user requirements and general system characteristics and assess whether they are realistic.

Early design phase. The next phase of the application cycle involves the creation of an *early* or *preliminary application design.* At this point we should have enough information to develop an approximate model of the application system and estimate its performance and capacity characteristics. Although we do not have all the details of the eventual design, the initial design should provide a good indication of general processing requirements. It should be possible to screen designs that cannot perform acceptably at this early stage.

During the early design phase, information should be available about general system flow, the general content of screen formats, and the type of processing anticipated for each screen interaction. We should be able to discover how many business units will be serviced each day and how many screen formats and transactions will be required for each.

In the preliminary design phase, enough information should be available to develop a general model of the system. Although all the detail of the eventual design is not yet known, the preliminary design can provide a good indication of the processing the system will require.

With preliminary design data, we can develop best- and worst-case scenarios. These will indicate whether the design will allow reasonable performance. Unreasonable designs may be adjusted more easily here than in later stages of the application life-cycle.

The mature design phase. The *mature* or *detail design* stage provides another opportunity to review the application performance. With added detail, it should be possible to develop a good estimate of both performance characteristics and capacity requirements. By this point, the application design should include details about programs and the resources they will use.

System test phase. During the *system and integration testing phase* it should be possible to measure selected portions of the system. We can verify whether profiles of resources and performance match expectations. We might not be able to evaluate performance in a test environment, but we should be able to decide whether transaction profiles match predicted values. In this phase, our emphasis should be on how well workload profiles match earlier models.

Implementation phase. Once the system moves to production, live production data should be compared to model estimates. Even if test results were consistent with projections, transaction profiles often change once systems are placed in production. The volume and mix of transactions can vary from that projected by application developers or users. A comparison of production performance data to estimates can provide feedback that can be helpful for the analysis of future systems. An analysis of significant deviances can help refine information gathering techniques.

It is worth noting that system activity during the first week may not match long-term patterns. Users often experiment with new systems and try features they may not normally use. Evaluations of activity and resource usage may need to wait until a system has been used for a few days or weeks.

Maintenance phase. As the application system matures, we can use SPE to estimate the effect of system revisions or volume changes. If projections of performance and resource usage reflect what occurred in production, we can use models to help forecast the impact of future changes.

8.4.1 SPE Models

In SPE, workloads are defined in terms of *workload specifications* and *software design*. *Workload specifications* provide a high-level definition of the application system. *Software design* identifies the specific work required to accomplish each function identified in the workload specifications.

Workload specifications. Workload specifications are the high-level definitions used to identify services and functions. They describe the system flow from a user perspective. In a CICS environment, workload specifications describe the screen formats and other processes seen by the user. Workload specifications include both the sequence in which the screens are processed and the probability that each screen could be executed.

In a system designed to enter information about claims, workload specifications would describe the screens that used to process a single claim. A screen used for one out of ten claims, would be entered 10 percent of the time. For planning and modeling, its activity would carry a weight of 10 percent.

> **Key Term:** *Workload specifications* describe data processing work in terms of events the user sees such as maps and screens.

Software design. Software design describes the application processing required to perform each user activity defined in the workload specifications. Software design describes the actual application processing needed to support the screens entered by users. In the early stages of application design, the software design will be general and approximate.

As the application design matures, more information will become available and details can be added.

Software design defines processing in terms of percentages and probabilities. The software required to process one screen (CICS map) might include reading two files every time and a third file 50 percent of the time. The software design for that screen would identify the three files and the percent (probability) each would be read when the screen was processed.

> **Key Term:** *Software design* describes the data processing activities required to perform each user function defined in the workload specifications.

The application processing described in software design includes events on external devices, CPU processing, and accesses to CICS facilities such as temporary storage and transient data. A profile will be developed for each user activity. Initial estimates will be rough approximations or even educated guesses. As the application design matures, more details can be included.

The software model. The *software model* combines the workload specifications and the software design and is a description of an application system in terms of the processing it will perform. By separating the model into descriptions of the user activities (workload specifications) and internal processes (software design), we can modify portions of the application design without having to redo the entire model. This separation allows us to identify functional and processing components of application models.

Software models describe systems in generic terms. *They do not define the environment in which the application will run or the specific hardware or software that will be required.* The purpose of a software model is to describe required services and processing — not what it will take to accomplish them.

> **Key Term:** *Software models* combine workload specifications and software design to describe workloads in terms of general processing required to do user functions.

The system model. The *system model* combines the software model with information about a specific hardware and software environment. In the system model, details about processor speed, specific hardware configurations, and internal structure are combined with the description of software defined in the software model.

System models assess how software models will perform in specific processing environments. System models are used to estimate resource utilization, queueing, and application performance in specific environments and/or hardware configurations.

> **Key Term:** *System models* combine information about software design with information about the environment in which it will run.

Later in this chapter we will look at how to build and assess software and system models for CICS systems. Although non-CICS systems are beyond the scope of this book, they, too, can be studied using SPE tools.

8.4.2 Performance Walk-Throughs

Performance walk-throughs provide a convenient and orderly method of gathering information about new systems. Whether done formally or informally, performance walk-throughs help ensure that information about new systems is accurate.

Normally, three groups need to be represented in performance walk-throughs. They are *system users*, *application developers*, and *performance analysts*.

System users provide information needed in the workload specifications. They are the best source of information about the way the system will be used and the level of performance they require. Users will be asked to describe how they expect to use the system and how frequently common functions will be used. They will be asked to identify which services they will use most heavily and which will be used infrequently. They also will be asked to identify performance goals and requirements.

Application developers translate user activities into data processing services. Their primary contribution will be a description of the processing that will occur for each user activity. Application developers will provide information about the processing required for each field on a screen, and the relationships between screens. During the early stages of system analysis and design, application developers will have limited information and only rough estimates of the data processing services that will be used. As the design matures, they can provide a clearer picture of application processing.

Performance analysts will normally be the ones facilitating the performance walk-throughs. They may be responsible for assembling data and compiling it into a useful format. At times they may need to draw information from users or application developers. In the early stages of analysis and design, when little is known about a system, performance analysts may need to ask creative questions to obtain the information they require.

8.5 IDENTIFYING PERFORMANCE GOALS

The primary reason for using SPE is to ensure that application systems *can meet performance goals*. SPE assumes that performance goals can be identified and quantified.

In most types of performance planning, CICS performance goals are expressed in terms of either internal or end-to-end *response time.* Typically, performance is measured in terms of average or percentile (e.g., 90th percentile) response times. However, in SPE, response time is only one way of defining performance objectives.

Another method of defining performance goals is in terms of *units of business activity that can be accomplished in a period.* Instead of concentrating on internal CICS response time, system developers may concentrate on user effectiveness. Instead of optimizing response time, they could optimize system effectiveness and the way users accomplish business functions. When a performance goal is stated in these terms, it *defines the effectiveness of the system.*

> **Key Point:** In SPE, performance goals go beyond transaction response times. A higher goal is to provide systems that allow users to achieve required levels of throughput. While response time is still an important measure, it is only a partial measure of service. SPE suggests that systems should be designed to support levels of user effectiveness. SPE is concerned with the effectiveness of an entire system, not just the performance of selected transactions.

The ultimate goal of most CICS application systems is to allow users to complete work correctly, quickly, and easily. Application systems must allow users to accomplish their business-related missions. They should both function correctly and have safeguards to ensure the integrity of data. And they must allow users to accomplish their work in a timely manner. System effectiveness implies optimizing the total time it takes users to accomplish business functions.

There are many ways to improve the effectiveness of application designs. Simple strategies like making it easy to get to common menus or grouping fields on a screen that are used together can make it easier for users to do their jobs. These strategies can make more of a difference in total user effectiveness than simple transaction response time. In Chapter 10, we will look at how SPE principles or guidelines can be used to produce effective application designs. Chapter 10 includes many suggestions to improve the effectiveness and efficiency of CICS applications.

As a rule, SPE concentrates more on total system effectiveness than on response time. It is possible to develop a system that delivers subsecond response time but does not allow users to accomplish strategic functions in a timely manner. With SPE, the emphasis is on the total function rather than on the response time of any specific transaction.

SPE is concerned with the effectiveness of an entire system, not just the performance of selected transactions.

Despite the overwhelming benefits of defining performance in terms of user effectiveness, usually it is *easier* to describe performance in terms of transaction response times. Even when performance goals are stated in terms of user effectiveness, CICS response time is still an important factor. Even if user work requirements can be satisfied, users will become dissatisfied if response is too slow. When work rates are used as SPE goals, transaction response time often will be stated as a secondary goal.

8.6 BUILDING AN SPE MODEL

The SPE approach suggests that we model the performance of new application systems as early as possible. With SPE, the emphasis is in screening unacceptable designs *before* much work has been done in the design or coding. Even with very limited information, it should be possible to find out whether an application has a reasonable chance of performing acceptably. We can be sure that early models will not be precise, but that is not their goal at this stage. Despite their imprecision, these models should let us see if the initial design is anywhere near acceptable.

In the SPE process, software models can be updated and refined as more detailed information becomes available. As details are added, it should be possible to refine estimates of application performance and resource requirements

User activities in the software model do not always correspond to CICS transaction IDs. CICS transactions often perform multiple functions, and several user functions identified in the workload specifications may have the same CICS transaction ID. In the design stage, categorizing user activities is more important than identifying CICS transaction IDs. However, if user activities can be defined as distinct CICS transaction IDs, it will be easier to compare model design to CICS transaction statistics during later phases of the application life-cycle.

8.6.1 Determining Application Workflow (Workload Specifications)

As we mentioned earlier in this chapter, software models have two distinct parts. One is a description of the application in terms of user activities. This is called *workload specifications,* which describes the screens and maps entered by users. The second is a description of the data processing work required for each user activity. This is called *software design*. The combination of the workload specifications and software design make up the *software model*.

Users are the best source of information about application workflow. Although they are often uncertain about exactly how they intend to use new application systems, user should know what work they hope to accomplish with them. At times, though, it may take special coaching to help users discover which screens they will use most frequently and in what order.

There always will be some uncertainty about how systems will be used, even at advanced stages of system development. Until users start to use systems in production, we do not know exactly how software will be used. Even so, users should be involved in the SPE process at an early stage if workload specifications are to be meaningful. Users normally are the best source of what they will do and how they intend to do it.

When considerable uncertainty exists, additional analysis may be required. If users have no idea how they will use systems, we can ask them to describe what type of business functions they hope to achieve with the system. Users normally will have some idea of the business units they perform and what it takes to accomplish them. Once we learn the nature of their mission, we can relate that to specific screen formats and other user activities. It may not always be easy, but users usually can provide a wealth of useful information about how they plan to use new systems.

Another way to learn how users will use systems is to develop prototypes of significant screens. Users could enter data and play-act standard workflows. This can help establish both workflows and timings. It can also help us discover if screen designs are easy to use or lend themselves to application work patterns. PC-based tools often simplify the process of application prototyping.

8.6.2 Build A Profile Of Application Processing (Software Design)

After developing a profile of the work to be done by users (the workload specifications), the next step is to estimate the processing required for each screen format. This is called the *software design*. The primary reason to develop software design is to identify the application paths that will be used most frequently and the resources they consume.

Typically, a few screen formats account for most processing. As few as two or three screen formats might account for over 90 percent of the transactions entered for a system. It is important to include descriptions of the most active transactions in the software design. It is not necessary to develop processing models of each screen. Unless infrequently used screens are expected to require a large amount of processing, they may be ignored or lumped into a miscellaneous category.

The software design is not necessarily a representation of program or transaction logic. It is a profile of the processing done to support specific user activities. The software design not only describes what is done, but how often it will be done. The goal is to establish the percentage of time data processing tasks will be performed for each significant user activity. The software design describes the transaction flow for significant user activities defined in the workload specifications.

In the software design, processing will be described in terms of three basic elements.[1] Together, these elements produce a profile of the software.

- *Actual processing* describes the processing and external events executed by the application. It is a statement of the data processing

---

[1] Dr. Smith's book [SMIT90] describes a more elaborate procedure for developing software design. Her approach is more rigorous than that presented here and should be used for more sophisticated structures than those discussed in this and the next two chapters.

tasks that will be performed for a user activity. Actual processing will include CPU processing, file accesses, database calls, temporary storage calls, and other data processing services.

- *Frequency* describes the probability that actual processing will be executed. Frequency is stated as a percent or probability.
- The *number of iterations* describes the number of times a data processing task will be performed when it is requested.

Let us look at an example of how these three elements are combined as part of a software design.

In an order entry system, one screen is used to enter information about new orders. About 10 percent of the orders are from international customers and require special processing. Each order from an international customer will require an average of six separate accesses to a file containing international information. The software design for this screen would show a frequency of .10 for international orders. The number of iterations for the international file would be 6 – the file would be read an average of six times each time an international order was processed. The combined effect would be that the international file will be accessed an average of 0.6 times each time this screen is processed.

Software design includes the actual work, the probability (frequency) it will be needed, and number of times it will be executed when it is needed.

Application developers normally are the best source of information about software design. They face the responsibility of turning user requirements into working application systems. As such, they should be able to identify the processing tasks required for each user activity.

With SPE, the approach is to make use of the best information available and try to develop estimates as early as possible. Even if specific information about application processing, files, and databases is not yet available, analysts usually will have a general idea of the processing that will be required. When specific information is lacking, analysts should be able to provide approximations, high and low estimates, or even educated guesses about resources to be used.

One challenge in building a model of software is that coding often starts before the entire analysis is complete. Time constraints may require programming to start when only part of the analysis has been completed. There can be considerable overlap between the analysis, design, and programming portions of a project.

A good way to deal with design overlap is to develop a picture of the system as soon as system requirements are defined. The model will be very rough. When additional detail is available, it can be added. It is important to remember that the goals of SPE are to screen unacceptable designs, provide effective systems, and assist in the capacity planning. It can be more difficult to achieve these goals when much of the coding is complete before the entire design is finished.

8.6.3 Building the Software Model

The software model combines the description of application activities (defined in the workload) specifications with the description of the processing for each activity (defined in the software design). For simple systems, models can be evaluated using the "back of the envelope" techniques suggested in this chapter and in Chapter 9. However, detailed models of large systems can become quite complex and difficult to resolve without the aid of sophisticated software. In this book, we will concentrate on techniques that can applied without the use of complex tools. If modeling tools are available, they can perform some tasks suggested in this chapter automatically.

The major task in building the software model is identifying the total amount of work required by each user activity. The process of estimating resource utilization and performance will take place later when the software model is combined with information about an operating environment to produce a *system model*.

8.6.4 Estimating Transaction Volume

In SPE, transaction volume is addressed in terms of workload specifications, or sequences of screens used for given functions. To estimate transaction volume, we first estimate the number of units processed (e.g., the number of invoices processed per hour, number of claims entered per day, etc.). Then we translate this into the number of user activities or screen sequences that would result. Transaction volume and sequences would be combined with the software design to produce a model of the work required by the application software.

If there is uncertainty about transaction volume, it is best to develop a range of probable activity. This will help establish best- and worst-case scenarios. It is usually wise to expect initial estimates of transaction volume to be low and to adjust estimates accordingly.

The number of business units entered per hour is usually a better planning tool than total business units processed in a day or week. Capacity and performance studies are normally associated with peak or recurring peak periods. Some of the techniques suggested in Chapter 4 can be used to estimate the amount of work that will be processed during peak hours.

For the purposes of estimating transaction volume, application systems can further be categorized by their intended use and audience. Some common categories include:

Information entry systems. Information entry systems are systems whose primary use is to enter data. These systems may be targeted to either a limited number of dedicated users or a large number of individuals who enter data intermittently. In either case, the number of transactions normally will be tied to some identifiable natural unit of work (e.g., orders, loans, or reservations). Once we know the number of business units, it should be easy to identify the corresponding number of transactions.

When users' primary duty is to enter data, the best indicator of work arrivals will be the number of users and the rate at which they work. Some experimentation with a simple work model may help assess user work rates.

When information is entered by *many users who use the system less regularly*, processing peaks might vary with peaks in business activity. When many infrequent users enter data, either the data will vary with business peaks or filter in sporadically. If the information relates directly to a primary activity, work will usually be entered as it happens or at least during the same day. If information is required periodically, work may be entered gradually over a period of time with a spike just prior to the reporting deadline.

Data transfer systems form a special type of information entry system. Remote systems, such as PCs, workstations, or midrange processors can drive information updates on the host. These systems can generate a considerable amount of transaction activity between the host and remote processors for short bursts of time.

Query systems. Query systems are designed to retrieve data from existing files and databases and return information to users. It is usually more difficult to project transaction activity for query systems than for information entry systems.

When query systems provide new, unique data services, it can be difficult to assess user demand. Once such systems are installed, they are often used more heavily than either users or application developers ever believed possible. Transaction rates for some query systems can be as much as an order of magnitude higher than initial forecasts.

With the advent of complex relational database systems, it is now possible to provide views of data that were never before practical. New queries may not only satisfy long-unsatisfied needs, but they might present new opportunities to streamline existing work procedures. When new useful information becomes easy to access, demand for the data may far surpass even optimistic expectations. Users commonly find applications for data that were never envisioned by the original project sponsors.

On the other hand, users sometimes ask for access to data, but system usage never materializes. A user may exaggerate the perceived need for a system to gain project approval. If systems are difficult to use or provide unpopular services, system usage may be less than anticipated.

In the past, query system would produce screen outputs, but today they also may include data transferred to other processors to support user information systems.

Full-function systems. Full-function systems provide for the entry and maintenance of data along with a range of queries. All of the nuances associated with both information entry and query systems are applicable to full-function systems.

The key to estimating user activity for new systems is to understand the way the system will be used and the type of users that will be entering transactions. It is important to know whether system work flow is determined primarily by the size of the staff using the system, the volume of a key business indicator, or the popularity of data.

In Chapter 4 we discussed techniques to estimate transaction volume. We suggested that *new systems* might *replace existing data processing systems, replace manual systems,* or *provide entirely new functionality.* Techniques for estimating transaction volume vary depending on the origin of the system.

Systems that replace existing data processing systems. When a new application replaces an existing data processing system, the existing system can be used to suggest a rough indication of workload activity. Chances are, though, that new systems will provide different functionality that may affect the way the system is used. For this reason, it is more important to identify the number of business units processed by the old system than the number of transactions. Combined with new workflow specifications, the number of business units can indicate how many total transactions will be entered.

Systems that replace manual functions. When manual systems are replaced by on-line systems, the manual systems can be used to estimate user activity. It is very likely, though, that query activity will be higher than on the manual system. Users are likely to take advantage of new data opportunities and convenience. If additional users can access data in the new system, query activity can be quite a bit higher than planned.

8.6.5 Estimating CPU Usage

The task of estimating CPU usage for new systems can be challenging. In theory, we can microanalyze programs and apply approximate path lengths for each minute function. It is very difficult, though, to estimate how much processing is required by each service requested by application programs. It is even more difficult to itemize all services that will be part of the application path length.

The use of I/O density can be a more practical method of estimating application CPU usage. In most CICS environments, there is a strong correlation between the number of I/O requests and the amount of CPU time used. Unless the operating environment or application development style changes significantly, the amount of processing per I/O request for new systems will usually be similar to that experienced by other systems in the same environment.

The term *I/O density* is used to describe the relationship between CPU usage and I/O requests. It is a measure of the amount of CPU time it takes to drive each I/O request. *Logical I/O density* deals the internal processing costs to drive logical I/O requests. *Physical I/O density* is a measure of total processing costs related to I/O events actually passed to external devices.

In a CICS environment, the ratio of both logical and physical I/Os to CPU usage will change over time. As a rule, the amount of CPU time used per *physical* I/O request will tend to increase as application complexity increases and as additional application data becomes resident in memory (less visits to external devices for the same amount of work). On the other hand, the amount of CPU time used per *logical* I/O request will tend to increase with application complexity, but decrease as data becomes resident in memory (the cost of retrieving data decreases when it can be accessed from memory).

In most CICS environments, several different forms of application programming will evolve, each with its own range of I/O densities. Some CICS applications will use only locally-defined VSAM files. Others might make extensive use of function shipping to access resources defined in other CICS regions. Fourth generation languages and DB2 also affect I/O density. Each application style will require different amounts of processing to accomplish application objectives. This will be reflected in differing levels of logical and physical I/O density.

To estimate CPU usage for new applications, one would calculate the I/O density for a similar CICS environment. Then I/O density would be multiplied by the number of I/Os projected in the software model to obtain an estimate of CPU activity. In most CICS environments, logical I/O density should provide a reasonable estimate of CPU usage.

8.6.6 Evaluating the Software Model

The best way to evaluate a software model is to use modeling software. Products such as Crystal (from BGS Systems), Performance Arkitect (from Windtunnel Software), or SNAPSHOT (IBM) are designed to evaluate the performance of complex application systems. In theory, models can be evaluated manually, but the effort can become intense.

We will briefly discuss how to evaluate simple CICS systems in this chapter and will continue with an illustration in Chapter 9. The reader is encouraged to apply these techniques for simpler systems. The reader is cautioned, though, that modeling software is almost essential when evaluating more complex situations.

Assuming that we have already produced a profile of user activity (*workload specifications*) and a description of the processing required for each user activity (*software design*), and compiled them into a *software model*, the next step is to estimate workload volume using the projected number of user activities. This should provide an indication of the total amount of activity and processing generated by the system.

With this information, we would have a description of the software requirements for a system. We could then begin to evaluate how the system would perform in a specific hardware and software environment. We might start with a simplified best-case analysis to see if the application system is close to reasonable. (Best-case analysis is discussed in more detail in Chapter 9.) After completing the best-case analysis, we would evaluate the software model in more detail and looking at specific hardware and software requirements.

If we were using a software modeling product, we would provide the product with information about our environment and let it do the rest of the work. If we are evaluating a model manually, we will need to calculate utilization and service parameters ourselves.

In a CICS environment, we will face four special challenges in evaluating system models. Some of these challenges are present in any environment, but are particularly complex for CICS workloads.

- *DASD service.* As we will discuss in Chapter 11, DASD performance is not always obvious from measurement data. There are many hidden quirks and arcane relationships that complicate the evaluation of DASD service.

- *MRO processing.* MRO relationships also provide challenges. Transactions running in one MRO region are often dependent on other CICS regions for resources and services. In an MRO environment, the interrelationship between CICS regions must be considered. Appendix D will discuss some of the issues affecting MRO performance.

- *DB2.* In many cases, DB2 represents a large "unknown" quantity. Slight variations in SQL parameters can make a major difference in processing requirements. Applications that run fine with small test tables sometimes "choke" when they have to deal with large production tables. Heavy update activity can affect the way DB2 data is distributed and change access patterns. Because of its complexity, it can be very difficult to manually assess the performance of DB2 SQL calls from CICS applications.

- *The interaction between closed systems.* The final challenge is that data processing systems are really closed queueing systems. This means that performance at one server usually affects activity at other servers. It also means that response affects the rate at which users can enter transactions. Without a modeling product, it can be difficult to project these relationships accurately.

Once all this information has been assembled, the next step is to map applications and resources to specific CICS regions, and files to specific hardware configurations. At this point in the evaluation, we can take several approaches. We can assume that the new application will be placed in its own CICS region, or we can look at placing it in an existing region. Similarly, we can either "place" files on known DASD volumes, assume they will be placed on empty volumes, or assume a constant service time and then configure a DASD environment to provide that level of service. If we had performed a best-case analysis, information from that analysis could help us decide which options were reasonable.

Assuming that DASD activity will be significant, we will need to evaluate activity for each file identified in the software model. We need to estimate each file's contribution to both device and channel utilization. As we will discuss in Chapter 11, both internal and external factors affect the amount of time DASD service times. LSR look-aside ratios affect the number of file requests passed to external storage. Cache read and write hit ratios affect both service time and contention for access to controllers. Refer to Chapter 11 for more information about CICS file service times.

After we have projected the number of visits to DASD, the easiest way to estimate DASD service time is to use service values from existing DASD volumes. Borrowing connect, disconnect, and pend time for similar volumes in the same configuration, we can project DASD utilization for modeled DASD.[2] We estimate device utilization by multiplying expected DASD activity by borrowed service information.

Using estimated resource utilization, we can use open queueing formulas (Table A.1) to estimate DASD service. If the volume is accessed exclusively by CICS applications, open queueing formulas will slightly *understate* true performance.[3] If the volume is also accessed by batch jobs during the period in question, service times can be much longer than those predicted by open queueing formulas.

The next step is to estimate CPU demand for the workload. The amount of CPU time used for each function can be calculated. Environmental factors, such as paging and MVS contention should be included. Chapter 7 showed how to estimate CPU demand.

After CPU demand, dispatch time per transaction, and delays associated with DASD have been calculated, the next step is to calculate a server return ratio for dispatch queueing within CICS. Chapters 6 and 7 showed how to do this. Using this server return ratio and CPU demand, we can extract a service multiplier for internal CICS queueing from Table

---

[2] As we will discuss in Chapter 11, volume utilization is a factor of connect time, disconnect time, pend time, and the number of requests per second.
[3] The reason for this is explained in Chapter 11.

B.9. This will allow us to estimate the total amount of CPU-related delay per transaction associated with a specific CICS environment.

We estimate response time by adding service times, including queueing for each element in a user activity. When estimated response time is too high, we may want to experiment with "splitting" processing between multiple CICS regions, "upgrading" processors, or adjusting the proposed DASD configuration until an acceptable solution can be found. If application performance still is not acceptable or if a cost-effective solution cannot be found, it may be necessary to adjust application design.

While we may dread the task of suggesting that a proposed design cannot be made to perform or will be too expensive to be viable, this is the primary reason for evaluating application design at an early point in the application life-cycle. When rough models are built at a very early point, less work will have been invested by application developers, and changes can be made more easily.

When performance is not evaluated until the design is complete and programming is already in progress, a considerable amount of rework may be necessary. The value of the SPE approach is that application performance can be assessed *before* most of the work has been done.

After we have evaluated the system model, we should have a good indication of whether software will perform acceptably. If we performed our analysis early in the design stage, we should review model data at later stages of the project life-cycle. It is likely that some assumptions made in early the design stage will change as the design is completed and programs are written.

8.7 SUMMARY

The primary reason for using Software Performance Engineering is to ensure that applications can deliver acceptable performance when installed in production. In this chapter, we have discussed SPE and outlined the steps that would be used to evaluate a new CICS application system.

We have suggested that SPE studies should begin as early as possible in the application life-cycle. A major reason for performing SPE studies is to identify performance deficiencies before most of the development work has been performed. This allows adjustments to application design when it is most cost effective.

In this chapter, we described the process of building an SPE model. Briefly, it consists of the following steps:

- *Identify user performance requirements.* This may be stated in terms of either user effectiveness or response times.

- *Define workload specifications.* Workload specifications define application processes in terms of user activities. In CICS systems, these activities are defined in terms of screen and map formats.

- *Identify the software design.* The software design is a description of the work required for each activity identified in the workload specifications.

- *Build the software model.* This is a combination of data from the software specifications and the software design. The software model describes an application system in terms of the work it will perform.

- *Evaluate the system model.* The system model evaluates the software model in the context of a specific software and hardware environment.

In Chapter 9, we will provide a comprehensive example of how the steps developed in this chapter can be applied.

SELECTED READING

[BELL88] Bell, Thomas E., "System Performance Engineering," *CMG Transactions,* Spring, 1988.

[SMIT90] Smith, Connie U., *Performance Engineering of Software Systems,* Addison-Wesley Publishing Company, Reading, Massachusetts, 1990.

Chapter 9

SPE — Application Design Example

9.1 OVERVIEW

Software Performance Engineering emphasizes the importance of designing performance into applications and evaluating performance early in the development life-cycle. In Chapter 8, we introduced general SPE concepts and discussed how to build SPE models. SPE models are used to evaluate application capacity and performance characteristics. In Chapter 9, we will develop an example illustrating how to build a SPE model for a new CICS application. Chapter 10 will look at SPE application design guidelines and how they can help develop responsive application systems.

Chapter 9 is almost completely devoted to a single example. It will show how to analyze applications under development and determine both their performance characteristics and capacity requirements. The example will follow the pattern developed in Chapter 8.

The techniques illustrated in this chapter are designed to be *simple and easy to apply*. They show how to develop quick estimates of performance and capacity. The purpose of these estimates is to screen out unacceptable application design before development is completed.

The application system presented in this chapter is limited in scope. Real-world applications usually will be more complex, involving more files and more elaborate interactions. Although it is possible to develop performance profiles manually, software modeling products simplify the task of resolving complex interactions. Even if advanced modeling tools are used, though, the same processes will be used to gather and analyze information about new application systems.

9.1.1 Primary Audience

This chapter will be useful to anyone interested in evaluating the performance and capacity of CICS applications early in their development. *Application developers* can see how to estimate what kind of service their applications will provide. *CICS systems programmers* will see how to determine whether a new application will fit into an existing software configuration. *Capacity planners* should find these techniques helpful in planning future resource requirements.

This chapter emphasizes that it is possible to estimate the performance of new systems, even early in the design stage. The earlier that new applications can be evaluated, the easier it will be to ensure acceptable performance. It is far less expensive to design for performance than to adjust for it after systems are developed.

9.2 REVIEW OF SPE CONCEPTS

Software Performance Engineering (SPE) involves the evaluation of performance and capacity throughout the application life-cycle. Beginning with the analysis of application requirements and continuing through system implementation, SPE suggests a process of developing and refining performance estimates. Estimates begin with skeletal information and are enhanced as better details become available.

Transaction workloads are defined in terms of two components: *workload specifications* and *software design*. Workload specifications describe applications in terms of user activities and the screen formats used to perform these activities. Software design describes the processing (CPU time, file requests, etc.) required to accomplish each user activity or screen.

> **Key point:** *Workload specifications* define what users see and use; *software design* defines the processing required for each user function.

The *software model* is a combination of the workload specifications and the software design. It is a picture of the processing required to accomplish user activities. The software model describes the system in terms of generic processing requirements. It details the data-processing tasks associated with activities viewed by users.

The *system model* is where application performance and capacity are evaluated. It combines the software model with information about a specific hardware and software environment. Details about CICS regions, DASD characteristics, and processors are used to evaluate the performance potential of the software design. In the system model, CICS applications can be appraised in real or proposed environments.

In Chapter 8, we introduced the concept of *performance goals*. Unlike traditional performance objectives, performance goals address performance in terms of required user productivity. They provide an indication of whether users can achieve their business-related activities in an acceptable time frame. Performance goals commonly include both response time and productivity requirements. With SPE, response time and user effectiveness are both measures of application performance.

9.2.1 Suggested SPE Procedure for Evaluating Sample CICS Application

This example outlines a procedure to estimate performance and capacity requirements of a new CICS application. It covers everything from the analysis of user requirements to the assessment of performance and capacity requirements. This procedure can be started at any stage in the application development life cycle, but as we mentioned above, should be started as early as possible. As the design and development of systems progress and as more complete information becomes available, models should be updated and reevaluated, especially for large or response-sensitive systems.

1. **Establish performance requirements.** One of the first, and perhaps most important, tasks in analyzing performance is to investigate user service needs. User service can be defined in terms of user effectiveness, response time, or both.

2. **Develop workload specifications.** This is a definition of screens and processes and the frequency of their use.

3. **Develop software design.** The software design describes the data processing work required for each of the screens or processes defined in the workload specifications.

4. **Build a software model.** The software model is created by combining the workload specifications and the software design. It represents the processing performed by the application system.

5. **Estimate best-case performance.** Using information in the software model, determine if the application system could provide appropriate service if it were running by itself in an ideal environment. This should be a comparatively easy task. Its purpose is to quickly screen the most unreasonable designs. If an application will not perform in an ideal environment, it certainly will not perform under production conditions.

6. **Estimate performance in the anticipated environment.** Combine information about the application with information about a specific software and hardware environment. This step will estimate resources used by the system and potential response time. It will also evaluate both how the new system will affect the performance of existing workloads and how they will affect the performance of the new system.

9.3 EVALUATING NEW APPLICATION SYSTEMS – AN EXAMPLE

Assume that we have been given the task of reviewing the performance needs and capacity requirements for a new invoice system. We have been approached fairly early in the project life-cycle and have been asked to assess whether the proposed system is capable of meeting user service requirements. The system will have to run on an existing processor along with other CICS systems currently in production. We would like to determine if this system can be placed in an existing CICS region (or if it will need to run in a separate CICS region) and whether files used by the system will require dedicated DASD. Of course, we would like to find out if the system will satisfy user service requirements.

In this example, we will refer to three classes of individuals. *Users* are representatives of the user community. They are the application sponsors who define the business needs to be satisfied by the system. *Application developers* are either systems analysts or programmers responsible for translating user requirements into working application systems. Because of variations in job titles and responsibilities at different installations, we will avoid the term analysts and programmers. *Performance planners* are those who represent the capacity planning, performance planning, systems programming, or SPE planning staff. The term is generic, referring to someone specializing in performance and/or capacity planning.

In this example, we will assume that the performance planner is coordinating the collection of data for the SPE model. Other individuals could have been responsible for this task, but in this example we will assume that this is the job of the performance planner, whose perspective we will follow throughout the example.

9.3.1 Establish Performance Requirements

The first thing we will do is determine what kind of service users will require. The best way to obtain this information is to meet with user representatives and application developers. Users will define what they hope to achieve from the system; application developers will translate user requirements into screen designs and processes; the performance analyst will collect and organize the information.

In our initial meeting with the users and application developers, we discovered that the users' main performance concern is that each clerk be able to process at least 75 invoices per hour. They plan to have a staff of 50 dedicated clerks entering invoice information. Users have stated that their staff will work an average of 6.9 hours a day, excluding breaks and other overhead. They also have indicated that they do not intend to hire more than 50 clerks to support current levels of business activity, which is about 26,000 invoices per day.

Based on the requirement to process 75 invoices per hour, we can see that a user will need to process an invoice in about 48 seconds. Table 9.1 summarizes the performance goals we identified for the invoice system.

Two elements control whether the 48-second goal can be achieved. The first is the way the system will be used, and the second is transaction response time. If the sum of user processing time (think time) and response time for the transactions for an invoice is 48 seconds or less, users should be able to achieve their performance goals. If an invoice cannot be completed in 48 seconds, it may be necessary to revise system design until an acceptable design alternative can be found. If an accept-

Table 9.1 User Performance Requirements for Sample System

Total invoices that must be processed each day	26,000
Number of clerks working invoice system	50
Hours per day each clerk works invoice system	6.9
Required work rate (invoices per hour)	75
Average time to complete one invoice (maximum acceptable value)	48 secs.

able design cannot be devised, users may need to rethink their performance requirements or the scope of the application system.

9.3.2 Develop Workload Specifications

In our interview with users and developers, we determined that three screen formats would be used heavily. Other screens were identified, but they will not be used very often. These other screens address exception processing that will be required only for a small percent of the invoices. None of these screens appear to have heavy processing requirements. At this time, we believe that we can ignore the exception screens since they will neither be used frequently nor require much processing.

The three screens have been designated screens 1, 2, and 3, respectively. Screen 1 is the first screen processed for each invoice. Users will always enter data on this screen before proceeding to other screens. About 20 percent of the time, data or keying errors will be detected on Screen 1. When this happens, Screen 1 will be redisplayed with error messages allowing users to correct or adjust data. Screen "1-N" in Table 9.2, represents the normal entry of Screen 1. It will be executed 100 percent of the time – once per invoice processed. Screen 1-E, error processing for Screen 1, will be executed 20 percent of the time. When errors are detected in Screen 1 input, it will be redisplayed so users can correct or reenter data.

Notice that although Screen 1 was involved in both screens 1-N and 1-E, they were identified separately. This is because users usually will enter much more data on the initial entry of an invoice than they will when they correct errors. The amount and type of processing for the two screens will be quite different.

Screen 2 also will be entered for each invoice, but users predict that only 10 percent of the screens will be redisplayed because of errors. Table 9.2 shows that 2-N will be entered 100 percent of the time and that

SPE — Application Design Example

Table 9.2 Summary of Screens Required to Process One Invoice

Screen Number	Type Processing	Screen Designation	Percent Used	Weighted Average
1	Normal	1-N	100%	1.0
1	Error	1-E	20%	.2
2	Normal	2-N	100%	1.0
2	Error	2-E	10%	.1
3	Normal	3	30%	.3
Total				2.6

2-E will be entered 10 percent. Screen 3 is provided for invoices requiring special processing. Users estimate that about 30 percent of all invoices will require this special processing.

Workload specifications for the invoice system are shown in Table 9.2. We have identified the significant user activities associated with entering a single invoice. The workload specifications show the most commonly used screens along with the percent of invoices for which each will be entered.

Table 9.3 summarizes average think time for each screen identified in the workload specifications. Although the time between user transactions is commonly called "think" time, users normally are not just sitting there looking at a screen and "thinking." They will be scanning sources of information, performing other business activities, or keying data. In this sense, "think" time is somewhat of a misnomer. A better name might be "user active time."

Table 9.3 Estimated User Think Time for One Invoice

Screen Designation	Weighted Average	User Think Time (Seconds)	Weighted Think Time
1-N	1.0	25	25.0
1-E	.2	8	1.6
2-N	1.0	15	15.0
2-E	.1	7	0.7
3	.3	9	2.7
Total	2.6		45.0

To obtain think times, screen prototypes were developed for each of the three screens and users were observed entering data. Based on user interaction with the screen prototypes, we believe that it will take about 25 seconds for a user to enter the data required on Screen 1-N. When an error occurs, it should take about 8 seconds for the user to find the source of the error and correct it. Screen 1-N is shown with a weighted "think" time of 25 seconds and 1-E of 1.6 seconds (8 seconds times the .2 probability that the screen will be entered). The results of our study suggest that it will take about 45 seconds of user activity to complete all the work associated with a single invoice.

Users had originally told us that each clerk would need to process about 75 invoices per hour. Therefore, the system should allow clerks to process each invoice in about 48 seconds. If estimates of user activity are correct, total response time for transactions 1-N, 1-E, 2-N, 2-E, and 3 will need to be about 3 seconds (48 seconds − 45 seconds) or less. Assuming that users were attached to local controllers or on high-speed communication lines, a total response time of 3.0 seconds might not be unreasonable for the average 2.6 transactions per invoice. We will continue our study to determine whether this is possible.

The information we have discovered so far would suggest that it might be wise to review application design. Since 45 of the allowed 48 seconds per invoice are associated with user activity, improvements in screen entry procedures might improve user effectiveness. It is possible that screen design could be improved to reduce the time it takes users to enter invoice data. Chapter 10 suggests several SPE application design guidelines to help build systems that are more efficient and effective as a whole.

For the purposes of this example, we will assume that SPE design guidelines had been used when the screens were designed and that further optimization is unlikely. Thus, our internal performance target will be to complete transaction processing for the 2.6 transactions in 3 seconds.

9.3.3 Develop Software Design

In our interviews with developers and users, we have learned that four files will be used for the new system. Three of the files will be VSAM key sequence datasets (KSDSs). The fourth file, also a KSDS, will contain an alternate index that will be updated when data in the base cluster changes. The developer told us that forward recovery and transaction backout would be required for all four files.

Since this system requires file recovery, CICS dataset journaling will be active. To allow the recovery of file data, CICS journal records will be written whenever records are added, updated, or deleted. In this example, we will assume that journal records are written asynchronously.[1]

Application design also requires that data on all files remain consistent with one another. Therefore, dynamic transaction backout (DTB) and file logging are required. As mentioned in the footnote below, file logging occurs synchronously. CICS applications must wait for logged data to be written to the system log before file updates are completed.

Table 9.4 summarizes the processing that will occur each time Screen 1-N is entered. The table shows that there will always be three read requests to FILEA. When edit routines do not detect any errors, a routine will be entered that updates FILEB. This routine will be executed 80 percent of the time — there is a 20 percent chance that edit routines will detect errors in Screen 1 and bypass updates. When the routine is executed, it will read FILEB an average of eight times, do an average of seven updates, and add one record. The routine also will "write" eight journal records and eight log records (one for each update and one for the add).

Table 9.4 also shows that the routine updating FILEC is performed 60 percent of the time. Each time it is executed it will read and update 10 records on FILEC. The final entry indicates that two additional records will be written to the system log for each task execution. These are associated with syncpoint processing.

Tables 9.5 to 9.8 provide software profiles for Screens 1-E, 2-N, 2-E, and 3, respectively. Table 9.5 shows that can one routine for Screen 1-E is executed 98 percent of the time and another 75 percent of the time. Profiles for other screens are shown in the other tables.

---

[1] An FCT option tells CICS to journal copies of records that have been updated, added, or deleted. Journaled data can be written either synchronously (journal records are sent to external storage before the file updates are performed) or asynchronously (data will be moved to a journal buffer and sent to external storage when the buffer is "full"). Asynchronous journaling is commonly used because it provides better service (applications do not normally have to wait for journal writes to be completed). Synchronous journaling commonly will be chosen when it is critical that file updates always be recoverable. File logging (for DTB and emergency restart), however, is always done synchronously. When updates are logged, journal data are committed to external storage before CICS actually performs the file update.

Table 9.4 Software Profile for Screen 1-N

Screen	Percent Used	Resource Name	Type of Activity	Avgerage Number	Weighted Average
1-N	100%	FILEA	read	3	3.0
	80%	FILEB	read	8	6.4
		FILEB	update	7	5.6
		FILEB	add	1	0.8
		Syslog	sync-write	8	6.4
		Journal	journal	8	6.4
	60%	FILEC	read	10	6.0
		FILEC	update	10	6.0
		Syslog	sync-write	10	6.0
		Journal	journal	10	6.0
	100%	Syslog	sync-write	2	2.0

It is important to note that profiles include not only what will occur for each screen, but the probability that certain logic paths will be executed. The result, shown in the "Weighted Average" columns of Tables 9.4 through 9.8 is the average number of times each data processing service will be executed per screen. This column represents the *software design* or profile portion of the software model. Each important user activity identified in *workload specifications* is defined in one of these tables.

Table 9.5 Software Profile for Screen 1-E

Screen	Percent Used	Resource Name	Type of Activity	Avgerage Number	Weighted Average
1-E	98%	FILEB	read	8	7.8
		FILEB	update	7	6.9
		FILEB	add	1	1.0
		Syslog	sync-write	8	7.8
		Journal	write	8	7.8
	75%	FILEC	read	10	7.5
		FILEC	update	10	7.5
		Syslog	sync-write	10	7.5
		Journal	write	10	7.5
	100%	Syslog	sync-write	2	2.0

Table 9.6 Software Profile for Screen 2-N

Screen	Percent Used	Resource Name	Type of Activity	Average Number	Weighted Average
2-N	100%	FILEA	read	1	1.0
	75%	FILEB	read	2	1.5
	90%	FILED	read	4	3.6
		FILED	update	4	3.6
		AIX-D	update	4	3.6
		Syslog	sync-write	4	3.6
		Journal	write	4	3.6
	100%	Syslog	sync-write	2	2.0

Table 9.7 Software Profile for Screen 2-E

Screen	Percent Used	Resource Name	Type of Activity	Average Number	Weighted Average
2-E	98%	FILED	read	4	3.9
		FILED	update	4	3.9
		AIX-D	update	4	3.9
		Syslog	sync-write	4	3.9
		Journal	write	4	3.9
	100%	Syslog	sync-write	2	2.0

Table 9.8 Software Profile for Screen 3

Screen	Percent Used	Resource Name	Type of Activity	Average Number	Weighted Average
3	100%	FILEA	read	1	1.0
	80%	AIX-D	read	5	4.0
		FILEC	read	5	4.0
	40%	FILEA	update	1	0.4
		Syslog	sync-write	1	0.4
		Journal	write	2	0.4
	100%	Syslog	sync-write	2	2.0

Notice that we have not mentioned CICS transactions in our discussion so far. All of the screens might be processed under the same transaction ID, or each screen could have its own transaction ID. Ideally, each screen identified with a separate user activity would run under its own transaction ID. This would allow us to map CICS transaction statistics to user activities identified in the model. Assuming that program logic can anticipate which processing will follow, tasks can set the appropriate transaction ID before returning to CICS.

9.3.4 Build a Software Model

The next step in this process is to combine the information about user activity in the *workload specifications* with the description of processing in the *software design* to create a *software model*. In essence, we will combine data in Table 9.2 with data in Tables 9.4 through 9.8. The software model, shown in Table 9.9, defines the average work required to process one invoice. It is a profile of the processing required per unit of business activity. This software model will be the basis of most of the performance analysis that follows.

The information in Table 9.9 was derived by multiplying the weighted number of file accesses for each screen by the percent (probability) the screen would be entered. For example, Screen 1-N is executed once per

Table 9.9 Average Resources Used by Each Screen for One Invoice

Resource	Type of Activity	1-N (100%)	1-E (20%)	2-N (100%)	2-E (10%)	3 (30%)	Total
FILEA	read	3.0		1.0		0.3	4.3
	update					0.1	0.1
FILEB	read	6.4	1.6	1.5			9.5
	update	5.6	1.4				7.0
	add	0.8	0.2				1.0
FILEC	read	6.0	1.5			1.2	8.7
	update	6.0	1.5				7.5
FILED	read			3.6	0.4		4.0
	update			3.6	0.4		4.0
AIX-D	read					1.2	1.2
	update			3.6	0.4		4.0
Total file requests		27.8	6.2	13.3	1.2	2.8	51.3
Syslog	sync-write	14.4	3.5	5.6	0.6	.7	24.8
Journal	journal	12.4	3.1	3.6	0.4	0.1	19.6

invoice. File accesses performed for Screen 1-N are multiplied by 100 percent and placed in the "1-N" column. Screen 1-E is executed for only 20 percent of the invoices. The file accesses shown in Table 9.5 are multiplied by 20 percent and placed in the "1-E" column.

The "Total" column in Table 9.9 lists the application processing to process one invoice. This represents most of the information required for the software model.

The information we have gathered so far has been generic. It defines the data processing activities required to accomplish a single user function. Next, information from the software model will be merged with specific data about hardware and software to evaluate performance and capacity requirements.

9.3.5 Estimate Best-Case Performance

Once we have identified the data processing work required to complete user activities, the next step is to evaluate its performance in a stand-alone environment. This will allow us to quickly screen unacceptable designs. If an application cannot perform acceptably when there is no competition for resources, it will not perform well under normal processing conditions.

Evaluating *best-case* performance is the first step in building the *system model*. In the best-case scenario, we will define the hardware and software platforms but will not consider other workloads.

Calculate the Number of Physical I/Os for Each File. Internal caching affects the number of I/O requests actually passed to DASD. The effect of internal caching should be considered when estimating the number of visits to external storage. Internal caching is discussed in Chapter 11.

In this example, we were told that three of the files (FILEA, FILEB, and FILED) will be accessed via LSR. They are all new files, and we feel comfortable that LSR access will be appropriate. However, we will need to access FILED via NSR. It is an existing file, and some older applications require NSR to prevent lock-outs.[2] We were told that there will be

---

[2] The most common LSR lock-out involves applications which browse a file and then attempt to update or delete records without first ending the browse. This will work under NSR but will cause the application to lock itself out under LSR. Other, more subtle application coding techniques can cause other problems with LSR that will not show up under NSR, some of which do not include updating the LSR file.

only two levels of index (the sequence set and the high-level index record) on all files.

Table 9.10 describes the I/O operations anticipated for each type of I/O request identified in the software model. It summarizes the physical I/Os that will be required for each type of request. The "buffer hit ratios" (or, more properly, "look-aside ratios," for LSR files) reflect the probability that CIs will be located internally in VSAM buffers thus saving I/O operations. A buffer hit ratio of 100 indicates that the CI will be located in memory 100 percent of the time (except for an initial read request to access it from DASD). A buffer hit ratio of 0 percent means that a physical I/O will be generated for each file request.

For the purposes of this illustration, we will assume that look-aside ratios were estimated using information about the current operating environment and estimates of activity for specific files.

Table 9.10 shows that we expect to access high-level index records for all four files from memory about 100 percent of the time. Normal access patterns for the LSR files (FILEA, FILEB, and FILEC) should keep the high-level index record for each file in memory. An extra index buffer has been allocated for the NSR file, FILEC, and its high-level index record also should be accessed from memory.

We will continue by estimating look-aside ratios for sequence set data. Based on file size and probable access patterns, it appears that a look-

Table 9.10 Analysis of I/O Accesses Required for VSAM Files

Resource	Type of Activity	File Access Activity						
		High-Level Index	Buffer Hit Ratio	Seq. Set CI	Buffer Hit Ratio	Data CI	Buffer Hit Ratio
FILEA	read	1	100%	1	95%	1	60%
	update	0		0		1	0%
FILEB	read	1	100%	1	90%	1	20%
	update	0		0		1	0%
	add	1	100%	1	90%	2	10%
FILEC	read	1	100%	1	0%	1	0%
	update	0		0		1	0%
FILED	read	1	100%	1	95%	1	50%
	update	0		0		1	0%
AIX-D	read	2	100%	2	95%	2	50%
	update					2	0%

aside ratio of 95 percent seems reasonable for FILEA's sequence set. Similar reasoning can be used for sequence set data on FILEB and FILED. Notice that Table 9.10 shows accesses to the index and sequence set CIs for record adds to FILEB. This is because VSAM must locate the index and data CI before a record can be added.

It is usually more difficult to project look-aside ratios for data components. We will assume that we reviewed the data for each file and how it normally would be accessed. We then use this information to estimate how often we could expect to locate CIs in memory. Next, we compare these projections with the look-aside ratios for other similar files. From all this, we estimate that about 60 percent of the data CIs for FILEA should be accessed directly from the buffer pool.

Combining the weighted averages of the three elements, we estimate that each read request to FILEA should take about .45 visits to external storage. This is explained as follows. No I/O requests will be required to read the high-level index; about 5 percent of the reads to sequence set CIs and 40 percent of the accesses to data CIs will require access to external storage. On the average, reads to FILEA will require .45 visits to external storage.

In Table 9.10, updates are shown with a 0 percent hit ratio. Update requests will reference external storage 100 percent of the time.[3]

FILEC will be accessed using NSR. Therefore, read hit ratios for sequence set and data CIs will be assumed to be zero.

Estimate DASD Service Time for Each Type of VSAM File Request. DASD service will be discussed in more detail in Chapter 11. In that chapter, we will discuss the many factors that influence DASD service and performance. We will see that typical DASD access patterns, complex interaction between components, and advanced features in modern controllers make it difficult to calculate service times for DASD.

In theory, it is possible to microanalyze each element of DASD service and calculate expected service times. However, as a practical matter, it may be a more complex task than one would believe. See Chapter 11 for a more complete discussion of elements affecting DASD service times.

For purposes of the *best-case analysis*, we will simply assume an average DASD service time of 15 to 20 ms per I/O event. In the context of

---

[3] Even if DASD fast write is being used, write requests will still need to be sent to the controller.   Table 9.10 a

this example, we will state that this range of service was derived by reviewing other DASD volumes in the same environment. Since this is a best-case analysis, we will assume that we can configure or tune DASD to achieve this level of service. Later, we will take a more realistic look at DASD performance.

Since our initial goal is to estimate *best-case performance*, it is reasonable to select good or average service times for DASD. A range of 15 to 20 ms service is a reasonable target for conventional DASD that is accessed randomly.

To keep this example simple, we have not considered cache or advanced controller features. However, if cache controllers are commonly used in our environment, we could assume they will be used, especially in the best-case analysis. We might assume a lower average DASD service time to adjust for the benefits of cache.

Table 9.11 shows estimates of the service times for file requests identified in the software model. We applied an average DASD service time of 15 to 20 ms to the buffer hit ratios shown in Table 9.10. The probability that an external I/O event will be required is 100 percent minus the buffer hit ratio. For example, a buffer hit ratio of 90 percent means that a component will be accessed from DASD only 10 percent of the time.

As shown in Table 9.10, read requests for the sequence set CI of FILEA will require access to external storage 5 percent of the time (100 - 95 percent). Assuming an average I/O service time of 15 to 20 ms per external I/O, average access time for sequence set records should be about 0.8 to 1.0 ms (.05 times 15 to 20 ms). Similarly, data CIs will be retrieved from external storage 40 percent of the time. This yields an average service time of 6 to 8 ms. Average service time for read requests to FILEA should average about 6.8 to 9.0 ms [(0.8 - 1.0) ms + (6 - 8) ms].

Estimate Total DASD Service Time per Invoice. Once we have estimated best-case service for each file, our next step is to estimate total file-related service time for each unit of work.

DASD service time could have been estimated separately for each transaction. However, in this example, our performance goal was to ensure that average response time did not exceed 3.0 seconds per invoice processed. Here, it is appropriate to estimate service time for the set of transactions required to process one invoice.

Table 9.12 summarizes the DASD service time required to process one invoice. The two rightmost columns identify a range of DASD service per invoice processed. Data in these columns are simply the product of

Table 9.11 Initial Calculation of Average Service Time per Logical I/O Request

Resource	Type of Activity	Average Service Time per I/O	Average Effective Service Time		
			Sequence Set	Data CI	VSAM I/O Request
FILEA	read	15-20 ms	0.8-1.0 ms	6-8 ms	6.8-9 ms
	update	15-20 ms		15-20 ms	15-20 ms
FILEB	read	15-20 ms	1.5-2.0 ms	12-16 ms	13.5-18 ms
	update	15-20 ms		15-20 ms	15-20 ms
	add	15-20 ms	1.5-2.0 ms	27-36 ms	28.5-38 ms
FILEC	read	15-20 ms	15-20 ms	15-20 ms	30-40 ms
	update	15-20 ms		15-20 ms	15-20 ms
FILED	read	15-20 ms	0.8-1.0 ms	7.5-10 ms	8.3-11 ms
	update	15-20 ms		15-20 ms	15-20 ms
AIX-D	read	15-20 ms	1.5-2.0 ms	15-20 ms	16.5-22 ms
	update	15-20 ms		30-40 ms	30-40 ms

activity and service time. Assuming that we can provide DASD service time of 15 to 20 ms per physical I/O, VSAM files should require between 900 and 1198 ms of DASD service per invoice.

Remember that this is a best-case analysis. We have intentionally chosen reasonable DASD service times and have ignored the effects of queueing. Our goal at this time is to determine whether the application can run in an ideal environment. In the best-case analysis, we are simply trying to screen for grossly unacceptable designs.

Estimate the Delays Associated with Journals, the System Log and Other System Datasets. Table 9.13 provides a general summary of DASD access patterns for various types of system files. It suggests ranges of values commonly experienced in many CICS environments.

Synchronous journal writes always require data to be passed to external storage. When a synchronous journal write is requested, the requesting CICS transaction will wait until journal data are sent to external storage.

Synchronous write requests will always wait for at least one I/O. If another write was already in progress to the same journal, the task will wait for that write to be satisfied as well. The number of times this

Table 9.12 DASD Service Time Required per File per Invoice

Resource	Type of Activity	Activity per Invoice (from Table 9.9)	Average Service Time per Request (from Table 9.11)	Minimum File Service Time per Invoice	Maximum File Service Time per Invoice
FILEA	read	4.3	6.8-9ms	29 ms	39 ms
	update	0.1	15-20 ms	2 ms	2 ms
	Total			31 ms	41 ms
FILEB	read	9.5	13.5-18ms	128 ms	171 ms
	update	7.0	15-20 ms	105 ms	140 ms
	add	1.0	28.5-38 ms	29 ms	38 ms
	Total			262 ms	349 ms
FILEC	read	8.7	30-40 ms	261 ms	348 ms
	update	7.5	15-20 ms	113 ms	150 ms
	Total			374 ms	498 ms
FILED	read	4.0	8.3-11 ms	33 ms	44 ms
	update	4.0	15-20 ms	60 ms	80 ms
	Total			93 ms	124 ms
AIX-D	read	1.2	16.5-22 ms	20 ms	26 ms
	update	4.0	30-40 ms	120 ms	160 ms
	Total			140 ms	186 ms
Total service time				900 ms	1198 ms

happens is strictly a factor of how much data are written to the journal. In the best-case analysis, we will ignore journal queueing.

The most common kind of synchronous journal activity is file logging. Data are written to the system log to support DTB and emergency restart. When files are logged, record images are written to the log synchronously, causing transactions to wait. Control will not be returned to the requesting task until the file request is satisfied and the corresponding data is written to the system log.

Asynchronous journal writes will wait only if the journal buffer is full (or in CICS/ESA, if both journal buffers are full). Most of the time, applications will not wait for asynchronous journal writes. They will simply move

Table 9.13 Analysis of Typical I/O Accesses Required for CICS System Files

Resource	Type of Activity	Percent of Requests that will Wait	Records per Write
System log	dataset logging (synchronous-write)	100%	1-50
Journal	asynchronous journal write	5-50%	1-50
Journal	synchronous journal write	100%	1-50
Temporary storage	write to auxiliary storage	0-50%	1-200
Temporary storage	write to auxiliary storage (recoverable data)	30-100%	1-200

data to a journal buffer. Applications will wait only when space is not available in a journal buffer to hold the journaled item.

Temporary storage is a very efficient medium for writing data to auxiliary storage. TS data will not be sent to external storage unless internal conditions (such as the need to reuse a buffer) force it to be written. Even recoverable temporary storage data are not sent to external storage immediately. It is collected with other TS write data and written when convenient. Of course, recoverable TS data will be forced to external storage when syncpoints are processed.

The invoice system will not access auxiliary temporary storage, but will use both synchronous and asynchronous journal writes. Table 9.9 shows an estimate of 24.8 synchronous writes to the system log and 19.6 asynchronous journal writes per invoice. If we assume that each DASD access will take 15 to 20 ms, synchronous writes to the system log should generate 372 to 496 ms in delays for each invoice processed. This is shown in Table 9.14. If we further assume that applications will wait for only 5 percent of asynchronous journal requests (remember, this is a best-case analysis), total journal-related time will be 387 to 516 ms.

Estimate the Amount of CPU Time Used by the Application. In this example we will use logical I/O density to estimate how much CPU time will be used by the application in CICS. *Logical I/O density* is a measure of how much CPU time is used by CICS transactions per logical I/O request. Logical I/O density does not include either CICS or operating system overhead. Logical I/O density is simply an indication of how much CPU activity occurs on the CICS primary TCB for each I/O request issued by applications. This information is excellent for sizing applications and estimating the load on CICS regions. It does not, however, reflect the total costs of running applications.

Other techniques could have been used to estimate the amount of CPU time used by CICS transactions. Using commercial modeling products, we could have described the logic of the application system in detail. It is possible, at least in theory, to create accurate descriptions of program logic and estimate total instructions executed. When we know very little about the specific details of application design, it is usually more practical to "borrow" CPU data from other similar systems. This is neither foolproof nor is it necessarily accurate. However, if we select systems that are fairly similar in structure and programming style, logical I/O density should provide a good indication of how much CPU time will be used by the application within CICS.

We will assume that we have reviewed several other similar applications running in the same environment and have tried to select applications written in the same programming language with similar design structures. We also were careful to select applications designed for information entry which did not have a large number of queries. Our goal was to find applications as similar in style to the invoice system as possible. We will assume that the applications we selected had a logical I/O density of about 1.5 ms per logical I/O. We could have selected a

Table 9.14 Delays Associated with CICS System Files

System file	Activity	Average Service Time per I/O	Total Requests	Portion of Requests That Will Wait for Writes to External Storage	Total Service Time
System log	Synchronous write	15-20 ms	24.8	1.00	372-496 ms
Journal	Asynchronous write	15-20 ms	19.6	.05	15-20 ms

SPE — Application Design Example

range of density values, if it had been obvious that this was necessary. We will assume, though, that logical I/O density for the systems we reviewed all had fairly consistent values.

> **Key Point:** *It very important to recognize that the logical I/O density of 1.5 ms per logical I/O selected in this example is very installation-dependent.* The same application could have a vastly different logical I/O density if run on a processor with a different engine speed. The 1.5 ms used in this example is intended only for use in this example and should not be used anywhere else. *If you are going to use logical I/O density to estimate CPU usage, you must calculate values that are appropriate for your environment.*

Table 9.9 shows that a total of *51.3 VSAM file requests* will be executed for each invoice processed. Assuming a logical I/O density of 1.5 ms of CPU time per file request, each invoice should accumulate about *77 ms of CPU time on the primary CICS TCB*.

User performance requirements stated that the system would need to support 50 clerks working 75 invoices per hour. This translated into 3,750 invoices per hour. Since each invoice is expected to use 77 ms of CPU time, 289 CPU seconds would be required each hour.

$$\text{Total CPU} = 3750 \times 77 \text{ ms} = 3750 \times 0.077 \text{ secs} \approx 289 \text{ secs}$$

This application will consume 289 CPU seconds per hour in a CICS region when users are working at anticipated work rates. Assuming that all this CPU time will be processed on the primary TCB, the invoice application would contribute about 8.0 percent CPU usage to that TCB (289 seconds / 3600 seconds per hour).

For the purposes of the best-case analysis, we can ignore CPU queueing if the amount of CPU time the application requires is relatively low. We can assume that if the application were placed in its own CICS region, CPU queueing would be insignificant. However, if the application required 30 percent or more of a processor engine, internal CPU queueing should be included, even in the best-case analysis.

We also have ignored the effect of operating system contention. We have assumed that we could give the application a high enough MVS dispatching priority to minimize systemwide contention if necessary.

Finally, we have ignored total processor capacity. If the application was being run on a uniprocessor, the 8 percent CPU usage would represent an 8 percent increase in total processor utilization. The percentage would be much less on a four- or six-engine processor.

It is acceptable to ignore specific environmental considerations in the best-case analysis. Later, when we perform a more detailed analysis of how the application would fit in an existing environment, we will need to consider all of these considerations. However, if it is obvious that some factors cannot be ignored in your environment, then they should be included in the best-case analysis.

> **Key Point:** The purpose of the best-case analysis is to provide a quick estimate of whether the application has the potential to perform at all. If it will not perform acceptably under ideal conditions, it will not deliver acceptable performance in a production environment.

Results of the Best-Case Analysis. So far, we have gathered information about the invoice application and its requirements. We have estimated internal CPU usage and "best-case" I/O times for VSAM files and journals. For DASD resources, we have assumed that we could configure a system capable of delivering 15 to 20 ms service time per I/O request. We have ignored CPU queueing and all other types of contention.

Our research has shown that VSAM files should require 900 to 1198 ms of "ideal" DASD service per invoice. Journals and the system log are expected to add another 387 to 516 ms of server delays. Each invoice should require about 77 ms of CPU time. Assuming that we have identified all resources used by the application, it should take *no less than* 1364 to 1791 ms processing to service one invoice. This is summarized in Table 9.15.

Our performance goal was to process invoices in 3 seconds or less. An average of 2.6 transactions will be entered for each invoice. Assuming that terminals are either locally attached to the host or on very high-speed lines and that total network delay is about 0.1 seconds per transaction, network delays would add about .26 seconds per invoice.

The results of the best-case analysis show that the invoice system should meet users' service requirements under ideal conditions. As long as we can configure a system capable of delivering 15 to 20 ms service time for DASD I/Os, can place the system in a lightly used CICS region, do not have intense competition from operating system tasks, and can

Table 9.15 "Best-Case" Analysis of the Invoice System

Item	Service time
VSAM files	900-1198 ms
Journals and system log	387-516 ms
CPU used by the primary TCB	77 ms
Total service time excluding queueing	1364-1791 ms

place users on local or high-speed lines, we can meet the service requirements for the invoice system.

The results would suggest that the invoice system has the potential to deliver acceptable performance under ideal conditions. This suggests that even if the system will not fit into a specific configuration, it can be made to perform with adequate hardware and software resources. On the other hand, if performance was not acceptable or marginal at this point, we might be want to examine the design more closely. Designs that do not run well under ideal conditions usually fail miserably on a loaded system.

9.3.6 Evaluate Performance in the Anticipated Environment

So far, the discussion in this chapter has shown how to develop a software model and then perform a best-case analysis of anticipated performance. Using these procedures, it should not be too difficult to determine if new CICS applications have the potential to perform in an ideal environment.

When new CICS applications are added into existing CICS environments, we must consider both how the application will fit in the environment and how it will impact existing applications. While it is possible to resolve complex relationships manually, modeling software will certainly simplify the task.

If a modeling package is available, the modeling software would be used to integrate information about the new system with information about the existing operating environment. Assuming that we had a calibrated model of the existing environment, information from the software models could then be introduced. The modeling package could then be used to project resource utilizations and response times and to evaluate various "what-if" scenarios.

When we are evaluating new CICS applications, we may need to review a number of options. New CICS applications may be placed in existing CICS regions or in separate regions. Applications may access resources locally in the same region or they may need to use MRO services. A number of interrelated factors affects the placement and performance of new and existing CICS applications.

Furthermore, files can be placed on dedicated volumes or on volumes with existing files. Different strings and controllers have different performance characteristics, and the presence of a new major workload can change these characteristics. Controller options (such as read caching and DASD fast write), the amount of cache storage, and existing DASD activity all can affect potential service. Read and write caching usually will improve DASD service, but unless access patterns support good cache-hit ratios, caching can actually degrade DASD service.

Processing by new systems will affect total CPU utilization and competition for the CPU among address spaces. New systems also affect DASD access patterns and contention among DASD components. All these factors need to be considered when evaluating how a new system will affect, and be affected by, an existing environment.

Placing the Invoice Application in a CICS Region. Data from the best-case analysis can be used to assess the size of new systems. This information can help us determine which options might be viable.

In the best-case analysis we estimated that each invoice will process an average of 2.6 transactions and should require 77 ms of CPU time. Overall, the system should require 289 CPU seconds per hour when users are processing 3,750 invoices per hour. A value of 289 CPU seconds translates into the equivalent of about 8 percent of a processor engine.

Even though we have estimates of user work rates and staff size, we should recognize that additional users may be hired or that users may work more quickly than originally projected. In either case, peak activity can be higher than projected. In our planning, we should be sensitive to the fact that our estimates may understate total requirements.

The first decision we will address is the placement of the application in a CICS region. One factor to consider is the location of resources accessed by the application. Three of the files used in the invoice application are new and can, at least in theory, be placed in any CICS region. FILEC already exists and is being used by other CICS applications. The new application is expected to use FILEC fairly heavily. To save MRO overhead, it might be worth placing the invoice application in the CICS region that owns FILEC. This, of course, assumes that FILEC does not live in either a *file owning region* (FOR) or *resource owning region* (ROR).[4]

If we decide to place the invoice application in an existing *application owning region* (AOR), we need to consider how it will affect CPU demand within that region. This is a two-step process.

The first step is to estimate the total increase in CPU utilization system-wide and how this affects CPU contention for CICS regions of the same or higher MVS dispatching priorities. The total CPU cost associated with running a CICS application (including overhead) typically will be 20 to 30 percent more than the CPU time directly charged to CICS transactions. CICS transaction statistics will not include CICS internal overhead (such as for CICS dispatching and terminal control) or MVS overhead (such as processing I/O interrupts). For small systems, these overhead values can be ignored. For larger, more resource intensive systems, some effort should be made to estimate these values.

In this example, we estimated that CICS transactions will use 8 percent of one processor engine. If we were running on a four-engine processor, this would translate to about 2 percent of the processor. Even if overhead were as much as 30 percent, the total load on the processor should be less than 3 percent.

For the purposes of this illustration, we will assume that the total CPU time used by equal- and higher-priority tasks was less than 70 percent and that the CPU time added by the new invoice system would not materially affect processor contention systemwide. If this had been a larger application or if total CICS-related CPU activity had been higher, techniques illustrated in Chapter 7 would be used to adjust for processor contention in this and other CICS regions.

Assuming that we will place the invoice application in an existing AOR, we must evaluate the effect of the application on the AOR. We start by converting CPU time to dispatch time. In this example, we have assumed that total systemwide CPU contention should not change significantly when this application is added. Therefore, the ratio of dispatch time to CPU time should in the AOR should not change significantly.

Assuming that dispatch time in the AOR has been 1.2 times as large as CPU time, we can estimate that dispatch time per invoice should be about

---

[4] A more complete discussion of CICS MRO strategies can be found in Appendix D.

92 ms. Similarly, the invoice application should add about 9.6 percent (1.2 x 8 percent) to CPU demand in the region.

At this point, we would use Table B.1 in Appendix B and the technique illustrated in Chapters 6 and 7 to estimate the effect of internal queueing on CICS performance. For the purposes of this illustration, suffice it to say that we will need to merge CPU demand for new and existing applications, estimate a new server ratio, and select a new service multiplier.

Scanning Table B.1 we see that an increase of 10 percent CPU demand (server utilization) will make a significant difference in queueing at higher levels of utilization. The table also shows that when server utilization (CPU demand) is 50 percent or less, a 10 percent change in server utilization will produce only a minor change in the service multiplier and queueing. It should not be hard to estimate whether the additional processing generated by the new system will have a material effect on dispatch processing in an existing CICS region.

The reader is encouraged to review those techniques illustrated in Chapters 6 and 7 to estimate the effect of CPU demand on CICS performance. The reader is also reminded that CICS represents a series of interrelated queueing systems. When service changes at any component, other components will be affected indirectly. Modeling tools help evaluate the effect of these relationships.

When evaluating how new CICS applications will perform in an existing environment, we should consider both systemwide and internal processor competition. First, we should consider increased competition among MVS tasks and its effect on CICS internal dispatching. Then we can evaluate delays associated with dispatch queueing in the CICS region in which the application will be placed. MVS processor competition will affect CICS CPU demand. This, along with the added workload will affect dispatch queueing and CICS response time. Techniques discussed in Chapters 6 and 7 can be used to estimate contention and delays.

One final comment: It is important to consider the effect of the new system on recurring peak periods.[5] We also should investigate whether the new workload could cause a shift in recurring peaks.

A More Realistic Look at DASD. When we performed the best-case analysis, we assumed the DASD environment could deliver 15 to 20 ms

---

[5] The importance of recurring peak periods for performance planning was discussed in Chapters 3 and 4.

SPE — Application Design Example   269

service per DASD I/O. We made no attempt to determine what it would take to accomplish that level of service.

As was the case for CPU activity, no event takes place in a vacuum. Increases in DASD activity on any volume affect the activity of other volumes sharing the same controller and channels. In Chapter 11, we will take a closer look at DASD service for CICS applications. We will show that, on the whole, DASD performance is very difficult to model or predict. Many factors that cannot be directly measured effect DASD service.

Now we will revise our estimates of DASD service and estimate resource utilization contributed by the invoice application. This is one situation where a modeling package can certainly make the job of estimating performance easier.

One way to estimate resource utilization is to summarize the components of DASD service that contribute to "device busy." For the purposes of this illustration, we can "borrow" values from the same string(s) on which the files will be placed. This will work acceptably for smaller systems. For major systems, the entire DASD subsystem should be reevaluated with the added workload.

Table 9.16 shows the estimated contribution of each type of file request to device busy. This table is constructed using percentages from Table 9.10 and a constant value of 13 ms per physical I/O. The 13 ms represents an estimate of seek time, rotational delay, data transfer time, and delays receiving a path to the volume. We will assume that we have "borrowed" this value from other volumes in the same environment running during the same time period. It might be more appropriate to use a range of values instead of selecting a single value (13 ms), but we will use a single value in this illustration.

> **Key Point**: The value of 13 ms used for DASD service above is valid only for this example and may not be valid in any other environment. To use this technique, you must determine appropriate values for your environment.

After estimating detailed service contributions for each logical event, we can estimate total service time for each file. Table 9.17 shows that FILEA receives little activity and should be capable of sharing a volume with other active files.

FILEB and FILEC will be used heavily by the new invoice system. FILEB is a new file and should be placed on a volume by itself or on a volume with little other activity. However, FILEC is an existing file used by

Table 9.16 Calculation of Average Volume Server Times for Logical Services

Resource	Type of Activity	Connect Time + Disconnect Time + Pend Time	Average Effective Service Time		
			Sequence Set	Data CI	VSAM I/O Request
FILEA	read	13 ms	0.7 ms	5.2 ms	5.9 ms
	update	13 ms		13 ms	13.0 ms
FILEB	read	13 ms	1.3 ms	10.4 ms	11.7 ms
	update	13 ms		13.0 ms	13.0 ms
	add	13 ms	1.3 ms	23.4 ms	24.7 ms
FILEC	read	13 ms	13.0 ms	13.0 ms	26.0 ms
	update	13 ms		13.0 ms	13.0 ms
FILED	read	13 ms	0.7 ms	6.5 ms	7.2 ms
	update	13 ms		13.0 ms	13.0 ms
AIX-D	read	13 ms	0.7 ms	13.0 ms	13.7 ms
	update	13 ms		26.0 ms	26.0 ms

other applications. For this reason, it is important to investigate how the invoice system will affect other users of the file. It might be necessary to split the file onto multiple volumes, place the file under cache, or alter application programs so that the file can be accessed via LSR.

We will not attempt to calculate DASD queueing at this point. It follows different patterns than those discussed so far in this book. Chapter 11 presents techniques for evaluating DASD service. The reader is encouraged to review that chapter for information on estimating total DASD service.

Modeling Tools. We have discussed many of the factors that should be considered when evaluating new CICS applications. We have seen that not only will new applications be affected by the environment in which they are placed, but they will influence the performance of existing applications.

Chapters 6 and 7 provide the basic tools needed to evaluate processing contention in CICS regions. Chapter 11 discusses the analysis of DASD performance. Appendix D discusses MRO considerations. In simpler situations, these principles can be applied to evaluate the performance and environmental effect of new application systems.

However, when large, new systems are placed into existing complex environments, the task of evaluating all of the interrelationships between processing components becomes very complicated. Modeling tools are designed to help resolve these types of situations.

The reader is certainly encouraged to perform quick estimates of the impact of new application systems. The techniques developed so far should allow rough evaluations of the effect of even major systems. For most smaller systems, the techniques suggested in this chapter for best-case and advanced studies will provide very useful results. However, when large, complex systems are incorporated into complex MRO environments, more advanced tools will be very helpful.

Table 9.17 Total Resource Requirements for Anticipated Level of User Activity

Resource	Activity	Number per Invoice	Est. Service Time	Invoices per Hour	Device Usage per Hour	Projected Utilization
FILEA	read	4.3	5.9 ms	3750	95 sec.	
	update	0.1	13.0 ms	3750	5 sec.	
	TOTAL			3750	100 sec.	3%
FILEB	read	9.5	11.7 ms	3750	417 sec.	
	update	7.0	13.0 ms	3750	341 sec.	
	add	1.0	24.7 ms	3750	93 sec.	
	TOTAL			3750	851 sec.	24%
FILEC	read	8.7	26.0 ms	3750	848 sec.	
	update	7.5	13.0 ms	3750	366 sec.	
	TOTAL			3750	1214 sec.	34%
FILED	read	4.0	7.2 ms	3750	108 sec.	
	update	4.0	13.0 ms	3750	195 sec.	
	TOTAL			3750	303 sec.	8%
AIX-D	read	1.2	13.7 ms	3750	62 sec.	
	update	4.0	26.0 ms	3750	390 sec.	
TOTAL				3750	452 sec.	13%

9.4 SPREADSHEETS

Much of the material presented in this chapter has been shown in the form of tables. As a practical matter, data of this type can be easily adapted to PC-type spreadsheet programs. Data from one table are commonly merged with data from other tables using simple "formulas." If the spreadsheet is set up properly, columns or rows can be easily combined with other data.

This author recommends the use of PC spreadsheets to simplify the task of collecting and organizing model data. It will require a little extra work the first time a spreadsheet is developed, but once the data are entered in rows and columns, it can be easily manipulated. What-if questions can be accomplished by simply copying and modifying data. Much of the effort of combining and manipulating data can be simplified with simple spreadsheet commands. Spreadsheet data can then be used to drive modeling software if it is available.

Most modern spreadsheet packages also contain graphic capabilities that can be requested with little effort. It can be handy to create pie charts or bar graphs to get a better view of data. It might be nice to see what portion of resource utilization belongs to each component.

9.5 SUMMARY

As new CICS applications are being designed, it is good practice to ensure that they can perform acceptably at an early point in their lifecycle. It is much easier and less expensive to address performance issues early in the design stage than after an application has been installed in production.

Modern CICS systems tend to be complex, including a wealth of functions and service. They tend to address complex business issues and include intricate processing schemes. CICS applications that take advantage of high-performance features, such as data tables, hiperspaces, or large LSR pools, can access large amounts of data and still deliver rapid response time. The relationship between application design, resource utilization, and performance is not always clear or easy to predict. All of this suggests that we should review potential performance before investing a large amount of time in system development.

In this chapter, we have developed a detailed example showing how to evaluate the performance of a new CICS system. In many cases, we might be tempted to perform our study, review the results, and do nothing further until the system is eventually installed. Although it will take some additional work, it should be worthwhile to update and evaluate the software model as better information becomes available. This can help ensure the accuracy of our forecasts. Loading model data into a spreadsheet or in modeling product will make it easier to reevaluate the model when the data changes.

The main reason for performing SPE studies is to screen for unacceptable designs before they become committed to code. Additional benefits include a better picture of the software and hardware needed when the system is finally implemented. Good planning improves the chances that application systems will perform acceptably when they are installed in production and helps prevent capacity-related surprises.

Chapter 10

SPE — Application Design Guidelines

10.1 OVERVIEW

In this chapter, we will examine the *principles of application design that lead to efficient and effective application systems.*[1] We will discuss the basic principles and show how each can be applied in a CICS environment. This chapter will show many specific ways the guidelines can be applied to CICS applications and to the CICS environment.

The application design principles, or guidelines, presented in this chapter can improve applications in three ways. They can help provide CICS application systems that will:

- Allow users to work more effectively
- Be more responsive (have better response time)
- Make more efficient use of computer resources

At the highest level, SPE design guidelines can be used to create systems that allow users to work more effectively. When applied to overall system design, SPE guidelines seek to optimize user workflow.

---

[1] Dr. Connie Smith ([SMIT87] and [SMIT90]) developed and published a set of seven general guidelines for responsive application systems. The material presented in this chapter starts with the general principles suggested by Dr. Smith and tailors them to a CICS environment.

Along with user productivity, SPE design guidelines help ensure that systems will be responsive. Although these guidelines do not guarantee that systems will perform acceptably, they do suggest structures that have a better chance of delivering acceptable service.

Finally, SPE design guidelines suggest approaches that allow efficient use of resources. In a CICS environment, one of the best ways to control the amount of CPU time used by application systems is through the judicious use of SPE guidelines.

SPE application design guidelines can improve user effectiveness, provide better application performance, and allow more efficient systems, *often at the same time*. Guidelines that make users more effective often use fewer resources as well. Some guidelines to improve performance also may improve application efficiency or allow users to work more effectively.

10.1.1 Primary Audience

On the surface it might appear that application design guidelines are directed primarily toward *application developers*. Without question, these guidelines should be valuable for those designing CICS application systems. However, many guidelines are global in nature and can be helpful to CICS *systems programmers* as well. SPE guidelines can be applied in locating system resources and setting up CICS regions. These guidelines also should be useful for *performance analysts* or *CICS systems programmers* who are involved in reviewing application design.

10.2 IMPROVING CICS APPLICATION PERFORMANCE

There are several ways to improve the performance of CICS applications. We will discuss five of them.

1. One way is to *add processor capacity or faster external storage media*. Faster hardware will usually improve application performance. Depending on the relative speed of the hardware and the amount of time applications spend waiting for services, hardware upgrades can make a significant difference in performance. However, hardware upgrades normally will help only when resources are overworked and applications or systems are queued or waiting for services. Of course, hardware upgrades can be one of the more expensive approaches to improving application performance.

2. A second method of improving application performance is *system tuning*. System tuning involves adjusting system parameters and access to resources. Examples of tuning include increasing the number of buffers in an LSR pool, turning off system facilities such as trace, controlling the maximum number of CICS tasks, adjusting internal (CICS) or external (MVS) dispatching priorities, moving applications to alternate configurations, and moving DASD files to reduce volume or channel contention. As with hardware upgrades, system tuning is effective only when CICS applications are actually affected by the resources being tuned.

3. Another way to improve performance is *detailed application (micro) tuning*. With microtuning, application code is modified or rewritten to improve efficiency. Typically, portions of programs are modified to make internal processing more efficient. Unfortunately, microtuning has limited potential in a CICS environment. We will discuss this later.

4. The fourth method of improving application performance is the practice of *designing performance into applications*. It is the method preferred by this author. When SPE application design guidelines are used, systems will perform better, use fewer resources, and leverage user efforts. Once applications have been designed, it can be difficult to go back and make them efficient. Big-picture efficiency can be achieved only through efficient application design.

   Big-picture efficiency can be called *macro-tuning* or *macro-efficiency*. Of course, macro-tuning is not really tuning but is the use of design principles that foster efficient, effective application systems.

5. A fifth method of improving application efficiency and performance is to *set installation coding standards.* Each installation should look for coding techniques that make sense in their environment and standardize their use. When microefficiencies are applied globally during application development, all applications will be slightly more efficient. Although it is usually not worth the effort to perform microtuning on existing applications, it may take very little work to select efficient techniques as applications are being developed. A small amount of processing saved in many application modules will help reduce CPU usage overall.

The first three methods of performance improvement deal with applications that are *already written*. At this point in the application life-cycle, the structure of the system and most application programs has been established and cannot be changed easily. System and application tuning and new hardware may or may not be able to resolve performance problems. The last two techniques address applications before they are written. The best opportunity to ensure acceptable performance and efficiency will come early in the application analysis and design stages.

10.2.1 Controlling CPU Usage in a CICS Environment

CICS transactions perform application processing and request CICS services such as file requests, program linkage, or screen mapping. Most CICS services invoke processing in several management modules or domains.

As a rule, several times more processing will occur in CICS system modules performing application requests than will occur in application code. Except for transactions that are unusually processor-intensive, much more processing will be spent performing CICS-related services than application processing.

Typically, no more than 5 to 15 percent of the processing in a CICS region is spent in actual application code. Most processing (75 to 90 percent) is spent in CICS management modules or domains supporting application requests.

Transaction statistics provided by CMF or other similar monitors show the amount of CPU time used by individual CICS tasks. The CPU time shown in transaction statistics includes processing performed by CICS management modules or domains called to service application requests. Usually, less than 15 percent of the CPU time shown in CMF transaction statistics will have been spent in actual application code. Most of the remainder of the time will be spent in CICS management modules performing application requests.

Because such a small amount of processing occurs in actual application code, most types of microtuning and code optimization have little effect in a CICS environment. Unless application processing is grossly inefficient, traditional application tuning opportunities will have limited potential to reduce CPU usage. Even if all processing in application programs could be eliminated, CICS CPU utilization would be reduced by no more than 5-15 percent.

Optimizers can usually reduce application CPU usage by 10 to 30 percent. Since application code normally accounts for only 5 to 15 percent of the CPU time used in a CICS region, code optimizers, in theory, should be able to reduce total CICS usage by no more than .5 to 4.5 percent. Unless application code is unusually processor-intensive, code optimization may have limited value for most CICS applications.

In contrast, SPE application design guidelines do have the potential to reduce the processing required in CICS applications. When applications are efficient as a whole, they will require fewer resources to accomplish the same amount of work.

This author does not by any means discourage using code optimizers or tuning application code. Any savings of resources can be beneficial. However, it is important to recognize that processes and activities to tune or optimize CICS application code may provide limited benefit. Unless significant inefficiencies can be identified, tuning application code will have a very small effect on total CICS CPU usage.[2]

10.3 GENERAL PRINCIPLES OF EFFECTIVE AND RESPONSIVE SOFTWARE

In the remainder of this chapter, we will explore the seven principles (or guidelines) of software design originally defined by Dr. Connie Smith [SMIT90]. Dr. Smith's principles are valid for most kinds of data processing systems. This chapter will present a brief description of each principle, along with examples of how the principles can be applied to CICS-based applications.

SPE application design principles or guidelines can be applied to high-level system design as well as to the design of individual application programs. They can influence the efficiency and performance of systems at several levels.

SPE design guidelines are more than a set of tricks that magically transform inefficient code into efficient code. SPE design principles present a *unified design philosophy* that will improve performance, resource utilization, and user effectiveness at several levels. The use of these

---

[2] A product called Strobe from Programmart can be used to identify processing inefficiencies in CICS transactions. Unless a tool of this kind is used, it can be very difficult to locate application tuning opportunities that will materially reduce CICS CPU usage.

design principles should not be viewed as a way of tuning efficiency, but rather as a methodology that can improve both user effectiveness and system performance.

In Chapters 8 and 9, we emphasized the importance of addressing performance issues early in the application life-cycle. When performance is addressed early in system design, little additional effort will be needed to develop responsive code. In this chapter we will look at the principles or guidelines that can be used to create efficient, effective systems.

> **Key Point:** When SPE design guidelines are used, systems will not only perform better, but they will usually be less resource-intensive and provide better user satisfaction.

10.4 PRINCIPLE 1 – THE FIXING-POINT PRINCIPLE

The *fixing-point principle* refers to the time the relationship between flexibility and performance is fixed or committed. This principle involves the *trade-off between application flexibility and performance*.

Per the fixing-point principle, there is a cost for flexibility in application programs. The more flexible the application design, the more it will cost to execute the program. The earlier commitments are made, the more efficiently they can be handled.

It is usually more efficient to make commitments as early as possible. Commitments made prior to program execution usually will be more efficient than those made during program execution. Relationships that are resolved at program execution time normally will require more resources than those that can be resolved ahead of time. It will take more processing when application programs need to resolve relationships that could have been established prior to execution.

> **The fixing-point principle.** There is a trade-off between application flexibility and application efficiency.

DB2 Binds. A traditional example of the fixing principle is the *time at which DB2 application binds take place*. When binds are done dynamically (at execution time), there will be more flexibility. Processes will not need to commit to specific processing until the SQL call is issued. This provides optimal flexibility. The primary drawback to dynamic SQL calls is that binding must take place each time an SQL call is executed. This not only wastes resources, but it slows response time.

In contrast, static binds are more efficient than dynamic binds. When application programs are bound prior to program execution, their paths are fixed by DB2. They are normally bound when they are placed in the execution library. When application programs are executed, there is no need to rebind SQL calls to the database thus saving the overhead of path selection on each bind.

There is no real need to suggest that static binds should be used in CICS application programs. This is very much the standard for most CICS applications. However, this illustration was used because it provides a good example of the trade-offs involved in the fixing-point principle.

Fourth-Generation Languages. Fourth-generation languages normally interpret commands instead of compiling them. Each time code is executed, the language must reinterpret each command. Code is not fixed until execution time. It remains flexible and can be changed up to the time it is executed.

In contrast, second- and third-generation languages (assemblers and compilers), analyze code once and commit it to a series of machine-executable instructions. Code is fixed during the compile. Because of these differences, interpretive languages usually use more CPU resources than compiled languages to accomplish similar functions.

> **Key Point:** The fixing principle is much broader in scope than the time DB2 binds occur or the choice of compilers. It applies to any situation involving trade-offs between general solutions and specific implementations.

Application Flexibility. Program developers commonly include extra logic, just in case programs ever need to be enhanced. This goes beyond good program structure that can be easily modified, but includes specific code within programs to facilitate added functionality that may be required at a later time.

The cost of additional flexibility is often longer development time and decreased application efficiency. While it does not take much processing to execute a few additional instructions occasionally, a design philosophy that permeates code with openings for expansion probably will be less efficient overall. There is a cost associated with increased flexibility.

Fixing during System Design. Systems are sometimes designed with additional flexibility because users are not sure how the systems will be used. Users may have trouble envisioning the way they will use features on new systems. They may ask request a wide variety of options and services because they do not know exactly how they will use their systems.

The result is that many CICS systems designed today include a variety of services, many of which will be used infrequently, if at all. Multiple options may be provided to perform the same service in different ways.

The fixing principle would suggest that application developers become more familiar with user needs early in the design process. From an SPE perspective, designers should learn not only what functions the user will require, but how frequently each will be used. It may not be acceptable to omit services needed by users, even if they will be used infrequently. However, it may be possible to limit the number of ways infrequently used functions can be performed.

Sorts. There is probably no such thing as a "good" sort in a CICS environment. It can take a substantial amount of processing and storage to sort many items. Large sorts should be avoided in CICS transactions. It is usually more efficient to maintain the data in sequence than to perform frequent sorts in CICS transactions.

Response Testing versus HANDLE CONDITION. When the command-level interface was first introduced, HANDLE CONDITION commands were the only way to check the results of CICS commands. HANDLE CONDITION commands specify the names of routines to receive control when specified conditions occur. If a condition occurs for which no HANDLE was issued, the transaction will be abnormally terminated with a standard error code.

The HANDLE CONDITION is a very general command. HANDLE CONDITION logic is invoked for each command issued within a program (unless RESP is specified). The primary advantage of the HANDLE CONDITION is that special routines can be defined in a program to deal with specific conditions. The major disadvantage is that, unless separate HANDLE CONDITION commands are issued pointing to different error routines, it can be difficult to tell which command caused the condition.[3] In time, the PUSH and POP options were issued to establish multiple

---

[3] One of the more difficult situations to debug is an application that receives control in a HANDLE CONDITION routine for an error from a command it was not prepared to deal with.

HANDLE environments. This simplified management of the HANDLE CONDITION.

The RESP option is available in current releases of CICS/MVS and CICS/ESA. When the RESP option is coded on a CICS command, HANDLE CONDITION logic will be bypassed, and control will be returned to the application program after the command is executed. The application program is then responsible for checking the response code and taking any action that might be required. The disadvantage of the RESP option is that the responsibility for all error handling rests in the application program.

The two major advantages of using the RESP option are improved program structure and reduced processing overhead. When the RESP option is used, it is easier to code standard program structures that are more stable and easier to debug. As far as the responsibility for handling all unusual response conditions, it is not difficult to write a common routine to take appropriate action (probably abending the task) for unusual conditions. Application programs can check common responses and then call the error routine for exceptional conditions.

The primary advantage of using the RESP option is that is it is quite a bit more efficient than using HANDLE CONDITION commands. As with many other general solutions, the HANDLE CONDITION uses more resources. The simpler, less general RESP option uses much less CPU time and is more straightforward.

> **Key Point:** The RESP option not only is more efficient than more general HANDLE CONDITION commands, but it allows improved program structure.

10.5 PRINCIPLE 2 — LOCALITY PRINCIPLE

To improve both performance and effectiveness, *resources should be kept close to the processes they support*. When resources are "close" to the processes that use them, both performance and resource utilization should be improved.

The locality principle addresses four types of locality or closeness. *Spatial locality* is closeness of *distance*. *Temporal locality* involves having processes and resources *close together in time*. *Effectual locality* includes techniques which *match services to their needs*. *Degree locality* provides resources that *closely match capacity requirements*.

The locality principle. Keep resources close to the facilities that use them.

10.5.1 Spatial Locality – Closeness of Distance or Function

In a CICS environment, the principle of *spatial locality* can be applied at many levels. Systems programmers can use this principle as they set up CICS regions and define resources. Application developers can apply this same principle to create user interfaces that are both easier to use and more efficient. And this principle also can be used when coding application programs.

When applications and the resources they use are kept close to one another, both performance and efficiency will be improved. Sometimes spatial locality can be achieved without much effort or planning. At other times it may take some work to achieve good spatial locality. Usually, though, it should not take much effort to achieve good spatial locality.

Menu Content. Spatial locality can be used in the design of on-line menus. Users will be able to locate related functions more rapidly when they are grouped on the same menu screen. Appropriate grouping of menu data simplifies access to application functions.

Menu Navigation. Many systems have a hierarchical menu structure. This may require users to return to higher-level menus before selecting other services. Users might need to navigate up and down through several menu screens before being allowed to select functions. Good spatial locality would suggest an easy access path between menu selections that are commonly used together.

Figure 10.1 illustrates how good spatial locality would allow easy navigation between menu functions. Providing users with the ability to navigate directly between panels can help improve productivity and reduce the number of transactions entered. This should reduce processing requirements by eliminating navigation through extra menu screens.

Another way to apply this guideline might be in hot keys between applications. A single program function key could allow users to navigate between commonly used applications. For example, on an invoice entry screen, a hot key could allow users to pull up frequently used customer information quickly. A separate hot key could return the user to the invoice application.

While it may not be practical to allow cross-navigation between unrelated systems, easy screen navigation within a single system normally is desirable. For new systems, interscreen navigation can be included early in the design phase with little extra work. For existing systems, though, options of this kind could be hard to introduce.

Screen Content. When designing screen formats, data that are used together should be kept on the same screen if possible. Users should not have to enter multiple screens to access data that are commonly used at the same time. The user is best served if all the data needed to answer a question, make a decision, or solve a problem are contained on a single screen. Users will also benefit when all processing for common updates can be entered from a single screen.

Early in the design stage, it may not be easy to determine which user functions will be used together. User work patterns may not become apparent until users actually start using their systems. It may be possible, though, to set up prototypes of screen formats and ask users to run through scripts to solve business-related problems. This process can help determine which services and functions would be used together.

If spatial locality is to be applied to screen content, data access patterns must be researched before screen designs are completed. Once screen designs are set and programming has started, it can be difficult to change the screen designs. It is hard to apply the principle of spatial locality to screen formats after the early portions of the design phase.

NO Spatial Locality
Between Menu Items

Spatial Locality
Between Menu Items

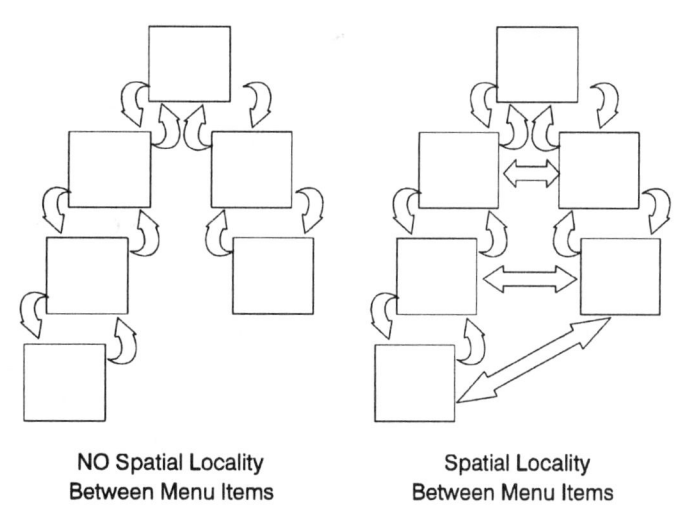

Figure 10.1 Spatial locality in menu navigation.

On the other hand, it may not always be wise to display related data. Unless data items are used together frequently, it may be wasteful to display them every time a query is made. If items are obtained from separate records or rows, additional I/O accesses may be required to obtain the data.

It takes some familiarity with the way users will reference data to design locality into screen formats. As a rule, the more that is known about how users will access systems, the more closely screens can be tailored to their needs.

Screen Design. Data fields that are commonly referenced together should be located close to one another on screen formats. Fields which are commonly entered together should be separated by no more than a single keystroke. User effort will be wasted when users need to tab through several fields to complete common transactions. The principle of locality would suggest that data items that are used together should be grouped together in the order users normally will reference them.

File Design. Spatial locality is useful in the design of files and databases. When data elements are frequently accessed together, it may be desirable to keep them in the same record or row. This will allow all related information to be referenced with a single physical access.

In relational database systems, normalization and theoretical flexibility must often be weighed against efficient access patterns. When data elements that are processed together can be stored in the same record or row, it will take less work to access data. Although the normalization of data can enhance application flexibility, designs with better data locality usually will perform better.

In theory, high locality in database and file designs might reduce data base flexibility but can make applications more efficient. These trade-offs need to be reviewed and evaluated.

CICS System Resources. The most efficient location for CICS resources normally is in the region in which they are accessed most frequently. It takes a considerable amount of overhead to access VSAM files, temporary storage, and transient data via MRO function shipping. In fact, in CICS/VS and CICS/MVS systems, it can take three to four times as much processing overhead to access files via function shipping as it does to access them locally. Similarly, MRO function shipping normally is more efficient than accessing data from another processor. The principle of spatial locality would suggest that the closer CICS resources are to the applications that use them, the more efficient accesses will be.

Although resources can be accessed most efficiently when they are defined locally, there are many reasons to place them in remote regions. One common reason is performance. When a resource, such as a VSAM file, is used heavily from two CICS AORs, it might not be wise to place the file definition in either AOR. If the AORs are heavily used, they may be constrained by high CPU demand, storage, or maximum tasks.

When a file is defined in an AOR, applications in that region will be able to access the file with minimal overhead. Other regions, though, might experience delays accessing the file. At times, it may be wise to place files in a FOR to guarantee reasonable service from multiple regions. The main drawback to placing files in an FOR is that it involves additional CPU overhead.

Another reason to place files in remote regions is application availability. In CICS/ESA, the idea of *resource-owning regions* (RORs) is becoming popular. When all CICS resources, such as files, transient data, and temporary storage are defined locally in RORs, it is possible to run the same applications in multiple AORs. The AORs then access resources contained in RORs and FORS. With the intelligent router program in CICS/ESA, if one AOR fails, transactions can be automatically routed to other AORs. Together, RORs and *redundant application regions* (RARs), can be used to improve application availability.

Defining all resources in the regions that use them is the most efficient and lowest-cost method of placing resources. ROR/RAR schemes are at the other extreme of cost, but provide better availability. In many CICS environments, the cost of accessing resources remotely is not as important as availability. When ROR/RARs are used, application availability is chosen over operating costs.

Linking Programs in Other CICS Regions. CICS/ESA release 3.3 provides new opportunities to improve spatial locality through use of the *dynamic program link* (DPL) facility. In modern CICS MRO environments, complex application functions often need to be performed in multiple CICS regions. Prior to DPL, CICS resources typically were defined in one region and accessed one-at-a-time via MRO or ISC from other regions. With DPL, CICS program links can be shipped directly between CICS regions or platforms, and a set of related logic can be performed in a single region owning the necessary resources.

As shown in Figure 10.2, the advantage of DPL is that a series of remote services can be accessed via a single request. Instead of shipping multiple file, temporary storage, or transient data requests between regions, a single request can be shipped that performs a logical block of work. Resources can be accessed locally in the server region, saving MRO overhead. DPL allows complex units of work to be defined in the most appropriate CICS region or platform and accessed as a unit from other CICS systems.

The trade-off between using DPL and simply accessing resources remotely will center on the amount of processing being done and the number of file accesses required. Distributing work indiscriminately can complicate the relationships between CICS regions and introduce unnecessary inter-region dependencies.

The use of CICS distributed program link (DPL) to pass requests between regions or platforms can provide better locality by keeping resources close to the code (routines) that access them.

Key Point: The principle of spatial locality suggests that it is more efficient to have resources close to applications. Sometimes it will be more efficient to keep copies of simple routines,

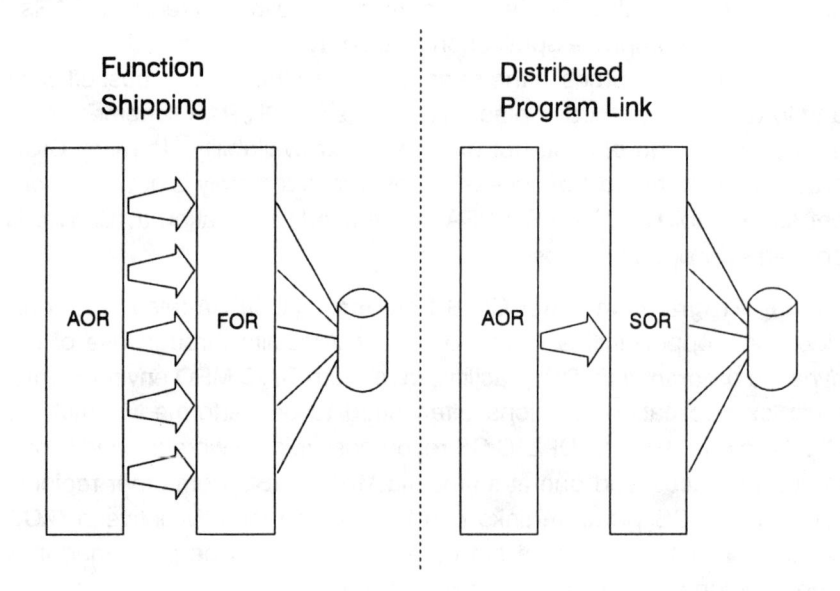

Figure 10.2 DPL versus function shipping.

such as date routines, in each CICS region to minimize cross-region overhead. As a general guideline, DPL will help locality when the overhead of several function shipping requests can be replaced by a single DPL call. It may not be efficient to use DPL simply to consolidate services into a single region.

Selecting Records from DB2 Tables. CICS applications that request records from DB2 databases can either request that DB2 return only selected records or select records themselves. Good spatial locality would suggest that DB2 perform record selection. This will save the overhead of passing unneeded records back to CICS. Not only will overhead be saved on record selection, but DB2's optimizer logic can choose the most efficient access path for the data selected.

Client-Server Applications. Spatial locality is especially important in the design of client-server applications. Client-server applications commonly use CICS facilities to support work on other platforms. CICS's powerful communication and file control options provide an ideal link for applications requiring access to data or processing on a host system.

In client-server applications, it is especially important to locate data close to where it will be used. Depending on network topography, the costs and delays associated with transferring data between nodes can be substantial. The amount of data that may be transferred between CICS and remote applications may be limited by transmission time across communication links. Decisions of where to place application processing and files (on the host, in the workstation, or on a remote file server) are important in client-server design.

Good locality would suggest that we avoid heavy access of data across telephone links. Systems designs that concentrate processing on multiple nodes and pass a limited number of packets across communication media probably will provide better performance and be less resource-intensive.

10.5.2 Temporal Locality — Closeness in Time

Temporal locality suggests that the order and timing of processing can affect application performance. Resources should be available when they are needed, and applications should take advantage of the natural order of data. Like spatial locality, temporal locality can be applied at several levels.

Menu Design. Users can be more effective if it is easy for them to access the functions they use most often. When systems are accessed primarily by casual users, it should be easy to locate common services. When the most popular services are on a very early menu, users can access them quickly without searching through multiple menus. Similarly, menu selections that are not used very often can be placed on lower or specialized menus. This will improve user service and save the cost of processing multiple menus.

Menu shortcuts will be beneficial for systems used primarily by experienced users. As illustrated in Figure 10.3, menu shortcuts allow users to select applications directly from the high-level menu even if they are defined on a lower menu. Instead of selecting item "2" on the first menu, item "5" on the second menu, and item "3" on the third menu, users would enter "2.5.3" and go directly to the chosen application. Temporal locality is improved by allowing users to access functions quickly.

Processing Data. Good temporal locality suggests that all related processing be performed at one time. This is done to avoid the additional overhead associated with reaccessing data. When possible, related processing should be concentrated in a single transaction. When this is not

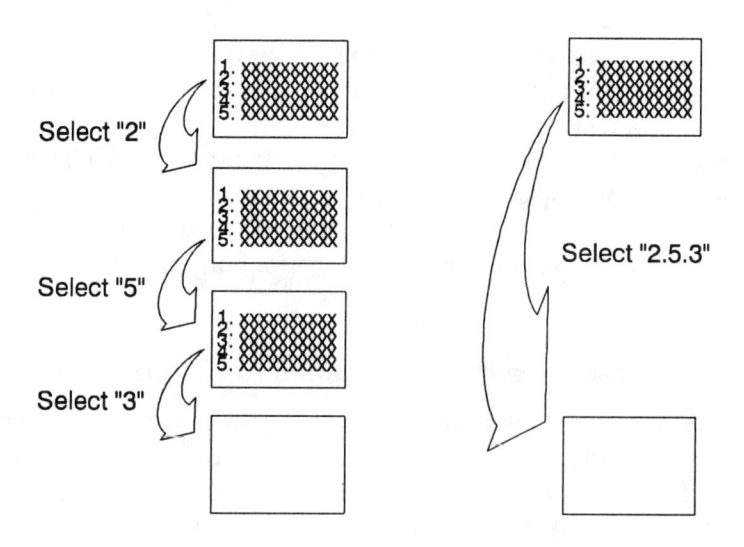

Figure 10.3 Simplified menu selection.

possible, processing should be continued in immediately subsequent transactions to optimize buffer and cache look-aside potential.

The Size of Buffer Pools. When users commonly perform a series of CICS transactions to accomplish a single function, much of the same data will be accessed in successive transactions. Many access facilities, such as local shared resources (LSR), auxiliary temporary storage, and DB2, allow data to be reaccessed directly from buffers. Since many applications process the same or similar data in a series of transactions, better locality will be achieved if buffer pools are large enough to retain data used by a series of transactions.

To achieve better temporal locality, buffer pools should be large enough to retain data accessed by a series of transactions. Records should be kept in memory long enough for subsequent transactions to reaccess them without revisiting DASD. Of course, the size of buffer pools is subject to other limitations, particularly that of real storage.[4]

Applications may be designed to allow users to concentrate on a particular unit. For example, users may enter a series of transactions for a particular city or state. As long as the user continues to work one locality, a similar set of records will be accessed. Once the user moves on to another set of data, he or she will access other data. Here, it is beneficial to have a large enough buffer pool to keep an appropriate set of records in memory.

Unless we know quite a bit about data access patterns and user behavior, it can be very difficult to predict data usage patterns. The best way to size buffer pools is to experiment and watch read-hit ratios. When additional buffers fail to improve look-aside values, the pool is probably as large as it needs to be. When natural data access patterns exist, there should be a fairly distinct point at which increases in pool size provide diminishing returns.

Depending on data access patterns, the number of buffers required to achieve good read-hit ratios can vary considerably. There are no magic look-aside targets that we should strive for. Data on some files are accessed in a truly random manner, and it might not be possible to achieve even a 20 percent read-hit ratio for this data, even with a very

---

[4] Temporary storage buffer pools are below the line in CICS/VS and CICS/MVS. Virtual storage may be the primary limitation to the size of the temporary storage buffer pools in these versions of CICS.

large pool. Other data may be reused so frequently that read-hit ratios can approach 100 percent.

For LSR pools, it is usually worthwhile to keep indexes and data in separate subpools.[5] Even when data CIs do not have good reaccess patterns, index CIs may have good read-hit ratios – even with a limited pool size. By separating indexes and data into separate subpools, each can be tuned separately.

10.5.3 Effectual Locality – Closeness in Purpose

Effectual locality suggests that processing we take advantage of performance-related features. Performance-related hardware and software features can improve application response time and efficiency. Effectual locality tends to be more closely associated with system functions and software options than with application design. In many ways, exploiting effectual locality is similar to system tuning.

Exploiting DASD Fast Write. Some DASD controllers provide a feature called *DASD fast write* (DFW). When DFW is active for a volume (or file, as the case may be), applications will not have to wait for data to be transferred to DASD devices. As soon as reconrds are transferred to the controller, applications will be allowed to continue processing. The controller will take responsibility for eventually storing the data on the appropriate DASD device.[6] When DFW is available, it can provide improved DASD service times for files with high write activity.

DFW is especially recommended for the *CICS system log*.[7] Typically, a large percent of writes to the system log are synchronous writes. Whenever CICS tasks update protected files, file updates are not scheduled until the "before-images" are written to the system log. When DFW is used, journal writes are considered complete as soon as log records are

---

[5] In CICS/VS and CICS/MVS systems, the only practical way to separate data and index CIs into separate buffer pools is to have different data and index CI sizes, forcing them into different-size subpools. Current releases of CICS/ESA allow data and indexes to be defined in separate subpools. By mapping index and data CIs into separate subpools, each can be tuned separately.
[6] When DASD fast write is being used, data integrity is ensured by the nonvolatile storage (NVS) in the controller. NVS is controller storage backed by a battery. Data will be held in NVS during power failures and can be written to DASD once power is restored.
[7] DASD fast write is commonly recommended for the CICS system log. However, DASD fast write is, at least in theory, a little less dependable than writes done directly to DASD. The reason for this is that if there were a prolonged power failure, in theory, data in the NVS could be lost. The chances of this happening should be very small, and DASD fast write is generally considered quite reliable.

transferred to the controller. This reduces journal-related delays and helps improve transaction response time.

Although DASD fast write is strongly recommended for the CICS system log, it may not provide much benefit for *CICS journals*. Although most writes to the system log are performed *synchronously*, much of the data written to other journals is written *asynchronously*. As shown in Figure 10.4, CICS tasks will not wait for asynchronous writes to the journal data set. CICS tasks will resume processing when journal records are moved to a journal buffer.

Since transactions seldom wait for asynchronous journal writes, there is little value in using DFW for CICS journals dominated by asynchronous write activity. On the other hand, when journal records are written synchronously, CICS tasks will wait while journal records are sent to external storage, and DFW can help improve CICS transaction response time.

The CICS *restart data set* is also a good candidate for DASD fast write. After CICS startup, most activity to the restart data set is write activity. DFW can help relieve a potential bottleneck.

Other candidates for DASD fast write are *VSAM files with high write activity*. ESDS data sets used to log data normally are good DFW candi-

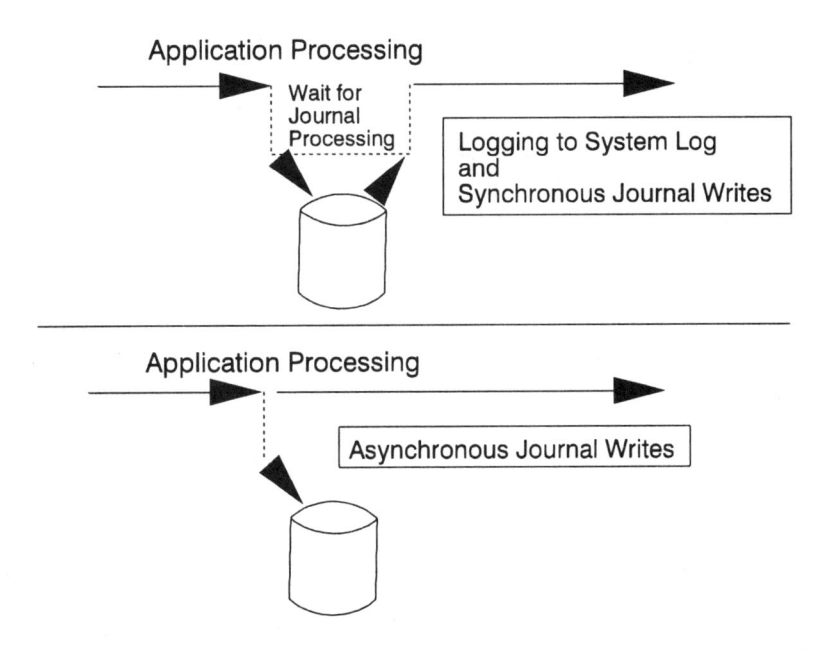

Figure 10.4 Asynchronous vs. synchronous journaling.

dates. However, VSAM KSDS files with very good data read-hit ratios may be *very poor* candidates for DFW. As explained in Chapter 11, when DFW is active, tracks will be staged when they are not already in cache for nonformatted writes (the type of writes normally performed by VSAM). This can cause a considerable amount of controller overhead when data subpools have high read-hit ratios, because they may not be mapped in the controller. This can actually degrade performance.

DFW is usually recommended for DB2 system logs. However, when DB2 log activity is extremely heavy, DFW may provide little benefit or even degrade performance. DB2 reference manuals should be consulted for more specific information.

DASD fast write is <u>definitely not recommended</u> for *DB2 data tables*. DB2 has its own rules for writing to data tables. Unless one of a few specific situations occurs,[8] output data may remain in DB2 buffers for a long time (even hours or days) without being committed to DASD. When DB2 does write data to tables, it attempts to write a large number of pages with each write request. DASD fast write provides no benefit for this type of activity. More important, though, the use of DFW for DB2 tables can monopolize the NVS while DB2 is writing to tables. This can hurt the performance of other applications using DFW.

> **Key Point:** DASD fast write is normally recommended for DB2 system logs but should <u>not</u> be used for DB2 tables.

Exploiting Features of Data Base Services. As a rule, most database systems have some options that produce good on-line service and some that do not. Where possible, applications should plan to use database features that provide high performance and low overhead. Doing this can make a dramatic difference in CICS performance.

Conventional wisdom suggests that simple relational structures perform better than complex ones. CICS applications designed to read or write a moderate number of database pages can receive excellent database service. However, applications that take advantage of complex database functions requiring large scans or sorts probably will deliver

---

[8] Updated DB2 data will be kept in the buffer pool and not written to DASD until it is triggered by one of the following: A buffer manager threshold is reached (such as 50 percent of the pool containing write data); a threshold is reached related to the number of pages updated for a specific table; a database being stopped; a quiesce is processed; or DB2 takes a system checkpoint.

less that exceptional response time. Furthermore, complex functions tend to be processor intensive.

Relational databases can be excellent companions for CICS application systems. When they are used with wisdom, database systems can deliver excellent service at an acceptable cost. When complex services are used, though, relational data bases can provide poor service and high resource costs.

Optimizing Network Data Streams. When CICS messages must travel across remote telephone lines, network transmission time can be a large part of response time. For lines with speeds of 9600 bps (bits per second) or less, it can take several seconds to transmit a full screen of data.

Network optimizers use various techniques to reduce the size of network data streams. Some optimizers can reduce the number of characters transmitted by over 50 percent. With fewer characters transmitted, user response time will improve, sometimes dramatically.

10.5.4 Locality of Degree — Matching Processing to Capacity

Degree locality involves matching hardware and software capacity to application requirements. Degree locality suggests that resources should be appropriately sized. They should be neither too large nor too small.

CPU Demand. For the best degree locality, CICS regions should be structured so that CPU demand during peak periods is neither too high nor too low. As discussed in Chapters 6 through 8, transaction response time will suffer when CPU demand is too high. Conversely, when peak CPU demand is very low, much of the processing will be consumed by CICS overhead, thus wasting CPU resources. This is called the "low utilization effect."

The goal of degree locality is to match resource capacity to application requirements. This will result in acceptable performance without wasting resources. A good target might be to have peak CPU demand in CICS regions between 25 and 40 percent.

Processor Engine Speed. A corollary of the CPU demand recommendation is that most CICS systems will perform better on faster processors. As a rule, when two processors have about the same amount of power, the processor with the faster engines will provide better CICS performance. For example, a three-engine processor with the equivalent power of an older six-engine processor should out-perform the six-engine processor for most CICS workloads. This principle was illustrated in the final example in Chap. 7.

> **Key Point:** CICS workloads will normally perform better on faster processor engines.

Processor Storage. Degree locality also calls for adequate processor storage to handle existing workloads. Not only is it important to have enough real and expanded storage to eliminate most external paging, but there should be enough real storage to keep page movement to and from expanded storage at reasonable levels.

Common Subroutines. Subroutines will be more efficient if they are tailored to perform a specific definable function. They should have a clearly defined purpose and clearly defined inputs and outputs. Common subroutines should be responsible for one specific function.

The purer the function of a common subroutine (or module), the better the chance that the module will perform that function correctly. As seen in Figure 10.5, subroutines should be coded as "black boxes" with a single function. All programs that access a subroutine should adhere to the same input and output conventions.

10.6 PRINCIPLE 3 — PROCESSING VERSUS FREQUENCY PRINCIPLE

The primary purpose of the processing versus frequency principle is to *minimize the total amount of resources used*. In achieving this purpose, this guideline *helps create systems that allow users to be more effective and productive*.

There is often a trade-off between the complexity of individual transactions and the total number of transactions executed. The trade-off involves balancing the amount of processing per transaction against the number of transactions users must enter to complete a business-related function. This principle suggests that we try to minimize the *product* of the number of transactions needed to complete a function and the average resources used per task. As a rule, it is better to optimize resource utilization for business functions than for single transactions.

"Black Box"

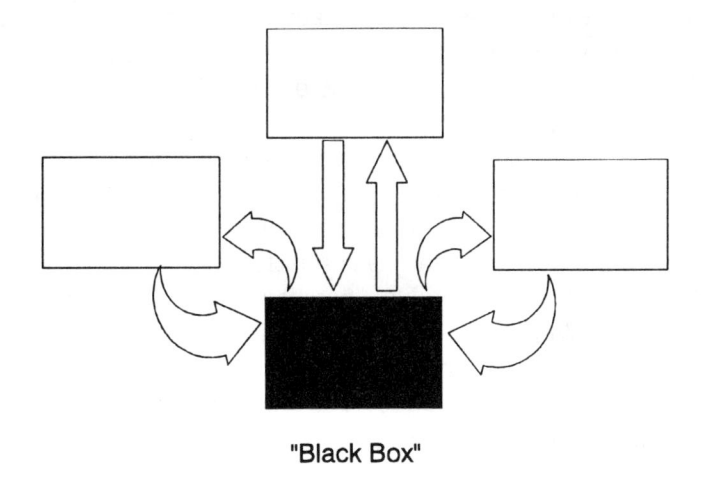

Figure 10.5 Common subroutines should be "black boxes."

The processing versus frequency principle. Balance the complexity of individual transactions against the number of transactions processed to minimize the total amount of resources used.

The Amount of Data Displayed. When inquiry-type transactions are designed, analysts must decide how much data will be displayed Certain information will be needed most of the time. Other information may be needed occasionally, and still other data may be almost never used. The processing-versus-frequency principle suggests that the choice of which information to display should weigh the cost of displaying information against the frequency at which it is used.

If information is seldom used, it might not be worth displaying every time. Not only will there be a cost to displaying data, but large amounts of optional data can clutter screen formats. This makes them less usable for casual users. Applications can be designed to display infrequently used data on separate screens or only when users enter special parameters.

The purposes of this guideline are to minimize total processing costs and improve user service. When information is already in memory (e.g., additional fields in records already being processed), there may be very little cost associated with moving it to display areas. The processing cost of providing users with potentially useful data would be almost nil. On the other hand, when nonessential information must be read from external storage, there will be a definite cost in terms of processing and response time. Not only will it cost more to execute transactions, but CICS internal response time will be longer.

Another factor is the way terminals are connected to the host. If terminals are connected locally or on high-speed lines, the total number of characters transmitted normally will have a minor effect on response time. However, when terminals are connected to slower lines, additional characters can make a noticeable difference in the response time experienced by users. When many infrequently referenced fields are displayed every time, users will wait longer to receive displays.

When user devices are connected to low-speed lines (e.g., 9600 bps of less), displaying large amounts of optional data can materially degrade user response time.

It is important to consider the total number of transactions as well as the number of characters in each screen format. When optional data will be used frequently and users must enter additional transactions to retrieve it, the cost of transmitting additional transactions may be more than the savings of not displaying optional data.

> **Key Point:** It is important to remember that *the goal of this guideline is to minimize total resource usage.*

10.7 PRINCIPLE 4 — THE CENTERING PRINCIPLE

In most CICS systems, a few transaction types will account for most CICS processing. Most activity will be concentrated in a few transaction IDs, and most application processing will be concentrated in a small number of application modules. Sometimes, as few as 5 to 10 percent of the application modules in a CICS region will be responsible for 90 percent or more of the processing in that region. In this context, the term "processing" includes the CPU time used directly by the application and by CICS management modules called by the application.

Moreover, in most application programs, a small portion of the code will be used very heavily. Much of the code in most programs will be executed infrequently, if at all. As little as 20 percent of a program's code may be responsible for 80 percent or more of the application processing.

The centering principle suggests that the best efficiency can be achieved by concentrating on the performance of the most heavily referenced programs and routines. The best candidates for tuning or optimization are those transactions or routines that are used most frequently. Efforts to improve frequently used transactions or routines normally have the greatest payback.

> **The centering principle.** Streamline access to the most commonly used processing and services.

Customizing Menu Paths. Functions that are commonly referenced should be the most easy to access. This is especially important when users may not be familiar with the content of menus or submenus. If possible, the most frequently accessed menu selections should appear on the highest-level menu. Services which are not commonly used are better placed on later menu entries. It might even be possible to dedicate program function (PF) keys to very popular functions. Quick access to popular functions will help users access system functions more effectively.

Customizing Screen Design. To achieve the best performance and lowest resource utilization, screens and menus that are frequently used should be free of data that are used less frequently. The most commonly used screens provide the best performance if they are customized to contain only essential data fields. Other, less essential data can be presented on separate screens. Only when specialized data are needed will additional screens be accessed. The goal of this principle is to allow heavily used screens to perform efficiently.

This guideline is similar to one discussed under the *processing versus frequency* principle (see page 297). However, in the centering principle, the emphasis is on high-volume transactions. Improvements in the efficiency of high-volume components have the greatest potential to improve overall performance and resource utilization.

When screens are tailored to expedite the services most frequently performed by users, the users' job can be simplified. When only necessary data fields are displayed, users will not need to deal with superfluous or confusing data elements. The following guidelines are suggested for application screen design:

- Optimize the workflow for those users who access the system most heavily.
- Streamline screens to benefit the most frequent users.

- Display only data necessary for users to perform predominant system functions.
- Reduce the number of keystrokes required to perform common services.

User effectiveness, overall transaction response time, and software efficiency can be improved by streamlining access to functions commonly referenced by high-volume users.

Optimizing CICS Application Processing. As a rule, programs should be designed to pass control to the predominant logic path as quickly as possible. If a certain function will be selected 90 percent of the time, the logic to select that function should occur very early in processing. Little extraneous processing should occur before selecting the predominant function.

Earlier in this chapter we stated that most CPU utilization in a CICS region occurs in CICS management modules. Processing within application programs accounts for a small portion of total CICS processor use. Consequently, application coding efficiencies by themselves usually have only a limited effect on either resource usage or performance.

However, streamlining program structure to make better use of CICS services can influence processing and responsiveness. Normally, the most effective application tuning strategy for CICS applications is to address overall program structure. Programs that apply SPE guidelines for overall efficiency will use fewer CICS resources and be more responsive.

Communications for Client-Server Applications. In client-server applications, communication between clients (workstations) and servers (the host — perhaps CICS) can be a key component of response time. The number of characters transmitted, even on higher speed lines, will influence application responsiveness.

The centering principle suggests we concentrate on improving the applications generating the most network traffic. APPC pairs that transmit large volumes of data between platforms can gain the most benefit from tuning and optimization. The more data transmitted, the higher the potential benefit.

From a large picture perspective, heavy network traffic in a client-server application may suggest that processing is not taking place on the optimal platform. While client-server architectures offer the ability to distribute processing to multiple platforms, some early implementations concentrate processing on a single platform (either the host or the work station). Client-server applications may be more effective if application processing occurs on multiple platforms. Heavy network traffic between nodes may indicate that either processing or data might be moved to different nodes or platforms.

10.8 PRINCIPLE 5 – THE ASYNCHRONOUS PROCESSING PRINCIPLE

In a CICS environment, it is sometimes better to split processing between transactions or regions. It may be beneficial to divide transactions into separate processing units to allow some processing to occur concurrently with other activity. The *asynchronous processing* principle suggests that *asynchronous processing involves trade-offs between response time and application complexity.*

In a classic sense, asynchronous processing involves dividing work so that it may be dispatched simultaneously on separate processors. However, this requirement is rare in a CICS environment. For CICS applications, asynchronous processing normally involves overlapping functions and distributing processing to transactions not associated with terminals.

> **The asynchronous processing principle.** There is a trade-off between the benefits of creating asynchronous processing units and the complexity and cost of controlling them.

Separating Nonessential Processing. With the complex application structures common in today's CICS systems, a single CICS transaction may be required to update data for several applications systems. This may cause a conflict between transaction response time and transaction functionality.

A common solution is to complete essential processing in the transaction initiated by the user and then start another CICS transaction (not associated with a terminal) to perform additional processing. Users will experience faster response times, and other processing can occur in parallel. The advantage is improved user productivity The cost is additional overhead and complexity. This technique is illustrated in Figure 10.6.

Additional overhead is required to start and run asynchronous tasks. When one or more asynchronous tasks are started for each terminal-

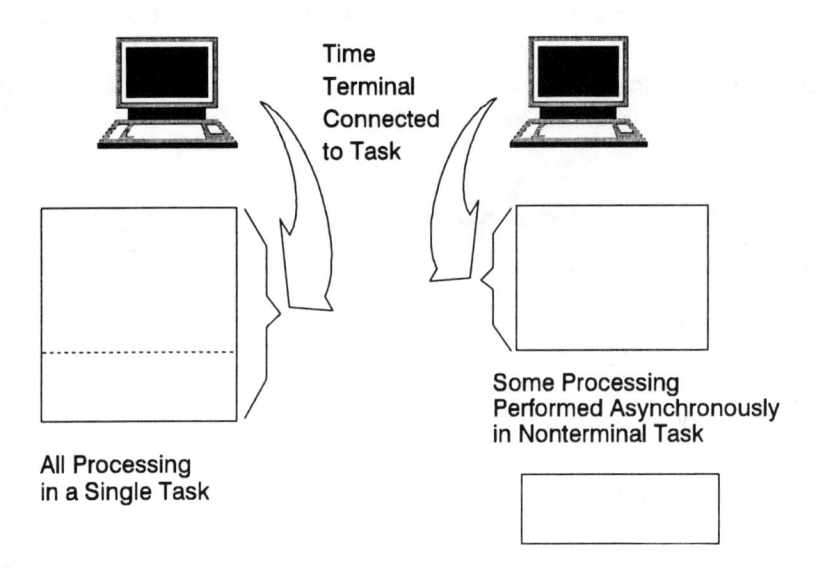

Figure 10.6 Moving work to an asynchronous task.

driven task, the cost of starting additional tasks could become substantial. Overhead costs will be even higher if the tasks are started in other CICS regions or on other processors.

The timing of updates can be an important factor with asynchronous processing. Updates performed by asynchronous tasks may not be completed before new terminal-related transactions are entered. Terminal-driven transactions must be designed to recognize that asynchronously updated data may not be available right away.

When data updated by asynchronous and terminal-driven transactions are closely related, special application processing may be required to maintain logical relationships between data. Application programs may need to handle situations where related data was not yet updated, incomplete, or inconsistent. Application systems may not need to be quite as complex when asynchronous tasks process data that are unrelated to the primary function of the terminal-driven transactions.

Another issue is that if an asynchronous task fails, there may be no way to back-out updates committed by the terminal-driven transaction. If data updated in terminal-driven tasks are related to data updated in asynchronous tasks, it may be difficult to ensure that data remain consistent.

SPE – Application Design Guidelines

A final concern is that asynchronous tasks compete with terminal-driven tasks for CICS resources, such as storage, max-tasks, VSAM strings, and dispatch service. Even if asynchronous tasks run at a lower dispatching priority, they will affect dispatch service and access to other resources. When asynchronous tasks run in separate CICS regions, they still compete indirectly for system resources. Processing in asynchronous tasks can influence response time in terminal-driven tasks.

Asynchronous tasks may be used to remove processing from terminal-driven transactions. Although this can reduce application response time, the asynchronous tasks will generate additional overhead, add application complexity, and require special planning.

Queueing Asynchronous Work. Instead of using asynchronous tasks to off-load processing from key transactions, work requests can be written to some kind of a queue and then processed asynchronously by batch processes (usually long-running CICS tasks). This scheme is easier to control than true asynchronous processing, and it uses fewer resources. Of course, issues of data integrity and synchronization are much the same when work is queued as when it is processed asynchronously.

There are some definite advantages to queueing work to a quasi-batch facility. If the CICS region is CPU- or storage-constrained, some processing can be moved to another CICS region. The amount of processing can be controlled by the number of tasks started to process queued data. This can smooth peak CICS processing requirements.

The primary value of queueing work to batch processes is to shorten user response time. However, when users need to access deferred data immediately, this technique may not provide an acceptable solution.

Used wisely, deferred processing can provide better response time for users, allow processing to be shifted to less-stressed CICS regions or less-expensive platforms, and reduce total capacity demands. However, deferred processing requires additional planning and invloves some processing overhead.

The VSAM Subtask or Concurrent TCB. The VSAM subtask in CICS/VS and CICS/MVS and the concurrent (CO) TCB in CICS/ESA allow certain VSAM requests to be processed under a separate MVS TCB. When the optional VSAM or CO subtask are active, selected VSAM processing can occur on the subtask TCB while the main or QR TCB continues to processing other work. Of course, there is a cost associated with dispatching the additional TCB and communicating between MVS tasks.

In CICS/MVS and CICS/ESA, VSAM subtasks process only update-type requests unless the primary TCB is quite busy. When the primary TCB is using at least 70 percent of a processor, CICS also sends VSAM read requests to the subtask. Since there normally are many times more read requests than write requests, the VSAM or CO subtasks will have limited use at lower levels of processor utilization.

The "70 percent" limitation is not as imposing as it might seem. CPU utilization data are updated very frequently (every one-half second). Even when overall CPU utilization is quite low, normal processing spikes can trigger occasional use of the subtask for read processing.

Asynchronous Processing with Database Subtasks. When IMS/DBCTL (CICS/ESA only) or DB2 are being used in a CICS region, a separate MVS TCB will be created for each database connection. When CICS tasks issue database calls, they are passed to the database TCBs for processing. This allows multiple database tasks to be processing concurrently with CICS transaction activity.

The number of database tasks that can be created is a factor of overhead. A common rule of thumb has been that no more than 15 database tasks should be defined per CICS region. The overhead of running more TCBs can be counterproductive. However, with later releases of DB2 (i.e., 2.3 and later) it appears that a larger number of tasks can be active without significant penalties.

10.9 PRINCIPLE 6 — SHARED RESOURCES PRINCIPLE

CICS provides an umbrella of services that allow sharing of resources under controlled conditions. When resource sharing is needed, resources can be accessed either with shared access or exclusive control. Shared access allows other CICS tasks to use a resource concurrently. Exclusive control implies that only one CICS task can access a resource at a time.

The goal of the *sharing principle* is to *improve systemwide performance by limiting the amount of time applications wait for shared resources.* The sharing principle is effective only when applications cooperate in a planned sharing strategy.

The primary method of limiting the effects of sharing is to control the amount of time exclusive control is held. This can be done by deferring requests for exclusive control as long as possible, releasing exclusive control as soon as possible, and performing as little processing as possible while exclusive control is being held. It is also beneficial to hold as few resources as necessary at any point in time.

> **The sharing principle.** Minimize the time applications wait for resources.

VSAM Files. VSAM files are the most common shared resources in most CICS systems. When records in a VSAM file are accessed for update, CICS will issue an ENQ to serialize access to the record. Additionally, VSAM will lock on the *control interval* (CI) when update processing is requested.

There are differences between the way VSAM *local shared resources* (LSR) and *nonshared resources* (NSR) control VSAM buffers. When NSR is being used, VSAM will lock on a CI *only* when an update request is being processed. Read and browse requests may access the same CI without going through the update lock. This permits applications to browse records on a VSAM file and update them without first releasing the CI.

In LSR, VSAM checks if the required CI is already in the buffer pool. If it is, VSAM will access the CI directly without rereading it from DASD. If the CI is being used by any task for browse or update processing, the requesting task will wait.

Two different techniques may be used in CICS to improve VSAM sharing. The first, and most obvious, is not to issue read-for-update commands until shortly before the update will actually be performed. Once the record has been read for update, it should be rewritten immediately. This will release the VSAM CI so that other tasks may access data within the CI.

The second technique is to limit the length of time browse operations hold a single CI for LSR files. Since browse processing under LSR holds a CI, no other transactions can access data records in that CI until the browse is ended or the browse moves to the next CI. When transactions browse a file and process other files between GETNEXT accesses, the CI can be held for a long time. When it is necessary to process other files, it might be beneficial to end file browses and restart them after completing other processing. By breaking up the time CIs are held, other CICS tasks will not wait as long when they need records in the CI.

In addition to the locks taken by CICS and VSAM, locking will occur when file logging and DTB are being used. Once an update-type operation occurs, the record will be held until a CICS syncpoint occurs. This will prevent other CICS tasks from accessing the record until after it is committed and could no longer be backed out.

As a matter of good programming practice, all updates and LSR file accesses occurring during a single unit of work (between the execution of syncpoints) should be performed in the same sequence by all CICS transactions. This is the preferred way of preventing deadly embraces. Whenever resources are accessed in different sequences, there is a chance that deadlocks will occur.

Another good practice is to bunch all update processing just prior to a syncpoint. This will limit the time records are unavailable to other tasks.

CI and CA Splits on VSAM Files. While CI or CA splits are being processed for VSAM files, various resources will be unavailable. At a minimum, a CI will be briefly unavailable to other applications. In the worst case, an entire CICS region may be suspended during split processing.

There is considerable difference between the impact of CI and CA splits in LSR processing versus NSR processing. When a file defined *in LSR* takes a CI or CA split, *only the affected portion of the file will be unavailable* while the split is taking place. When a file is defined under NSR, *the TCB requesting the update that caused the split will be suspended for the duration of the CI or CA split*. If VSAM subtasking or the concurrent TCB were active, the subtask would be suspended; otherwise, the primary TCB would be suspended for the duration of the split. In essence, when an NSR file takes a CI or CA split, all processing will be suspended on one of the CICS TCBs while the split was occurring.

The actual DASD processing for CI and CA splits is more efficient with NSR than with LSR. However, the consequences of taking a split are far more serious under NSR.

The principle of sharing would suggest that the number of splits, the duration of the splits, and the number of resources made unavailable all be minimized for performance. The best way to minimize CI and CA splits is through appropriate key design. When new records are to be added at only a few locations in a VSAM file, insert activity can cause many CI and CA splits. There is very little that can be done to overcome poor key design.

When key design allows a reasonable distribution of new key values, appropriate free space can help prevent CI and CA splits. It is even possible to define different amounts of free space for different portions of a file. However, when key design places most new records in few locations, it may not be possible to reduce CI and CA splits, regardless of how much free space is allocated.

If splits must occur, it is best to prevent CA splits. CI splits can be processed much more quickly than CA splits. They have less of an impact than CA splits. Whenever possible, CA splits should be almost totally eliminated by key design and free space.

Finally, files that experience many CI or CA splits should not be accessed using NSR. With NSR, CI and CA splits can restrict processing on one of the CICS TCBs. If NSR is being used for files experiencing CI and CA splits, the VSAM subtask or CO TCB should be active.

Key Point: CI and CA splits should be minimized for VSAM files. The best way to do this is through good key design and proper allocation of free space. If VSAM CI and CA splits cannot be avoided, it is best minimize CA splits. NSR should not be used for VSAM files that require many CI or CA splits.

Some Notes on Sharing VSAM Data. The discussion above has addressed VSAM processing with a single open ACB. When multiple address spaces open the same VSAM file, sharing data with integrity becomes close to impossible. VSAM file integrity is possible only when a file is defined in a single CICS region and accessed via MRO or ISC from all other regions. Updates performed in one region may not be available to other regions unless the file is open in a single region and accessed via MRO or ISC services.

The following quotation is taken from the question and answer portion of IBM LINK (Article Q504735):

> *VSAM has never provided concurrent access to VSAM datasets from both CICS and non-CICS address spaces.* [Emphasis added.] Multiple CICS address spaces may only access VSAM datasets concurrently through the facilities of CICS function shipping. . . .
>
> VSAM files can be shared, with integrity, between batch and CICS if there is no update activity by any participant. If there is any update activity, integrity cannot be assured.

When *all* CICS regions and batch jobs perform only read or browse functions, a VSAM file can be opened with integrity by multiple sources. However, if any source updates data on the file, sharing with integrity can become a problem.

> **Key Point:** If VSAM files are to be shared between CICS regions, they should be defined in one CICS region and accessed via MRO or ISC from all other CICS regions.

When VSAM files must be accessed by batch jobs, they normally should be closed to CICS before the batch job executes. However, several commercial program products address sharing VSAM data between CICS and batch jobs. In most products, batch accesses to VSAM data are passed to by special mirror transactions of one type or another and then processed using standard CICS file control services. One product works quite differently, though, intercepting VSAM requests and processing them directly in its own address space.

DB2 and Resource Sharing. DB2's rules for sharing are unique. Although data are accessed at the row (logical record) level, locks are held at the page (physical block) level. When multiple rows need to be updated in the same table, it is very difficult to prevent page deadlocks between transactions. The only possible suggestion with current releases of DB2 is to perform updates in the same sequence and do a small number of updates to the same table between syncpoints (commits).

Recoverable Transient Data. Few resources create a greater potential resource bottleneck than recoverable transient data queues. In essence, recoverable transient data is a single-server resource for write activity. When any CICS transaction writes to a queue, no other CICS task can write to that queue until the first task issues a syncpoint.

10.10 PRINCIPLE 7 — THE INSTRUMENTATION PRINCIPLE

The final principle does not specifically address performance or capacity issues. Instead the *instrumentation principle* suggests that *programs include logic to document how frequently key services are performed.*

In a CICS environment, there is a wealth of information available about CICS transactions and the type work they perform. However, single transaction types commonly perform several different functions, and they do not necessarily correspond to business functions. Statistics at a transaction level may not provide sufficient detail for performance analysis or workload forecasting.

The instrumentation principle is easier to implement for batch jobs than for CICS transactions. Batch programs can collect statistical data and produce a simple report at job or step completion. CICS programs, though, are not designed to produce batch reports. There are few inexpensive ways to record instrumentation data for CICS applications. One is to write data to some kind of journal or file that would be analyzed offline later. Another option would be to keep statistics in common storage, such as the CWA, and have a started task dump or record information periodically. A third option would be to use CICS standard exits or exits provided by monitors to store information in user data fields.

Instrumentation is important primarily for transactions that are either executed frequently or use large amounts of resources. There is little justification for documenting internal processing on small, low-volume applications.

> **The instrumentation principle.** It can be useful to document workload information for high volume transactions.

Different Types of Transaction Activity. Some transactions perform many separate functions all under a single transaction ID. For performance analysis and capacity planning purposes, it may be hard to determine which of the multiple functions were performed by a transaction. Providing instrumentation within the transaction, it may be possible to document the number of times each function was performed. In the Chapter 8, when we identified workload components, we did not concentrate on transaction IDs, but on units of work. Good instrumentation can help support subsequent planning and projections.

Other Information. Other information that can be useful is the number of significant business units processed in a transaction. Many transactions process a variable number of units in a single transaction. It is often difficult to learn the average number of units per transaction or their distribution. When these data are instrumented, it can help track and project future workload growth. The number of business units per transaction can be an important planning factor.

10.11 SUMMARY

There is an opportunity to influence performance, system efficiency, and user effectiveness, when applications are being designed. In this chapter we have examined some techniques that can be used to design efficient application systems. The guidelines suggested in this book are more than tricks to make applications perform well. They are the basis of a philosophy that can be applied to all levels of application and system design. When they are used wisely, they will help provide responsive, resource-efficient systems.

SELECTED READING

[IBM000] IBM Technical Information Search items Q421763, Q480337, Q504735.

[SMIT87] Smith, Connie U., "General Principles for Performance Oriented Design", *CMG '87 Proceedings*, 1987.

[SMIT90] Smith, Connie U., *Performance Engineering of Software Systems*, Addison-Wesley, Reading, Massachusetts, 1990.

Chapter 11

CICS and the DASD Subsystem

11.1 OVERVIEW

When CICS applications experience performance problems, chances are that DASD will be part of the problem. Although DASD delays may be a significant portion of CICS performance, DASD problems usually can be corrected more easily than CICS processing constraints. Even so, DASD capacity planning requires as much attention as other types of planning.

The focus of this chapter will be on the DASD activity commonly found in a CICS environment. The chapter will discuss both the components of DASD service and CICS internal factor such as internal caching. This chapter will not discuss all aspects of DASD service, but will examine DASD services and access patterns commonly used by CICS application and system files.

11.1.1 Primary Audience

The primary audience of this chapter is the *CICS systems programmer* or other technician concerned with DASD performance. However, the examples in this chapter do point out some features of cache performance that should be useful to *capacity planners*.

Application developers may not control DASD configurations but should provide input for the placement of their data. Developers are often the first to hear complaints about application response time. Thus it is valuable to understand how DASD service can affect application performance.

11.2 THE CICS I/O ENVIRONMENT

In CICS systems today, only a portion of application I/O requests actually involve access to spinning storage. Multiple layers of caching commonly stand between an application I/O request and actual DASD devices. Data is commonly cached internally by facilities such as LSR and temporary storage and externally by cache controllers.

When application files use CICS data tables, service time should be less than 0.1 ms on a "25 mip" uniprocessor. When VSAM file requests can be satisfied entirely from VSAM buffers without visiting DASD, service time would be about 0.5 ms on the same processor. If data is retrieved from storage in cache controllers, DASD service time for a VSAM file should include 2 to 3 ms per physical I/O; the total CPU cost of performing the I/O can be close to 1 ms. When neither of these caching techniques is effective, it usually will take at least 15 ms to complete each I/O request. If both the VSAM data and index components must be read from DASD, application file service time will be at least 30 ms (two I/O requests of 15 ms each). Figure 11.1 suggests minimum service times for each type of access.

Average file service time experienced by CICS applications will be influenced by internal and external caching. In the material below, we will look at the different factors that commonly influence file service time in a CICS environment.

11.3 MAJOR COMPONENTS OF I/O SERVICE TIME

A series of events must occur for each I/O to DASD, but only a few have much influence on performance. Many events are very short and seldom influenced by queueing. Some events, though, are frequently affected by hidden delays and queueing. These are the most common causes of service degradation.

The following list summarizes the more significant components of I/O service time for uncached DASD devices. Chances are that, when DASD service time is slow, one or more of these components will be the cause. We will examine the influence of caching later in this chapter.

CICS File Access Times

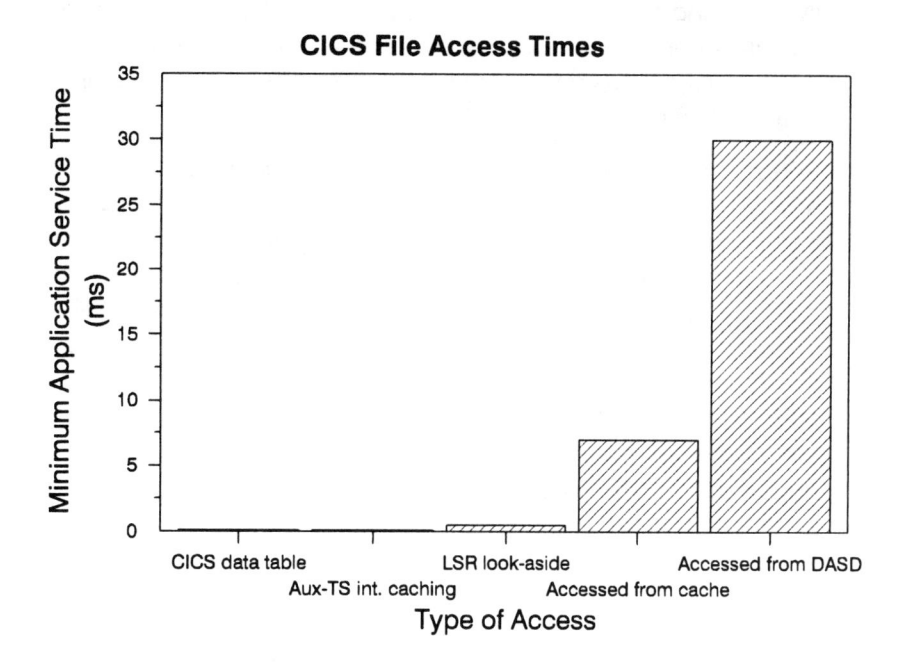

[Bar chart: Minimum Application Service Time (ms) vs Type of Access. CICS data table / Aux-TS int. caching ≈ 0; LSR look-aside / Accessed from cache ≈ 7; Accessed from DASD ≈ 30.]

Figure 11.1 Experted service times for I/O requests.

- *Queue for the device.* Time spent waiting for the device is called *IOS queue time*. This is the time I/O requests are queued because another I/O request from the same system already is being processed by the device.

- *Time waiting for path to device.* MVS makes no effort to determine if any paths are available to a device when it starts an I/O. The subchannel will wait until a path is available to the device.

- *Device being used by another system.* When DASD is shared between processors, there is a chance that a device needed by one system will be reserved by another system. When another system is using the device, the I/O request must wait until the device becomes available.

- *Seek time.* Seek time is a measure of the time is takes to move the read-write head to the appropriate cylinder and select the appropriate head. Seek time is affected by the distance the head must travel.

- *Latency.* Once the read-write head is positioned at the appropriate cylinder and track, the volume will need to rotate until the correct data is under the head. Average rotational delay, or *latency*, is commonly estimated as one-half the time it takes the volume to complete one revolution.

- *RPS reconnect.* DASD tracks are divided into *sectors*. Most DASD accesses will disconnect from the channel once the proper track has been selected. While the volume is rotating, the channel and controller are free to transfer data for other devices. When the actuator rotates to a point close to the requested sector, the device will attempt to reconnect to the channel. If at least one channel path is available, the device will reconnect and transfer data. If no channel path is available, the device will complete another revolution, and then reattempt the connection. Each *RPS miss* will add at least 16 ms (on a 3380-class device) or 14 ms (on a 3390-class device) to I/O service time.

- *Transfer data.* This is the time it takes to transfer data to or from a device. It will take less than 3 ms (even on 3-megabyte channels) to transfer most types of data commonly processed by CICS systems. Only VSAM files with large CI sizes or large CICS journals should have much larger transfer times.

Key Point: The components of DASD I/O service that contribute most heavily to service time are *queue time for the device*, *RPS reconnect time*, *seek time*, *latency*, *time trying to get a path to the device*, *data transfer time*, and *contention for the device from another system*.

11.4 COMMON MEASURES OF DASD SERVICE

It would be nice if hardware and software provided precise measures of everything that contributes to DASD service time. Some measures do exist that correspond fairly closely with the delays mentioned above. Unfortunately, the information available does not tell us everything we might like to know. It usually requires analysis of known data, queueing delays, and a few assumptions to obtain a complete picture of DASD performance.

11.4.1 Data About DASD Volumes (RMF Type 74 Records)

RMF is a good source of information about DASD performance. RMF Type 74 records summarize information about DASD volumes for each RMF interval. Some useful data contained in Type 74 records include:

- *Average IOS queue time*. In essence, this is an estimate of how long I/O requests are queued for devices. A queue is maintained by MVS for each device. When an I/O request arrives and an I/O event is already in progress, IOS[1] places the new request on the queue. IOS queue time is an indication of how long I/O requests spend on that queue.

  IOS queue time is not measured directly, but is calculated indirectly from other measures. RMF keeps track of the number of I/O requests queued for the device and then uses Little's law (see Chapter 5) to calculate IOS queue time. Even though IOS queue time is calculated, it should be reasonably accurate.

  IOS queue time represents time queued for I/O events scheduled *from the same system*. Contention from I/O events started by other processors will not be contained in IOS queue time, but in pend time.

  IOS queue time does not reflect queueing within application software. For example, when VSAM file requests wait for strings or buffers, queueing for resources will occur within CICS. This queueing will affect the time it takes to complete logical I/O requests but will not be reflected in IOS queue time.

- *Pend time*. Pend time is the interval between when the operating system sends an I/O to a subchannel and the I/O is able to establish a connection to the device. If channel paths are heavily used, if the device is being accessed from other processors, or if staging is being done on a cache controller, the connection can be delayed. RMF (release 3.3 and above) contains separate accumulators for each of the three types of pend time.

---

[1] IOS is a generic name for the MVS modules that pass the I/O to the channel subsystem and process the interrupt when it finishes.

Normally, pend times of less than 1 ms are common for DASD dedicated to CICS workloads. Most CICS volumes are not accessed from other processors and, hopefully, are not on heavily used channels or controllers.

- *Disconnect time.* Disconnect time is the time a volume is disconnected from the channel. It includes the time I/O requests are waiting for the head to be positioned on the correct track and cylinder. Most disconnect time is associated with seeking (moving the read-write head) or waiting for rotational positioning. Disconnect time also includes more obscure delays, such as cache staging and destaging (which we will discuss later in this chapter).

  A portion of disconnect time will be associated with seek time. The remainder will be for rotational delay, missed RPS connections, and other delays. Average seek time should be 3 to 15 ms, depending on the device type and data access patterns. Latency (rotational delay) will account for about one-half the time it takes to complete one revolution, which should be about 6 to 8 ms, depending on the type of device. Delays for RPS misses will be the product of the time it takes to complete one revolution multiplied by the percent of requests that experience RPS misses. The remainder of disconnect time should be associated with other delays such as staging and destaging.

- *Connect time.* Connect time is the time the device is connected to a channel path. The largest portion of connect time is the time it takes the device to transfer data.

  Connect times of 1 to 3 ms are common for CICS-related data. Most CICS system and application files are accessed via simple channel programs. They usually involve the transfer of a single block or VSAM CI per physical I/O request. Larger connect times might reflect large VSAM CI sizes or journal blocks.

11.4.2 Data About Channels (RMF Type 73 Records)

RMF Type 73 records contain data about channel activity. The primary information of interest in Type 73 records is the *percent channel busy*. On properly configured 3390 class DASD and 3380 J/K devices, there are four channel paths to each device. The average (mean) utilization of the four paths (or the sum of the four utilizations compared to 400 percent) define channel busy as seen by the volume.

If volumes on a string can be accessed from multiple processors, channel activity from all processors should be considered. Assuming similar RMF intervals, RMF Type 73 data should be merged. One caution is that RMF interval start times often vary by a few seconds from processor to processor and adjustments may need to be made for these differences. When merging RMF data from multiple processors, this author includes logic to round any RMF interval start-time within a few seconds of the start of a minute to exact start of the minute; this allows merging of similar data from multiple processors.

11.5 CACHE CONTROLLERS

At one time, cache controllers only improved response time for read accesses to data on DASD storage. Today, controllers not only provide read caching, but they also support write caching, dual copies, and many other functions. At the time of this writing, controllers have been announced with features that support point-in-time backups running concurrently with on-line updates. Controllers no longer merely store and transfer data to the host, but they provide a wide range of optional services.

With all the diversity of services, not all vendors' controllers are exactly alike. Differences in controllers affect both basic operations and total functionality. In this book, we will focus only on IBM 3990 and 3880 cache controllers. Because of the limited scope of this discussion, we will ignore differences in controllers produced by other vendors. As a whole, cache controllers function approximately the same, but there are variances in the specifics of implementation.

11.5.1 Cache Controller Operation — Read Requests

Cache functions in controllers can enhance DASD service times significantly. When a read request is received for a volume or dataset controlled by cache, one of three conditions can occur:

- A *read hit*. A read hit occurs when the data requested by a read request are already in cache storage. On a read hit, the requested block will be transferred directly from the controller to the processor. Total service time will consist of transfer time plus channel and control unit pend time (if any), IOS queueing, and channel and control unit protocol. I/O service times of 2 to 3 ms are common when data can be accessed directly from cache storage.

- A *read miss*. A read miss occurs when the requested data are not in the cache. For read misses, the channel is disconnected while the standard commands are executed to locate and retrieve the data. The record is transferred to the host and the cache *simultaneously*. After the record has been transferred, *the remainder of the track will be read from DASD into the cache*. Records on the track before the requested data will not be transferred to cache.

The transfer of the remainder of the track to cache is called *promotion* or *staging*. The device will be disconnected from the channel while the staging is taking place. The volume will appear to MVS as being free at this time, even though it cannot be accessed. Requests for data in cache can be satisfied while staging is occurring, but the volume itself cannot be accessed. When I/O operations wait for staging, the delay will be recorded as disconnect time.

- A *front-end miss*. When a read misses occur (see above), only a portion of the track is transferred to cached storage. When a read request is received for a record in the portion of a track that had not been staged, a front end miss occurs. On a front-end miss, the front portion of the track is transferred to cache and the record is then transferred to the host.

11.5.2 Cache Controller Operation — Write Requests

While most cache controllers function similarly for read operations, write operations will be treated differently depending on whether write caching is supported. Most vendors now have cache controllers that support write caching, but not all controllers have this capability.

There are two basic types of write commands. *Formatted writes* write new data on a track and then erase the remainder of the track. *Nonformatted writes* rewrite blocks of data that already exist but do not disturb the remainder of the track. Formatted writes are common for sequential output files and journals. Nonformatted writes are used for VSAM update and record-add processing.

The following conditions can occur for writes to cached devices:

- A *write hit*. When the record being written resides in cache, a write hit occurs. On 3990-3 controllers, the record is updated in the cache. If DASD fast write is not active, the record will be transferred to DASD. If DASD fast write is active, the record will be saved in nonvolatile storage and written to DASD at a later time. On 3880-23 controllers, when a write hit occurs, the record will be transferred to DASD but not to cache. Cache data will be marked as invalid.

Formatted writes are always treated as write hits. Since all trailing data on the track will be erased, there is nothing to be staged.

- *A write miss.* A write miss occurs when a non-formatted write references a track that is not already in cache. On 3990-3 controllers, data will be transferred to DASD, and the remainder of the track will be staged into cache. This is similar to what happens on a read miss. Even when DASD fast write is active, data will be transferred directly to DASD on a write miss. On 3880-23 controllers, data is simply transferred to DASD on a write miss.

Write misses should not be that common for the type of writes commonly generated by CICS applications. Typically, records are read from DASD before being updated. Once they have been read, there is a good chance they will still be in cache a short time later when they are updated.

When VSAM files are accessed from large LSR pools, it is possible that records may be retained in an LSR pool longer than they are retained in cache. Cache misses can occur when these records are updated, if the records had been flushed out of the cache controller. Temporary storage data can be another source of write misses. Temporary storage CIs are not necessarily read before being written to DASD.

11.5.3 Common Cache Controller Measurement Data

The IBM 3990 cache controller maintains several useful statistics. A command is sent to controllers once each RMF reporting period to capture statistics, and data is then written to SMF. Of the many cache statistics available, the following are most useful in typical CICS environments:

- *Read hit ratio (nonsequential).* Cache controllers can be accessed sequentially or nonsequentially (randomly). The nonsequential read hit ratio is the number of nonsequential read requests satisfied from cache divided by the number of nonsequential read requests. Most CICS accesses to cache data are non-sequential.

- *Read hit ratio (sequential)*. One would hope that there is not much sequential (batch) processing on volumes accessed randomly by CICS applications. The sequential read hit ratio usually should not contain much useful information for volumes dedicated to CICS workloads unless there are many sequential reads.

- *DASD fast write ratio hit ratio (nonsequential)*. This is the percent of DFW writes experiencing cache hits. DFW will provide benefit only for formatted writes or non-formatted writes when records being written either are already in cache. Low DFW write-hit ratios may suggest that DFW is degrading DASD service instead of helping it.

- *Read/write ratio*. This is simply the number of read requests divided by the number of write requests. On earlier controllers, the ratio of read-to-write activity was quite important. In 3880-23 controllers, writes would cause additional overhead and invalidate cache data. In 3990-3 controllers with DFW, write activity will not degrade performance as long as there is a reasonable write cache-hit ratio.

Key Point: When DASD volumes are controlled by cache controllers, DASD service time will be a factor of how frequently data are found in cache storage. In fact, read-hit ratios, write-hit ratios, and read/write ratios can have a greater influence over DASD performance than traditional DASD delays, such as seek time or latency. Service can be improved significantly by good read- and write-hit ratios. Very poor hit ratios can actually degrade performance.

11.6 QUEUEING THEORY AND DASD WORKLOADS

As a rule, DASD volumes make poor queueing systems. All major queueing disciplines assume some kind of consistent access patterns. They require that arrival rates and services times be distributed randomly or share some identifiable pattern. Unfortunately, DASD access patterns are seldom either random or consistent.

For example, on a single volume, some datasets may be accessed randomly, others sequentially (by batch jobs or browse requests), and still others both randomly and sequentially. Volumes may alternate between short, mostly random accesses, heavy sequential processes, and even intensive high-speed data transfers. Many DASD volumes experience a mix of short random accesses and lengthy sequential processing.

CICS and the DASD Subsystem   321

Device utilization and service times reported by RMF or other monitors contain information summarizing many unlike events. Consider a volume that is used primarily by CICS workloads but is also accessed by occasional batch jobs that copy or update datasets. The device might be 10 to 15 percent busy when it is accessed only by CICS transactions. However, when batch jobs are accessing the volume, it might be 80 to 90 percent busy for several minutes. Over a fifteen minute period, the volume might be busy an average of 30 to 35 percent busy. However, that average in itself provides little indication of the actual activity occurring on the volume.

> **Key Point**: It is difficult to apply standard queueing formulas to DASD access patterns. The nature of DASD workloads generate access patterns that violate many of the assumptions of most standard queueing systems.

Moreover, even "random" accesses by CICS applications are not truly random. Each time a VSAM KSDS is accessed, VSAM will read one or more high levels of index, the sequence set CI, and a data CI. In CICS, high level indexes usually are retained in memory and accessed without visiting DASD.[2] Thus, a typical read request might access only one sequence set and one data CI from DASD.

When indexes are imbedded (a common practice for VSAM files accessed by CICS[3]), the sequence set CI will reside on the same cylinder as the corresponding data CIs. Typically, a read for a sequence set CI will be followed immediately by a read for a data CI on the same cylinder. Any update would follow shortly and reference the same cylinder. Thus, a DASD access to a sequence set CI probably will be followed by one or two accesses to data CIs on the same cylinder.

LSR also can play a part in access patterns. If LSR pools are large enough to provide good look-aside ratios, many file requests may need

---

[2] With LSR, it is likely that the high-level indexes will be retained in memory; with NSR, high level indexes will be retained in memory if enough index buffers are provided.
[3] At one time indexes for KSDS files accessed randomly by CICS systems were almost always imbedded. Even though an entire track would be consumed by each sequence set record, only one seek would be required per data access, and sequence set CIs could be retrieved more quickly. Today, when LSR internal caching can eliminate most sequence set reads for some files, imbedded indexes can be wasteful. Furthermore, when embedded indexes are read on cached volumes (or datasets), an entire track's worth of data will be consumed in cache storage for a single sequence set CI. For these reasons, this previously popular option may be losing favor in modern CICS systems.

to access DASD for only the data CI. Some file reads would require one I/O, some would require two, and some might be satisfied entirely from memory. Another source of skewing can be CICS transactions that access multiple records in the same area of the file. There are several reasons that accesses to VSAM data are not purely random. Accesses will arrive in groups, and activity will not be spread evenly over all files on a volume.

DB2 databases display even more erratic access patterns than VSAM files. When DB2 databases are accessed randomly, short simple channel programs are used. Tablespace scans, however, use long channel programs that access many pages in a single operation. And when DB2 finally decides to write data,[4] many pages will be written via a single I/O request.

It is hard to select a queueing system that will accurately mirror DASD service. As a rule, DASD access patterns vary greatly and are influenced by several factors. Queueing systems that work well at one time of the day may be wildly inaccurate at another, and prediction techniques are seldom repeatable from day to day. Even queueing systems that are designed to account for bunching will not produce repeatable results. In some cases, estimates may match actual service times, but often not for the right reason.

11.6.1 DASD Queueing Systems

Although DASD volumes as a whole are not good candidates for queueing analysis, volumes dedicated to CICS system files or VSAM application datasets, are usually better behaved. Although it is hard to find queueing formulas that consistently explain DASD performance, they can help approximate the controlled, "random" accesses common for volumes dedicated to CICS systems.

Two interrelated queueing systems affect DASD service. The first is the set of channel paths to the device. In theory, this should form a multi-server queueing system. Delays, such as channel pend time and RPS misses should follow some kind of random queueing algorithm. As we will see later, this is not really the case. In addition to normal queueing for

---

[4] As we mentioned in a previous chapter, DB2 will not write data for database tables until one of several conditions exist. When it does write data, it will do so rapidly using lengthy channel programs.

resources, there are several obscure factors that influence channel-related delays.

The second queueing system is for the device itself. There are two elements in this queueing system. The first is the actual time it takes to accomplish an I/O. This includes connect and disconnect time (the time it takes to position the device and transfer data) and pend time (a measure of environmental contention for access to the device). The second element is the time queued waiting to get to the device.[5]

Examples are included later in this chapter that illustrate both types of queueing systems.

11.7 ANALYSIS OF I/O SERVICE TIME

In this section of the chapter, we will take a detailed look at a few DASD volumes. The illustrations demonstrate the types of delay commonly generated by CICS workloads. All the examples have been drawn from volumes that were used almost exclusively for CICS application or system datasets. Two of the volumes process a limited amount of batch work besides normal CICS activity. None of the three volumes contain complex data such as DB2 tables.[6]

The volumes shown in this chapter have been chosen for their wide range of activity. This gives a better representation of queueing trends than would be possible with volumes that were less active. All three exhibit what would normally be considered "poor" service for many sample periods. This helps illustrate the value of planning DASD configurations used by CICS systems.

11.7.1 DASD Example 1

The first volume contains only VSAM data sets used exclusively by CICS applications. The volume is attached to a cache controller, and read

---

[5] It has been argued that pend time should be included with IOS queue time as a total measure of contention for the device. While this does provide a better measure of total contention, it ignores the fact that there are really two separate but interrelated queueing systems. One system represents the system-wide contention that affects average server time for the device; the other represents queueing on the host for the device. We can get a better appreciation of the specific factors influencing performance if we separate contention into its separate components.
[6] Two excellent reference sources for a more general approach to DASD performance are suggested in the Selected Reading at the end of this chapter. See the works by Johnson and Johnson [JOHN92] and Houtekamer and Artis [HOUT93].

caching is turned on at the volume level. No batch processing occurs for the volume during the periods measured. Table 11.1 describes the volume and its environment.

Figure 11.2 shows DASD service time including queueing for Volume 01. Each point on the plots shown in this chapter represents one 15-minute interval. DASD service time appears to vary from a few milliseconds when the volume is lightly used to over 70 ms when the volume is very active. The single observation at 70 percent busy may either be an outlier or an indication that service has hit a queueing threshold.

DASD service times of 40 to 60 ms are common when this volume is over 40 percent busy. For an uncached volume, this would be a normal range of service. This level of service might be expected just because of queueing for the device.

However, on this volume, basic DASD service time is very low in some situations. When the volume is less than 10 percent busy, service time can be as low as 2 to 3 ms. When the volume is 50 to 60 percent busy, service times are 20 to 30 times as high as when it is lightly used. Differences of this magnitude cannot be explained by queueing for the device alone.

To continue the analysis, we will look at IOS queue time for this volume. IOS queue time is an estimate of the time I/O requests are queued for a device. Figure 11.3 shows that IOS queue time is fairly large at higher levels of device utilization. It appears to represent a large portion of service time at higher levels of utilization.

Figure 11.4 provides additional insight into the elements influencing response time. Disconnect time increased to about 18 to 20 ms when the volume was 20 percent busy. It remained at this level until the volume was over 50 percent busy.

Table 11.1 Description of Environment for Volume 01

Type of data	Several VSAM files
Data accessed by	CICS applications only
Primary access	Random
RMF reporting interval	15 minutes
Amount of data collected	3 hours each day, 7 days a week
Type volume	3380-K
Type controller	3990 Mod 3
Cache	Volume

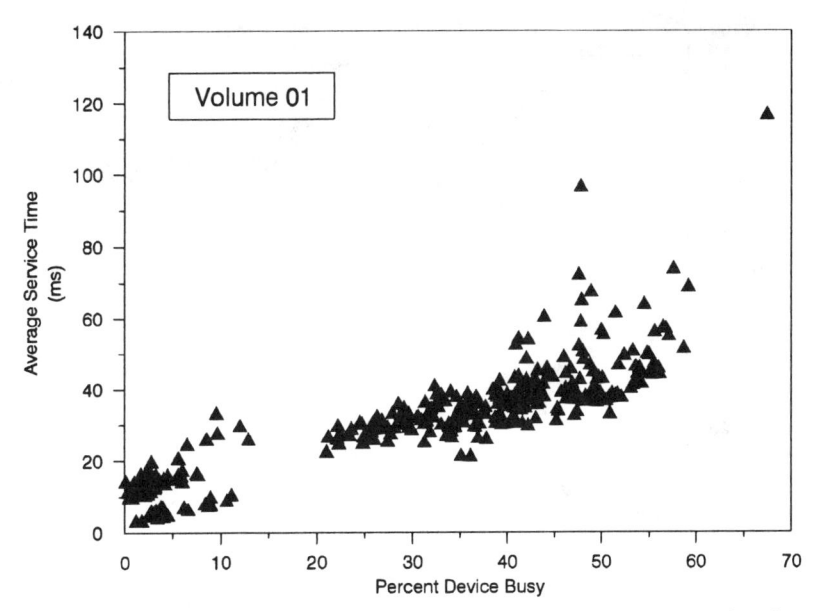

Figure 11.2 Average DASD service time versus percent device busy (Volume 1).

Disconnect time includes delays for head movement, latency (rotation), missed RPS reconnects, and cache staging. It is hard to tell from the information given what portion of disconnect time was caused by each factor.

Next, we will look at connect time. Average connect time consists primarily of data transfer time for VSAM files. Figure 11.5 shows average connect time for this file. Notice that connect time was slightly lower when the volume was less than 20 percent busy. However, average connect time did not vary much and was typically between 2.0 and 3.0 ms for most sample periods.

A similar analysis was performed on pend time. Pend time represents the time waiting to obtain a path to the volume. Figure 11.6 shows only the portion of pend time associated with channel contention. Even at its worst, channel-related pend time was less than 0.6 ms. Pend time for control unit and volume contention from other systems was negligible and is not shown.

Figure 11.6 seems to show a correlation between volume activity and channel-related pend time. The explanation for this is that CICS applications tend to use multiple volumes concurrently. Some of these share the same strings and channel paths. As transaction activity increases, not

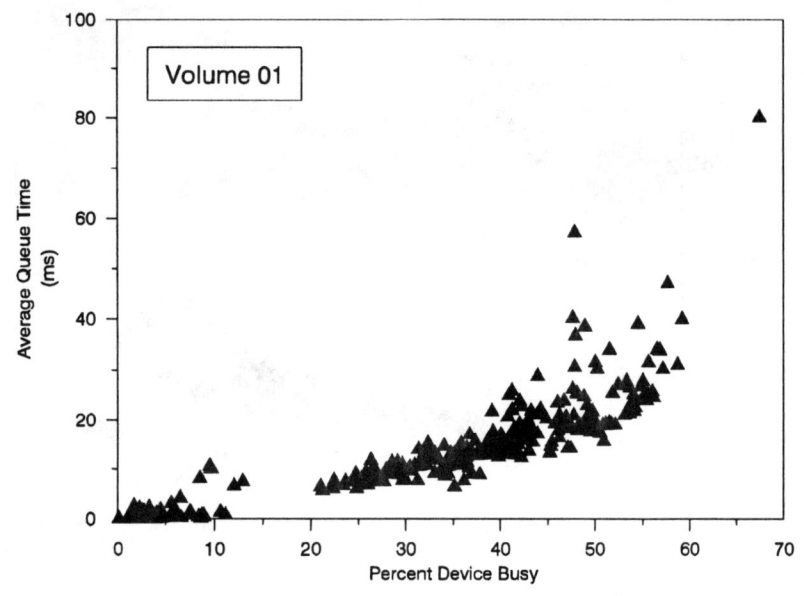

Figure 11.3 IOS queue time versus percent device busy (Volume 1).

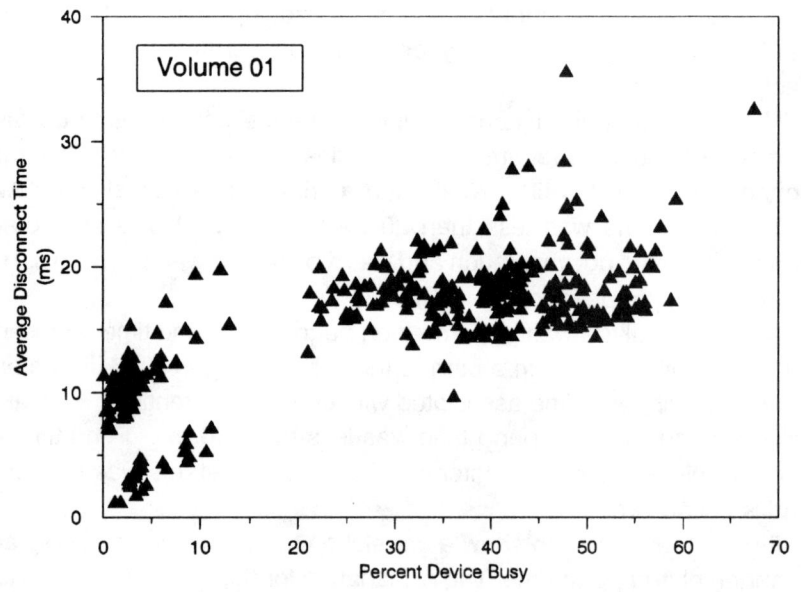

Figure 11.4 Average disconnect time versus percent device busy (Volume 1).

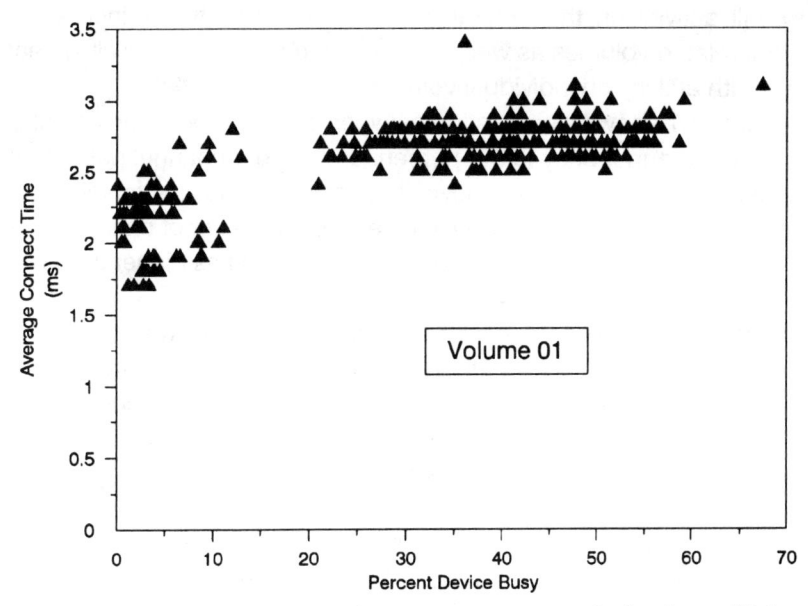

Figure 11.5 Average connect time versus percent device busy (Volume 1).

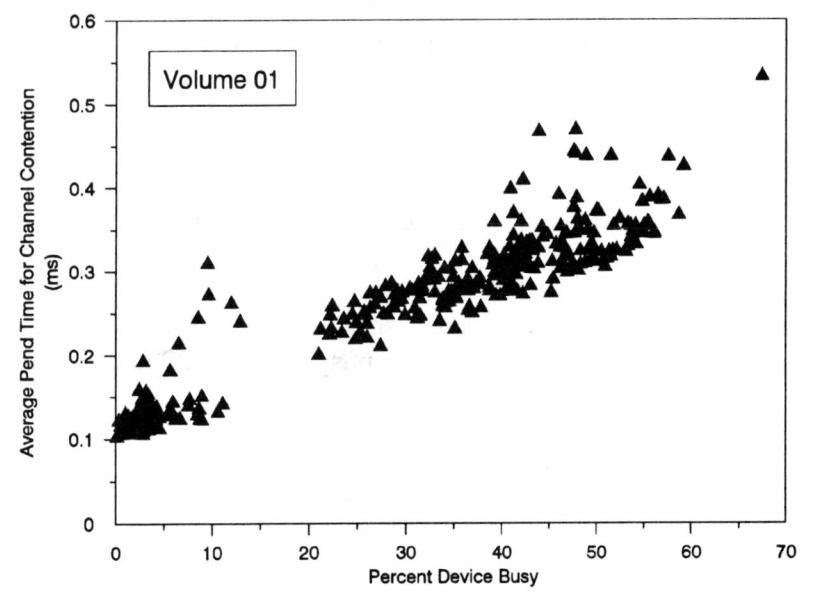

Figure 11.6 Average pend time versus percent device busy (Volume 1).

only will activity on this volume increase, but activity will increase on several related volumes as well. As a result, channel activity will increase along with activity on individual volumes.

Figure 11.7 shows a correlation between channel pend time and channel busy. Channel busy is the percent that all four channel paths to the device are busy. This figure shows that channel pend time tends to grow proportionately with channel busy time. When the set of channels is 40 to 50 percent busy, channel pend time is several times higher than when there is very little channel activity.

In theory, a set of channel paths to a volume should form a multi-server queueing system. However, there is more to this process than can be explained by random queueing. Tables B.4 and A.1 both suggest that the service multiplier should be no more than 1.1 for a multiserver system (with four server) that is 50 percent busy. If random queueing were the cause of the delays, channel pend time should be no more than 1.1 times as high when channel paths were 50 percent busy overall as it would when the device was lightly used. Figure 11.7 suggests a much higher multiplier.

Figure 11.8 shows a correlation between total disconnect time and channel activity. Overall, disconnect time appears to increase proportionately with channel busy. However, disconnect time is composed of three factors, only one of which is directly related to channel activity.

Perhaps the most significant graph in this series is Figure 11.9. Figure 11.9 shows the ratio of total DASD service time divided by device busy time.

The sum of connect time, disconnect time, and pend time are the time it takes to start and complete an I/O. This is also the time the device is considered busy. In a queueing system, it would be considered *average server time* (the time spent at the server). IOS queue time is an estimate of the time I/O events were queued waiting for access to a device (server). Total service time is the sum of device busy time and IOS queue time.

Total service time = device busy time + IOS queue time
= (connect + disconnect + pend time) + IOSQ time

Figure 11.9 shows that the ratio of total service time to average server time appears to form a somewhat well-behaved queueing system. The graph appears similar to the graph of service multipliers for open single server systems shown in Figure 11.10.

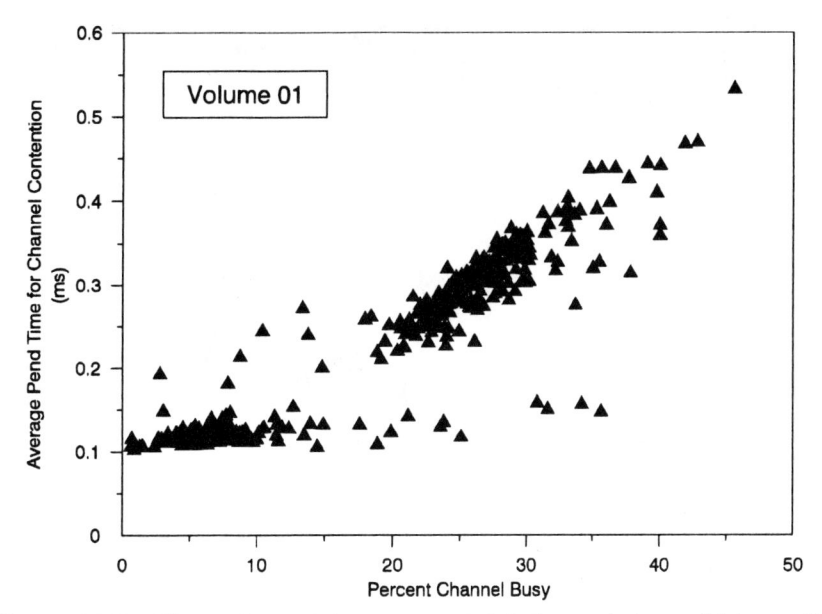

Figure 11.7 Channel pend time versus total channels busy (Volume 1).

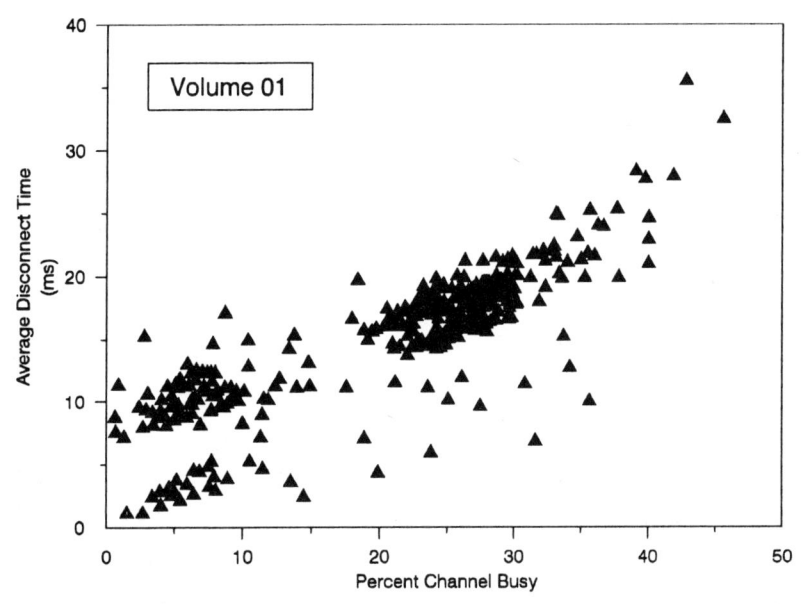

Figure 11.8 Channel disconnect time versus total channels busy (Volume 1).

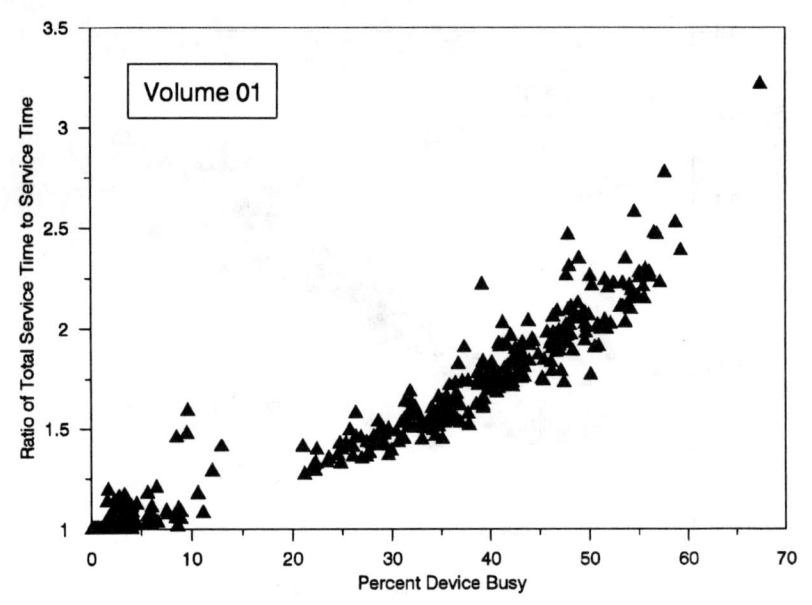

Figure 11.9 Ratio of total device service time (including queueing) to service time at the device (Volume 1).

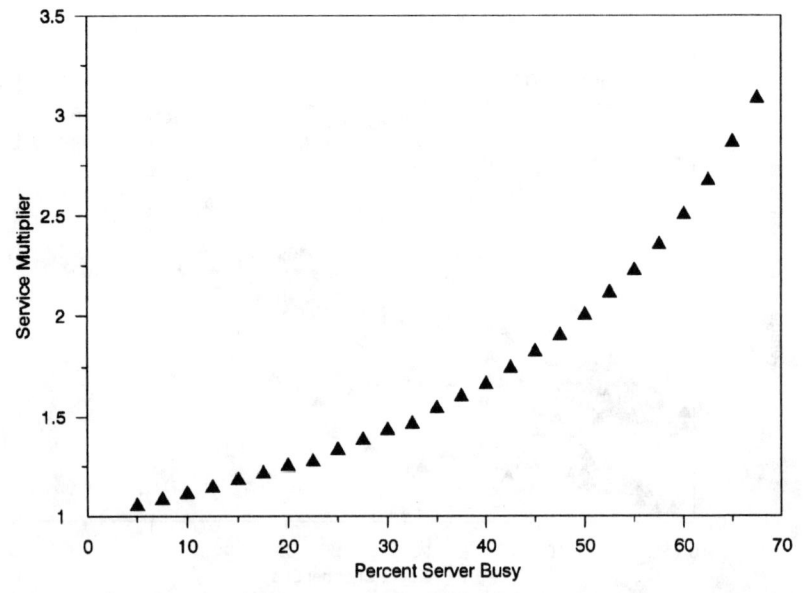

Figure 11.10 Standard service multipliers for open single-server queueing systems.

CICS and the DASD Subsystem 331

Combining the data we reviewed with some information about the volume, we can make the following observations:

- The graphs show three distinct patterns of activity. Figure 11.2 shows two distinct sets of service patterns when the device was less than 10 percent busy and a third when device utilization was over 20 percent busy.

  The series of graphs shows data for the same 3-hour period 7 days a week. On normal workdays, CICS transaction activity kept both the volume and its channel paths busy. On Saturdays and Sundays, activity for both the system as a whole and for the systems using this volume was light. For some weekend periods, there was almost no activity in application systems. The lowest set of service times reflect these periods; the periods with higher service time and low device utilization were from normal weekend periods with moderate activity. Weekdays accounted for periods when device busy and service times were higher.

- One reason that device service time was so good on weekends was that there was very little competition for memory on the cache controller. Cache data are not shown, but read-hit ratios for data on the volume were typically over 80 percent on weekends. On weekdays, cache read-hit ratios were commonly 30 to 50 percent or less. A cache read-hit ratio of 30 percent is considered very low, and a much larger percentage of the I/O requests on weekdays resulted in visits to DASD than did on weekends.

- An old rule of thumb is that on-line DASD service time should be less than 25 ms. A large portion of this volume's service exceeds this ROT. A large part of the service time is associated with device queueing (IOS queue time), and it would be easy to blame device busy for the higher service. One obvious solution might be to move some datasets to another the device. This would reduce total activity and queueing for the device.

- From all the information we have, though, it appears that other factors should be considered. As seen in Figure 11.4, disconnect time was over 20 ms for about one-fourth of the intervals. Figure 11.8 shows that this occurred when the channels were more than 30 percent busy. This is an indication that channel activity is only a small part of the cause of high disconnect time. We mentioned above that the cache-hit ratio on weekdays was usually less than 50. Cache hit ratios for other cached volumes on the string were also lower. This suggests that read-miss and write-miss staging are contributing to disconnect time.

- At least some data on this volume has good cache characteristics. When total controller activity was very light on weekends, the volume had a good cache read-hit ratio. In the presence of other work, the read-hit ratio declined.

If a much larger cache was installed, service times on this and other volumes on the controller would improve. An improved read-hit ratio would cause total service time to improve for several reasons:

- The number of I/O requests satisfied from cache would increase.
- Since each I/O request would keep the logical volume busy for a shorter time, total device utilization would be lower. The average number of I/O requests queued for the volume would be lower, and IOS queue time would decrease.
- When cache read-hit ratios are high, there will be less staging of data. Paths to the device will be free a larger percent of the time.
- There also will be fewer RPS misses. Not only will data satisfied from cache not have to compete for path availability, but reduced staging will improve the availability of DASD paths.

- If cached volumes are under the control of *system managed storage* (SMS), it might be helpful to perform caching at the dataset level instead of at the volume level. When there are several files on a volume, it is likely that they will have different access patterns and different cache-hit potential.

11.7.2 DASD Example 2

The previous illustration showed a volume containing VSAM datasets used only by CICS applications. The volume was dedicated to CICS processing, and no batch workloads used the volume during the periods examined. As much as possible, the volume serviced "random" VSAM I/O requests for several files. All accesses were generated by a single homogeneous workload.

The volume examined in this example contains several VSAM data used primarily by CICS. However, Volume 02 is also accessed by batch jobs. The batch jobs read data sequentially and are generally "detuned" (they run with only a few buffers and do not use high-speed copy operations). The volume is attached to a cache controller, and read caching is turned on at the volume level. Table 11.2 describes the volume and its environment.

Data for Volume 02 was collected for the same time frame as Volume 01. The periods when the device was less than 30 percent busy occurred on weekends.

Figure 11.11 shows average service time for Volume 02 compared to volume busy. Clearly this volume is quite busy a large percent of the time. It appears that the volume is more than 30 percent busy for more than half of the 15-minute sample periods. Not only is device utilization high, but service time is high. Many samples show service times over 50 ms, and some over 100 ms.

Figures 11.12 and 11.13 show that queue time and disconnect time account for large portions of Volume 02's service time. Figure 11.13 shows an interesting pattern. Disconnect time shows two tiers of values for most levels of activity. Assuming a fairly consistent delay for seek time, this is an indicator that channel contention and cache staging have varying effects on disconnect time during different periods.

Figure 11.14 shows channel-related pend time for the device vs. channel busy percents for the four channel paths. This is similar to the pattern shown for Volume 01.

Figure 11.15 shows the ratio of total service time to device busy time. This ratio reflects the service multiplier for the DASD volume. We can see that the service multipliers are more aggressive than would be predicted

Table 11.2   Description of Environment for Volume 02

Type of data	VSAM files
Data accessed by	CICS applications and batch jobs
Primary access	Random with some sequential batch
RMF reporting interval	15 minutes
Amount of data collected	3 hours each day, 7 days a week
Type volume	3380-J density
Type controller	3990 Mod 3
Cache	Volume

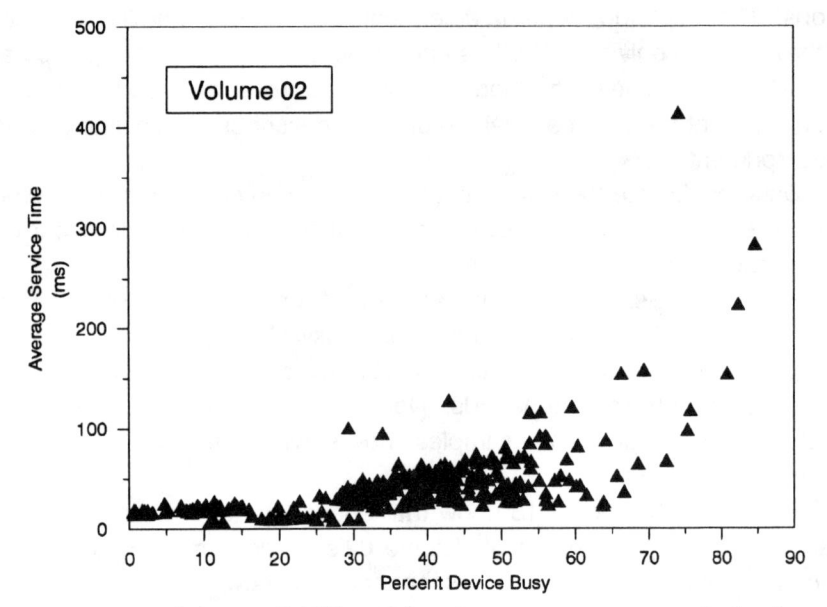

Figure 11.11 Average DASD service time versus percent device busy (Volume 2).

by open queueing formulas (see Table A.1). For example, when the device is 50 percent busy, Figure 11.15 shows the response/service ratio (service multiplier) to be between about 2 and 3. The corresponding service multiplier for an open queueing system is 2.0.

In essence, open queueing formulas set a theoretical maximum for systems in which queueing is determined only by the random arrival of customers. The actual service multipliers for this volume were larger than what would be predicted by open queueing systems. This tells us that queueing delays were caused by something other than the random arrival of events.

Earlier in this chapter, we mentioned that DASD activity does not follow random patterns. We suggested that work arrives in bursts (especially for batch jobs). We also suggested that individual I/O requests often generate multiple physical I/Os. The result is that DASD devices do not actually service a stream of random I/Os requests. Instead, they process clusters of activity.

When activity arrives in groups or clusters, servers will behave as if they were busier than averages might suggest. Since performance data is commonly collected in 15-minute to 2-hour intervals, the averages they show are the composite of many small dissimilar periods. A device that

CICS and the DASD Subsystem   335

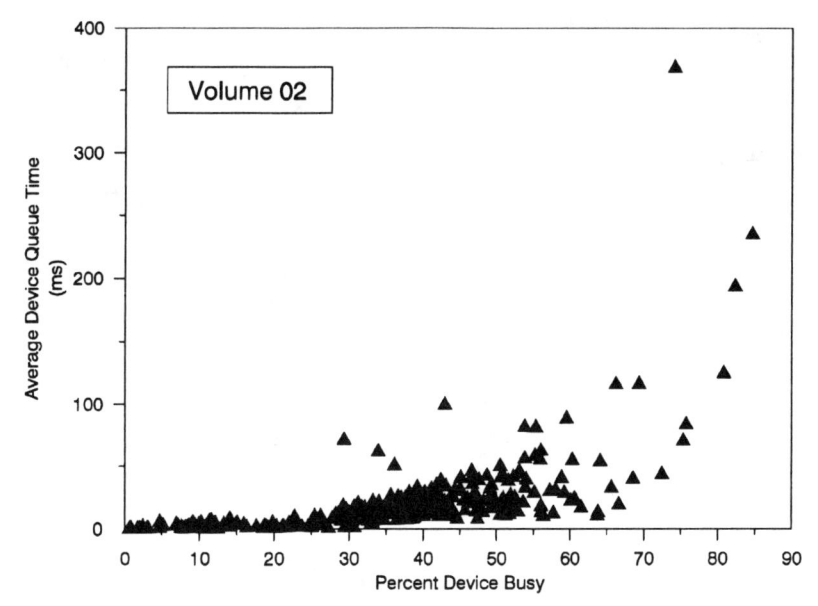

Figure 11.12 Average IOS queue time versus percent device busy (Volume 1).

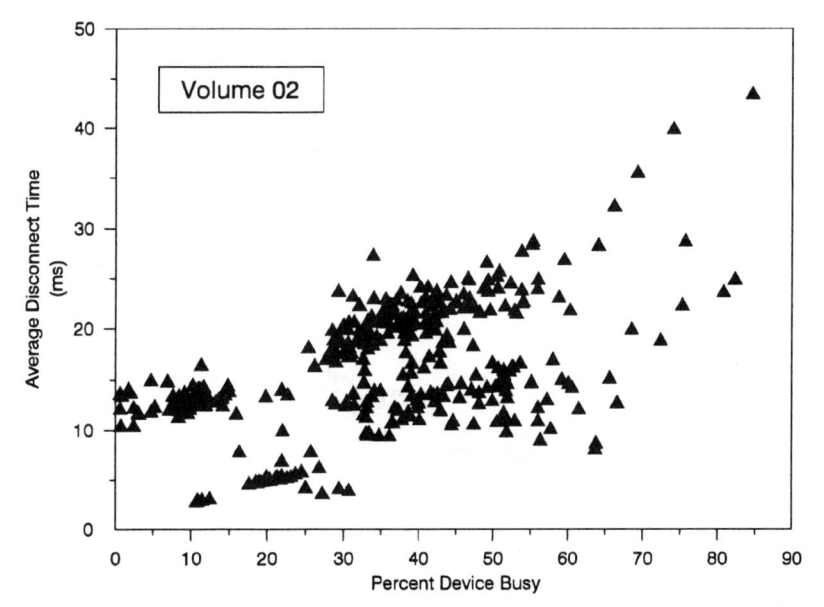

Figure 11.13 Average disconnect time versus percent device busy (Volume 1).

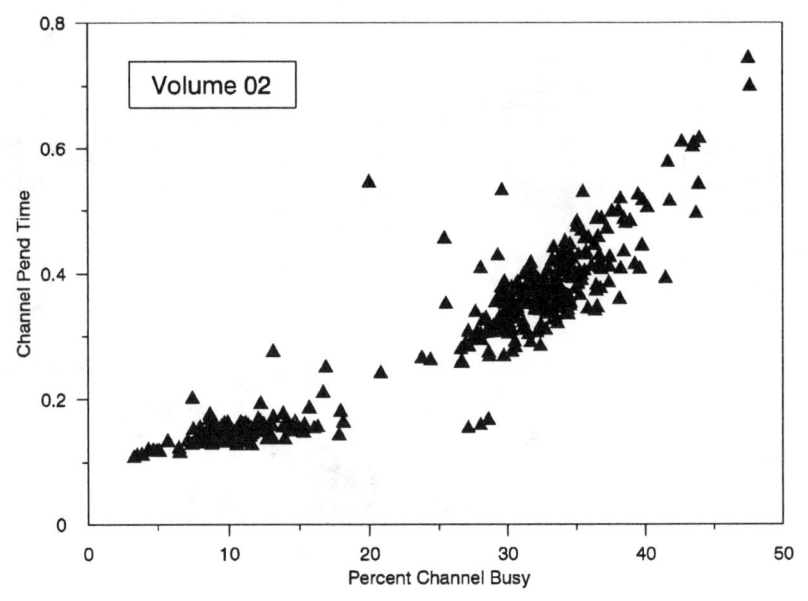

Figure 11.14 Channel pend time versus total channels busy (Volume 2).

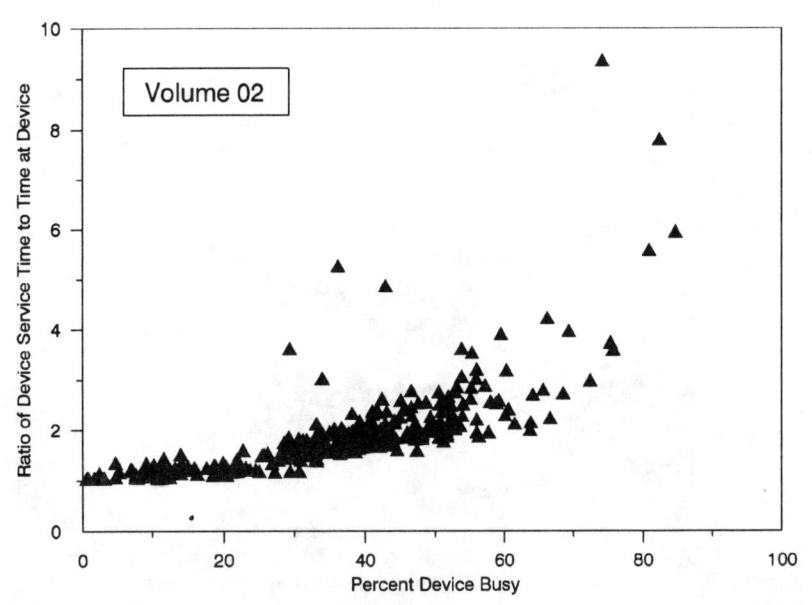

Figure 11.15 Ratio of total device service time (including queueing) to service time at the device (Volume 2).

was 40 percent busy overall might be 20 percent busy half the time and 60 percent busy the other half. Queueing delays would be higher than the average would indicate.

There are several different queueing systems that can be used to predict delays of this type. However, in most cases, it is difficult, if not impossible, to collect the information needed to use such systems. Furthermore, since averages represent a collection of unlike intervals, any set of formulas will be valid only as long as the mix of unlike data remained consistent. This is normally not the case with complex DASD workloads.

If a more in-depth analysis is to be performed on DASD activity, some type of detailed trace will be needed. This can be accomplished by using GTF trace or a trace produced by certain MVS monitors.

The data for Volume 02 suggests the following:

- Figure 11.15 shows that service multipliers for this volume are significantly higher than would be predicted by open queueing formulas. Figure 11.9 showed that service times for Volume 01 are just slightly greater than those predicted by open queueing. Volume 01 contains only VSAM files used exclusively by CICS applications. Volume 02 is accessed by batch jobs as well as CICS applications.

- The ratio of total service time to device busy time is high because of extremes in bunching.

- The more variation in workload mix, the more difficult it will be to forecast service times accurately. Volume 02 shows a wider range of service multipliers than Volume 01 for each level of utilization. Not only are service multipliers higher for Volume 02, but they are less consistent.

11.7.3 DASD Example 3

The volume in this example not only has CICS data and some batch access, but it shares its controller with another processor. Volumes 01 and 02 were located on cache controllers accessed only from a single processor dedicated to CICS applications. For the most part, Volumes 01 and 02 were not exposed to the type of contention generated by TSO, heavy batch, and ad hoc workloads. However, Volume 03 was on a string used heavily by these workloads. The controller was driven by activity that was not conducive to sharing with CICS applications.

Figure 11.16 shows average service time for Volume 03. Notice that service appears worse at any level of volume utilization than it does for either Volume 01 and 02. In this example, contention for channel paths is a major factor in service for the volume.

Figure 11.17 shows the service time to device busy ratio (similar to that shown in Figures 11.9 and 11.15). Notice that service multipliers were both more aggressive and more varied than those for Volumes 01 and 02. The competition on the channels and controllers from heavy batch and ad hoc work contribute to the behavior of this queueing system.

Overall, we can conclude the following:

- DASD datasets used for CICS workloads will receive the best service if they are placed on DASD volumes and channels dedicated to CICS workloads.

- Batch work can degrade performance on volumes serving random workloads.

- CICS datasets are placed on volumes using channels accessed heavily by TSO, DB2, or batch workloads can receive less than acceptable service.

11.8 CICS INTERNAL CACHING

11.8.1 LSR Access of VSAM Files

We have discussed *local shared resources* (LSR) in several other chapters. LSR is the default (and preferred) method of accessing VSAM files in CICS. Not only can LSR conserve I/Os (compared to NSR), but it will save CPU time and can potentially reduce the working set size. There are situations in which LSR cannot be used or has some disadvantages. These have been discussed in other chapters.

In LSR, VSAM buffers are divided into pools and subpools defined in the *file control table* (FCT). Each pool is divided into one or more subpools. Each subpool contains a set of buffers of the same size and is shared by one or more files. CIs from each file are mapped into appropriate subpools based on index and data CI sizes. Data are retained in each subpool using a *least recently used* (LRU) algorithm. This suggests that when LSR selects a buffer, it will use the buffer that was least recently referenced. An LRU algorithm tends to keep the most recently referenced data in storage.

Whenever a CI is accessed, LSR will determine if the CI is in the appropriate subpool. Records that are commonly accessed will tend to

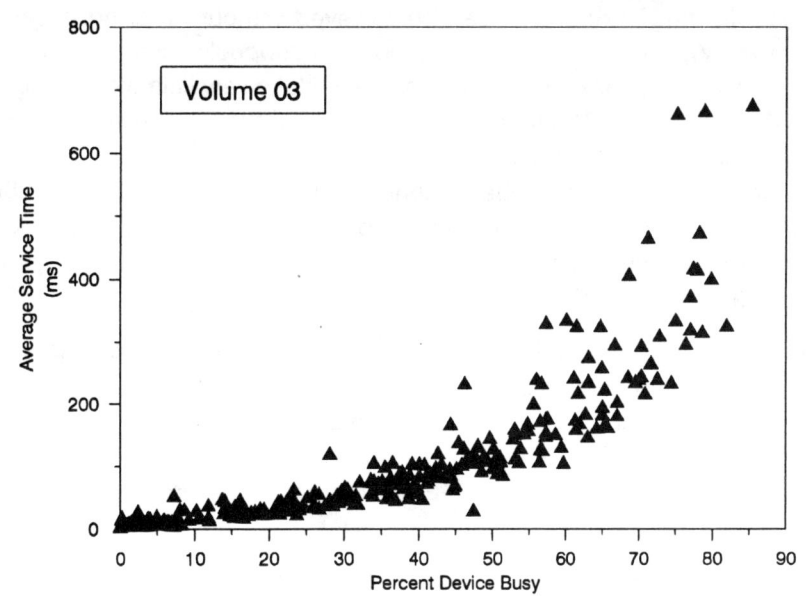

Figure 11.16 Average DASD service time versus percent device busy (Volume 3).

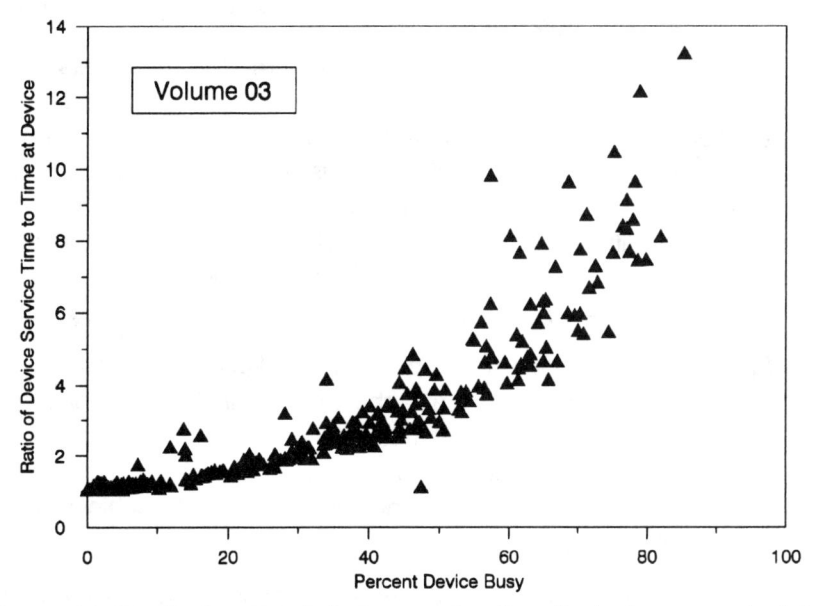

Figure 11.17 Ratio of total device service time (including queueing) to service time at the device (Volume 3).

remain in the subpool and can be retrieved without revisiting external storage. When records are accessed from subpools, effective application service time will be very good, and it will take very little processing to satisfy the request. The more data that can be retrieved directly from LSR buffers, the better the service that will be provided.

VSAM performance will be influenced by the look-aside ratios of LSR subpools. *Look-aside* is the feature of LSR that allows it to use CIs already in buffers. The following suggestions are offered as ways to improve the look-aside ratio:

- Separate data and index CI sizes into separate subpools. No subpool should contain both data and index CIs. It is normally possible to achieve look-aside ratios of 80 to 99 percent for index CIs. Data CIs usually will experience lower ratios. When index and data buffers share the same subpool, data CIs may replace index CIs and reduce the overall look-aside ratio.

  In current releases of CICS/ESA, separate subpools can be specified for data and index buffers. In CICS/MVS and CICS/VS systems, it is usually possible to force VSAM to use different CI sizes for data and index CIs, thus forcing them into separate subpools. Data CI sizes of 4k to 8k are generally preferred along with index CI sizes of 2k or less.

- Concentrate first on tuning the look-aside ratio for index data. This is accomplished by first ensuring that index data are in their own subpool and then increasing the number of buffers in the subpool until an acceptable look-aside ratio is achieved. Alternately, IBM SEs have a buffer analysis aide that can be used to estimate the benefits of different sizes of buffer pools. For most small to medium size files, it should be possible to achieve look-aside ratios of 95 percent or more for index data.

- Increase data subpools to improve the look-aside ratio; group files by reference patterns. As a rule, there is a point of diminishing return for most data subpools. Increasing the size of LSR subpools will provide noticeable benefit up to a certain point. Beyond that point, it will take a large number of additional buffers to achieve much additional benefit.

  It is possible to get very high look-aside ratios for data CIs, but this tends to be the exception rather than the rule. Unless data reference patterns are highly localized or the total amount of data in the files is quite small, it may not be possible to achieve high data look-aside ratios. If records are accessed randomly on large files, look-aside ratios may be as low as 10 to 20 percent, even with very large subpools (hundreds or even thousands of buffers).

Each file has a *locality pattern*. In some files, records are read randomly and not referenced again for a long time. This would be the locality pattern for a large table in which all data had about the same chance of being read. Commonly, though, a small portion of a file is used more heavily than others. An example of this might be a Zipcode file in which many customers were in the same geographic area. Some application systems access the same or similar records multiple times in a series of transactions. In interactive transactions, a user might look at a customer's record in one transaction and update it in the next. If the LSR subpool was large enough to retain the record between transactions, only the first transaction in a series would need to retrieve the record from DASD.

The key to this discussion is that the locality pattern for each file will be different. By combining files with similar locality patterns into the same subpool, subpools can be given enough buffers to accommodate common access patterns. Once subpools are large enough to accommodate typical locality, though, additional buffers will provide little additional benefit.

- Be cautious of files with heavy browse activity. If these files are accessed via LSR, they should be segregated into their own subpools. If not, they can dominate and pollute a subpool. Not only will files of this type receive little benefit from LSR, but they will tend to steal buffers from files that would otherwise benefit from look-aside.

- Place files with high read activity in a separate pool (or subpool) if they have either a very good or very bad look-aside ratio. If the look-aside ratio is poor, highly active files will pollute the buffer pool and prevent other files from benefiting from LSR. Not only will they receive little benefit, but they will disrupt service for other files. It is probably best to place them in a small pool dedicated to files of this type. They will not benefit materially from having a large number of buffers and should not be allowed to disrupt the performance of other files.

Highly active files with good look-aside ratios will benefit from LSR but will tend to dominate the pool in which they are defined. They should be placed in a separate pool or subpool and given enough buffers to allow a good look-aside ratio for all files.

- Concentrate on improving the service of those VSAM files that are used most heavily. Saving 10 percent of the I/Os for a file issuing 1,000,000 read requests per day will have a greater impact than saving 90 percent of the I/Os for a file issuing 50,000 read requests.
- Do not be misled by percentages. Increasing the look-aside ratio from 90 to 95 percent will reduce the number of I/Os by one-half.
- Be aware that files with good LSR look-aside ratios may be poor candidates for cache controllers. If most of the good caching occurs in LSR, all that remains for external (controller) cache is random activity with poor reference patterns.

One of the easiest ways to improve CICS performance is to tune LSR pools and subpools. If there is sufficient memory to support large LSR buffer pools, LSR look-aside can not only reduce visits to external storage, but it can reduce total CPU usage. A considerable amount of CPU time can be saved by avoiding the processing associated with accessing data from external storage.

11.8.2 CICS Temporary Storage

Temporary storage (TS) is CICS's scratch-pad facility. It is widely used by application programs, program products and internal CICS functions to hold data for short periods of time. Because the use of TS is so pervasive, its performance can affect most applications.

Of all the services running in a CICS region, temporary storage is one of the most efficient. Many innovative (almost brilliant in this author's opinion) techniques allow auxiliary temporary storage to perform many times better than native VSAM for scratch-pad data.

Auxiliary temporary storage is so efficient that some records will be written, updated, and deleted without ever referencing DASD. Not only are read requests cached internally, but write requests are also cached. As an added benefit, when DASD activity is required, temporary storage uses more efficient access techniques than standard VSAM.

CICS supports two major classes of TS data — main and auxiliary temporary storage. In MVS/XA and MVS/ESA systems, main-TS will be placed in storage above the 16-meg line. In CICS/ESA, main-TS will reside in a DSA above the line. In CICS/MVS, OS getmains will be used for main-TS. The amount of main-TS that can be used depends on the amount of real storage available to support it.

The second class of TS data is auxiliary temporary storage (aux-TS). Data in aux-TS *nominally* reside in an entry sequenced dataset (ESDS) maintained by CICS using special control interval processing. Data in the aux-TS dataset may be retained between executions of CICS with warm or emergency restarts.

Auxiliary temporary storage is designed to minimize visits to DASD and store and access data very efficiently. Control blocks are designed to permit rapid, low-cost access to data. In fact, aux-TS processing is so efficient, that its performance can be comparable to that of CICS data tables.

When applications issue TS write requests, TSP (temporary storage program) will attempt to move the data to a buffer in memory. If space can be found in a write buffer, the data simply will be moved to the buffer. It will not be written to external storage at that time.

Applications will not wait for temporary storage to be written. Even write requests for recoverable data will not be forced to DASD immediately. Only when TSP either needs to use the buffer or when recoverable data for the same task resides in multiple TS buffers will recoverable TS data be committed to DASD. Of course, the last recoverable data will be forced out to DASD when a syncpoint is taken.

TS items that are not recoverable will not be written to DASD unless TSP needs to write the buffer for some other reason. Some data will never be written to DASD and will remain in buffers for its entire life.

TSP also uses a very efficient output selection algorithm. When the aux-dataset is less than 75 percent full, TSP will always select the first empty CI when it needs to start a new buffer. Since TSP maintains a table reflecting the status of each CI in the dataset, it can easily locate the first free CI. And since TSP knows that the CI is empty, it does not need to access it from DASD – it simply formats an empty area and starts moving data into it. TSP can do this because it uses special CI processing that allows it to bypass normal VSAM requirements.

For the sake of comparison, let us look at the difference in writing five records to aux-TS versus writing them to a VSAM KSDS Let us assume that all five records could fit into a single CI. The VSAM KSDS will require that the sequence set and data component be accessed five times each. Additionally, at least five writes to external storage will be necessary.

Even if LSR look-aside could locate all CIs in memory and DASD fast write would be used on the volume, the CI would need to be transferred to the controller five times. If there were any CI or CA splits, the process would take even longer.

Ignoring the effect of other workloads, the five records could all be placed into the same CI (assuming it was empty and nothing else was placed into the CI). If the CI needed to be written after the five data records had been moved to the buffer, a single I/O would be required. Instead of multiple reads and writes, aux-TS might require only one or two writes to store the same data.

TSP is even more efficient deleting aux-TS than writing it. It simply locates the index identifying the queue element and marks the queue as deleted. No actual reference will be made to the data. TSP is smart enough to reuse freed space when it needs to. Without getting into the detail, it is sufficient to say that a clever technique allows deletion of aux-TS queue elements without actually referencing those elements.

When TSP needs to read an item, it will first check if the item is already in a buffer. If it is not, it will read the CI into a buffer. If necessary, it will clear or write an existing buffer to make space for the buffer being read. The percentage of records requiring DASD access will depend on data access patterns, the size of data, the number of buffers, and the delay between data accesses.

Table 11.3 summarizes when auxiliary temporary storage will require access to external storage.

As a rule, aux-TS is one of the most efficient vehicles for storing and accessing DASD data. Only a small percent of write requests will require access to DASD and many read requests will be satisfied internally. Auxiliary temporary storage provides rapid, low-cost access to temporary data used by CICS applications.

The only major limitation to auxiliary temporary storage is that in CICS/VS and CICS/MVS, the temporary storage buffer pool resides below the 16-megabyte line. This limits the number of buffers that can be defined. This limitation was removed with CICS/ESA.

One interesting side note is that a small number of aux-TS buffers often can provide excellent internal read-hit and write-hit ratios. Depending on the type of data being stored and its average life, a limited number of aux-TS buffers can provide excellent service.

Table 11.3 DASD Accesses for Auxiliary Temporary Storage

Type TS Queue	Type Request	When Access to DASD Required
Non-recoverable	Write	When eligible write buffers do not contain enough space to hold new TS element; existing data in a write buffer will be forced to DASD to allow new element to be placed in a buffer.
	Read	Only when the requested TS element in not already in a buffer.
	Delete	Never.
Recoverable	Write	1. Same as non-recoverable. 2. When recoverable data written for the same task resides in multiple TS buffers, the oldest data will be forced to DASD.
	Read	Only when the requested TS element in not already in a buffer.
	Delete	Never

11.9 ESTIMATING EFFECTIVE FILE SERVICE TIME FOR CICS APPLICATIONS

As we have seen, several factors affect file service time in CICS. The first is the type of operation being performed. The second is the percentage of each type of access that will be satisfied internally. LSR look-aside and temporary storage buffer management usually can reduce the number of physical I/Os significantly.

The third factor is the effect of caching in DASD controllers (if cache controllers are being used). Good read and write cache hit-ratios can make a significant difference in total service time. Bad hit-ratios can penalize service as much as help it.

The fourth factor is the specific components of DASD service and their contribution to service, including queueing. We spent considerable time discussing these factors in this chapter.

It is very difficult to estimate DASD service time by simply assembling information about workloads. DASD reference patterns can be difficult to estimate without seeing the actual interaction between workload components. It may not be easy to estimate LSR look-aside ratios, cache hit ratios, and the number of I/O requests actually sent to DASD. For this reason, it can be hard to assess actual access patterns and their effect on seek and disconnect time. Furthermore, factors like back-end staging and DFW promotion cause delays that are difficult to measure, much less predict.

This author would recommend the use of modeling software to account for the delays associated with new DASD workloads. The interaction and dynamics of workload mixes makes it difficult to estimate DASD service with any accuracy. Particularly when DASD is heavily used or advanced features are active, DASD service can be less than predictable.

An alternative approach might be to compare new DASD files and volumes to existing volumes in the same configuration. It might be safer to extrapolate from existing workload data than to try to predict service empirically.

11.10 RECOMMENDATIONS

This author would make several recommendations when configuring DASD for CICS systems:

- **Take advantage of internal caching wherever possible.** Nothing can do more to improve the performance of application file requests than accessing data directly from memory. Specific suggestions include CICS data tables, large VSAM LSR subpools, and appropriately sized temporary storage buffer pools (especially under CICS/ESA). Where appropriate, pools for database systems also should also be large enough to ensure good access to data.

    At one time, large LSR buffer pools were CPU intensive because VSAM look-aside logic scanned buffer pools. However, with later versions of DFP, a hashing technique allows direct access to data, and LSR can handle large buffer pools very efficiently. As long as sufficient memory is available to map buffers, larger LSR pools should not only improved file service, but they should reduce total CPU usage (assuming that they reduce the number of physical I/O requests).

- **Isolate DASD components that access on-line (CICS) data.** This author would suggest that DASD devices contain only CICS data, strings be dedicated to random, on-line type work, and that controllers not serve multiple types of systems. The more you can isolate and protect CICS data, the better the chance that you will not face DASD-related performance problems.

Perhaps the most important component to protect is the DASD volume. Normally it is a good idea to keep CICS system files, VSAM data, journals, and DB2 data all on separate volumes. Furthermore, none of these classes of data should share volumes with batch, TSO, or ad hoc workloads. In essence, separate pools should be maintained for each of these classes of data, and they should all be separated from other workloads.

It probably will not hurt to have most types of CICS system files on the same volumes with VSAM application files. However, there is probably wisdom in not allowing application files and CICS journals share volumes. If journals and applications files are on the same volume, a DASD failure could destroy both the data and the journal records needed to recover it. Furthermore, on most types of DASD, each actuator will contain two volumes. It is wise to keep journal and application files on separate actuators.

Almost all accesses to CICS systems files, journals, and VSAM application files are random. They typically involve simple channel programs accessing a single block or CI at a time.[7] Such DASD access supports rapid access to data and efficient sharing of channels and controllers.

Many other types of DASD access involve complex channel programs that can dominate both devices and channels. Channel programs designed for batch work, for example, tend to optimize throughput and dominate volumes for longer periods of time. Depending on the number of buffers, batch applications can transfer several tracks at a time. This can put CICS accesses sharing the same volume at a disadvantage. Even though priority scheduling can favor higher-priority CICS work, CICS work will still have to wait for long channel programs to complete.

---

[7] Large data CIs may consist of a number of blocks, but they will be retrieved by a single channel program.

DB2 frequently generates long channel programs that can interfere with other types of work. DB2 can manage access to its own data, but can interfere with other types of random access.

It is also good to keep channels and control units free from other types of work. Of course, in today's large system environments, a large amount of data will sit behind a single controller. It may not be practical or even possible to totally separate CICS from other workload types. Nevertheless, most controllers have four paths, and it only takes two or three batch jobs each dominating a path (especially batch jobs doing high-speed backups) to affect performance on the whole controller.

- **Try to keep utilization below 35 percent for volumes accessed randomly by CICS applications.** Higher utilization causes queueing and degrades device service time. Remember that DASD accesses seldom follow true random patterns, and actual service is usually worse than that predicted by open queueing systems.

- **If cache controllers are being used, try to get at least a 70 percent cache read-hit ratio.** Lower ratios tend to force high rates of back-end staging. This is a hidden delay that can affect the performance of both the volume and the controller. When DASD service time is unacceptable and no other cause can be found, look for poor read-hit ratios on the controller.

- **Plan your DASD environment.** At the time of this writing, it is probably necessary to plan the placement of critical high-activity files.

11.11 DB2 DASD PATTERNS

Conventional RMF measures of DASD activity are not very useful for DB2 databases. DB2 can access data in several different ways and will build vastly different channel programs to handle each.

Some data will be accessed randomly in response to simple queries. Here, DB2 will build simple channel programs that may access a single page (block) on DASD. When applications issue SQL calls that require tablespace scans, DB2 builds lengthy channel programs to read those portions of tables not already in DB2 buffers. DB2 does not perform write activity all the time (as we mentioned earlier, DB2 will not write data to tables until certain thresholds are reached), but when it does, it attempts to write data to tables very rapidly with long, complex channel programs.

The point of this discussion is that it is not easy to look at conventional performance information and determine whether DASD containing DB2 data is functioning acceptably. It is not at all unusual to see service times of 100 ms or more for DASD volumes dedicated to DB2. The largest part of the service time may be associated with connect and disconnect time. This can be entirely natural for DB2 data. The long service times may be more an indication of DB2 building long, optimized channel programs than a problem in the DASD subsystem.

11.12 SUMMARY

In this chapter, we looked at factors that influence DASD service in a CICS environment. We examined both the internal and external components of DASD service time from a CICS perspective. The more significant elements of DASD service were discussed in detail, and three examples were provided to demonstrate how to evaluate DASD performance in a CICS environment.

The material in this chapter does not present a methodology for predicting DASD performance. Instead, it shows how to analyze DASD service for existing CICS applications and discusses the factors that affect performance.

The purpose of this chapter was not to show how to model DASD service, but how to recognize the factors that affect performance.

SELECTED READING

[FAIR90] Fairchild, Bill, "The Anatomy of an I/O Request," *CMG '90 Proceedings*, 1990.

[HOUT93] Houtekamer, Gilbert E. and H. Pat Artis, *MVS I/O Subsystems*, McGraw-Hill, Inc., New York, 1993.

[IBM000] IBM Technical Information Search items Q565363, Q500334, Q555349, Q555340.

[JOHN92] Johnson, Robert H and R. Daniel Johnson, *DASD: IBM's Direct Access Storage Devices*, McGraw-Hill, Inc., New York, 1992.

[KELL89] Keller, Ted C., "CICS Temporary Storage Performance," *Mainframe Journal*, April, 1989.

[MAJO92] Major, Joseph B., "The M/G/1 Model and DASD I/O Response Time," *CMG Transactions*, Spring, 1992.

[MERR87] Merrill, H. W. "Barry," *Merrill's Guide Supplement*, SAS Institute Inc., Cary, NC, 1987.

Appendix A

Open Queueing Tables

Data in Table A.1[1] have been compiled from the open queueing formulas found in *Probability, Statistics, and Queueing Theory with Computer Science Applications* by Dr. Arnold Allen. A SAS program to produce these service multipliers for open queueing systems is included in Appendix E.

---

[1] While every effort has been made to ensure the accuracy of the numbers in Table A.1, no warranty is made of their accuracy or of their applicability in specific circumstances. This table is provided to help the reader estimate delays in selected data processing applications. As noted several places in the text, open queueing formulas will provide reasonable approximations of queueing service only when certain basic assumptions (such as the random arrival of events and unlimited customer population) are satisfied. The reader assumes all risks in the use of data in this table.

Table A.1 Service Multiplier for Open Queueing Systems

Server Utilization	SERVICE MULTIPLIER Number of Servers							
	1	2	3	4	5	6	7	8
.01	1.01	1.00	1.00	1.00	1.00	1.00	1.00	1.00
.02	1.02	1.00	1.00	1.00	1.00	1.00	1.00	1.00
.03	1.03	1.00	1.00	1.00	1.00	1.00	1.00	1.00
.04	1.04	1.00	1.00	1.00	1.00	1.00	1.00	1.00
.05	1.05	1.00	1.00	1.00	1.00	1.00	1.00	1.00
.06	1.06	1.00	1.00	1.00	1.00	1.00	1.00	1.00
.07	1.08	1.00	1.00	1.00	1.00	1.00	1.00	1.00
.08	1.09	1.01	1.00	1.00	1.00	1.00	1.00	1.00
.09	1.10	1.01	1.00	1.00	1.00	1.00	1.00	1.00
.10	1.11	1.01	1.00	1.00	1.00	1.00	1.00	1.00
.11	1.12	1.01	1.00	1.00	1.00	1.00	1.00	1.00
.12	1.14	1.01	1.00	1.00	1.00	1.00	1.00	1.00
.13	1.15	1.02	1.00	1.00	1.00	1.00	1.00	1.00
.14	1.16	1.02	1.00	1.00	1.00	1.00	1.00	1.00
.15	1.18	1.02	1.00	1.00	1.00	1.00	1.00	1.00
.16	1.19	1.03	1.01	1.00	1.00	1.00	1.00	1.00
.17	1.20	1.03	1.01	1.00	1.00	1.00	1.00	1.00
.18	1.22	1.03	1.01	1.00	1.00	1.00	1.00	1.00
.19	1.23	1.04	1.01	1.00	1.00	1.00	1.00	1.00
.20	1.25	1.04	1.01	1.00	1.00	1.00	1.00	1.00
.21	1.27	1.05	1.01	1.00	1.00	1.00	1.00	1.00
.22	1.28	1.05	1.01	1.00	1.00	1.00	1.00	1.00
.23	1.30	1.06	1.02	1.01	1.00	1.00	1.00	1.00
.24	1.32	1.06	1.02	1.01	1.00	1.00	1.00	1.00
.25	1.33	1.07	1.02	1.01	1.00	1.00	1.00	1.00
.26	1.35	1.07	1.02	1.01	1.00	1.00	1.00	1.00
.27	1.37	1.08	1.02	1.01	1.00	1.00	1.00	1.00
.28	1.39	1.09	1.03	1.01	1.00	1.00	1.00	1.00
.29	1.41	1.09	1.03	1.01	1.00	1.00	1.00	1.00
.30	1.43	1.10	1.03	1.01	1.01	1.00	1.00	1.00
.31	1.45	1.11	1.04	1.01	1.01	1.00	1.00	1.00
.32	1.47	1.11	1.04	1.02	1.01	1.00	1.00	1.00

Table A.1 Service Multiplier for Open Queueing Systems (continued)

Server Utilization	SERVICE MULTIPLIER Number of Servers							
	1	2	3	4	5	6	7	8
.33	1.49	1.12	1.04	1.02	1.01	1.00	1.00	1.00
.34	1.52	1.13	1.05	1.02	1.01	1.00	1.00	1.00
.35	1.54	1.14	1.05	1.02	1.01	1.01	1.00	1.00
.36	1.56	1.15	1.06	1.03	1.01	1.01	1.00	1.00
.37	1.59	1.16	1.06	1.03	1.01	1.01	1.00	1.00
.38	1.61	1.17	1.07	1.03	1.02	1.01	1.00	1.00
.39	1.64	1.18	1.07	1.03	1.02	1.01	1.01	1.00
.40	1.67	1.19	1.08	1.04	1.02	1.01	1.01	1.00
.41	1.69	1.20	1.08	1.04	1.02	1.01	1.01	1.00
.42	1.72	1.21	1.09	1.05	1.02	1.01	1.01	1.01
.43	1.75	1.23	1.10	1.05	1.03	1.02	1.01	1.01
.44	1.79	1.24	1.11	1.05	1.03	1.02	1.01	1.01
.45	1.82	1.25	1.11	1.06	1.03	1.02	1.01	1.01
.46	1.85	1.27	1.12	1.06	1.04	1.02	1.01	1.01
.47	1.89	1.28	1.13	1.07	1.04	1.02	1.02	1.01
.48	1.92	1.30	1.14	1.07	1.04	1.03	1.02	1.01
.49	1.96	1.32	1.15	1.08	1.05	1.03	1.02	1.01
.50	2.00	1.33	1.16	1.09	1.05	1.03	1.02	1.01
.51	2.04	1.35	1.17	1.09	1.06	1.04	1.02	1.02
.52	2.08	1.37	1.18	1.10	1.06	1.04	1.03	1.02
.53	2.13	1.39	1.19	1.11	1.07	1.04	1.03	1.02
.54	2.17	1.41	1.20	1.12	1.07	1.05	1.03	1.02
.55	2.22	1.43	1.22	1.13	1.08	1.05	1.04	1.03
.56	2.27	1.46	1.23	1.14	1.09	1.06	1.04	1.03
.57	2.33	1.48	1.25	1.15	1.09	1.06	1.04	1.03
.58	2.38	1.51	1.26	1.16	1.10	1.07	1.05	1.04
.59	2.44	1.53	1.28	1.17	1.11	1.08	1.05	1.04
.60	2.50	1.56	1.30	1.18	1.12	1.08	1.06	1.04
.61	2.56	1.59	1.31	1.19	1.13	1.09	1.06	1.05
.62	2.63	1.62	1.33	1.21	1.14	1.10	1.07	1.05
.63	2.70	1.66	1.36	1.22	1.15	1.11	1.08	1.06
.64	2.78	1.69	1.38	1.24	1.16	1.11	1.08	1.06

Table A.1 Service Multiplier for Open Queueing Systems (continued)

Server Utilization	SERVICE MULTIPLIER Number of Servers							
	1	2	3	4	5	6	7	8
.65	2.86	1.73	1.40	1.25	1.17	1.12	1.09	1.07
.66	2.94	1.77	1.43	1.27	1.19	1.13	1.10	1.08
.67	3.03	1.81	1.45	1.29	1.20	1.15	1.11	1.09
.68	3.13	1.86	1.48	1.31	1.22	1.16	1.12	1.09
.69	3.23	1.91	1.51	1.33	1.23	1.17	1.13	1.10
.70	3.33	1.96	1.55	1.36	1.25	1.19	1.14	1.11
.71	3.45	2.02	1.58	1.38	1.27	1.20	1.16	1.12
.72	3.57	2.08	1.62	1.41	1.29	1.22	1.17	1.14
.73	3.70	2.14	1.66	1.44	1.32	1.24	1.19	1.15
.74	3.85	2.21	1.71	1.47	1.34	1.26	1.20	1.16
.75	4.00	2.29	1.76	1.51	1.37	1.28	1.22	1.18
.76	4.17	2.37	1.81	1.55	1.40	1.31	1.24	1.20
.77	4.35	2.46	1.87	1.59	1.43	1.33	1.26	1.21
.78	4.55	2.55	1.93	1.64	1.47	1.36	1.29	1.24
.79	4.76	2.66	2.00	1.69	1.51	1.40	1.32	1.26
.80	5.00	2.78	2.08	1.75	1.55	1.43	1.35	1.29
.81	5.26	2.91	2.16	1.81	1.60	1.47	1.38	1.32
.82	5.56	3.05	2.26	1.88	1.66	1.52	1.42	1.35
.83	5.88	3.21	2.37	1.96	1.72	1.57	1.46	1.39
.84	6.25	3.40	2.49	2.05	1.79	1.63	1.51	1.43
.85	6.67	3.60	2.62	2.15	1.87	1.69	1.57	1.48
.86	7.14	3.84	2.78	2.27	1.96	1.77	1.63	1.53
.87	7.69	4.11	2.96	2.40	2.07	1.86	1.71	1.60
.88	8.33	4.43	3.17	2.56	2.20	1.96	1.80	1.68
.89	9.09	4.81	3.42	2.74	2.35	2.09	1.90	1.77
.90	10.00	5.26	3.72	2.97	2.52	2.23	2.03	1.88
.91	11.11	5.82	4.09	3.24	2.74	2.42	2.18	2.01
.92	12.50	6.51	4.55	3.59	3.02	2.64	2.38	2.18
.93	14.29	7.40	5.15	4.03	3.37	2.94	2.63	2.40
.94	16.67	8.59	5.94	4.63	3.85	3.33	2.97	2.70
.95	20.00	10.26	7.05	5.46	4.51	3.89	3.44	3.11

Table A.1 Service Multiplier for Open Queueing Systems (continued)

Server Utilization	SERVICE MULTIPLIER							
	Number of Servers							
	1	2	3	4	5	6	7	8
.96	25.00	12.76	8.71	6.70	5.51	4.72	4.15	3.73
.97	33.33	16.92	11.49	8.79	7.17	6.10	5.34	4.77
.98	50.00	25.25	17.04	12.95	10.50	8.88	7.72	6.85
.99	100	50.25	33.71	25.45	20.50	17.21	14.86	13.10

SELECTED READING

[ALLE90] Allen, Arnold O., *Probability, Statistics, and Queueing Theory with Computer Science Applications*, 2d ed., Academic Press, San Diego, 1990.

Appendix B

Closed Queueing Tables

Data in the tables that follow[1] has been compiled from the machine repair (closed) queueing formulas found in *Probability, Statistics, and Queueing Theory with Computer Science Appliations* by Dr. Arnold Allen.

Tables B.1 (one server) through B.8 (eight servers) show service multipliers ("Svc. Mult.") for sets of fixed server return ratios. The number of customers was varied for each server return ratio to generate the closest server utilizations ("Svr. Util.") to those shown in the "Approx. Server Utilization" column. Server utilizations are approximate because only whole numbers of customers could be calculated.

For example, in Table B.1, the service multiplier ("Svc. Mult.") for a system that is approximately 50 percent busy with a server return ratio of 20 would be approximately 1.76. The closest server utilization possible would be .506. Refer to Chapters 6 and 7 for explanations and examples of how to use these table.

Table B.9 contains a set of service multipliers for fixed numbers of customers in closed single-server systems. Server return ratios were varied to calculate values very close to the "Approx. Server Utilization."

---

[1] These tables are provided as an aid in estimating closed queueing systems. While every effort was made to ensure the accuracy of this data, no warranty is made of their accuracy or applicability in specific circumstances. The reader assumes all risks for use of data in these tables.

Table B.1 Service multipliers for closed queueing systems with fixed server return ratios and variable numbers of customers

Number of Servers = 1

SERVICE MULTIPLIERS

Approx. Server Utilization	Return ratio = 10		Return ratio = 15		Return ratio = 20		Return ratio = 25		Return ratio = 30	
	Svr. Util.	Svc. Mult.	Svr. Util.	Svc. Mult.	Svr. Util.	Svc. Mult.	Svr. Util.	Svc. Mult.	Svr. Util.	Svc. Mult.
.10	.091	1.00	.125	1.06	.095	1.05	.115	1.08	.097	1.07
.15	.180	1.09	.125	1.06	.142	1.10	.153	1.12	.161	1.14
.20	.180	1.09	.186	1.13	.189	1.16	.191	1.17	.192	1.18
.25	.268	1.20	.247	1.21	.236	1.22	.266	1.28	.256	1.28
.30	.268	1.20	.307	1.30	.282	1.29	.304	1.34	.287	1.33
.35	.353	1.32	.366	1.40	.328	1.36	.341	1.41	.350	1.44
.40	.436	1.47	.424	1.51	.418	1.54	.414	1.56	.412	1.57
.45	.436	1.47	.424	1.51	.462	1.64	.450	1.65	442	1.65
.50	.515	1.64	.481	1.64	.506	1.76	.486	1.74	.503	1.82
.55	.515	1.64	.536	1.79	.548	1.89	.556	1.96	.562	2.02
.60	.591	1.85	.590	1.96	.590	2.04	.591	2.09	.591	2.14
.65	.662	2.09	.641	2.16	.631	2.20	.657	2.40	.648	2.40
.70	.727	2.38	.690	2.38	.708	2.60	.689	2.57	.703	2.73
.75	.727	2.38	.737	2.64	.744	2.84	.750	3.00	.755	3.13
.80	.785	2.73	.820	3.30	.811	3.43	.806	3.53	.803	3.62
.85	.837	3.15	.855	3.70	.841	3.78	.856	4.20	.847	4.23
.90	.916	4.20	.887	4.17	.893	4.63	.899	5.04	.904	5.41
.91	.916	4.20	.914	4.70	.915	5.13	.917	5.53	.904	5.41
.92	.916	4.20	.914	4.70	.915	5.13	.917	5.53	.920	5.89
.93	.943	4.84	.936	5.29	.934	5.70	.933	6.07	.934	6.41
.94	.943	4.84	.936	5.29	.934	5.70	.933	6.07	.946	6.99
.95	.943	4.84	.954	5.96	.950	6.32	.947	6.67	.946	6.99
.96	.964	5.57	.954	5.96	.963	7.00	.959	7.32	.957	7.61
.97	.964	5.57	.969	6.68	.973	7.74	.969	8.02	.966	8.29
.98	.978	6.36	.979	7.47	.981	8.54	.977	8.77	.981	9.78

Closed Queueing Tables 359

Table B.1 Service multipliers for closed queueing systems with fixed server return ratios and variable numbers of customers (continued)

Number of Servers = 1
SERVICE MULTIPLIERS

Appr. Server Util.	Return ratio = 40		Return ratio = 50		Return ratio = 60		Return ratio = 70		Return ratio = 90	
	Svr. Util.	Svc. Mult.	Svr. Util.	Svc. Mult.	Svr. Util.	Svc. Mult.	Svr. Util.	Svc. Mult.	Svr. Util.	Svc. Mult.
.10	.097	1.08	.098	1.08	.098	1.09	.098	1.09	.099	1.10
.15	.146	1.13	.156	1.15	.147	1.15	.155	1.16	.154	1.16
.20	.194	1.20	.195	1.21	.196	1.21	.197	1.22	.197	1.23
.25	.242	1.27	.253	1.30	.245	1.29	.252	1.31	.252	1.31
.30	.290	1.35	.292	1.36	.293	1.37	.294	1.38	.295	1.39
.35	.338	1.44	.350	1.47	.358	1.50	.350	1.49	.350	1.50
.40	.409	1.59	.407	1.60	.406	1.61	.405	1.62	.404	1.63
.45	.455	1.71	.445	1.70	.453	1.74	.446	1.73	.447	1.75
.50	.502	1.85	.501	1.88	.501	1.89	.501	1.91	.500	1.92
.55	.547	2.01	.557	2.08	.548	2.07	.555	2.11	.554	2.13
.60	.592	2.20	.593	2.24	.594	2.27	.595	2.30	.596	2.34
.65	.658	2.54	.647	2.53	.655	2.61	.647	2.60	.648	2.64
.70	.701	2.81	.700	2.88	.699	2.93	.699	2.97	.699	3.02
.75	.742	3.14	.750	3.32	.756	3.46	.749	3.44	.749	3.52
.80	.800	3.76	.798	3.88	.797	3.97	.797	4.04	.796	4.16
.85	.852	4.58	.857	4.86	.848	4.85	.853	5.07	.851	5.23
.90	.898	5.65	.895	5.85	.904	6.39	.902	6.53	.899	6.77
.91	.912	6.07	.907	6.24	.914	6.78	.910	6.89	.914	7.42
.92	.924	6.54	.918	6.66	.923	7.19	.919	7.27	.920	7.78
.93	.935	7.04	.928	7.11	.932	7.63	.927	7.68	.927	8.16
.94	.935	7.04	.938	7.60	.940	8.11	.942	8.59	.939	9.00
.95	.946	7.58	.946	8.12	.947	8.62	.948	9.09	.951	9.93
.96	.963	8.80	.961	9.29	.961	9.75	.960	10.18	.961	10.98
.97	.970	9.48	.968	9.93	.972	11.02	.970	11.41	.969	12.14
.98	.981	10.95	.978	11.33	.980	12.43	.979	12.76	.980	14.11

Table B.2 Service multipliers for closed queueing systems with fixed server return ratios and variable numbers of customers

Number of Servers = 2

SERVICE MULTIPLIERS

Approx. Server Utilization	Return ratio = 10		Return ratio = 15		Return ratio = 20		Return ratio = 25		Return ratio = 30	
	Svr. Util.	Svc. Mult.	Svr. Util.	Svc. Mult.	Svr. Util.	Svc. Mult.	Svr. Util.	Svc. Mult.	Svr. Util.	Svc. Mult.
.10	.091	1.00	.094	1.00	.095	1.00	.096	1.00	.097	1.01
.15	.136	1.00	.156	1.01	.143	1.01	.154	1.02	.145	1.01
.20	.182	1.01	.187	1.02	.190	1.02	.192	1.03	.193	1.03
.25	.272	1.04	.249	1.04	.261	1.05	.250	1.05	.258	1.06
.30	.316	1.06	.311	1.07	.308	1.08	.307	1.08	.306	1.08
.35	.361	1.09	.342	1.09	.355	1.11	.345	1.11	.353	1.12
.40	.405	1.12	.403	1.14	.402	1.15	.401	1.16	.401	1.16
.45	.448	1.16	.463	1.20	.448	1.20	.458	1.22	.449	1.21
.50	.491	1.20	.493	1.23	.494	1.25	.495	1.27	.496	1.27
.55	.533	1.25	.552	1.32	.539	1.32	.550	1.35	.542	1.35
.60	.615	1.38	.609	1.42	.606	1.45	.605	1.46	.604	1.47
.65	.654	1.46	.637	1.48	.650	1.55	.658	1.60	.649	1.59
.70	.692	1.56	.692	1.63	.692	1.68	.693	1.71	.693	1.74
.75	.764	1.79	.744	1.81	.753	1.91	.743	1.91	.750	1.98
.80	.797	1.93	.793	2.03	.791	2.11	.807	2.28	.805	2.32
.85	.856	2.27	.858	2.48	.845	2.49	.850	2.64	.855	2.77
.90	.905	2.71	.896	2.87	.905	3.20	.901	3.29	.899	3.38
.91	.905	2.71	.912	3.09	.905	3.20	.913	3.49	.909	3.56
.92	.925	2.98	.927	3.34	.918	3.42	.923	3.71	.918	3.76
.93	.925	2.98	.927	3.34	.930	3.66	.933	3.94	.927	3.97
.94	.942	3.27	.940	3.61	.941	3.92	.942	4.19	.944	4.45
.95	.956	3.59	.952	3.91	.950	4.20	.950	4.46	.951	4.71
.96	.956	3.59	.962	4.23	.959	4.50	.958	4.75	.958	4.99
.97	.968	3.95	.970	4.58	.973	5.17	.971	5.39	.969	5.60
.98	.977	4.33	.977	4.95	.979	5.54	.981	6.11	.978	6.29

Table B.2 Service multipliers for closed queueing systems with fixed server return ratios and variable numbers of customers (continued)

Number of Servers = 2

SERVICE MULTIPLIERS

Approx. Server Utilization	Return ratio = 40		Return ratio = 50		Return ratio = 60		Return ratio = 70		Return ratio = 90	
	Svr. Util.	Svc. Mult.	Svr. Util.	Svc. Mult.	Svr. Util.	Svc. Mult.	Svr. Util.	Svc. Mult.	Svr. Util.	Svc. Mult.
.10	.098	1.01	.098	1.01	.098	1.01	.099	1.01	.099	1.01
.15	.146	1.02	.147	1.02	.147	1.02	.148	1.02	.148	1.02
.20	.195	1.03	.196	1.03	.197	1.03	.197	1.04	.198	1.04
.25	.256	1.05	.255	1.06	.254	1.06	.253	1.06	.253	1.06
.30	.304	1.09	.303	1.09	.303	1.09	.302	1.09	.302	1.09
.35	.353	1.12	.352	1.13	.352	1.13	.351	1.13	.351	1.13
.40	.401	1.17	.401	1.17	.400	1.17	.400	1.18	.400	1.18
.45	.449	1.22	.449	1.23	.449	1.23	.449	1.23	.449	1.24
.50	.497	1.29	.497	1.30	.498	1.30	.498	1.30	.498	1.31
.55	.556	1.39	.555	1.40	.554	1.40	.553	1.41	.552	1.41
.60	.603	1.49	.602	1.50	.602	1.51	.601	1.52	.601	1.53
.65	.649	1.62	.649	1.64	.649	1.65	.649	1.66	.649	1.67
.70	.705	1.82	.704	1.84	.703	1.86	.703	1.87	.702	1.89
.75	.749	2.03	.749	2.07	.749	2.09	.749	2.11	.749	2.14
.80	.802	2.38	.801	2.42	.801	2.46	.800	2.49	.800	2.53
.85	.852	2.85	.850	2.92	.849	2.98	.849	3.03	.849	3.10
.90	.896	3.52	.902	3.78	.900	3.87	.899	3.94	.898	4.07
.91	.912	3.85	.909	3.93	.912	4.15	.910	4.21	.911	4.42
.92	.920	4.03	.921	4.27	.917	4.31	.920	4.50	.919	4.68
.93	.927	4.23	.927	4.45	.928	4.65	.929	4.82	.930	5.12
.94	.940	4.66	.939	4.85	.938	5.03	.942	5.37	.941	5.63
.95	.952	5.15	.949	5.30	.952	5.67	.950	5.79	.951	6.20
.96	.963	5.70	.959	5.80	.960	6.16	.961	6.49	.960	6.86
.97	.972	6.31	.971	6.66	.970	6.98	.970	7.39	.971	7.86
.98	.982	7.33	.980	7.64	.979	7.92	.981	8.53	.980	9.04

Table B.3 Service multipliers for closed queueing systems with fixed server return ratios and variable numbers of customers

Number of Servers = 3

SERVICE MULTIPLIERS

Approx. Server Utilization	Return ratio = 10		Return ratio = 15		Return ratio = 20		Return ratio = 25		Return ratio = 30	
	Svr. Util.	Svc. Mult.	Svr. Util.	Svc. Mult.	Svr. Util.	Svc. Mult.	Svr. Util.	Svc. Mult.	Svr. Util.	Svc. Mult.
.10	.121	1.00	.104	1.00	.095	1.00	.103	1.00	.097	1.00
.15	.152	1.00	.146	1.00	.143	1.00	.154	1.00	.151	1.00
.20	.212	1.00	.208	1.01	.206	1.01	.205	1.01	.204	1.01
.25	.242	1.01	.250	1.01	.254	1.01	.256	1.02	.247	1.01
.30	.303	1.02	.291	1.02	.301	1.02	.295	1.02	.301	1.03
.35	.363	1.03	.353	1.04	.349	1.04	.346	1.04	.354	1.05
.40	.392	1.04	.395	1.05	.396	1.06	.396	1.06	.397	1.06
.45	.452	1.07	.456	1.09	.443	1.08	.447	1.09	.450	1.10
.50	.510	1.11	.496	1.11	.505	1.13	.498	1.13	.503	1.14
.55	.539	1.13	.557	1.17	.551	1.17	.548	1.18	.545	1.18
.60	.596	1.19	.596	1.21	.597	1.23	.597	1.24	.597	1.25
.65	.651	1.26	.654	1.30	.657	1.33	.646	1.32	.649	1.33
.70	.704	1.36	.692	1.37	.700	1.42	.694	1.42	.700	1.45
.75	.755	1.47	.747	1.51	.757	1.58	.752	1.59	.749	1.60
.80	.803	1.62	.799	1.69	.797	1.74	.797	1.78	.800	1.88
.85	.846	1.81	.847	1.93	.848	2.02	.849	2.09	.850	2.15
.90	.902	2.19	.902	2.37	.903	2.52	.896	2.53	.899	2.64
.91	.902	2.19	.914	2.51	.913	2.64	.913	2.76	.913	2.86
.92	.918	2.35	.925	2.66	.922	2.78	.921	2.88	.920	2.97
.93	.932	2.51	.935	2.82	.931	2.92	.928	3.02	.933	3.23
.94	.945	2.70	.945	2.99	.939	3.08	.942	3.31	.939	3.37
.95	.945	2.70	.953	3.18	.953	3.42	.948	3.47	.950	3.68
.96	.956	2.90	.961	3.38	.960	3.61	.960	3.83	.960	4.02
.97	.973	3.36	.968	3.60	.971	4.03	.970	4.23	.969	4.41
.98	.980	3.61	.979	4.07	.980	4.49	.981	4.90	.979	5.06

Table B.3 Service multipliers for closed queueing systems with fixed server return ratios and variable numbers of customers (continued)

Number of Servers = 3

SERVICE MULTIPLIERS

Approx. Server Utilization	Return ratio = 40		Return ratio = 50		Return ratio = 60		Return ratio = 70		Return ratio = 90	
	Svr. Util.	Svc. Mult.	Svr. Util.	Svc. Mult.	Svr. Util.	Svc. Mult.	Svr. Util.	Svc. Mult.	Svr. Util.	Svc. Mult.
.10	.098	1.00	.098	1.00	.098	1.00	.099	1.00	.099	1.00
.15	.146	1.00	.150	1.00	.148	1.00	.150	1.00	.150	1.00
.20	.203	1.01	.203	1.01	.202	1.01	.202	1.01	.201	1.01
.25	.252	1.02	.248	1.02	.251	1.02	.249	1.02	.249	1.02
.30	.301	1.03	.300	1.03	.300	1.03	.300	1.03	.300	1.03
.35	.349	1.05	.353	1.05	.349	1.05	.352	1.05	.351	1.05
.40	.398	1.07	.398	1.07	.398	1.07	.399	1.07	.399	1.07
.45	.454	1.10	.450	1.10	.447	1.10	.450	1.10	.450	1.11
.50	.502	1.14	.502	1.14	.502	1.15	.501	1.15	.501	1.15
.55	.550	1.19	.547	1.19	.550	1.20	.548	1.20	.548	1.20
.60	.598	1.26	.598	1.26	.598	1.27	.599	1.27	.599	1.28
.65	.653	1.36	.649	1.36	.652	1.37	.649	1.37	.649	1.37
.70	.699	1.47	.699	1.48	.699	1.49	.699	1.50	.699	1.51
.75	.752	1.64	.749	1.65	.751	1.67	.749	1.67	.749	1.69
.80	.797	1.85	.803	1.91	.802	1.93	.802	1.95	.801	1.97
.85	.852	2.23	.848	2.25	.851	2.31	.848	2.32	.851	2.40
.90	.903	2.83	.901	2.90	.900	2.96	.900	3.01	.900	3.09
.91	.909	2.93	.911	3.07	.913	3.11	.910	3.22	.911	3.33
.92	.920	3.13	.920	3.26	.921	3.37	.921	3.47	.919	3.55
.93	.930	3.36	.929	3.47	.928	3.57	.931	3.75	.930	3.88
.94	.940	3.62	.941	3.83	.939	3.89	.941	4.06	.941	4.26
.95	.949	3.90	.949	4.09	.949	4.27	.950	4.42	.950	4.69
.96	.961	4.38	.960	4.54	.961	4.84	.960	4.97	.959	5.20
.97	.971	4.94	.969	5.06	.969	5.34	.970	5.61	.969	5.93
.98	.980	5.58	.981	6.07	.980	6.31	.980	6.55	.979	6.99

Table B.4 Service multipliers for closed queueing systems with fixed server return ratios and variable numbers of customers

Number of Servers = 4

SERVICE MULTIPLIERS

Approx. Server Utilization	Return ratio = 10		Return ratio = 15		Return ratio = 20		Return ratio = 25		Return ratio = 30	
	Svr. Util.	Svc. Mult.	Svr. Util.	Svc. Mult.	Svr. Util.	Svc. Mult.	Svr. Util.	Svc. Mult.	Svr. Util.	Svc. Mult.
.10	.091	1.00	.094	1.00	.095	1.00	.096	1.00	.097	1.00
.15	.159	1.00	.156	1.00	.155	1.00	.154	1.00	.153	1.00
.20	.205	1.00	.203	1.00	.202	1.00	.202	1.00	.202	1.00
.25	.250	1.00	.250	1.00	.250	1.00	.250	1.00	.250	1.01
.30	.295	1.01	.297	1.01	.297	1.01	.298	1.01	.298	1.01
.35	.341	1.01	.343	1.01	.345	1.02	.346	1.02	.347	1.02
.40	.408	1.02	.406	1.03	.404	1.03	.403	1.03	.403	1.03
.45	.453	1.04	.452	1.04	.451	1.05	.451	1.05	.451	1.05
.50	.497	1.06	.498	1.06	.498	1.07	.499	1.07	.499	1.07
.55	.542	1.08	.544	1.09	.545	1.10	.546	1.10	.539	1.10
.60	.607	1.13	.604	1.14	.603	1.15	.602	1.15	.602	1.16
.65	.649	1.17	.649	1.19	.649	1.20	.649	1.21	.649	1.21
.70	.691	1.22	.707	1.27	.705	1.29	.703	1.30	.703	1.31
.75	.751	1.32	.749	1.36	.748	1.38	.748	1.40	.748	1.41
.80	.807	1.47	.803	1.51	.801	1.54	.800	1.57	.799	1.58
.85	.858	1.66	.852	1.72	.850	1.77	.849	1.80	.848	1.83
.90	.902	1.92	.896	2.01	.902	2.16	.900	2.21	.899	2.26
.91	.915	2.02	.906	2.10	.910	2.24	.907	2.29	.911	2.40
.92	.915	2.02	.916	2.19	.918	2.33	.920	2.45	.922	2.55
.93	.927	2.14	.934	2.41	.932	2.53	.932	2.64	.932	2.73
.94	.938	2.26	.941	2.53	.939	2.64	.937	2.74	.942	2.92
.95	.948	2.40	.949	2.65	.951	2.87	.948	2.95	.951	3.14
.96	.957	2.54	.962	2.93	.962	3.14	.962	3.33	.959	3.38
.97	.971	2.87	.973	3.25	.971	3.44	.970	3.62	.970	3.78
.98	.982	3.24	.981	3.60	.981	3.95	.980	4.10	.981	4.41

Table B.4 Service multipliers for closed queueing systems with fixed server return ratios and variable numbers of customers (continued)

Number of Servers = 4

SERVICE MULTIPLIERS

Approx. Server Utilization	Return ratio = 40		Return ratio = 50		Return ratio = 60		Return ratio = 70		Return ratio = 90	
	Svr. Util.	Svc. Mult.	Svr. Util.	Svc. Mult.	Svr. Util.	Svc. Mult.	Svr. Util.	Svc. Mult.	Svr. Util.	Svc. Mult.
.10	.098	1.00	.098	1.00	.098	1.00	.099	1.00	.099	1.00
.15	.152	1.00	.152	1.00	.152	1.00	.151	1.00	.151	1.00
.20	.201	1.00	.201	1.00	.201	1.00	.201	1.00	.201	1.00
.25	.250	1.01	.250	1.01	.250	1.01	.250	1.01	.250	1.01
.30	.299	1.01	.299	1.01	.299	1.01	.299	1.01	.299	1.01
.35	.347	1.02	.348	1.02	.348	1.02	.348	1.02	.349	1.02
.40	.402	1.03	.402	1.03	.401	1.03	.401	1.04	.401	1.04
.45	.451	1.05	.451	1.05	.450	1.05	.450	1.05	.450	1.06
.50	.499	1.08	.499	1.08	.499	1.08	.499	1.08	.500	1.08
.55	.547	1.11	.548	1.11	.548	1.11	.548	1.12	.549	1.12
.60	.601	1.16	.601	1.16	.601	1.17	.601	1.17	.601	1.17
.65	.649	1.22	.649	1.23	.649	1.23	.649	1.23	.649	1.24
.70	.702	1.32	.701	1.32	.701	1.33	.701	1.33	.701	1.34
.75	.748	1.43	.748	1.44	.749	1.45	.749	1.46	.749	1.47
.80	.799	1.61	.799	1.63	.799	1.64	.799	1.66	.799	1.67
.85	.848	1.88	.852	1.94	.851	1.96	.851	1.98	.851	2.01
.90	.898	2.33	.901	2.44	.900	2.48	.900	2.52	.899	2.57
.91	.911	2.52	.909	2.55	.910	2.63	.911	2.70	.911	2.77
.92	.920	2.65	.920	2.73	.920	2.80	.920	2.86	.920	2.96
.93	.929	2.81	.930	2.94	.929	2.99	.930	3.10	.931	3.22
.94	.941	3.06	.940	3.18	.940	3.29	.940	3.38	.941	3.53
.95	.951	3.36	.949	3.45	.951	3.63	.950	3.70	.951	3.89
.96	.961	3.70	.961	3.87	.961	4.02	.961	4.16	.960	4.32
.97	.970	4.08	.970	4.36	.969	4.48	.970	4.72	.971	5.03
.98	.979	4.68	.980	5.08	.980	5.30	.980	5.52	.980	5.92

Table B.5 Service multipliers for closed queueing systems with fixed server return ratios and variable numbers of customers

Number of Servers = 5

SERVICE MULTIPLIERS

Approx. Server Utilization	Return ratio = 10		Return ratio = 15		Return ratio = 20		Return ratio = 25		Return ratio = 30	
	Svr. Util.	Svc. Mult.	Svr. Util.	Svc. Mult.	Svr. Util.	Svc. Mult.	Svr. Util.	Svc. Mult.	Svr. Util.	Svc. Mult.
.10	.109	1.00	.100	1.00	.095	1.00	.100	1.00	.097	1.00
.15	.145	1.00	.150	1.00	.152	1.00	.146	1.00	.148	1.00
.20	.200	1.00	.200	1.00	.200	1.00	.200	1.00	.200	1.00
.25	.255	1.00	.250	1.00	.248	1.00	.246	1.00	.252	1.00
.30	.291	1.00	.300	1.00	.295	1.00	.300	1.00	.297	1.00
.35	.345	1.01	.350	1.01	.352	1.01	.346	1.01	.348	1.01
.40	.400	1.01	.400	1.01	.400	1.02	.400	1.02	.400	1.02
.45	.454	1.02	.449	1.02	.447	1.03	.453	1.03	.451	1.03
.50	.507	1.04	.499	1.04	.504	1.04	.499	1.04	.502	1.05
.55	.543	1.05	.548	1.06	.551	1.06	.552	1.07	.547	1.07
.60	.596	1.08	.597	1.09	.597	1.09	.598	1.10	.598	1.10
.65	.648	1.11	.645	1.13	.653	1.14	.650	1.14	.649	1.15
.70	.699	1.17	.704	1.19	.698	1.20	.702	1.21	.699	1.21
.75	.748	1.24	.750	1.27	.752	1.29	.753	1.30	.748	1.30
.80	.794	1.33	.805	1.40	.803	1.42	.802	1.44	.801	1.45
.85	.852	1.50	.846	1.54	.852	1.61	.849	1.63	.853	1.67
.90	.902	1.75	.902	1.86	.902	1.94	.898	1.96	.900	2.02
.91	.913	1.83	.910	1.92	.909	2.00	.909	2.06	.909	2.12
.92	.924	1.91	.918	2.00	.922	2.13	.920	2.18	.919	2.23
.93	.933	2.00	.933	2.15	.928	2.20	.930	2.32	.932	2.42
.94	.942	2.10	.940	2.24	.939	2.36	.939	2.47	.940	2.56
.95	.950	2.21	.952	2.44	.950	2.54	.948	2.63	.951	2.80
.96	.958	2.32	.958	2.54	.959	2.74	.960	2.91	.962	3.07
.97	.970	2.57	.972	2.90	.971	3.07	.970	3.24	.970	3.39
.98	.980	2.85	.980	3.17	.980	3.46	.981	3.74	.980	3.87

Closed Queueing Tables

Table B.5 Service multipliers for closed queueing systems with fixed server return ratios and variable numbers of customers (continued)

Number of Servers = 5

SERVICE MULTIPLIERS

Approx. Server Utilization	Return ratio = 40		Return ratio = 50		Return ratio = 60		Return ratio = 70		Return ratio = 90	
	Svr. Util.	Svc. Mult.	Svr. Util.	Svc. Mult.	Svr. Util.	Svc. Mult.	Svr. Util.	Svc. Mult.	Svr. Util.	Svc. Mult.
.10	.102	1.00	.102	1.00	.102	1.00	.101	1.00	.101	1.00
.15	.151	1.00	.149	1.00	.151	1.00	.149	1.00	.149	1.00
.20	.200	1.00	.200	1.00	.200	1.00	.200	1.00	.200	1.00
.25	.249	1.00	.251	1.00	.249	1.00	.251	1.00	.251	1.00
.30	.302	1.00	.302	1.01	.302	1.01	.301	1.01	.301	1.01
.35	.351	1.01	.349	1.01	.351	1.01	.349	1.01	.349	1.01
.40	.400	1.02	.400	1.02	.400	1.02	.400	1.02	.400	1.02
.45	.448	1.03	.451	1.03	.449	1.03	.451	1.03	.450	1.03
.50	.502	1.05	.501	1.05	.501	1.05	.501	1.05	.501	1.05
.55	.550	1.07	.548	1.07	.550	1.07	.549	1.07	.549	1.07
.60	.598	1.10	.599	1.11	.599	1.11	.599	1.11	.599	1.11
.65	.651	1.16	.649	1.16	.651	1.16	.649	1.16	.649	1.16
.70	.699	1.22	.699	1.23	.699	1.23	.699	1.24	.699	1.24
.75	.750	1.32	.748	1.32	.750	1.33	.751	1.34	.751	1.35
.80	.801	1.47	.800	1.48	.800	1.49	.800	1.50	.800	1.51
.85	.849	1.69	.851	1.72	.849	1.73	.850	1.75	.850	1.77
.90	.898	2.07	.901	2.15	.901	2.19	.900	2.21	.900	2.25
.91	.910	2.20	.911	2.27	.911	2.37	.910	2.34	.909	2.39
.92	.921	2.35	.920	2.41	.919	2.45	.921	2.53	.920	2.58
.93	.931	2.52	.931	2.61	.929	2.63	.930	2.70	.929	2.77
94	.941	2.71	.940	2.78	.939	2.84	.940	2.95	.940	3.03
95	.950	2.93	.950	3.05	.950	3.15	.950	3.24	.949	3.33
.96	.959	3.18	.960	3.36	.960	3.51	.960	3.58	.960	3.76
.97	.971	3.66	.970	3.81	.970	3.94	.969	4.07	.969	4.29
.98	.979	4.12	.980	4.47	.980	4.68	.980	4.87	.980	5.13

Table B.6 Service multipliers for closed queueing systems with fixed server return ratios and variable numbers of customers

Number of Servers = 6

SERVICE MULTIPLIERS

Approx. Server Utilization	Return ratio = 10		Return ratio = 15		Return ratio = 20		Return ratio = 25		Return ratio = 30	
	Svr. Util.	Svc. Mult.	Svr. Util.	Svc. Mult.	Svr. Util.	Svc. Mult.	Svr. Util.	Svc. Mult.	Svr. Util.	Svc. Mult.
.10	.106	1.00	.104	1.00	.103	1.00	.103	1.00	.102	1.00
.15	.152	1.00	.146	1.00	.151	1.00	.147	1.00	.151	1.00
.20	.197	1.00	.198	1.00	.198	1.00	.199	1.00	.199	1.00
.25	.242	1.00	.250	1.00	.254	1.00	.250	1.00	.247	1.00
.30	.303	1.00	.302	1.00	.302	1.00	.301	1.00	.301	1.00
.35	.348	1.00	.354	1.00	.349	1.00	.353	1.00	.349	1.00
.40	.394	1.01	.396	1.01	.397	1.01	.397	1.01	.398	1.01
.45	.454	1.01	.448	1.01	.452	1.02	.448	1.02	.451	1.02
.50	.499	1.02	.499	1.02	.499	1.03	.499	1.03	.500	1.03
.55	.544	1.03	.551	1.04	.547	1.04	.550	1.04	.548	1.04
.60	.603	1.06	.602	1.06	.601	1.07	.601	1.07	.601	1.07
.65	.647	1.08	.652	1.10	.648	1.10	.651	1.11	.648	1.11
.70	.704	1.13	.702	1.14	.701	1.15	.701	1.16	.702	1.14
.75	.745	1.18	.751	1.21	.746	1.21	.750	1.23	.751	1.21
.80	.799	1.27	.798	1.30	.797	1.34	.797	1.33	.798	1.30
.85	.848	1.40	.851	1.46	.853	1.50	.849	1.51	.851	1.46
.90	.903	1.63	.898	1.70	.903	1.79	.901	1.82	.898	1.70
.91	.912	1.69	.913	1.80	.908	1.83	.911	1.91	.913	1.80
.92	.921	1.76	.920	1.86	.919	1.93	.920	2.00	.920	1.86
.93	.930	1.83	.932	1.98	.930	2.05	.929	2.10	.932	1.98
.94	.938	1.90	.938	2.05	.940	2.17	.941	2.28	.938	2.05
.95	.953	2.07	.950	2.20	.949	2.31	.949	2.41	.950	2.20
.96	.959	2.16	.960	2.37	.961	2.55	.959	2.63	.960	2.37
.97	.970	2.37	.968	2.56	.971	2.82	.971	2.97	.968	2.56
.98	.979	2.60	.979	2.88	.980	3.14	.981	3.38	.979	2.88

Table B.6 Service multipliers for closed queueing systems with fixed server return ratios and variable numbers of customers (continued)

Number of Servers = 6

SERVICE MULTIPLIERS

Approx. Server Utilization	Return ratio = 40		Return ratio = 50		Return ratio = 60		Return ratio = 70		Return ratio = 90	
	Svr. Util.	Svc. Mult.	Svr. Util.	Svc. Mult.	Svr. Util.	Svc. Mult.	Svr. Util.	Svc. Mult.	Svr. Util.	Svc. Mult.
.10	.102	1.00	.101	1.00	.101	1.00	.101	1.00	.101	1.00
.15	.150	1.00	.150	1.00	.150	1.00	.150	1.00	.150	1.00
.20	.199	1.00	.199	1.00	.199	1.00	.200	1.00	.200	1.00
.25	.248	1.00	.248	1.00	.249	1.00	.249	1.00	.249	1.00
.30	.301	1.00	.301	1.00	.301	1.00	.300	1.00	.300	1.00
.35	.350	1.00	.350	1.00	.350	1.01	.350	1.01	.350	1.01
.40	.398	1.01	.399	1.01	.399	1.01	.399	1.01	.399	1.01
.45	.451	1.02	.451	1.02	.451	1.02	.451	1.02	.450	1.02
.50	.500	1.03	.500	1.03	.500	1.03	.500	1.03	.500	1.03
.55	.548	1.05	.549	1.05	.549	1.05	.549	1.05	.549	1.05
.60	.601	1.07	.600	1.08	.600	1.08	.600	1.08	.600	1.08
.65	.649	1.11	.649	1.11	.649	1.11	.649	1.12	.649	1.12
.70	.700	1.17	.700	1.17	.700	1.17	.700	1.17	.700	1.18
.75	.752	1.25	.751	1.25	.751	1.26	.751	1.26	.751	1.26
.80	.802	1.37	.798	1.37	.801	1.39	.801	1.39	.801	1.40
.85	.850	1.56	.850	1.58	.850	1.59	.850	1.60	.850	1.62
.90	.899	1.90	.901	1.96	.901	1.98	.900	2.01	.900	2.04
.91	.909	1.99	.909	2.05	.910	2.09	.911	2.13	.910	2.16
.92	.921	2.15	.920	2.18	.919	2.21	.920	2.26	.921	2.33
.93	.930	2.27	.930	2.33	.930	2.38	.930	2.43	.930	2.49
.94	.942	2.47	.940	2.51	.940	2.58	.941	2.65	.940	2.72
.95	.950	2.64	.951	2.77	.950	2.82	.949	2.87	.950	3.00
.96	.960	2.90	.959	3.01	.961	3.16	.960	3.24	.960	3.38
.97	.970	3.28	.970	3.43	.970	3.57	.970	3.70	.970	3.85
.98	.979	3.74	.981	4.05	.980	4.15	.980	4.34	.980	4.59

Table B.7 Service multipliers for closed queueing systems with fixed server return ratios and variable numbers of customers

Number of Servers = 7

SERVICE MULTIPLIERS

Approx. Server Utilization	Return ratio = 10		Return ratio = 15		Return ratio = 20		Return ratio = 25		Return ratio = 30	
	Svr. Util.	Svc. Mult.	Svr. Util.	Svc. Mult.	Svr. Util.	Svc. Mult.	Svr. Util.	Svc. Mult.	Svr. Util.	Svc. Mult.
.10	.104	1.00	.098	1.00	.102	1.00	.099	1.00	.101	1.00
.15	.156	1.00	.152	1.00	.150	1.00	.148	1.00	.152	1.00
.20	.195	1.00	.196	1.00	.197	1.00	.198	1.00	.198	1.00
.25	.247	1.00	.250	1.00	.252	1.00	.247	1.00	.249	1.00
.30	.299	1.00	.304	1.00	.299	1.00	.302	1.00	.300	1.00
.35	.351	1.00	.348	1.00	.347	1.00	.352	1.00	.350	1.00
.40	.402	1.00	.402	1.00	.401	1.00	.401	1.01	.401	1.01
.45	.454	1.01	.446	1.01	.449	1.01	.450	1.01	.451	1.01
.50	.506	1.01	.500	1.02	.503	1.02	.500	1.02	.502	1.02
.55	.544	1.02	.553	1.03	.550	1.03	.549	1.03	.548	1.03
.60	.595	1.04	.597	1.04	.597	1.05	.598	1.05	.598	1.05
.65	.646	1.06	.649	1.07	.651	1.08	.652	1.08	.648	1.08
.70	.695	1.09	.701	1.11	.697	1.11	.700	1.12	.702	1.13
.75	.756	1.16	.751	1.17	.749	1.17	.748	1.18	.751	1.19
.80	.802	1.23	.800	1.25	.799	1.27	.799	1.28	.803	1.30
.85	.845	1.33	.846	1.37	.848	1.40	.849	1.43	.850	1.44
.90	.903	1.55	.902	1.62	.898	1.64	.899	1.69	.900	1.73
.91	.912	1.60	.909	1.66	.908	1.71	.912	1.79	.911	1.82
.92	.920	1.65	.921	1.75	.918	1.79	.920	1.87	.918	1.89
.93	.928	1.70	.932	1.86	.932	1.93	.932	1.99	.929	2.00
.94	.942	1.83	.938	1.91	.940	2.03	.939	2.08	.941	2.18
.95	.949	1.90	.948	2.03	.948	2.14	.949	2.24	.950	2.33
.96	.960	2.05	.961	2.24	.959	2.34	.959	2.42	.961	2.56
.97	.970	2.22	.972	2.48	.969	2.56	.970	2.70	.970	2.84
.98	.979	2.41	.981	2.76	.979	2.90	.981	3.12	.980	3.24

Table B.7 Service multipliers for closed queueing systems with fixed server return ratios and variable numbers of customers (continued)

Number of Servers = 7

SERVICE MULTIPLIERS

Approx. Server Utilization	Return ratio = 40		Return ratio = 50		Return ratio = 60		Return ratio = 70		Return ratio = 90	
	Svr. Util.	Svc. Mult.	Svr. Util.	Svc. Mult.	Svr. Util.	Svc. Mult.	Svr. Util.	Svc. Mult.	Svr. Util.	Svc. Mult.
.10	.101	1.00	.101	1.00	.101	1.00	.101	1.00	.100	1.00
.15	.150	1.00	.151	1.00	.150	1.00	.151	1.00	.151	1.00
.20	.199	1.00	.199	1.00	.199	1.00	.199	1.00	.199	1.00
.25	.251	1.00	.249	1.00	.251	1.00	.249	1.00	.250	1.00
.30	.300	1.00	.300	1.00	.300	1.00	.300	1.00	.300	1.00
.35	.348	1.00	.350	1.00	.349	1.00	.350	1.00	.350	1.00
.40	.401	1.01	.401	1.01	.400	1.01	.400	1.01	.400	1.01
.45	.449	1.01	.451	1.01	.450	1.01	.451	1.01	.450	1.01
.50	.498	1.02	.501	1.02	.501	1.02	.501	1.02	.501	1.02
.55	.550	1.03	.551	1.03	.550	1.03	.551	1.03	.551	1.04
.60	.599	1.05	.599	1.05	.599	1.05	.599	1.05	.599	1.06
.65	.650	1.08	.649	1.08	.650	1.09	.649	1.09	.649	1.09
.70	.702	1.13	.701	1.13	.701	1.13	.701	1.13	.701	1.14
.75	.749	1.19	.751	1.20	.749	1.20	.750	1.21	.750	1.21
.80	.799	1.30	.799	1.30	.799	1.31	.799	1.31	.799	1.32
.85	.851	1.47	.849	1.48	.850	1.50	.849	1.50	.851	1.52
.90	.900	1.77	.899	1.78	.901	1.84	.901	1.85	.900	1.88
.91	.911	1.87	.911	1.91	.909	1.92	.909	1.95	.910	1.99
.92	.919	1.96	.920	2.02	.921	2.06	.920	2.08	.920	2.12
.93	.930	2.09	.929	2.14	.930	2.20	.930	2.23	.930	2.29
.94	.940	2.25	.940	2.30	.939	2.36	.939	2.40	.941	2.50
.95	.950	2.43	.949	2.51	.950	2.59	.950	2.65	.950	2.75
.96	.960	2.69	.960	2.80	.961	2.90	.960	2.94	.960	3.05
.97	.970	3.01	.970	3.16	.971	3.29	.970	3.36	.970	3.53
.98	.980	3.46	.980	3.66	.980	3.84	.980	3.94	.980	4.19

Table B.8 Service multipliers for closed queueing systems with fixed server return ratios and variable numbers of customers

Number of Servers = 8

SERVICE MULTIPLIERS

Approx. Server Utilization	Return ratio = 10		Return ratio = 15		Return ratio = 20		Return ratio = 25		Return ratio = 30	
	Svr. Util.	Svc. Mult.	Svr. Util.	Svc. Mult.	Svr. Util.	Svc. Mult.	Svr. Util.	Svc. Mult.	Svr. Util.	Svc. Mult.
.10	.102	1.00	.102	1.00	.101	1.00	.101	1.00	.101	1.00
.15	.148	1.00	.148	1.00	.149	1.00	.149	1.00	.149	1.00
.20	.205	1.00	.203	1.00	.202	1.00	.202	1.00	.202	1.00
.25	.250	1.00	.250	1.00	.250	1.00	.250	1.00	.250	1.00
.30	.295	1.00	.297	1.00	.298	1.00	.298	1.00	.298	1.00
.35	.352	1.00	.352	1.00	.351	1.00	.351	1.00	.351	1.00
.40	.398	1.00	.398	1.00	.399	1.00	.399	1.00	.399	1.00
.45	.454	1.00	.453	1.01	.452	1.01	.452	1.01	.452	1.01
.50	.500	1.01	.500	1.01	.500	1.01	.500	1.01	.500	1.01
.55	.556	1.02	.546	1.02	.547	1.02	.548	1.02	.548	1.02
.60	.601	1.03	.600	1.03	.600	1.04	.600	1.04	.600	1.04
.65	.645	1.05	.646	1.05	.653	1.06	.652	1.06	.652	1.06
.70	.700	1.08	.699	1.09	.699	1.09	.699	1.09	.699	1.10
.75	.753	1.12	.751	1.14	.751	1.14	.751	1.15	.750	1.15
.80	.804	1.19	.802	1.21	.801	1.22	.801	1.23	.800	1.24
.85	.852	1.30	.850	1.33	.849	1.35	.849	1.36	.849	1.37
.90	.903	1.48	.900	1.53	.898	1.57	.902	1.62	.901	1.64
.91	.911	1.52	.911	1.60	.912	1.65	.909	1.67	.911	1.71
.92	.919	1.57	.922	1.67	.921	1.72	.920	1.76	.920	1.80
.93	.933	1.66	.932	1.76	.929	1.80	.931	1.86	.929	1.89
.94	.939	1.71	.942	1.85	.941	1.92	.941	1.98	.940	2.03
.95	.951	1.83	.951	1.96	.952	2.07	.950	2.11	.951	2.20
.96	.962	1.96	.959	2.08	.961	2.24	.961	2.32	.963	2.45
.97	.971	2.11	.970	2.28	.970	2.43	.971	2.56	.969	2.63
.98	.981	2.36	.981	2.59	.979	2.72	.981	2.92	.980	3.03

Table B.8 Service multipliers for closed queueing systems with fixed server return ratios and variable numbers of customers (continued)

Number of Servers = 8

SERVICE MULTIPLIERS

Approx. Server Utilization	Return ratio = 40		Return ratio = 50		Return ratio = 60		Return ratio = 70		Return ratio = 90	
	Svr. Util.	Svc. Mult.	Svr. Util.	Svc. Mult.	Svr. Util.	Svc. Mult.	Svr. Util.	Svc. Mult.	Svr. Util.	Svc. Mult.
.10	.101	1.00	.100	1.00	.100	1.00	.100	1.00	.100	1.00
.15	.149	1.00	.150	1.00	.150	1.00	.150	1.00	.150	1.00
.20	.201	1.00	.201	1.00	.201	1.00	.201	1.00	.201	1.00
.25	.250	1.00	.250	1.00	.250	1.00	.250	1.00	.250	1.00
.30	.299	1.00	.299	1.00	.299	1.00	.299	1.00	.299	1.00
.35	.351	1.00	.350	1.00	.350	1.00	.350	1.00	.350	1.00
.40	.399	1.00	.399	1.00	.400	1.00	.400	1.00	.400	1.00
.45	.451	1.01	.451	1.01	.451	1.01	.451	1.01	.451	1.01
.50	.500	1.01	.500	1.01	.500	1.01	.500	1.01	.500	1.01
.55	.548	1.02	.549	1.02	.549	1.02	.549	1.02	.549	1.02
.60	.600	1.04	.600	1.04	.600	1.04	.600	1.04	.600	1.04
.65	.651	1.06	.651	1.07	.651	1.07	.651	1.07	.651	1.07
.70	.700	1.10	.700	1.10	.700	1.10	.700	1.11	.700	1.11
.75	.750	1.16	.750	1.16	.750	1.16	.750	1.17	.750	1.17
.80	.800	1.25	.800	1.25	.800	1.26	.800	1.26	.800	1.27
.85	.849	1.40	.851	1.41	.851	1.42	.851	1.43	.850	1.44
.90	.900	1.67	.900	1.69	.899	1.71	.899	1.73	.900	1.76
.91	.910	1.75	.910	1.78	.910	1.81	.910	1.83	.910	1.86
.92	.920	1.85	.920	1.89	.921	1.92	.919	1.93	.920	1.98
.93	.930	1.96	.930	2.01	.931	2.06	.930	2.07	.930	2.12
.94	.941	2.21	.940.	2.16	.940	2.21	.940	2.24	.940	2.30
.95	.949	2.27	.950	2.36	.950	2.40	.950	2.47	.950	2.53
.96	.959	2.48	.960	2.60	.960	2.66	.960	2.75	.960	2.84
.97	.970	2.80	.970	2.94	.970	3.03	.970	3.10	.970	3.27
.98	.980	3.24	.980	3.43	.980	3.54	.980	3.71	.980	3.89

Table B.9 Service multipliers for closed queueing systems with fixed numbers of customers and variable server return ratios

Number of Servers = 1

SERVICE MULTIPLIERS

Approx. Server Utilization	10 Customers		20 Customers		30 Customers		40 Customers		50 Customers	
	Svr. Util.	Svc. Mult.	Svr. Util.	Svc. Mult.	Svr. Util.	Svc. Mult.	Svr. Util.	Svc. Mult.	Svr. Util.	Svc. Mult.
.10	.100	1.10	.100	1.10	.100	1.11	.100	1.11	.100	1.11
.15	.150	1.15	.150	1.17	.150	1.17	.150	1.17	.150	1.17
.20	.200	1.21	.200	1.23	.200	1.24	.200	1.24	.200	1.24
.25	.250	1.28	.250	1.31	.250	1.32	.250	1.32	.250	1.32
.30	.300	1.35	.300	1.39	.300	1.40	.300	1.41	.300	1.41
.35	.350	1.43	.350	1.48	.350	1.50	.350	1.51	.350	1.52
.40	.400	1.52	.400	1.59	.400	1.61	.400	1.62	.400	1.63
.45	.450	1.62	.450	1.71	.450	1.74	.450	1.76	.450	1.77
.50	.500	1.73	.500	1.84	.500	1.89	.500	1.91	.500	1.93
.55	.550	1.85	.550	2.00	.550	2.06	.550	2.10	.550	2.12
.60	.600	1.99	.600	2.18	.600	2.27	.600	2.32	.600	2.35
.65	.650	2.15	.650	2.40	.650	2.51	.650	2.58	.650	2.63
.70	.700	2.33	.700	2.66	.700	2.81	.700	2.91	.700	2.97
.75	.751	2.56	.750	2.97	.750	3.19	.750	3.32	.750	3.42
.80	.801	2.82	.800	3.37	.800	3.66	.800	3.86	.800	4.00
.85	.850	3.15	.850	3.89	.850	4.31	.850	4.59	.850	4.80
.90	.900	3.60	.900	4.61	.900	5.23	.900	5.67	.900	6.00
.91	.910	3.72	.910	4.80	.910	5.47	.910	5.95	.910	6.33
.92	.920	3.84	.920	5.01	.920	5.74	.920	6.27	.920	6.69
.93	.930	3.98	.930	5.25	.930	6.04	.930	6.63	.930	7.09
.94	.941	4.15	.940	5.50	.940	6.39	.940	7.04	.940	7.56
.95	.950	4.31	.950	5.81	.950	6.80	.950	7.53	.950	8.12
.96	.960	4.52	.960	6.18	.960	7.29	.960	8.12	.960	8.79
.97	.970	4.79	.970	6.64	.970	7.89	.970	8.87	.970	9.65
.98	.980	5.13	.980	7.25	.980	8.73	.980	9.87	.980	10.83

Table B.9 Service multipliers for closed queueing systems with fixed numbers of customers and variable server return ratios (continued)

Number of Servers = 1

SERVICE MULTIPLIERS

Approx. Server Utilization	60 Customers		70 Customers		80 Customers		90 Customers	
	Svr. Util.	Svc. Mult.	Svr. Util.	Svc. Mult.	Svr. Util.	Svc. Mult.	Svr. Util.	Svc. Mult.
.10	0.111	1.12	0.111	1.12	0.111	1.12	0.111	1.12
.15	0.150	1.17	0.150	1.17	0.150	1.17	0.150	1.17
.20	0.200	1.24	0.200	1.25	0.200	1.25	0.200	1.25
.25	0.250	1.32	0.250	1.33	0.250	1.33	0.250	1.33
.30	0.300	1.42	0.300	1.42	0.300	1.42	0.300	1.42
.35	0.350	1.52	0.350	1.52	0.350	1.52	0.350	1.53
.40	0.400	1.64	0.400	1.64	0.400	1.65	0.400	1.65
.45	0.450	1.78	0.450	1.78	0.450	1.79	0.450	1.79
.50	0.500	1.94	0.500	1.95	0.500	1.96	0.500	1.96
.55	0.550	2.13	0.550	2.15	0.550	2.16	0.550	2.16
.60	0.600	2.37	0.600	2.39	0.600	2.40	0.600	2.41
.65	0.650	2.66	0.650	2.68	0.650	2.70	0.650	2.72
.70	0.700	3.02	0.700	3.06	0.700	3.08	0.700	3.11
.75	0.750	3.48	0.750	3.54	0.750	3.58	0.750	3.62
.80	0.800	4.10	0.800	4.19	0.800	4.26	0.800	4.31
.85	0.850	4.97	0.850	5.10	0.850	5.22	0.850	5.31
.90	0.900	6.28	0.900	6.51	0.900	6.70	0.900	6.87
.91	0.910	6.63	0.910	6.88	0.910	7.10	0.910	7.30
.92	0.920	7.02	0.920	7.32	0.920	7.56	0.920	7.78
.93	0.930	7.48	0.930	7.80	0.930	8.09	0.930	8.34
.94	0.940	8.01	0.940	8.37	0.940	8.70	0.940	8.99
.95	0.950	8.62	0.950	9.05	0.950	9.42	0.950	9.76
.96	0.960	9.38	0.960	9.87	0.960	10.32	0.960	10.71
.97	0.970	10.34	0.970	10.92	0.970	11.46	0.970	11.93
.98	0.980	11.65	0.980	12.38	0.980	13.03	0.980	13.62

SELECTED READING

[ALLE90] Allen, Arnold O., *Probability, Statistics, and Queueing Theory with Computer Science Applications*, 2d ed., Academic Press, San Diego, 1990.

Appendix C

Modified Closed Queueing Tables

This author's research has shown that contention caused by MVS dispatching delays often is less than delays predicted by closed queueing systems. This author's experience has been that this type of queueing tends to be more deterministic in nature (less variable) than the random parameters upon which closed queueing systems are based. Since this author could not locate standard queueing formulas to describe this type of multi-server queueing system, simulation studies were used to develop the numbers.

The numbers in Tables C.1 through C.8[1] were generated by a simulated model of closed queueing systems that was modified to restrict the randomness of average service time. The result was a set of queueing data with total service times lower than those of true closed (machine repair) queueing systems.

Tables C.1 through C.8 contain service multipliers that can be used to calculate the effect of MVS dispatch contention on queueing in many

---

[1] The data in Tables C.1 through C.8 reflect the results of simulation models. As such, they represent approximate indicators of specialized performance data. Although his data was designed for use estimating MVS dispatching delays, it may be useful for other queueing systems. The reader assumes all risks related to the use of this data or its application to other areas.

dedicated CICS environments. They also can be used in others situations in which closed queueing formulas tend overstate true performance. Chapter 7 discusses how to use data in these tables.

Table C.1   Service Multipliers Designed to Emulate Competition for MVS Dispatch Service In Dedicated CICS Environments

Server Utilization	Number of Servers = 1						
	SERVICE MULTIPLIERS						
	Number of Customers						
	10	20	30	40	50	70	90
.10	1.05	1.05	1.06	1.06	1.05	1.05	1.05
.15	1.06	1.09	1.09	1.09	1.08	1.08	1.08
.20	1.09	1.12	1.13	1.13	1.11	1.12	1.11
.25	1.11	1.15	1.17	1.16	1.14	1.17	1.15
.30	1.13	1.20	1.22	1.20	1.19	1.22	1.22
.35	1.18	1.24	1.28	1.24	1.23	1.27	1.27
.40	1.22	1.29	1.33	1.31	1.30	1.33	1.33
.45	1.24	1.33	1.38	1.34	1.37	1.40	1.39
.50	1.26	1.38	1.43	1.41	1.44	1.48	1.47
.55	1.28	1.43	1.49	1.49	1.52	1.56	1.56
.60	1.30	1.48	1.57	1.58	1.60	1.66	1.68
.65	1.32	1.53	1.62	1.67	1.71	1.78	1.83
.70	1.35	1.58	1.68	1.78	1.81	1.93	1.96
.75	1.37	1.64	1.77	1.88	1.94	2.11	2.17
.80	1.40	1.71	1.87	2.00	2.08	2.30	2.37
.85	1.43	1.79	1.99	2.15	2.26	2.54	2.64
.90	1.48	1.88	2.12	2.34	2.48	2.79	2.98
.91	1.49	1.91	2.16	2.39	2.54	2.87	3.06
.92	1.50	1.93	2.20	2.44	2.59	2.95	3.15
.93	1.51	1.97	2.24	2.49	2.65	3.03	3.26
.94	1.53	2.01	2.29	2.55	2.71	3.12	3.38
.95	1.55	2.05	2.34	2.61	2.79	3.24	3.51
.96	1.57	2.09	2.41	2.69	2.88	3.36	3.67
.97	1.60	2.14	2.48	2.78	3.01	3.51	3.84
.98	1.64	2.22	2.59	2.91	3.18	3.69	4.09

Table C.2 Service Multipliers Designed to Emulate Competition for MVS Dispatch Service In Dedicated CICS Environments

Number of Servers = 2

SERVICE MULTIPLIERS

Server Utilization	Number of Customers						
	10	20	30	40	50	70	90
.10	1.01	1.01	1.01	1.01	1.01	1.01	1.01
.15	1.01	1.01	1.01	1.01	1.01	1.01	1.01
.20	1.02	1.02	1.03	1.02	1.02	1.02	1.02
.25	1.03	1.04	1.04	1.03	1.03	1.04	1.04
.30	1.04	1.05	1.06	1.05	1.05	1.05	1.06
.35	1.04	1.06	1.07	1.07	1.07	1.07	1.08
.40	1.05	1.08	1.09	1.09	1.09	1.09	1.10
.45	1.06	1.09	1.11	1.11	1.12	1.13	1.13
.50	1.06	1.11	1.14	1.13	1.15	1.16	1.17
.55	1.07	1.13	1.17	1.17	1.19	1.19	1.21
.60	1.08	1.15	1.19	1.20	1.23	1.25	1.27
.65	1.08	1.17	1.22	1.24	1.27	1.31	1.33
.70	1.09	1.20	1.26	1.29	1.32	1.37	1.40
.75	1.10	1.23	1.30	1.34	1.38	1.46	1.48
.80	1.11	1.25	1.34	1.40	1.45	1.55	1.59
.85	1.12	1.29	1.39	1.47	1.53	1.66	1.71
.90	1.15	1.34	1.46	1.56	1.64	1.79	1.88
.91	1.15	1.35	1.47	1.58	1.66	1.83	1.92
.92	1.16	1.36	1.49	1.60	1.69	1.86	1.97
.93	1.17	1.38	1.51	1.63	1.72	1.90	2.02
.94	1.18	1.40	1.54	1.67	1.76	1.95	2.07
.95	1.19	1.42	1.57	1.70	1.80	2.00	2.13
.96	1.21	1.44	1.60	1.74	1.84	2.06	2.21
.97	1.23	1.47	1.65	1.79	1.91	2.14	2.30
.98	1.25	1.52	1.71	1.86	1.98	2.23	2.42

Table C.3 Service Multipliers Designed to Emulate Competition for MVS Dispatch Service in Dedicated CICS Environments

Number of Servers = 3

Server Utilization	SERVICE MULTIPLIERS Number of Customers						
	10	20	30	40	50	70	90
.10	1.00	1.00	1.00	1.00	1.00	1.00	1.00
.15	1.00	1.00	1.00	1.00	1.00	1.00	1.00
.20	1.00	1.01	1.01	1.01	1.01	1.01	1.01
.25	1.01	1.01	1.01	1.01	1.01	1.01	1.01
.30	1.01	1.02	1.02	1.02	1.02	1.02	1.02
.35	1.01	1.02	1.03	1.02	1.03	1.03	1.03
.40	1.02	1.03	1.04	1.04	1.04	1.04	1.05
.45	1.02	1.04	1.05	1.05	1.05	1.06	1.06
.50	1.02	1.05	1.06	1.06	1.07	1.07	1.09
.55	1.02	1.06	1.07	1.08	1.10	1.10	1.11
.60	1.02	1.07	1.09	1.10	1.12	1.13	1.15
.65	1.03	1.08	1.11	1.12	1.14	1.16	1.19
.70	1.03	1.09	1.13	1.15	1.17	1.21	1.24
.75	1.04	1.11	1.15	1.18	1.21	1.26	1.29
.80	1.04	1.12	1.18	1.22	1.25	1.31	1.34
.85	1.05	1.14	1.21	1.26	1.30	1.38	1.42
.90	1.07	1.17	1.25	1.32	1.37	1.47	1.53
.91	1.08	1.18	1.27	1.34	1.39	1.50	1.56
.92	1.08	1.19	1.28	1.35	1.40	1.52	1.59
.93	1.09	1.20	1.29	1.37	1.42	1.55	1.63
.94	1.10	1.21	1.31	1.39	1.45	1.58	1.66
.95	1.11	1.23	1.33	1.41	1.48	1.61	1.70
.96	1.12	1.25	1.35	1.44	1.51	1.65	1.76
.97	1.14	1.27	1.38	1.47	1.55	1.71	1.82
.98	1.17	1.31	1.42	1.52	1.61	1.77	1.90

Table C.4 Service Multipliers Designed to Emulate Competition for MVS Dispatch Service in Dedicated CICS Environments

Number of Servers = 4

SERVICE MULTIPLIERS

Server Utilization	Number of Customers						
	10	20	30	40	50	70	90
.10	1.00	1.00	1.00	1.00	1.00	1.00	1.00
.15	1.00	1.00	1.00	1.00	1.00	1.00	1.00
.20	1.00	1.00	1.00	1.00	1.00	1.00	1.00
.25	1.00	1.00	1.00	1.00	1.00	1.00	1.01
.30	1.00	1.01	1.01	1.01	1.01	1.01	1.01
.35	1.00	1.01	1.01	1.01	1.01	1.01	1.02
.40	1.00	1.01	1.02	1.02	1.02	1.02	1.02
.45	1.01	1.02	1.02	1.02	1.03	1.03	1.04
.50	1.01	1.02	1.03	1.03	1.04	1.04	1.05
.55	1.01	1.03	1.04	1.04	1.05	1.06	1.07
.60	1.01	1.03	1.05	1.06	1.07	1.08	1.09
.65	1.01	1.04	1.06	1.07	1.09	1.10	1.12
.70	1.01	1.05	1.07	1.09	1.11	1.13	1.15
.75	1.02	1.06	1.09	1.11	1.13	1.16	1.19
.80	1.02	1.06	1.10	1.13	1.16	1.20	1.24
.85	1.03	1.08	1.13	1.16	1.20	1.25	1.29
.90	1.04	1.10	1.16	1.20	1.25	1.32	1.37
.91	1.04	1.10	1.17	1.22	1.26	1.33	1.39
.92	1.05	1.11	1.18	1.23	1.27	1.35	1.41
.93	1.05	1.12	1.19	1.24	1.29	1.37	1.43
.94	1.06	1.13	1.20	1.25	1.30	1.40	1.46
.95	1.07	1.14	1.21	1.27	1.32	1.42	1.49
.96	1.08	1.15	1.23	1.29	1.35	1.45	1.53
.97	1.09	1.17	1.25	1.32	1.38	1.49	1.57
.98	1.11	1.20	1.29	1.36	1.42	1.54	1.63

Table C.5 Service Multipliers Designed to Emulate Competition for MVS Dispatch Service in Dedicated CICS Environments

Number of Servers = 5

Server Utilization	SERVICE MULTIPLIERS						
	Number of Customers						
	10	20	30	40	50	70	90
.10	1.00	1.00	1.00	1.00	1.00	1.00	1.00
.15	1.00	1.00	1.00	1.00	1.00	1.00	1.00
.20	1.00	1.00	1.00	1.00	1.00	1.00	1.00
.25	1.00	1.00	1.00	1.00	1.00	1.00	1.00
.30	1.00	1.00	1.00	1.00	1.00	1.00	1.00
.35	1.00	1.00	1.01	1.01	1.01	1.01	1.01
.40	1.00	1.01	1.01	1.01	1.01	1.01	1.01
.45	1.00	1.01	1.01	1.01	1.01	1.02	1.02
.50	1.00	1.01	1.02	1.02	1.02	1.02	1.03
.55	1.00	1.01	1.02	1.03	1.03	1.04	1.04
.60	1.00	1.02	1.03	1.04	1.04	1.05	1.06
.65	1.00	1.02	1.04	1.05	1.06	1.06	1.08
.70	1.01	1.02	1.04	1.06	1.07	1.09	1.10
.75	1.01	1.03	1.05	1.07	1.09	1.11	1.13
.80	1.01	1.04	1.07	1.09	1.11	1.14	1.17
.85	1.01	1.05	1.08	1.11	1.14	1.18	1.21
.90	1.02	1.06	1.10	1.14	1.17	1.23	1.27
.91	1.02	1.07	1.11	1.15	1.18	1.24	1.29
.92	1.02	1.07	1.12	1.16	1.19	1.25	1.30
.93	1.02	1.08	1.13	1.17	1.21	1.27	1.32
.94	1.02	1.08	1.14	1.18	1.22	1.29	1.34
.95	1.03	1.09	1.15	1.19	1.24	1.31	1.36
.96	1.03	1.10	1.16	1.21	1.26	1.33	1.39
.97	1.04	1.12	1.18	1.23	1.28	1.36	1.43
.98	1.05	1.14	1.21	1.27	1.32	1.40	1.48

Table C.6 Service Multipliers Designed to Emulate Competition for MVS Dispatch Service in Dedicated CICS Environments

Number of Servers = 6

SERVICE MULTIPLIERS

Server Utilization	Number of Customers						
	10	20	30	40	50	70	90
.10	1.00	1.00	1.00	1.00	1.00	1.00	1.00
.15	1.00	1.00	1.00	1.00	1.00	1.00	1.00
.20	1.00	1.00	1.00	1.00	1.00	1.00	1.00
.25	1.00	1.00	1.00	1.00	1.00	1.00	1.00
.30	1.00	1.00	1.00	1.00	1.00	1.00	1.00
.35	1.00	1.00	1.00	1.00	1.00	1.00	1.00
.40	1.00	1.00	1.00	1.00	1.01	1.01	1.01
.45	1.00	1.00	1.01	1.01	1.01	1.01	1.01
.50	1.00	1.01	1.01	1.01	1.01	1.02	1.02
.55	1.00	1.01	1.01	1.02	1.02	1.02	1.03
.60	1.00	1.01	1.02	1.02	1.03	1.03	1.04
.65	1.00	1.01	1.02	1.03	1.04	1.05	1.06
.70	1.00	1.01	1.03	1.04	1.05	1.06	1.07
.75	1.00	1.02	1.03	1.05	1.06	1.08	1.10
.80	1.01	1.02	1.04	1.06	1.08	1.10	1.12
.85	1.01	1.03	1.05	1.08	1.10	1.13	1.16
.90	1.02	1.04	1.07	1.10	1.13	1.17	1.21
.91	1.02	1.05	1.08	1.11	1.14	1.18	1.22
.92	1.02	1.05	1.08	1.12	1.14	1.19	1.23
.93	1.03	1.06	1.09	1.12	1.15	1.21	1.25
.94	1.03	1.06	1.10	1.13	1.17	1.22	1.26
.95	1.04	1.07	1.11	1.14	1.18	1.24	1.28
.96	1.04	1.08	1.12	1.16	1.19	1.26	1.31
.97	1.05	1.10	1.14	1.18	1.22	1.28	1.34
.98	1.07	1.12	1.16	1.20	1.25	1.32	1.38

Table C.7 Service Multipliers Designed to Emulate Competition for MVS Dispatch Service in Dedicated CICS Environments

	Number of Servers = 7						
	SERVICE MULTIPLIERS						
Server Utilization	**Number of Customers**						
	10	20	30	40	50	70	90
.10	1.00	1.00	1.00	1.00	1.00	1.00	1.00
.15	1.00	1.00	1.00	1.00	1.00	1.00	1.00
.20	1.00	1.00	1.00	1.00	1.00	1.00	1.00
.25	1.00	1.00	1.00	1.00	1.00	1.00	1.00
.30	1.00	1.00	1.00	1.00	1.00	1.00	1.00
.35	1.00	1.00	1.00	1.00	1.00	1.00	1.00
.40	1.00	1.00	1.00	1.00	1.00	1.00	1.00
.45	1.00	1.00	1.00	1.00	1.01	1.01	1.01
.50	1.00	1.00	1.01	1.01	1.01	1.01	1.01
.55	1.00	1.00	1.01	1.01	1.01	1.02	1.02
.60	1.00	1.01	1.01	1.01	1.02	1.02	1.03
.65	1.00	1.01	1.01	1.02	1.03	1.03	1.04
.70	1.00	1.01	1.02	1.03	1.03	1.04	1.05
.75	1.00	1.01	1.02	1.03	1.04	1.06	1.07
.80	1.00	1.01	1.03	1.04	1.06	1.08	1.10
.85	1.01	1.02	1.04	1.06	1.07	1.10	1.12
.90	1.01	1.03	1.05	1.07	1.10	1.13	1.16
.91	1.01	1.03	1.06	1.08	1.10	1.14	1.17
.92	1.02	1.03	1.06	1.09	1.11	1.15	1.18
.93	1.02	1.04	1.07	1.09	1.12	1.16	1.20
.94	1.02	1.04	1.07	1.10	1.13	1.17	1.21
.95	1.03	1.05	1.08	1.11	1.14	1.19	1.23
.96	1.03	1.06	1.09	1.12	1.15	1.21	1.25
.97	1.04	1.07	1.11	1.14	1.17	1.23	1.27
.98	1.06	1.09	1.13	1.17	1.20	1.26	1.31

Table C.8 Service Multipliers Designed to Emulate Competition for MVS Dispatch Service in Dedicated CICS Environments

Number of Servers = 8

SERVICE MULTIPLIERS

Server Utilization	Number of Customers						
	10	20	30	40	50	70	90
.10	1.00	1.00	1.00	1.00	1.00	1.00	1.00
.15	1.00	1.00	1.00	1.00	1.00	1.00	1.00
.20	1.00	1.00	1.00	1.00	1.00	1.00	1.00
.25	1.00	1.00	1.00	1.00	1.00	1.00	1.00
.30	1.00	1.00	1.00	1.00	1.00	1.00	1.00
.35	1.00	1.00	1.00	1.00	1.00	1.00	1.00
.40	1.00	1.00	1.00	1.00	1.00	1.00	1.00
.45	1.00	1.00	1.00	1.00	1.00	1.00	1.00
.50	1.00	1.00	1.00	1.00	1.01	1.01	1.01
.55	1.00	1.00	1.00	1.01	1.01	1.01	1.01
.60	1.00	1.00	1.01	1.01	1.01	1.02	1.02
.65	1.00	1.00	1.01	1.01	1.02	1.02	1.03
.70	1.00	1.01	1.01	1.02	1.02	1.03	1.04
.75	1.00	1.01	1.02	1.02	1.03	1.05	1.05
.80	1.00	1.01	1.02	1.03	1.04	1.06	1.07
.85	1.01	1.01	1.03	1.04	1.06	1.08	1.10
.90	1.01	1.02	1.04	1.06	1.08	1.11	1.13
.91	1.01	1.02	1.04	1.06	1.08	1.11	1.14
.92	1.01	1.03	1.05	1.07	1.09	1.12	1.15
.93	1.02	1.03	1.05	1.07	1.09	1.13	1.16
.94	1.02	1.04	1.06	1.08	1.10	1.14	1.17
.95	1.02	1.04	1.06	1.09	1.11	1.15	1.19
.96	1.03	1.05	1.07	1.10	1.12	1.17	1.20
.97	1.04	1.06	1.09	1.11	1.14	1.19	1.23
.98	1.06	1.08	1.11	1.14	1.17	1.21	1.26

Appendix D

Miscellaneous Notes on MRO

D.1 BACKGROUND

CICS's *multiple region option* (MRO) was originally used as a tool to help relieve virtual storage constraint in CICS regions. Resources defined in one CICS region could be accessed in other regions, allowing CICS applications to be split between regions. Terminal definitions could be defined in one region, applications in another region, and files, transient data, and temporary storage in yet another.

Today, MRO allows us to separate CICS activity and resources into multiple regions for many different reasons. A wide range of objectives can be achieved using MRO services.

D.2 MRO SERVICES

MRO provides several services that allow communication between CICS regions. These services include:

- **Transaction routing.** With transaction routing, transactions are started in one region and routed to other CICS regions. Typically, transactions are started or received in a *terminal-owning region* (TOR) and routed to an *application-owning region* (AOR). When transactions are passed between regions, a copy of the terminal information, if any, is passed along with the transaction. The terminal control table or its equivalent resides only in the TOR. Each AOR contains terminal information for active transactions.

- **Function shipping.** Function shipping allows applications running in one CICS region to access resources defined in another region. With function shipping, files, transient data, and temporary storage can be accessed by command-level programs running in other CICS regions. Normally, function shipping occurs automatically, where CICS tables or resource definition on-line (RDO) definitions contain the system identifier (SYSID) of remote CICS regions. Alternately, application programs can specifically route requests to other regions, specifying remote SYSID themselves.

- **Distributed transaction processing.** Distributed transaction processing (DTP) allows CICS tasks to communicate directly with tasks in other regions using LU 6.1 peer-to-peer communication. DTP allows true inter-task communication and can be the basis of cooperative processing structures.

- **Dynamic program link.** Dynamic program link (DPL) allows CICS applications to link to programs defined in other CICS regions or on other CICS platforms. Introduced in CICS/ESA 3.2.1, DPL allows transactions to separate processing between CICS systems, allowing work to be executed in the most appropriate environment. DPL can be driven by RDO definitions or explicitly requested by applications.

Transaction routing and function shipping have been the most commonly used MRO facilities. DPL is new, but probably will become very popular as people find new ways to apply it.

D.3 COMMON REASONS TO CREATE MULTIPLE CICS REGIONS

Over the years, there have been many reasons to create multiple CICS regions. In the earliest days, separate organizational units might have separate CICS systems, each with its own terminals, files, and applications. With high-function, integrated applications, today it is often necessary to split single CICS workloads across multiple regions.

Although there are many good reasons to split or create CICS regions, there are a few strategies that are commonly found in many CICS environments. A few of these include:

- **Overcome virtual storage constraint.** *Virtual storage constraint* (VSC) was the principal reason most installations began using MRO services. As mentioned in Chapter 2, VSC is seldom more than an annoyance in most CICS shops today. With the coming of MVS/XA, MVS/ESA, and CICS releases that progressively exploited addressing above the 16-megabyte line, VSC is usually a problem only when extended addressing features have not been exploited. In CICS/MVS, and especially in CICS/ESA release 3.2.1, most significant storage areas have been placed above the 16-megabyte line.

    From a technical perspective, VSC has almost ceased to be a problem. By CICS/ESA 3.2.1, nearly all system constraints have been resolved. Where VSC still exists, application language and coding constraints are usually the primary cause. As installations convert to languages that can run and use storage above the 16-megabyte line, VSC should cease to be an issue.[1]

- **Overcome processor constraint.** As VSC problems were solved, individual CICS regions could run more work, allowing the CICS main TCB (CICS/VS and CICS/MVS) or QR TCB (CICS/ESA) to do more processing. When CPU activity in CICS regions reaches a critical level (see chapters 6 and 7), splitting applications between CICS regions can help relieve processor constraint. This option is usually preferred to upgrading processor speed.

- **Segregate unusual technology.** When CICS applications use new or unusual technology, it may be wise to place them in separate CICS regions. New technology may not always be stable or may place unusual demands on CICS regions. It is often better to isolate other applications from the effects of new or experimental technology.

---

1 OS/VS COBOL was perhaps the most popular of the older languages that required storage below the 16-megabyte line. IBM has announced that this product will not be supported in IBM products released after June 30, 1994. This implies that releases of CICS that become available after that date will not support OS/VS COBOL. This should be one of the remaining frontiers in the battle of VSC relief.

- **Support applications with different availability requirements.** CICS applications often have differing availability requirements. Separating applications in different CICS regions is one way to allow shutting down the application systems when they are not needed.

- **Isolate application systems for security.** In all releases of CICS existing at the time of this writing, applications can look at all storage owned by other applications in the same CICS region. Therefore, CICS applications processing sensitive data are often placed in separate CICS regions to isolate them from other applications. Future releases or maintenance levels of CICS will allow storage protection for CICS tasks, but whether they will provide security against looking at data in memory is unknown at the time of this writing.

- **Allow applications to run under different releases of CICS.** Sometimes it is necessary to run multiple releases of CICS for different CICS applications. One good example is for macro-level applications that cannot be run on CICS 3.2.1 or beyond. They can run in CICS/MVS regions.

These are but a few of the reasons various organizations have multiple CICS regions today.

D.4 THE COST OF MRO OVERHEAD

MRO services require a considerable amount of processing overhead. It takes more total CPU time to ship requests between regions than to process them locally in the same CICS region. In fact, it takes more total processing to ship most requests between CICS regions than it does to process the requests themselves. MRO overhead occurs in the sending region, the receiving region, and operating system overhead.

Table D.1 summarized the results of a series of benchmark tests conducted by the author. The purpose of the tests was to compare the amount of CPU time required to perform VSAM READ requests locally and using CICS/MVS and CICS/ESA function shipping. The tests showed that MRO overhead was typically at least twice as high as the actual cost of performing a command-level READ. The tests confirm reports that MRO overhead is much less under CICS/ESA than it was under CICS/MVS.

The benchmarks were run on a dedicated Amdahl 1400 processor. The only workloads active on the processor were the CICS test regions

Table D.1 The Relative Costs of Performing File READ Requests Using MRO Function Versus Accessing the File Locally

Type of Activity	CICS Release		Total CPU Cost per VSAM READ
	AOR	FOR	
Local VSAM READ	CICS/MVS 2.1.1	n/a	1.6 ms
Local VSAM READ	CICS/ESA 3.3	n/a	1.7 ms
VSAM READ accessed via MRO function shipping	CICS/MVS 2.1.1	CICS/MVS 2.1.1	6.0 ms
VSAM READ accessed via MRO function shipping	CICS/MVS 2.1.1	CICS/ESA 3.3	4.9 ms
VSAM READ accessed via MRO function shipping	CICS/ESA 3.3	CICS/ESA 3.3	4.8 ms

Note: All CPU costs shown in Table D.1 are derived from RMF Type 70 data and include all CICS and system overhead. The Monitor for CICS was active during the benchmarks.

and the facilities necessary to support them. Both the CICS/MVS 2.1.1 and CICS/ESA 3.3 regions were active (but not necessarily running transactions) during all benchmark runs. This was done to simplify the comparison of different benchmark runs. Various controls were included in the test (such as measuring quiet base-level periods). Different series of tests included transactions with different numbers of random READ commands, to allow separation of fixed costs per transaction and costs per VSAM READ command. The same VSAM data was accessed in all benchmark runs using a randomizing routine with a common seed, and the same number of VSAM buffers was allocated to each CICS region. The Monitor for CICS was active for both the CICS 2.1.1 and CICS 3.3 regions.

CPU data in Table D.1 were derived from RMF Type 70 data. This provides a measure of total CPU time used systemwide, and includes the total costs of all commands including both CICS and MVS overhead.

The results of this benchmark suggest that function shipping overhead consumes about two to three times more total CPU time than the actual VSAM READ commands. The benchmark also suggests that function shipping in CICS/ESA is significantly more efficient than it is in CICS/MVS. It appears that similar savings in overhead occurred when the FOR was converted to CICS/ESA, regardless of which version was being used for the AOR.

Most literature on CICS/ESA seems to indicate that CICS/ESA is more efficient than CICS/MVS and that CPU costs have been reduced. This seems at least partially confirmed with the reduction in MRO overhead experienced in these tests. However, Figure D.1 shows a slightly higher CPU time for local READ commands in CICS/ESA than in CICS/MVS. This may be because the benchmarks were run with an early (beta) version of TMON. Early CICS/ESA releases of this monitor were reported to have high overhead.

The results of this test should not be used as an absolute indicator of performance. For one thing, LSR pools in all tests were intentionally small, and LSR data look-aside ratios were low. Additionally, the environment was pure and did not include competition from other workloads. And, other environments with different software and monitors would have incurred different overhead costs per transaction.

> **Key Point:** Specific results will vary from installation to installation. However, the costs of MRO overhead can be substantial, and are often higher than the cost of the actual services being performed remotely. In CICS/ESA, MRO overhead is quite a bit lower than it was in previous versions of CICS, but it can be, nonetheless, substantial.

D.5 MRO STRATEGIES

Several different approaches or strategies can be taken when planning CICS/MRO configurations. MRO strategies can be designed to minimize CPU overhead, maximize availability, or optimize performance. Depending on the needs of different organizations, some combination of strategies can be used. Different configurations can be developed for each of these strategies.

D.5.1 MRO Strategy 1: Minimizing CPU Overhead

When the primary goal is to minimize MRO overhead, efforts would be made to minimize the number of MRO requests between CICS regions. Traditionally, this would be achieved by defining resources locally in the CICS regions that use them most heavily.

When we are trying to minimize MRO overhead, it is usually wise to define resources in the CICS regions that access them the most. As shown in Table D.1, there is more total CPU time associated with MRO overhead than there is in the actual execution of READ commands for VSAM files. Resources should be defined locally in the regions that use them the most and accessed via MRO from all other regions.

With DPL in CICS/ESA, new techniques can be used to minimize MRO calls. Groups of file accesses and related processing can be collected in selected CICS regions, and access to units of processing can be accomplished with a single MRO link. With DPL, entire packages of work can be shipped between regions. With some planning, DPL can be used to eliminate multiple interregion requests.

Another way to reduce MRO overhead involves VSAM datasets that are *not updated in any CICS region* (or by any batch jobs while the files are open to CICS). When read-only VSAM files are heavily accessed by multiple CICS regions, it may be beneficial to define them locally in each CICS region, thus saving MRO overhead. Of course, there are drawbacks to doing this. For one thing, additional memory will be required for redundant control blocks in each region. Another drawback is that the collective LSR buffer look-aside ratio of several smaller pools might not be as large as it would be if the pools were combined in a single region.

One challenge in minimizing overhead is the grouping of files and application systems in various CICS regions. In cases where application systems are relatively independent of one another or can be contained in a single CICS region, it is easy to plan file and application placement. When systems are closely interrelated and share common files, it may be difficult to plan which applications are placed together and which files are contained with them. The best way to deal with this is to analyze which files are used most heavily and try to group applications to minimize MRO overhead for these files.

As we will see below, strategies that attempt to minimize CPU overhead will not always yield the best performance or availability, even though they use the least amount of CPU time.

D.5.2 Maximizing Availability

CICS/ESA introduced support for an intelligent router program. With this support, the router program can route transactions to multiple CICS application regions. With a little intelligence, the router program can detect CICS regions that are not responding and route work automatically to other CICS regions.

In CICS/ESA, the intelligent router program and reduced MRO overhead made the idea of *resource owning regions* (RORs) more practical. RORs contain only resources (such as file definitions, temporary storage, and transient data) and contain no application processing. *Redundant application regions* (RARs) contain only application processing, but rely on RORs for all resources.

Normally, two or more copies of each RAR will be available to process a given set of transactions. The intelligent router program will route transactions to RARs based on activity or some other measure. When the router suspects that a RAR is not responding, the router can automatically route transactions to one of the remaining RARs. If a single RAR failed, application processing could continue in other RARs.

The key to improved availability is to separate all processing from all resource ownership. Regions containing only resource definitions are not as likely to fail as regions containing application processing. As long as a failing RAR owned no resources needed by other RARs, processing could continue in other RARs, uninterrupted by the failure of a single CICS region. Since resources needed to execute transactions all would be contained in RORs, they should be available most of the time.

RAR/ROR configurations also can help resolve capacity such as CPU or storage constraint. With a little work, it should be possible to run additional RARs during periods of heavier demand. When heavy workloads are expected, additional RARs can be active. When there is little activity, fewer regions will be needed.

The RAR/ROR approach is perhaps the most expensive in terms of CPU overhead. Every access to CICS resources will require MRO function shipping overhead. However, ROR/RARs can provide improved availability.

D.5.3 Providing Optimal Performance

In most environments, the best performance is provided by local resource accesses. No only do local accesses require less CPU overhead than remote accesses, but they occur more quickly. However, when a resource is accessed heavily by programs in multiple CICS regions, other approaches may be more appropriate.

When a CICS region is constrained by CPU activity, max-tasks, or virtual storage, it may not be wise to use that region as a resource server for other CICS regions. When resources must be accessed from constrained regions, they can suffer delays getting into the region and accessing resources.

In such situations, application response time may be improved by moving resource definitions to FORs or RORs. FORs and RORs normally are not constrained by CPU activity, virtual storage, or max-tasks conditions. As such, they usually can deliver good, consistent service. Although overhead costs may be higher, service times can be acceptable.

When resources are accessed lightly to moderately by other regions, performance will probably be better if they are defined in the AOR using them most frequently. However, when resources are accessed heavily from multiple regions, total service time can be improved by placing resources in FORs or RORs.

With a strategy to optimize performance, local file access is usually preferable. When resources must be accessed heavily by other regions and the AOR owning the resource is constrained, it might be better to define the file in a FOR or ROR. There may be more overhead when files are defined in FORs or RORs, but performance can usually be good.

Appendix

E

SAS Program to Calculate Open Queueing Delays

The SAS program[1] presented on the following page is offered to as an aid in calculating queueing delays for open queueing systems. The program should provide accuracy to at least three digits for queueing systems with up to eight servers. The author has not verified results for larger numbers of servers and would not recommend use of this program for systems with large numbers of servers (e.g., 50 or more).

The formulas used to develop this program can be found in *Probability, Statistics, and Queueing Theory with Computer Science Applications* by Dr. Arnold Allen.

---

[1] While selected output produced by this program has been verifired, no warranty is made of the accuracy of its output or of its applicability is specific circumstances. As noted several places in the text, open queueing formulas will provide reasonable approximations of queueing service only when certain basic assumptions (such as the random arrival of events and unlimited customer population) are satisfied. The reader assumes all risks for use of this program.

398 Appendix E

```
/*  Program to generate M/M/C (Open) service times */

data openque(keep= c rho avgsvc response servmult);

    avgsvc = 1;  /* average time it takes to       */
                 /*   receive service at server.   */
                 /* When avgsvc is 1.0, calculated */
                 /* wait times can be used as      */
                 /* service multipliers.           */

    c = 4;       /* c is the number of servers    */

    do rho = .01 to .99 by .01;
/* rho represents average server utilization       */
/*    This example calculates a series of          */
/*    utilization values from .01 to .99.          */

       u = rho * c;
/*  u represents traffic intensity, i.e., the      */
/*     amount of work that arrives per unit of     */
/*        time.                                    */

       lambda = u / avgsvc;
/*  lambda represents the rate at which customers  */
/*     arrive in a queueing system.                */
/*     Note that:  rho = (lambda * avgsvc) / c     */

          sysuc = 1;       /* calculate (u**c)/c! */
          do i = 1 to c by 1;
             sysuc = (sysuc * u) / i;
          end;
/* calculate the sum of (u**n)/n! from 0 to c-1 */
/*  Note that by successively multiplying and    */
/*     dividing, higher values of u and c can be */
/*     calculated without losing accuracy.       */
          sumun = 0;
          do j = 0 to (c-1) by 1;
            if j = 0
              then i1 = 1;
              else do;
                i1 = 1;
                do i = 1 to j by 1;
                   i1 = (i1 * u) / i;
                end;
              end;
            sumun = sumun + i1;
```

```
              end;

/*   the probability that all servers are busy     */
     prob     = sysuc / (sysuc + (1-rho) * sumun);
/*   time spent waiting on a queue                 */
          queuetim = (prob * avgsvc)/ (c * (1 - (rho)));
     response = queuetim + avgsvc;
     servmult = response / avgsvc;
  output openque;
  end;

  label
     c        ='SERVERS'
     rho      ='UTILIZATION'
     avgsvc   ='AVERAGE*TIME AT*SERVER'
     response='SERVICE TIME*INCLUDING*QUEUEING'
     servmult='SERVICE*MULTIPLIER';

proc print data=openque split='*';
title 'LIST OF SERVICE TIMES FOR M/M/C QUEUEING
SYSTEMS';
   id c rho avgsvc;
   var response servmult;
```

Index

A

Absolute peaks:
  (See Peak periods, absolute peaks)
AOR:
  (See Application-owning regions)
Application-owning regions, 7, 28, 52, 287, 387, 392, 395
Arrival rate:
  (See Queueing systems, workload arrival rate)

B

Bell, Thomas E., 217
Best-case analysis:
  (See Software performance engineering, best-case analysis)
Bottleneck analysis, 96, 103–105
  performance debugging, 105

C

Cache controller operations:
  formatted writes, 318
  front end misses, 318
  nonformatted writes, 318
  read hits, 317
  read-hit ratio, 319–320, 332, 348
  read misses, 318
  read/write ratio, 320
  staging, 318–319, 331, 348
  track promotion, 318
  write hits, 318
  write misses, 319
  write-hit ratio, 320, 331–332
Cache controllers, 317–320, 331
Capacity and performance:
  difference between, 166–169
Capacity planning, 5
CDSA, 27
CI and CA splits, 306–307

CI and CA splits (Cont.):
  effect on dispatch time, 176, 188, 203, 205, 214
  effect on dispatch time on, 188
CICS
  file open and close commands, 19
  history of, 12
  internal dispatching, 11, 14–17
  internal dispatching priorities, 160–161
  management of virtual storage, 11
  storage compression, 23–24
  versions of, 4
CICS and the DASD subsystem, 311, 321–323, 345–348
CICS as a queueing system, 141, 143–154, 156–160
  three task states, 142
CICS as a queueing system:
  (See Queueing systems, CICS as a queueing system)
CICS asynchronous tasks, 301–303
CICS close commands, 134
CICS dispatch time, 140, 142, 147–148, 150
CICS dispatching:
  disruptive tasks, 161–162
CICS file open and close commands:
  effect on dispatch time, 175
CICS internal architecture, 2
CICS internal caching, 338, 340–345
CICS journals, 293, 347
CICS main TCB, 15–17, 19, 132
CICS monitor facility, 58–60, 278
CICS open commands, 134
CICS primary TCB, 132–133, 139
CICS restart data set, 293
CICS temporary storage, 342–344
CICS workloads, 34
Client-server applications, 289, 300
CMF:
  (See CICS monitor facility)
CO TCB, 20, 53, 132, 175–176
Code optimizers, 279
Command-level interface, 29

Comparing CICS performance on different processors, 200–214
Competition from MVS tasks:
  effect on CICS performance, 3, 165, 176–180
Controlling CPU usage in a CICS environment, 278–279
CPU delays for other TCBs, 159
CPU demand, 139, 150–151, 156, 171
  effect MVS competition on:
  (See Competition from MVS tasks)
  effect of CI and CA splits
  (See CI and CA splits, effect on dispatch time)
  effect of page faults on
  (See Page faults, effect on CICS performance)
CPU demand calculations:
  calibration of, 194–195
CPU measurement:
  CMF in CICS/ESA, 138–139
  CMF in CICS/VS and CICS/MVS, 136–137, 139
  end-of-day statistics, 139
  uncaptured time, 178, 187
CPU utilization:
  measurement of, 135–137

D

DASD architecture, 4
DASD fast write, 292–293, 320
DASD service:
  channel activity, 316–317, 322, 325, 328, 331, 333, 338, 348
  components of, 324–325
  connect time, 316, 323, 328
  DASD workloads as queueing systems, 320–323, 328, 331–334, 337
  data transfer time, 314
  DB2 databases, 322, 338, 347–349
  disconnect time, 316, 323, 325, 328, 331
  examples analyzing, 323–325, 328, 331–334, 337
  IOS queue time, 313, 315, 324, 328
  latency, 314, 316, 320, 325
  locality patterns, 341
  major components of, 312
  measures of, 314–316
  pend time, 313, 315, 322, 325, 328
  recommendations for, 346–348
  RPS reconnect, 314, 322
  seek time, 313

DASD service (Cont.):
  service time, 4
Database subtasks, 160
Database subtaskss, 20
DB2 binds, 280
DB2 data tables, 294
DB2 databases, 20
DB2 subtasks, 20–21, 137
DCA:
  (See Dispatch control area)
DFW:
  (See DASD fast write)
Dispatch control area, 160
Dispatch task area, 160
Dispatch time:
  (See CICS dispatch time)
Distortions to the utilization relationship, 102
Distributed transaction processing, 388
Domains:
  in CICS/ESA, 138
DPL:
  (See Dynamic program link)
DPSC:
  (See Dynamic program storage compression)
DSA:
  (See Dynamic storage area)
DTA:
  (See Dispatch task area)
Dynamic program link, 287–288, 388, 393
Dynamic program storage compression, 25–27
Dynamic storage area, 23–24

E

ECDSA, 27
EDSA, 25
End-of-day statistics, 139–140
Environmental factors:
  effect on CICS performance, 165
ERDSA, 27
EUDSA, 27

F

FEPI:
  (See Front end programming interface)
Fetch (product from Axios), 30

Index

File service time:
    estimating for CICS applications, 345
File-owning regions, 7, 29, 286, 391, 395
Fixed priority dispatching in MVS, 180
FOR:
    (See File-owning regions)
Forecasting workload changes, 3
Fourth generation languages, 281
Front end programming interface, 20
Function shipping, 29, 53, 388, 390–391, 394

G

Growth bias, 3, 44–46, 62–64, 76, 78–80, 92–93
    an organization's predisposition to change, 44
    structural forces, 44

H

Handle condition commands, 282–283
Hardware bottlenecks, 6
Historical data:
    analysis of, 41–46, 48–53
    dangers with use of, 41–44
How DASD effects CICS performance, 312
How to use this book, 8

I

Improving CICS application performance, 276, 278
Internal processing delays, 3
Intersystem communication, 22, 28
ISC:
    (See Intersystem communication)

L

Lambda:
    (See Queueing systems, average service time)

Library look-aside facility, 20
Little's law, 121
LLA:
    (See Library look-aside facility)
Loader domain, 25
Local shared resources, 29–30, 86, 102, 176, 255, 291, 305–307, 319, 321, 338, 340–341, 343, 345–346
    suggestions for performance improvements, 338, 340–342
Logical I/O density, 86, 238, 262–263
Low utilization effect, 102, 295
LSR:
    (See Local shared resources)

M

Machine repair model:
    (See Queueing systems, closed queueing systems)
Macro-efficiency, 277
Macro-level, 13, 390
Macro-tuning:
    (See Macro-efficiency)
Management Information Control System, 59
Merrill's Expanded Guide, 60
Microtuning, 277
MRO:
    (See Multiple region option)
Multiple region option, 13, 22, 25, 28–29, 31, 387–395
    cost of MRO overhead, 390–392
    difference between CICS/ESA and CICS/MVS overhead, 391–392
    minimizing CPU overhead, 392
    reasons to create multiple CICS regions, 388–390
MVS, 160
MVS CSA, 21
MVS dispatching algorithms, 177
MVS paging, 18
MVS private area, 21
MVS SQA, 21
MVS subtasks:
    (See MVS TCBs)
MVS TCBs, 14, 132–133
    CICS/ESA use of, 19–20, 135, 138–139, 144, 146, 175
    CICS/VS and CICS/MVS use of, 15–17, 19, 135, 144, 146
MXG:
    (See Merrill's Expanded Guide)

N

Natural forecasting units, 66–67, 74
Network data streams, 295
NFUs:
    (See Natural forecasting units)
Nonshared resources, 29, 176, 255, 305–307
NSR:
    (See Nonshared resources)

P

Page allocation map, 23
Page faults, 133
    CPU cost associated with moving pages, 174
    effect on CICS performance, 165, 170–175, 188, 190, 198, 201, 203–204
    effect on CPU demand, 171
    page movement time, 173–175
    satisfied from expanded storage, 173–175
    satisfied from external storage, 171–173
Page movement time:
    (See Page faults, page movement time)
Paging:
    (See Page faults, satisfied from external storage)
PAM:
    (See Page allocation map)
PDB:
    (See Performance database)
Peak periods, 53
    absolute and recurring types, 53
    absolute peaks, 54, 56
    difference between types of peaks periods, 54
    length of, 56–57
    planning for, 54
    recurring peaks, 53–54, 56, 69
Performance and capacity:
    difference between, 166–169
Performance database, 57–59, 61
Performance groups, 135
    control performance groups, 135
Performance management, 5
Performance planning, 5
    reasons to do, 7
Performance surprises, 6
Periodic review of performance data, 87–88, 92–93
Physical I/O density, 86, 237–238
Primary TCB, 171, 176
    competition with operating system tasks, 135
Processor differences:
    (See Comparing CICS performance on different processors)
Processor rating scales, 52, 203–204
Processor speed:
    effect on CICS performance, 165

Q

QR TCB, 19, 53, 132, 139–140, 175–176
Queueing systems, 107–117, 119–124, 126
    arrival of work, 107, 109, 124–126
    arrival rate versus resource utilization, 97, 100
    average arrival rate, 108, 121–122
    average service time, 108, 121, 123–124, 144
    bunching, 123, 125
    calibration of CPU demand calculations, 195
    CICS as a queueing system, 142–144
    closed queueing parameters, 114–115, 144–145
    closed queueing systems, 110–111, 114–117, 119, 141, 143–147, 150–152, 169
    closed queueing tables, 357, 359, 361, 363, 365, 367, 369, 371, 373, 375
    differences between, 166–170
    disruptive workloads, 194–195, 203, 333–334, 337
    distortions to queueing assumptions, 333, 337–338
    estimating delays caused by priority workloads, 181–190, 194–205, 209–212
    example of use, 126–128
    factors effecting utilization in closed systems, 145, 150–152, 155–159, 180
    interaction between, 157–159, 239
    interarrival time, 122
    iterative approach to estimating CICS dispatch service, 153–156
    maximum dispatch related service, 148, 150–151

Index   405

Queueing systems (Cont.):
  maximum server return ratio, 148, 150–151, 153–155
  mean time to failure, 114, 116, 122
  minimum server return ratio, 148, 150–151, 153–155
  modified closed queueing tables, 377
  multiserver systems, 108, 119, 166–169, 328
  open queueing systems, 110, 112–113, 119, 167–169
  open queueing tables, 351, 353, 355
  preemptive resume priorities, 180–181
  priority-based schemes, 161–162
  program to calculate open queueing delays, 397
  random arrival of events, 122–123, 334
  random distribution, 125–126
  random service times, 123–125
  resource utilization, 97–100, 117
  server return ratio, 117, 147–148, 152–154, 157, 169
  server utilization, 109, 112, 127, 152, 169
  servers, 106, 144
  service multipliers, 111, 116–117, 119, 127, 145, 149, 155, 167–168, 328, 333, 337–338
  significance of random patterns, 125–126
  single-server systems, 107–108, 112–114, 119, 146, 166–169, 322
  think time, 116, 169–170
  total wait time, 111, 113, 146, 168–169
  traffic intensity, 109, 127
  using tables to estimate CPU-related delays, 160
  workload arrival rate, 96–97, 99–100
Queueing theory, 3, 106
  a set of estimation techniques, 121
  assumptions behind, 121–126, 321
  definition of basic terms, 106
  what is queueing theory?, 106
Quick Fetch, 30

R

Recurring peaks:
  (See Peak periods, recurring peaks)
Redundant application regions, 287, 394
Resource management facility, 61

Resource projections for new systems, 83–84
Resource utilization:
  (See Queueing systems, resource utilization)
Resource-owning regions, 7, 287, 394–395
RESP option, 283
RMF:
  (See Resource management facility)
RMF type 70 data, 61, 391
RMF type 72 data, 61, 135, 175, 178
RMF type 73 data, 61, 316–317
RMF type 74 data, 61, 315
RO TCB, 19, 53, 133
ROR:
  (See Resource-owning regions)
ROT:
  (See Rules of thumb)
Round-robin dispatching, 160
Rules of thumb, 103, 105

S

SAS, 89
Service level agreements, 61
Service multipliers:
  (See Queueing systems, service multipliers)
  the key to simplified performance estimation, 111, 123
Short-on-storage condition, 24–25
SLA:
  (See Service level agreement)
Smith, Connie U., 217, 232, 275, 279
Software bottlenecks, 6
Software performance engineering, 4, 217–241, 243–244
  application design example, 243–248, 250–255, 257–270, 272
  application design guidelines, 275–309
  best-case analysis, 238, 240, 246, 255–265
  choosing a CICS region, 266
  common subroutines, 296
  communications, 300
  creating responsive applications, 218, 220, 275–276, 279–284, 286–287, 289–301, 303, 306–309
  design principles, 4
  effectual locality, 292–295
  estimating CPU time, 261–264

Software performance engineering (Cont.):
  estimating DASD service, 257–259, 269
  estimating delays associated with CICS journals, 259–260, 268
  evaluating application performance, 218, 220, 222–223, 225–241, 243–255, 257–270, 272
  evaluating performance in a specific environment, 265–269
  identifying performance goals, 232
  locality of degree, 295–296
  menu and screen design, 285, 290, 297–300
  modeling tools, 270
  overlap of life-cycle phases, 233–234
  penalties of poor performance, 219
  performance goals, 229–230, 245, 247, 296, 301–302, 304
  performance walk-throughs, 228
  procedure to evaluate CICS application, 257
  procedure to evaluate CICS applications, 245–270, 272
  processing versus frequency principle, 296–297
  risks of not using, 222–223
  shared resources principle, 304–308
  sizing application systems, 220
  software design, 244, 246, 250–252
  software model, 245–246, 254–255
  spatial locality, 284–289
  stages in the application life cycle, 245–246
  strategy for assessing application performance, 223–225, 227–230
  system model, 227, 238–241, 245–246, 265
  temporal locality, 289–291
  the centering principle, 298–300
  the fixing point principle, 280–283
  the instrumentation principle, 308–309
  the locality principle, 283–296
  the processing versus frequency principle, 299
  the use of spreadsheets, 272
  what is it?, 218–219
  why needed for today, 221–223
  why SPE was not needed in the past, 220–221
  workload specifications, 244–245, 248, 250
Software performance engineering models, 226–241

Software performance engineering models (Cont.):
  building an SPE model, 230–241
  DB2 considerations, 239
  dealing with uncertainty, 231–232
  estimating CPU usage, 237
  estimating DASD service times, 239–240
  estimating transaction volume, 234–237
  evaluating the software model, 238
  MRO processing, 239
  persons involved, 228–229
  software design, 226–227, 231–233, 238, 250
  software model, 227, 232–241
  the software model, 227, 231
  workload specifications, 226–227, 231, 234, 238, 248–249, 252
SOS:
  (See Short-on-storage condition)
SPE:
  (See Software performance engineering)
Stages of application life-cycle:
  early design phase, 224–225
  implementation phase, 225
  maintenance phase, 226
  mature design phase, 225, 231
  requirements definition phase, 224
  system test phase, 225
Storage addressability:
  16-megabyte limitation, 21–23, 26, 30, 32
Storage manager domain, 25
Subsystem storage protection, 27–28
System managed storage, 332
System under stress message, 24
SZ TCB, 53

T

Task control block, 14
  (See also MVS TCBs)
TCB:
  (See Task control block)
TCB processing:
  restrictions on, 14
Temporary storage, 29–30, 233, 287, 291, 312, 319, 387, 394
Terminal-owning region, 52
Terminal-owning regions, 7, 28
The processor complex as a queueing system, 179–180
Timeused facility, 138

Index   407

TOR:
  (See Terminal-owning regions)
Traffic intensity:
  (See Queueing systems, traffic intensity)
Transaction arrival patterns, 69, 72, 74, 76
Transaction routing, 28, 387–388
Transactions that use large amounts of CPU time, 158–159
TS:
  (See Temporary storage)
Tuning, 5

U

UDSA, 27
Uncaptured time:
  (See CPU measurement, uncaptured time)
Using tables to estimate CPU-related delays, 146, 148, 152, 154, 156–159

V

Variance:
  institutional changes, 89, 92
  random, 89–90, 92
  time-related, 89–90, 101
VCS:
  (See Virtual storage constraint)
Virtual look-aside facility, 20
Virtual storage access method:
  (See VSAM)
Virtual storage constraint, 11, 21–22, 24, 32, 389
Virtual storage constraint relief, 28
VLF:
  (See Virtual look-aside facility)
von Mayrhauser, Anneliese, 217
VSAM sharing, 305–308
VSAM subtask, 15, 17, 20, 29–30, 132, 212
VSCR:
  (See Virtual storage constraint relief)
VSP:
  (See VSAM subtask)

W

Workload characterization, 2, 35
Workload classification, 2, 35–39, 41
Workload growth:
  affect of response time on, 77
  assumptions behind, 98, 100–101
  base period, 48–49, 81
  business activity versus transaction processing, 69
  calculating components of, 48–51
  changes associated with levels of staffing, 74
  changes associated with new systems, 83–87
  changes in complexity/overhead, 78–81, 83
  changes in components of, 64
  complexity/overhead component, 45–46, 48–49, 64
  components of, 45, 63
  estimating number of transactions, 84–85
  exceptional situations, 52–53
  factors influencing number of transactions, 64–67, 69, 72, 74, 77–78
  gathering information, 78
  negative growth, 50
  new systems component, 45, 48
  processor differences, 51–52
  transaction arrival patterns, 72, 74, 76
  transaction profiles for new systems, 85–86
  translating business activity into workload peaks, 72
  types of change, 89
  variations in business activity, 65
  volume component, 45, 48–49
  volume-related changes, 64–67, 69, 72, 74, 76–78
Workloads, 3
  homogeneity in, 37–39, 41
  what is a workload, 34

X

XA-Relo, 30